FOUR BRANCHES

OF

GOVERNMENT

IN OUR FOUNDING FATHERS' WORDS

FOUR BRANCHES

OF

GOVERNMENT

IN OUR FOUNDING FATHERS' WORDS

A Document Disguised as a Book
That Will Return the Power of Government
to "We the People" and to Petition the Government
for a Redress of Grievances

Steven King

authorHOUSE®

AuthorHouse™
1663 Liberty Drive
Bloomington, IN 47403
www.authorhouse.com
Phone: 1 (800) 839-8640

Published by AuthorHouse   10/13/2015

ISBN: 978-1-5049-1927-2 (sc)
ISBN: 978-1-5049-1926-5 (hc)
ISBN: 978-1-5049-1928-9 (e)

Library of Congress Control Number: 2015910145

Print information available on the last page.

TABLE OF CONTENTS

1) Interpretation of Preamble...1
2) The U.S. Government Is a Four Branch System 2
3) Power schematics of a Three and Four Branch Systems......11
4) Four Branches of Government Equation............................12
5) The House of Representatives Is Truly a Reflection
   of the People 17
6) The Senate...24
7) supreme Court's Accumulation of Power For the
   Federal Government..28
8) The President...59
9) Congress...66
10) The Origin of Political Parties..68
11) The Power of Government 84
12) In Our Founding Fathers' Words; Love, Humor,
    Culture and Deceit 92
13) Checks and Balances of the Constitution.........................105
14) Branches Beyond the Four 107
15) The Evolution of America...109
16) Unions..125
17) Politics, Pollution, Climate Change, EPA and Economy....127
18) Over Population...151
19) Immigration..155
20) Assimilating into America 160
21) America's Exceptionalism...165
22) Education...170
23) Religion and Science 174
24) Political Views on Government.......................................182
25) Political Correctness...191

26) Freedom of Speech 193
27) Government has Become a High-End Welfare System 199
28) The National Debt is a Borderline Ponzi Scheme 201
29) The Liberal's Disabled America 203
30) Liberal Ideology vs. Conservative Ideology 207
31) Left, Right; Extremes and the Economy 211
32) Liberal Creativity 225
33) Today's Liberalism is a Developmental Issue 228
34) Socialism, Communism vs. The Freedom of
    Americanism 243
35) The Results of Liberal Democrat Policies 246
36) Liberal Politics in Conflict with Liberal Policies 250
37) The Topic of Race 255
38) Local Police and the Judicial System 266
39) A Liberal King, A UN-Constitutional President 287
40) The "Wars on" Will Never End 303
41) The Ying & Yang of Republican Decisions 304
42) Responsibilities of Choice 310
43) The Flaws of the Constitution 316
44) Some Corrections of the Constitution 322
45) The Liberal Ending of America 336
46) Conclusion to Four Branches of Government and
    Equation 337
47) Ending Note from Me to You 339

This book has many intentions but the truth is in the forefront of each. To correct history as it has been perceived or rewritten through our history. From the structure of our government to the procedures of the Constitution, at times seen through the eyes of our Founding Fathers. From tracing certain political ideologies thru history, to applying these same ideologies and their results on portions of our society. It shows how religion and science do not oppose each other but walk hand in hand through history with each leading the way at times, exposing the world's history. It uses these topics and others to trace the history of our American society and how political agendas have and are affecting that same society. Society cannot save society from society without society's help!

INTERPRETATION OF PREAMBLE

In the Preamble of the Constitution what are listed are just 6 excerpts out of many purposes, goals or a future product of the Constitution, not functions of government. Most all of the purposes are listed in the Constitution's Article I, Section 8 and are what the Founding Fathers deemed necessary at that time period for the people. The document also allowed for change through legislation for future generations. Those items listed are what the Founding Fathers wanted government to legislate through legislation once the government was formed by elections. The Founding Fathers did not feel they should legislate on any of the needs of government presented in Article I, Section 8 because their duty was to form the framework of government. It would then be the duty of the newly elected government by "We the People" who then would represent "We the People" to legislate laws to meet the needs the Founding Fathers included in the Constitution.

The powers of the Constitution are handed down to government bodies and once assigned to a body of government that power then becomes a function of that government body and only that government body the power is assigned. The 6 functions of government are as follows: to execute government, interrupt laws via of the Constitution's written words and an administration of justice, to legislate laws and to execute the powers not shared by the House of Representatives and Senate. Without following these 6 functions of government none of the items in Article I, Section 8 or anything else which legislatively followed the Constitution would have been passed into law. When using one or a combination of these 6 functions this creates a designed process for government to achieve the needed goals of government; to protect the people with a military, create a lawful society with a judicial system, establish a monetary system, etc. The Founding Fathers put forth this process as a recipe for good government of the people. To deviate from this process creates a chaotic process with the people not being represented through our government system.

The functions of the human body's organs allow the processes of breathing, walking, thinking, etc. It is these processes that allow mankind to create products such as homes, planes, airports, the "Constitution", etc. For man to change these body functions and how they work, to intermingle them, changes the processes and alters nature's product (normally not for the better) being the human body. This description I offer is what has happen to the "Constitution". A intermingling of the powers (functions) of government that has changed the process (procedures of government) which alters the quality of the product being the laws of government that rule "We the People".

THE U.S. GOVERNMENT IS A FOUR BRANCH SYSTEM

I include very little opinion in my writings of the branches of government. I have backed every statement with an example of how our government works mathematically as a four branch system and can't be duplicated using a three branch system. It includes a mathematical equation that supports my conclusion and the words of the Founding Fathers that name the four branches. The book includes a dead on description of how the "government system" has changed through history that even the Founding Fathers' writings support with their fears of a centralized accumulation of power being the Federal Government. My writings support the same fear and how it is happening.

The Founding Fathers passed away centuries ago and left many questions unanswered. Some questions can be answered, some may never be answered. My intentions are to reveal and correct history to our nation of citizens. To stimulate "the People's" minds in a effort to inform the informed with correct insights and engage the uninformed with material that might spark a renaissance in the learning's of the Constitution and the Founding Fathers intent of the document known as the Constitution for the Betterment of our Nation.

During my research of the Constitution, I never came across any structural information in regards to the Constitution other than what is written in the Constitution. To my knowledge no Founding Father ever wrote anything, before, during or after the writing of the Constitution that mentioned three or four branches or the executive branch, legislative branch or branches and judicial Branch. I also could never pinpoint the time or source of who named the three branches as our government is perceived to be in its history. When and where was the first three branch schematic used to explain the government structure? To begin a defense of the three branch system it would need to start with the answers to these questions. No three branch or bicameral government has a veto overrule of the country's leader. In a bicameral style of government, I believe all legislation is done with all parties in the room and is debated and agreed upon verbally before it is actually written and then voted on. This ensures that the bill will pass after it is written unless the wording or something has changed from the original verbal agreement. The veto overrule is a huge correction of power in our government structure and is what sets our government apart from all other governments of the world.

I first want to say "the ability for someone to change their mind displays an intellect to adapt to a changing situation when based upon correct information and it is what you base your disagreement on that shows your intelligence or ignorance", are you an independent critical thinker or a herd follower. Secondly "I think everybody needs to read the U.S. Constitution in an encyclopedia to help them understand the powers of each branch of government. Then they need to compare the actual U.S. Constitution as written using an encyclopedia as a reference so they can see the differences between the two, one being the actual document and the other being a teaching tool."

The words that describe and name our branches of government in the Constitution's Articles I, II and III are the following in order of appearance: Congress, **Senate, House of Representatives**, Representative, Representatives, Senators, Senator, Vice President, the **President** of the United States, each House, either House, neither

House, two Houses, that House, the other House, both Houses, a *President* of the United States of America, said House, the *President*, one supreme *Court* and those are all the words.

The names chosen by the Founding Fathers for our branches of government being the *President, House of Representatives* and supreme *Court* had never been used before in the history of world governments. Why did they feel the need to have names for government bodies that had never been used in a previous government system? Because the government they were creating also had never been done in history! Using three names that had never been used before in government, unique unto themselves, why would the Founding Fathers use a three branch system which had repeatedly failed throughout the history of the world? They didn't! They created the first four branch government system in the world's history. The Founding Fathers' choice to reuse the word *Senate* was to honor the world's first Republic government. The first Government to use the word in government was established within the Roman Empire and was a historical milestone as the first attempt at a self governing government by the people. Exactly what the Founding Fathers wanted as an end product of the Constitution, self governing by the people. To think the Founding Fathers after putting great thought into the names they chose would turn around and rename them with as mundane names as executive, legislative and judicial absolutely makes no sense (does an injustice to our Founding Fathers) and is not supported by the wording of the Constitution which is what they hoped to be a historical document. The only way for it to be a historical document is for it to continually function throughout the history of a lasting great nation.

The four government bodies have six powers or functions given to them by "We the People" in the powers of the Constitution; to execute government, interrupt laws via of the Constitution and administer justice, legislate laws and execute the powers not shared by the House of Representatives and Senate. Without using a combination of these six functions absolutely nothing happens in government. Anything that comes out of government is a purpose, a goal, a law, a product of a combination of these six functions. Now this doesn't make our government a six branch system and it doesn't make it a three branch system because someone picked out the three major functions of the six functions of government and used them to name the branches of government. The same three major functions just happen to be the second word in the first sentence of Articles I, II and III but is not the subject of any of the sentences. The "Constitution" has three main powers of government described in the document, they are distributed among four government bodies or branches of government. Our branches of government are not determined by the number of powers granted to government by the Constitution but the independent government bodies (branches) named in the Constitution by the Founding Fathers that possess an assigned power or may share a specific power of government independently of the other body or branches of government. The powers are what they are, powers, not the branches or bodies of our government. Why have all other forms of government been classified by our educational entities using their bodies of government and ours has been classified by the existing main powers of government? Keep in mind the descriptive boxes in the power schematic of our government usually have descriptions of what that branch does in government being the words executive, legislative & judicial which are adjectives and normally according to the rules of the English language describes what they do and is not the name for who they are. When these adjective words being executive, legislative and judicial are combined with the word "branch", or in my argument being "branches", were put there as a teaching tool by teachers and/or the news papers of some time period for novices (children's education and/or an uneducated public of that time regarding the Constitution) that might not understand what the **President, House of Representatives, Senate**, and supreme **Court** do in the scheme of government in relation to the highest law of the land, the United States' Constitution.

Now with a little history and math I will show how each are a branch of our government and the House of Representatives and the Senate are NOT combined under the **Descriptive Phrase** "Legislative Branch". When using this **Descriptive Phrase** being executive branch, legislative branch & judicial branch it implies three branches of government.

When you are told over and over something you begin to believe it and at some point you accept it as the Truth. There is a difference between being told and being taught. "Being told is **INDOCTRINATION** into a certain way of thinking without any supporting facts. Being **TAUGHT** is backing the curriculum with **FACTS** that support the **SUBJECT** allowing the **TRUTH** to be seen"!

You may still say Congress consists of the Senate & the House of Representatives which is true BUT only when they convene (assemble) or in the "Constitution" when the Founding Fathers used the term describing their shared legislative powers. Legislating laws is the first function of their two constitutional powers. The second function is to execute the powers not shared by each house and they may or may not need (depending on what power is being executed) to convene (assemble) as Congress to execute their powers given to them in the "Constitution". When the House of Representatives and the Senate convenes to form Congress that doesn't mean the House of Representatives and Senate disappear from government when becoming "Congress". The exact opposite is true! That "Congress" disappears from government when the House of Representatives and Senate are not convened. That is why the President can do recess appointments (judges, department heads) to the judicial system and government agencies or departments because congress no longer exists. To argue that our government is a three branch system means that the House of Representatives and Senate are always one under Congress. Therefore the House of Representatives and Senate would not need to convene (assemble) to legislate laws because they are one branch of government all the time which is not true. The reason they convene as Congress is because they are two separate branches of government.

After the "New World" (North America) was discovered the main people who immigrated (in the beginning) to this land were from England. What they were fleeing from was a government with absolute power dispensed by a King. They thought an ocean would separate them from that oppressive form of government but it didn't. So they fought the War of Independence to gain their freedom from that King & Country.

The Founding Fathers had to form a government that would not transform into something that repeated the form of government they fled and fought against. The Founding Fathers needed to form an elected government with separated powers. What they were worried with most was giving one body of government too much power (three versus four branches, four branches divides power even more among the branches) especially the body of government (President) that might create another King or Supreme Ruler. The Founding Fathers were much smarter than many of today's educated people that don't give them the credit they deserve for writing a document that up until my writings they didn't even understand. They had to disburse power and the functions of government evenly to government bodies or what many today refer to as "branches" of government. Now if you have three branches (Executive, Legislative, Judicial) each branch would have a percentage of power being 33 1/3% if disbursed evenly. That means the Senate and House of Representatives would each have 16.66...% of power. When convened as Congress would not have the power to overrule a President's veto with a 2/3 super majority vote of the Senate (16.66...%) and House of Representatives (16.66...%) because their powers combined would only equal that of the President (33.33...%). In a 3 branch government how does the Senate not concur or disagree with a President's appointment when the Senate's power in government is only 16.66...% and the President's power in government is 33.33...% being twice that of the Senate's power in government? When you have four branches of equal power (25% each) each branch can only agree or disagree; concur or not concur. With Presidential appointments, the President picks his choice, the Senate either agrees or disagrees; concurs or does not concur. Neither branch has the power to force its choice on the other branch. This is also true for the House of Representatives (25% of power) and the Senate (25% of power) when Congress legislates laws each branch must agree or concur to pass the bill on to the President. Congress' power must be greater than the President's power to reflect Congress's ability to overrule a President's (25% of power) veto with a 2/3 vote thus Congress' joined powers equaling 50% of government's total power.

A four branch government can easily have the perception of a three branch government when the House of Representatives and

Senate continually agree or can compromise on their differences. It is when the House of Representatives and Senate continually disagree and won't compromise on their differences that it becomes evident causing perception to fade into reality and the four branches of government become evident in the reality of government. With four branches being the *President*, *House of Representatives*, *Senate* and supreme *Court* each branch now has 25% of the power if disbursed evenly. How each branch uses these powers given through the Constitution will demonstrate the four branches of government with evenly disbursed powers. The best and most direct way to do this is with the most fundamental aspect of government, the stop and start of government. This is referred to as "government shutdown" which can only happen each time a yearly budget bill (funding for government) or a national debt bill (borrowing to fund government) needs to be addressed by government.

How many branches of government can shutdown government? The answer is three branches.

The ***President*** (25% of power) by vetoing the yearly budget bill or national debt bill. This can be overruled by Congress with its 50% of power when and only when Congress agrees with a super majority 2/3 vote of "Yea" by both the Senate and the House of Representatives to pass the bill into law without the President's signature.

The ***House of Representatives*** (25% of power) by not introducing or not responding to a yearly budget bill or a national debt bill or by passing a yearly budget or national debt bill to the senate that the Senate won't vote on or will vote on but not pass. Neither the Senate nor the President separately or together can do anything to restart government.

The ***Senate*** (25% of power) by not introducing (see Article I, Section 7) or not responding to a yearly budget bill or a national debt bill or by passing a yearly budget or national debt bill to the House of Representatives that the House of Representatives won't vote on or will vote on but not pass. Neither the House of Representatives nor the President separately or together can do anything to restart government.

This shutdown of government formula can NOT be duplicated under a three branch system because the mathematical powers of the House of Representatives and the Senate will be different not allowing it mathematically to happen.

The Founding Fathers' actual process of legislation is that all three branches must concur (agree) to pass a bill into law. When this is accomplished each branch individually of the other two has exerted its 25% of power in government with a concurring vote or decision. If the first two legislative branches can't agree on the bill then the bill will never reach the third branch being the President. When a written bill is passed by the legislative branches to the President he either concurs with his signature or not concurs with a veto of the bill. Once a vetoed bill is returned to the House from which it originated, a legislative decision is needed. It is now the two legislative branches that can combine their individual powers of Government (25% each = 50% combined overruling power) with a 2/3's concurring vote of both branches to overrule the President's (25% of power) veto thus allowing the bill to become law without the President's concurring signature as designated by "We the People's" Constitution.

The true power of Congress (50% of power) in government is to take the power of government out of the hands of one man and one branch of government, the President ("Too see the true character of a man give him power"), and place it in the hands of 535 people and two branches of government being the House of Representatives (435 people) and the Senate (100 people). "It is a lot easier to corrupt the mind of one person than it is to corrupt the minds of 535 people".

Now you should be able to see the proper **Descriptive Phrase** to describe our branches of Government is executive branch, legislative branches (meaning two or more and both branches, House of Representatives and the Senate, convene to form Congress to legislate laws under the powers of the Constitution given to both branches) and judicial branch. These words are not the bodies or branches of our government but are the three major powers of the six powers given to our government by the Constitution. So the words executive, legislative & judicial are nothing more than a teaching tool for the powers of our branches of government inserted into the power schematic and then were intentionally or unintentionally picked as our three branches of government.

If the House of Representatives is not an equal branch of government how did a inferior co-branch of government shutdown government in 2013 trying to stop or delay the implementation of the Affordable Care Act, aka Obamacare? It wasn't the Senate or Congress or the legislative branch (it actually was one of the legislative branches, which one? Having to ask and then answer this question to get the correct answer is an admission of four branches in itself!) or the President or the supreme Court or any terrorist organization as Barack Obama & Democrats described the Republican controlled House of Representatives. The House of Representatives is an equal branch of government and so is the Senate because the Senate mirrors the House of Representatives in shared powers and both have powers unique unto themselves. The Senate and House of Representatives are each fifty percent of the power of Congress which legislates one hundred percent of all bills and laws. It is alarming how through our country's history, educational system and/or news papers this phrase used as a teaching tool sneaked right into our perception of how our government's power schematic is laid out. The phrase "Executive Branch, Legislative Branch or Branches & Judicial Branch" should not be between the top tier "Government" and the bodies of government in the power schematic and when removed reveals the true names for our four branches. To avoid future confusion in our educational system they should be below the ***President***, ***House of Representatives***, ***Senate*** and supreme ***Court*** because these are the names of the branches of the United States of America's Government.

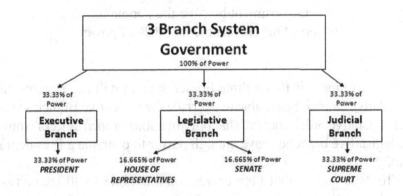

3 Branch System Government
100% of Power

| 33.33% of Power | 33.33% of Power | 33.33% of Power |

| Executive Branch | Legislative Branch | Judicial Branch |

| 33.33% of Power | 16.665% of Power | 16.665% of Power | 33.33% of Power |
| PRESIDENT | HOUSE OF REPRESENTATIVES | SENATE | SUPREME COURT |

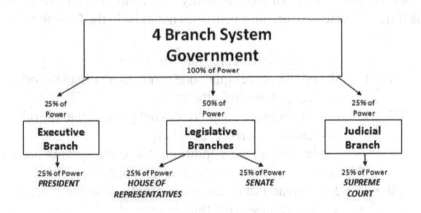

4 Branch System Government
100% of Power

| 25% of Power | 50% of Power | 25% of Power |

| Executive Branch | Legislative Branches | Judicial Branch |

| 25% of Power | 25% of Power | 25% of Power | 25% of Power |
| PRESIDENT | HOUSE OF REPRESENTATIVES | SENATE | SUPREME COURT |

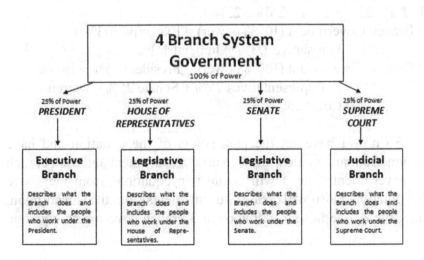

4 Branch System Government
100% of Power

| 25% of Power | 25% of Power | 25% of Power | 25% of Power |
| PRESIDENT | HOUSE OF REPRESENTATIVES | SENATE | SUPREME COURT |

| Executive Branch | Legislative Branch | Legislative Branch | Judicial Branch |
| Describes what the Branch does and includes the people who work under the President. | Describes what the Branch does and includes the people who work under the House of Representatives. | Describes what the Branch does and includes the people who work under the Senate. | Describes what the Branch does and includes the people who work under the Supreme Court. |

Constitution (100% power) given to
Government by "We the People"
to form Our Government (100% of power)

My argument is that a three branch system will not support the
Legislative Branch being able to overrule the Executive Branch's veto
of a legislative bill. I contend that only in a four branch system would
the legislative branches have enough power to overrule a President's
veto.

To demonstrate that I am correct on this issue I will create two
complete mathematical equations. The first equation is a 3 branch and
4 branch government without the ability to overrule a President's veto
as if the 2/3 vote to overrule a veto does not exist in the Constitution.

Mathematical Equation Setup
1 = 1   : the numbers are equal, one is not greater than the other,
            one cannot overrule the other.
1/3 = 1/3 : the numbers are equal, one is not greater than the other,
            one cannot overrule the other.
            Under the above conditions the only options are to
            agree or disagree, concur or not concur.
50 > 25 : 50 is greater than 25, one is greater than the other, the
            greater can overrule the lesser.
100% = 1/3% or 33.3...% + 1/3% or 33.3...% + 1/3% or 33.3...%
100% = 25% + 25% + 25% + 25%
3 Branch Government (100% power) = Executive 1/3% +
            Legislative 1/3% + Judicial 1/3%
4 Branch Government (100% power) = President 25% + House
            of Representatives 25% + Senate 25% + supreme
            Court 25%

So now I have set the parameters of the equation and have
assigned a mathematical value to all of government and each branch
of government. Now I will create two equations from the above
information. I also will create two statements from the Constitution,
one true & one false. I will apply a 3 branch government equation

and a 4 branch government equation to each statement then apply that to the Constitution. Mathematics is the universal language of the universe, it has no opinion, there will only be one correct answer and the others will be incorrect.

Legislative Branch 1/3% = Executive Branch 1/3% = Statement = Controlled Statement
House of Representatives 25% + Senate 25% > President 25% = Statement = Controlled Statement

Controlled Statement = <u>What the Constitution States</u>

<u>What the Constitution States</u>
Remember, as if the 2/3 vote to overrule a veto <u>does not</u> exist in the Constitution
1). House of Representatives 25% + Senate 25% > President 25% = legislative branches can't overrule executive branch
2). House of Representatives 25% + Senate 25% > President 25% = legislative branches can overrule executive branch
3). Legislative Branch 1/3% = Executive Branch 1/3% = Legislative Branch can overrule Executive Branch
4). Legislative Branch 1/3% = Executive Branch 1/3% = Legislative Branch can't overrule Executive Branch

The 1st Equation: The math states the Legislative Branches can overrule the President but the statement states the Legislative Branches can't overrule Executive Branch and the statement is correct by the Constitution. The math doesn't support the statement. So the equation is incorrect.

The 2nd Equation: The math states the Legislative Branches can overrule the President. The statement states the Legislative Branches can overrule Executive Branch. The Constitution states it can't. The Constitution doesn't support the math or the statement. So the equation is incorrect.

The 3rd Equation: The math states the Branches are equal and one can't overrule the other. The statement states Legislative Branch can overrule the Executive Branch. The Constitution says it can't. The math and the Constitution doesn't support the statement. So the equation is incorrect.

The 4th Equation: The math states the Branches are equal and one can't overrule the other. The statement states the Legislative Branch can't overrule Executive Branch and the Constitution supports the math and the statement. All three support each other. So the equation is _CORRECT!_

Again, mathematics is the universal language of the universe, it has no opinion, there will only be one correct answer and the others will be incorrect.

What the Constitution States

Now, lets do the equation as the 2/3 vote to overrule a veto <u>does</u> exist in our Constitution.

1). House of Representatives 25% + Senate 25% > President 25% = legislative branches can't overrule executive branch

2). House of Representatives 25% + Senate 25% > President 25% = legislative branches can overrule executive branch

3). Legislative Branch 1/3% = Executive Branch 1/3% = Legislative Branch can overrule Executive Branch

4). Legislative Branch 1/3% = Executive Branch 1/3% = Legislative Branch can't overrule Executive Branch

The 4th Equation: The math states the Branches are equal and one can't overrule the other. The statement states Legislative Branch can't overrule Executive Branch but the Constitution states it can. The Constitution does not support the math or the statement. So the equation is incorrect.

The 3rd Equation: The math states the Branches are equal and one can't overrule the other. The statement states Legislative Branch can overrule Executive Branch. The Constitution states the Legislative Branch can overrule the Executive Branch. The math doesn't support the statement or the Constitution. So the equation is incorrect.

The 1st Equation: The math states the Legislative Branches can overrule the President. The statement states Legislative Branches can't overrule Executive Branch. The Constitution states the Legislative Branch can over Executive Branch. The math and the Constitution do not support the statement. So the equation is incorrect.

The 2nd Equation: The math states the Legislative Branches can overrule the President. The statement states Legislative Branches can overrule Executive Branch. The Constitution supports the math and the statement. All three support each other. So the equation is *CORRECT!*

Conclusion: Without the 2/3 vote to overrule a President's veto the equation chose a three branch government. With the 2/3 vote to overrule a President's veto the equation chose a four branch government. Again a three branch government will not support a 2/3 vote to overrule a President's veto because the branches have equal power of 1/3% each. The United States of America's form of government created by the Constitution has a 2/3 vote to overrule the President's veto in the Constitution so the United States of America's form of Government must be four branches with the branches being the ***President, House of Representatives, Senate and*** supreme ***Court.***

With this mathematical equation you now have three options and three options only on which too make an ***intellectually educated*** decision on how many branches exist in our government.

1). The equation is wrong and that is how I managed to get the conclusion I desired. But to say this you must pinpoint the flaw in the equation, just saying so is not enough.
2). The equation is correct but the answer is wrong. Be very careful with this option because now you are stating that mathematics is flawed and this has never happened throughout the history of mathematics.
3). The equation is correct, the answer is correct meaning everything I have written in regards to the United States' form of government being a four branch system is correct.

Unbelievable as it may seem there are people that will still insist on the three branches and yet they will not read any portion of what I have written. There are others who after reading portions of it still try to develop an argument which ends right back at what they were taught in school being first through twelfth grade or college and what they were taught can't be wrong. They paid good money for that college education. I even had one person high up in our local school system educated at Ole Miss with a History Degree compare what I wrote to a actual tree and its branches, it was amazing to me the stupidity of his argument. Yet there are many including principals in our local school systems who were stunned after reading this because a light went off in their head allowing them to see the truth of what I had written. For the ones who disagreed, in their defense, none including the people who agreed with just what was written had seen the equation or the sentence breakdown of Articles I, II and III because I had not written them yet. This also shows that throwing money at an educational system doesn't guarantee a good education if the curriculum being taught is flawed. This ought to open our government's eyes to how essential a correct curriculum is because without it there is no reason to teach.

There is absolutely nothing wrong with questioning what you are being taught especially if there are no facts being introduced on the subject. If the teacher has no answers for the questions chances are the teacher was indoctrinated by that same thought process without answers or **Facts** meaning what was and is being **taught** is only a **theory** and **shouldn't be portrayed as the Truth**. Even with facts, are the facts limited to a set of perceptions which predetermine the outcome of the answer? If so, then the answer is incorrect because the facts were intended to be limited by the source in regards to the subject to achieve a certain predetermined outcome. In other words, **Indoctrination!**

THE HOUSE OF REPRESENTATIVES IS TRULY A REFLECTION OF THE PEOPLE

Our two government branches that legislate bills and the one branch that decides if it wants to execute the bill which may become law are each elected in three separate ways under the original Constitution for a purpose. It was for a representational format. The time of term in office also has a purpose. The President is elected by an electoral system selected by the peoples' vote of the states for a national position for a term of four years. The President, one person one home, if or when he/she goes home does so to one state, one county, one city or town. So their only true contact with the people may just be a selection from those options. True, he/she may own a vacation home or shake hands while on the campaign trail. But where he/she grew up in a town or county, they truly have the same values and beliefs because they all shared the same environment, so they truly have the President's ear. Of course his/her donors also have an ear, but that ear is bought and paid for. So the President is either belief motivated and/or money motivated or a combination thereof.

The Senate, two Senators are elected by the people from each State to represent the whole state for a term of six years. Again, one state, two people two homes, two counties, two towns or cities and everything else from the above paragraph also applies to the Senators.

The House of Representatives is elected for a two year term by the people to represent a district which covers a predetermined area of a county or counties within a state. The number of Representatives is determined by the population of the state. The result is a House of Representatives' member and his/her office is guaranteed to live and be within a short proximity of a voter and what is mentioned in the first paragraph also applies to the Representatives. The two year terms of the House of Representatives was created by the Founding Fathers because the direction of government can be altered by "We the People" every two years instead of waiting four years for a Presidential election or six years for a Senator's election. For the House of Representatives alone to alter the direction of government it must be 50%, along with the Senate (50%), of the branches that form Congress (100%) that write and pass all bills to the President to become law or vetoed. A do nothing Congress, as described by today's Democrats, does not exist and never will. What does exist are two branches of government with two different ideologies and each is not willing to compromise their ideas on or of government. So because they will not pass legislation promoting the others ideology they are "a deadlocked Congress" in regards to those issues. Sometimes doing nothing is doing something. The Founding Fathers' belief was "no law being passed is better than a bad law being passed". That is why the Founding Fathers designed checks and balances of legislation that are divided between two legislative branches which encourage a deadlock of government instead of promoting bad government that passes bad legislation. So a "deadlocked government" can be and is a normal aspect of government when needed and is not an act of terrorism as described by Barack Obama. When government is divided in such a way as Barack Obama has divided it there are only two positions, one is right and one is wrong with very little shared in between and the Founding Fathers knew of this concept when writing the "Constitution".

It is the voter's responsibility to break the deadlock with elected officials that support the "People's" views. The 2010 election that changed the House of Representatives from Democrat to Republican control and the 2014 election that changed the Senate also from Democrat to Republican control by "We the People" was a change in direction of the views of "We the People". Also a low turnout of voters of one party is essentially a vote for a lack of faith in that party or the party's leaders without having to put forth the effort of voting. Elections do have consequences Mr. President whether you agree with it or not, Barack Obama. It seems Barack only agrees with something when it works in his favor, how convenient.

The intent by the Founding Fathers was for the Legislative Branches to travel home and collect information as too the needs of the people along with ideas for solutions from the people who know the problems they are encountering and then write legislation regarding those ideas, a bottom up solution of governing. Because of this the Founding Fathers wanted the House of Representatives' voice in government to be at least as loud if not louder because of their numbers (435) than the Senate (100) and the President (1). The Founding Fathers would not and did not dilute the strongest voice of "We the People" by combining the House of Representatives with the second strongest (335 less people) voice of government, the Senate, under one branch. The Fathers' favorite son is the House of Representatives and wanted to ensure this thought by making it and the Senate equal branches in government because these two branches are the closest to "the People". Because of this 4.35 to 1.0 ratio of the House of Representatives to Senate members is the Founding Fathers reason for this following statement. Article I, Section 7 of the Constitution States:

"All Bills for raising Revenue shall originate in the House of Representatives; but the Senate may propose or concur with Amendments as on other Bills".

The Founding Fathers wanted the branch closest to the people to be the branch that controlled the wallet (spending) of "We the People". This was changed in the early to mid 1900's (I think) by congress but not by an Amendment to the Constitution but an agreement of Congress which obviously was and still is, by over stepping their powers, a violation of the Constitution. Again an example of the Federal Government by doing this has shifted the flow of thoughts and ideas from the bottom up, the people to government, to a top down, government to the people, form of government. The Founding Fathers also gave the last say in government to Congress with a 2/3 overruling vote of a veto of the President.

How has this changed over the years? With technology, the invention of radio, television, the internet and higher speeds of travel from horse back to train to Air Force One. Just to show how technology has effected our government lets ask and answer a couple of questions. This example was used by one of my social professors at Pensacola Jr. College to demonstrate that the size of government can be reduced without any repercussions to government or "We the People". Which State of the fifty states has the most counties or parishes? That would be Texas. Which State of the fifty states has the least amount of counties or parishes? That would be Alaska our largest state. Now you ask how can that be? When our country brought the country of Texas into the Union of the States in 1845 the main mode of transportation was horseback. The reasoning for the many county seats was to be able to reach a county seat in 1 day's horseback ride from anywhere in the State. When Alaska was brought into the Union of the States in 1959 the main mode of transportation was the high winged, short takeoff and landing capabilities of the Bush Plane that can reach the seat of government also in one day from anywhere in the State. Even today this mode of transportation is the fastest and most reliable for the people of that state.

In the early days of government the President rarely left the vicinity of Washington D.C. due to the time required for such travel. The President had to be close to government to address any unforeseen event such as an attack on the country. At this point in government history it was the House of Representatives that were the President's eyes and ears. The technological advances have allowed the President a larger view of the country in the President's perspective. But the President will never be entrenched among the "People" as the House of Representatives are entrenched among the "People". This lack of insight by many individuals that have become President is what has caused a President to lose the support of the "People" during his presidential term or terms. This larger perceived Presidential view has negated the House of Representatives and Senate as the eyes and ears of the President. Thus the legislative branches have become more of a political foe in regards to government and a Presidents Agenda, whether deemed good or bad, instead of an asset if used properly. These inventions have given the President a larger and louder bullhorn than the legislative branches which was never the intent of the Founding Fathers and the framework of which the Founding Fathers created our government through the Constitution. The Fathers couldn't foresee these inventions, and the shifting balance of the power of speech has changed from the legislative branches to leaning much more towards the President. This is happening for two reasons. First is that the legislative branches spend much less time in and amongst the people so the problems are not truly heard along with the peoples' ideas for solutions. The legislative branches are now spending more time in and assimilating too the Washington D.C. environment thus un-assimilating with the area and people they represent. The second reason is that the inventions mentioned allows the President a larger and louder voice to express his ideas to the nation's voters but he gets very little feedback or solutions directly from the people. In the earlier period of time the legislators got all the feed back and all the ideas from "the People". They then would return to Washington D.C. to correct the problems to "the People's" satisfaction. As I mentioned earlier the Constitution was designed as a bottom (We the People) up form of governing and these inventions have created a more of a top (President) down form of governing which muffles the voice of "the People". Thus we have now created a form of government not intended by the Founding Fathers. This has also given the Federal Government the power to rule over "We the People" versus a government of "the People" who identify their problems and suggested ideas to our legislators to legislate laws to solve the problems "the People" face. The end result is laws, executive orders, regulations or rules and unconstitutional supreme Court rulings that now create problems for "the People" to have to navigate around and makes the nation much less productive as a whole. Less productive equals less innovations, fewer jobs, less pay, less wealth, a lower standard of living, a lower class of people being the unemployed, etc.

Article V of the Constitution was written into the Constitution to correct what has changed to our form of government. The Founding Fathers could not foresee these inventions or the changes they would create to our form of government. They did foresee the possibility of such a situation becoming a reality. It is not just the creation of a King they did not want but a Federal Government with runaway powers that may also become "King", not in name but in the reality of government as a whole.

Article V of the Constitution is the intent of the Founding Fathers to return the ideas of government and how "We the People" want to be governed back to "We the People". Each state has more State

Representatives and Senators than they do Federal Government "House of Representatives" and "Senators". These State elected Officials live right in and amongst us in greater numbers and have greater contact with each and every one of us. They are closer to us thus they are even more likely to represent our views than our Federal elected Officials. That is exactly why the Founding Fathers empowered the States by a Convention to overrule the Federal Government with Amendments to the Constitution because the Federal Government is no longer listening to "We the People". "The People" continually try to elect new legislators to replace the ones not hearing us but because of the small numbers of turn over by the time we send a new legislator to Washington D.C. the ones "the People" had earlier elected have now assimilated into the Federal Government "System" so they seem too no longer hear "the People". We have now created this vicious cycle that causes nothing to be done for "The People" and everything being done for government. This cycle is what has caused the less fortunate of "We the People" to become disenchanted with government and the private sector in regards to opportunity. It is businesses and jobs which leads to wealth and upward mobility in society thus out of self preservation they will turn to any means including government for their survival. Yet it is government that created their situation with high taxes on businesses making it harder to create or maintain a business thus less job opportunities. Government has now seized on this situation as a means of buying votes to keep the legislators that have been assimilated into the Washington D.C. environment as the "keepers of the People" and hoping to ensure their place in Government and Society at a cost too and of "We the People".

There are two philosophies by which an elected official may govern. The first is "the voters elected me to do a job and my job includes making these type of decisions for the voters because I know what is best for everyone involved". The 2nd is "the voters elected me to make my decisions based on what I hear from the majority of my constitutes. That seems to be the best decision for the majority of my constitutes". Those are the two and of course all the distance in-between the two statements too get from one statement to the other statement.

In my opinion our government started as a second philosophy nation and at some point started moving towards the first philosophy and in the last 50 years has accelerated towards a government being run more by the first philosophy. More of a "do as I say not as I do" type of government which makes every citizen not in government a substandard citizen. To return government back to the correct path of the Founding Fathers intent of government the States should use Article V as a means to change the path of government and the nation. First with a balanced budget, Second with term limits and Third to limit the powers of the Federal Government. If not, the nation will collapse under the burden of government itself or the people not willing to live under the type of government we have been heading towards will rise up in revolt.

The Constitution twice relinquishes power civilly to the greater number of people in government. Beginning with the President and his one branch it passes the power to the two legislative branches being the House of Representatives and the Senate with their ability to overrule a President's veto, it then again passes power from the Federal government to the Government of the States with Article V of the Constitution; a Convention of the States and the power to amend the Constitution with a Amendment of the Constitution. Each time it relinquishes that power it relinquishes it to a larger body of government who are closer to the people which is self governing by the people. The Constitution is a document designed to govern the people from the bottom (the people) up not from the top (the President) down, the people have the ultimate and last say in government. The last step in relinquishing of power is a failure of our elected representatives and government not to govern for the people and by the people under the guidelines of the Constitution thus causing a revolt by the people or a State or States aka a Civil War. Possibly a break up of the Union of the States with a economic melt down causing the government to collapse thus creating a weak or no government. All because our federal government won't abide by the procedures and rules of the Constitution that allow for the Proper Representation of "We the People" of Our Nation.

THE SENATE

The Senate is one of two legislative branches with 100 members. Two elected officials for a 6 year term from each State of the U.S. of America. The Senate is the second largest branch of government with the second largest voice of the "People". It is also the Founding Fathers second favorite son based strictly on its smaller size. The Senate was designed by the Founding Fathers as each "States" voice in government during the process of writing everyday legislative federal "common laws". Under the Founding Father's Constitution Senators were elected or appointed by each "State's Legislative Body" to represent the interest's of each "State" in Federal Government. In 1913 with the passage of the 17th Amendment under the powers of the "Constitution" the Congress voted to allow the voting public of each "State" to elect their Senate officials. Even though it was done constitutionally the purpose of the Senate was to represent the "State's Government" not the "States people" but while serving the greater "State" you ultimately indirectly serve "the people" of the State. "The people" are also represented by their elected members of the other federal legislative branch of the United States being the House of Representatives. The "States Legislative" body should know the needs of the "State's" people as a whole better than the "People" in a single city or town would. The "State's Legislative" body then has some real time input for everyday Federal "Common Law" being legislated by their U.S. Senators from the State's Capital building. The "Senators" know the "State's Legislative body" can end their appointment at the end of their term if the Senator went against the State's interest. With that "State Power", the "State's Senators" when acting as a majority of all 50 states were able to act as a Check & Balance on the Federal Government. Once that power was transferred from the "State" to "We the People" of the state it allowed the "Senators" to act freely of the "State's Legislative body" and then answer to the "People" after the fact of federal legislation with the damage already done to the States and "the People". If "the People" can't keep track of their U.S. Senator's daily vote or much less can't have any pre-vote input towards those daily votes then that real time power that the "State" once possessed and managed for "the people" of the State over the Senators is now lost to the Federal Government and special interest groups. This allowed the U.S. Senate to answer to a unknowing, forgetful, sometimes not caring, time restricted because of their own jobs, "People of a State" that can't keep track of what their Senator is doing legislatively on a day to day bases which is exactly what the "States" did for "We the People". The difference being as the "States" lost their powers to the Federal Government the "States" were not able to fight back against the encroaching powers of the Federal Government. The "Senate" has now become part of the Federal Government elected by the people which before that was one of the checks and balances of the Founding Fathers original Constitution. The "People" unknowingly relinquished some of their own power in government by ending their partnership with their "State" Legislative Representatives to combat the growing powers of the Federal Government. The "People" thought they were still getting a larger voice in government because they would elect the "Senators" but they sacrificed the voice and powers of their "State" that existed in doing so. As I said before "the People" must be engaged to elect a creditable official. How many times a year do you talk directly to your State Senator? How many times have you left a message or had to speak to an assistant? When the Senators answered to the "States" they made sure they were in direct contact as much as needed for a real time update to ensure their positions in government. Now the Senator doesn't have to answer for the rights of their "States" which now leaves the "States" voiceless and "We the People" whining about our loss of freedom to our Federal Government. This was a major shift in power from the "States" and "We the People" to the "Federal Government". "The People" and "the States" of that time period didn't have a true understanding of how government would change when doing it in the name of "the People". The basic agreement that formed the Union of the States was between the States and the

"Constitution" that the States allowed to Unite them, not a Federal Government that didn't exist. That means each time there is a abuse of the "Constitution" the "States" are given another option too reject (opt out) the agreement which formed the "Union of the States" in my opinion.

With Obamacare aka the Affordable Care Act there are 34 states that didn't set up State Healthcare Exchanges due to the future costs that the States would incur. If you have additional State's cost of government additional revenue must be raised to pay for it. Now if the "States" had control of their 2 Senators as originally designed in the Constitution the vote on the ACA Bill that passed the Senate would have failed with a vote of about 68 against to 32 in favor. Under the Founding Fathers form of government the Senators were there to stop the Federal Government from imposing its will on the States. Obamacare is a tax placed on the States that set up healthcare exchanges. Sure the Federal Government covers the cost in the beginning but after a number of years the cost goes to the States. This is an expense to the States that now must find funding for this expense which means the Federal Government has now forced the States to tax the "People" in the name of the Federal Government to pay for an expense created by the Federal Government. Do you understand how changing something that was not understood by the elected officials who wanted and changed the Founding Fathers' formula to governing was an act of stupidity allowed or encouraged by the People?

The second problem is the "Senate" being allowed to create "legislative" spending bills out of the Senate house. This happened sometime in the early to mid 1900's with an agreement between both houses. Unlike the 17th Amendment this was done illegally by the House of Representatives of that time period because they can't relinquish that power without a Constitutional amendment. The Founding Fathers intentionally put this power in the hands of the branch closest to the people for a purpose. So now with these changes it allows the "Senate" to legislate spending bills aimed at the "State" to force the "State" into a program of which it might not be able to afford without the "State Government" having a voice on how their own resources are spent. This will cause a "State" to raise taxes to afford the matching funds for a Federal Government program such as what was done with the Affordable Care Act. So a richer "State" may get money collected from all 50 states while a poorer "State" loses its contribution of the Federal Tax monies because of its lack of resources to participate. If our national Senators were controlled by the "State" using the "Affordable Care Act" as an example would not have passed in the Senate.

The Founding Fathers wrote these processes into the "Constitution" for a reason. That reason was to ensure that the Federal Government's powers would not encroach on a "State" or "States" Rights as a *sovereign* *"State"* of the *United States* of America. History definitely shows the loss of "States Rights" to the Federal Government's ever increasing powers which are now encroaching on "We the People's" Rights with one less option to limit the powers of the Federal Government.

In my personal opinion I believe the Founding Fathers had a much greater knowledge and understanding of government than anyone that followed in government after that era. Their knowledge on government checks and balances far out weights that of our current government officials. To correct these imbalances the "Constitution" should be returned to its original form in regards to these topics to restore "States Rights" and the "Power of the Purse". Also for future Amendments to the "Constitution" my opinion is they cannot change the basic form or processes of government drawn out by the Founding Fathers in the "Constitution". The elected officials should not change a document that they don't truly understand which causes an undesired effect of which the Founding Fathers warned us about over 200 years earlier, a centralized accumulation of government power being the Federal Government.

The "States" may have brought this on themselves by creating laws that were so different than the other states that formed our union of states. An example of today's state's laws being used to harass a citizen of another state is the following. A citizen from state "A" travels thru states "B" and "C" using a recreational vehicle to get to state "D" for vacation. While driving thru the two states a state's law enforcement officer or county sheriff's deputy pulls this person over based strictly on the looks of the person behind the wheel of a $1/4 million dollar RV. Once stopped and searched for anything illegal nothing is found except for a single solitary beer in the refrigerator. Now needing to excuse the officer's own actions to justify the stop the officer must write the RV owner a ticket for illegal transportation of liquor across state lines. The stupidity of this action is also backed by the county or state court using the situation as a source of protection and revenue. The main reason to uphold the statute of these types of laws is the fact that the citizen was subject to an illegal stop and search and without the ticket it opens up the county or state to a lawsuit. By the States not addressing these issues even in today's society it allowed the Federal Government to intervene with its powers to correct situations between the "States" even though this situation I use as an example has never been correct by the county, state or federal government for the reason I listed. Government and the people involved in the running of government will always protect government because that is protecting themselves and their actions. The right's of a citizen and the abuse of that citizen's rights will almost always take a back seat to the unwritten or unconstitutional right's and the will of government being local, state or federal.

SUPREME COURT'S ACCUMULATION OF POWER FOR THE FEDERAL GOVERNMENT

The Founding Fathers did not view the supreme Court as they did the other three branches of government for two reasons. First reason is the Court is not elected by "We the People". The second reason is the Court is Bound and Restricted to what it can do by the Words of the "Constitution" and the processes thereof. The States agreed to be governed by the written words of the Constitution allowing a Union of the States creating our country being the United States of America.

What makes the supreme Court think, with its 25% of power in government, it can *change* a written "Common Law" that required 50% or 75% of the total power of government to pass a legislated bill into Law? What makes the supreme Court think it can *change* a Article or Amendment of "We the People's" Constitution when the

Constitution states it takes a minimum of 38 States to *change* "We the People's" Constitution? Will the supreme Court please render its *Interpreted decision* or a *Constitutionally worded decision* on this Question!

If the supreme Court gives a interpreted decision for a answer it *will* come up with a *unconstitutional reason*. If the supreme Court gives a decision based on the written words of "We the People's" Constitution it *will not* be able to come up with a *Constitutional reason*.

This is the fourth *"check and balance"* of the Four Branches of our Government's legislative process. No branch of the four has power over the other branches except for Congress's veto overrule of the President as described in the Constitution. The Constitution is a document of *concurring or not concurring power only*, because of the equally divided power among the four branches. This is the Founding Fathers' concept of *"Balance"* written into "We the People's" Constitution. With four branches (100% of Government) concurring on a legislated law, the law must be a good law. With three branches concurring, being both legislative branches (50% of Government doing so in a required greater number of two thirds of each government body) and the supreme Court (25% of Government) concurring on its Constitutionality, the law must be a good law. Anything less is seen as a bad law. Just remember, there is nothing that is perfect in government, politics, nature or the world and societies will never change this thought because societies are a large part of that imperfection.

This sets up the supreme Court for its own checks and balances in our system of government. Without the ability to impose its own power of government on any of the other branches because they are all equal in power it must abide by the same set of rules. Thus the supreme Court can only concur or not concur in regards to a legislated common law as the other three branches are only allowed in the legislative and executive voting process. When the supreme Court concurs, being nothing more than a continuation of the legislative and executive voting process it states that the common law is Constitutional under the worded guidelines of "We the People's" Constitution. When not concurring, again being nothing more than a vote, it states that the common law doesn't meet the requirements under the worded guidelines of "We the People's" Constitution. In not concurring the supreme Court can only render a statement as to *what* in the common law made it *unconstitutional* being the reason the *entire law* was *deemed unconstitutional*. This is almost the same conditions the President faces when using a veto except the supreme Court can't be overruled by government as designated by "We the People's" Constitution. Anything beyond these two actions (constitutional or unconstitutional) is above and beyond what the other three branches are allowed to do which is to concur or not concur in the legislative and executive voting process. Thus anything beyond these two actions is a *unconstitutional action of the supreme Court*. The only difference is a law doesn't go in front of the supreme Court until it has been challenged in the Courts. So it is a delayed but continued process of the legislative voting process of any common law, which may or may not occur depending on the written legislated law itself. If it is seen as Constitutional by society it may never be challenged in the Courts.

The supreme Court can't just determine every law's Constitutionality when laws are passed by a vote of the other three branches in the legislative voting process. First, until the law has exerted its power in society who knows if it is Constitutional unless the law has something in it that is obvious. Second, the Court system requires a complainant to file the proper paperwork to contest anything in a Court. So it is society's job to contest any law it sees as unfair or unfavorable to society. That is why the Court System must remain affordable to society so the process is not determined by wealth alone.

This explains why the supreme Court can't use its decision or ruling on a common law to create a perceived alteration or change of the law in any way. When doing so, it is done through "thought only" because the law itself remains as written regardless of what the supreme Court's ruling states with a non concurring decision. This act is not a procedure of "We the People's" Constitution. With four branches of equal power (25% each) in government the only option available to each branch is to agree or disagree, concur or not concur with each other. Any allowed deviation from this process is written into "We the People's" Constitution being "Congress's 2/3 veto overrule" and the supreme Court "having the final say" only on the common law's Constitutionality. That is why the supreme Court must base its rulings on the written words of the common laws comparing them to the written words of the Articles and Amendments in our Constitution because it can only concur or not concur with judiciary "Constitutionality".

When using this Constitutional format of governing, a "Common Law" will pass the "Complete Legislative Government Voting Process" with either 75% or 100% of total government power supporting the law as designated by the Constitution. But also the Constitution states that 25% of government power can overrule the 50% or 75% of government power that concurred on a legislated Common Law. This is based on the Law's "Constitutionality" only, with only a non-concurring vote of the supreme Court that strikes down the entire law.

Why were the Founding Fathers comfortable with the supreme Court being just 25% of government having the ability to strike down a law that may have 75% of government support when voted on by Congress (50%) and signed by the President (25%)? The first responsibility of the supreme Court is to the "Constitution". All its decisions of constitutionality regarding "common laws" originate from the words within our "Constitution" so their decisions should be constitutionally based, not politically or personally based. Remember the Founding Fathers would rather have no law versus a bad law. This is because 90% of the laws legislated being good or bad restrict the freedom of choice thus no law means no restrictions. So the Founding Fathers were comfortable with the supreme Court making a bad decision striking down a law because in doing so the Court would error on the side of society's freedom. But the Founding Fathers are turning over in their graves when the supreme Court uses its decision as a change to the law instead of striking down the law based on "Constitutionality". At this point in this unconstitutional process with only 25% support of the Complete Legislative Government Voting Process, being the supreme Court, a law has been enacted without the "People's" representatives being involved in the Complete Legislative Government Voting Process. Thus the "People" are now dealing with a un-constitutionally altered or changed law with little or no recourse for the "People".

Normally government has no problem passing good laws when they are supported by a concurring vote of the House of Representatives and the Senate, a concurring signature of the President and a concurring "Constitutionality" ruling, decision or opinion (all are one in the same) of the supreme Court being 100% of the Complete Legislative Government Voting Process. That is why the Founding Fathers' Constitution requires a minimum of 75% of the Complete Legislative Government Voting Process to support the law with the last step being the "Constitutionality of the Law" for the Law to remain active within Society. Also with just 75% support of the Complete Legislative Government Voting Process, what is overruled by the process is One man's vote or signature (again one in the same), the President, whose position in government was the least trusted by our Founding Fathers in our form of government. Now with the supreme Courts decisions being just 5 of 9 Justices used by the Court to alter or change a law, which now creates a new law in "Thought Only", due to a Presidential lawsuit. What the supreme Court is doing is creating a new and different law, bypassing the Complete Legislative Government Voting Process, now being supported by just 25% of government. Even if you include the President because he brought the lawsuit that government support only rises to 50% of government support which is still less than the 75% required by the "Constitution" to pass a legislated common law. Again the supreme Court's decision now being used to alter or change a law is nothing more than a opinion of the Court. Justices are no more immune to human faults than society is immune to human faults and society has a saying as to what "opinions are like". The supreme Court's decision may change "case law" or set "a precedent in law" but neither of these terms can be found in "We the People's Constitution". So neither the supreme Court or these terms have any legal status within or over the "Constitution". Only a supreme Court's non-concurring ruling (vote) regarding "Constitutionality" will remove a common law from the Registry of Laws in the Library of Congress which contains our written laws as described by the Constitution. So any and all written "common laws" in the Registry of Laws overrules any common law altered or changed by a "Thought Only" "Opinion" of the supreme Court. Where in the Constitution does it state "Opinion trumps Written Law" even if it is the supreme Court's opinion? The Court can use its "Opinion" to strike down a law based on "Constitutionality" but not to enact a New Law. This un-Constitutional bypassing of the Complete Legislative Government Voting Process by the executive and judicial branches have and are corrupting the processes of "We the People's" Constitution. Thus "We the People" are now being ruled by a Corrupted Government of as few as 6 people (5 Justices and 1 President) that are bypassing the two legislative branches being our 535 Representatives of "We the People". The Founding Fathers never conceived a process within the "Constitution" in which as few as 6 and as many as 10 (9 Justices and 1 President) people in government can rewrite and enact a common law or bypass the words of our Articles and Amendments within our Constitution.

When the Criminal Judicial System adjudicates a individual, the Judge or Jury must first determine guilt or innocence according to the "Constitution" and "Common Law" before it can impose a sentence. If innocent the individual is set free to function in society as the individual did before. If guilty the individual faces the next step being sentencing. Sentencing is so the individual must pay his or her debt to society for the crime the individual was convicted.

Now lets put a "Common Law" on trial for "Constitutionality" by again using the same structure of the Judicial system. A Legislated "Common Law" comes before a inferior or supreme Court for adjudication regarding Constitutionality. Judges must first determine guilt being innocent (Constitutional) or guilty (unconstitutional) according to our Constitution regarding the "Common Law's Constitutionality". If innocent (Constitutional) the "Common Law" is set free to function in society as the "common law" did before. If guilty (UN-Constitutional) the "Common Law" can only be struck down (KILLED) as a punishment and removed from the Library of Congress's Registry of Laws. There is no sentencing phase for punishment allowing for either Court's decision or ruling to change or alter the "Common Law". The sentence or punishment is predetermined with the guilty verdict, being Killed or Struck Down to no longer function among society. Thus the supreme Court can't alter or change a "Common Law" because it should already be dead. You can't alter or change something that no longer exists. The Court's ruling or decision itself shows the Court either believed the "Common Law" was unconstitutional (guilty) allowing it to be Struck Down or

Needed the guilty (the common law being unconstitutional) verdict of the common law too unconstitutionally change or alter the "Common Law". Now applying the Court's decision or ruling to the "Common Law" and how off base the decision or ruling is to the "Common Law" determines the reason for only one of the two actions. Was it really unconstitutional or was it deemed unconstitutional for the reason of "Change". If the "Constitutional Common Law" was Struck Down there never would have been a "Change" that meets the supreme Court's "Thought" in Ideology.

When a "Common Law" is brought before a Court, it is brought there only for the _reason_ to determine the "Common Law's" "**_Constitutionality_**"! It was **_Not_** brought before the inferior Courts or supreme Court for the _reason_ of "**_Change_**"! _Thus the "Common Law" can only **live** or **die**! There is **No** in-between_! It can't be a _little Constitutional_ or a _little Un-Constitutional_! Either it is or it isn't **_CONSTITUTIONAL_**!! Just like a Woman can't be a little pregnant, she is or she isn't pregnant!!

Perhaps the supreme and inferior Court's Justices believe they are still in a Criminal Court when passing down a sentence of "**_Change_**" on a "Common Law" that has no debt too repay too society!!

For the rest of this chapter remember everything in regards too who has the ability to _Write_ legislation and who has the ability to pass legislation under our Constitution keeping in mind the "Complete Legislative Voting Process of Government" being the "concurring or not concurring only" format of our Constitution. As I said earlier the Founding Fathers were much smarter in the formation of government than what our society has to offer today. The legislative branches have the ability to _Write_ legislation but all four branches then have the ability to concur or not concur on the Bill or later Law in regards too three reasons. The House of Representatives and the Senate House vote only on the legislation of the Bill. The President votes on the Bill in regards too "Implementation" only. The supreme Court votes on the now _Law_ in regards to "Constitutionality" only. These two thoughts of "the power of legislation" and the "Complete Legislative Voting Process of Government" will reveal unconstitutional governing by the supreme Court.

The supreme Court's interpreted rulings in regards to the "Constitution" and legislated "common law" must be fact checked against the "Constitution" and the "Common Law". That interpreted opinion is nothing more than the Court's reason to deem a common law Constitutional or not by concurring or not. So the first mistake was not striking the law down when deemed unconstitutional.

Every active law is stored in the Library of Congress's Registry of Laws. One way for the law to be removed as a Active Law is to pass another law of the same power in government that replaces the Law as was done with the XI, XIII, XIV, XVII, XX, XXV Amendments of the Constitution. The only other way to remove a active Common Law is for the "Common Law" to be deemed unconstitutional by the supreme Court. When the supreme Court rules on a law with a decision that alters or changes a Common Law it does so only in "Thought", being perception. The supreme Court's decision or ruling is the reason it should of ruled the Law Un-Constitutional, if it truly was Un-Constitutional. The decision or ruling is not the reason the supreme Court can rewrite the "Common Law". I say this because the Common Law still exists in its entirety, word for word as written in the Registry of Laws. In Law, which carries the power of law, a written and signed contract or a verbal contract? The written and signed, by those who possess the power of Legislation, contract carries the weight of Law in "We the People's" Constitution. So any verbal alterations or changes to the "Common Law" do not carry the weight of Law as does the Written Legislated Contract being the "Written Common Law".

The word "Ambiguous" was a term I believe developed in "Case Law" by our judicial system for judging "Common Law". If the wording of a legislated common law is ambiguous that still doesn't let the supreme Court rule using its ruling as now a rewritten in "Thought only" common law. If the law is ambiguous which means the Court can't make a decision because of how the law is written. Then because of the language used in the written law the Court has no choice but to strike the law as Unconstitutional because the Court can't determine its true meaning. The Court can't make the law Constitutional or Unconstitutional in its ruling. The Court can't determine someone's guilt or innocence based on a law that has multiple meanings! By following one meaning it proves guilt but by following the other it proves innocence. Thus when in doubt the tie goes to the "innocent until proven guilty" clause. This aspect of law is addressed in the Constitution by who in government has the powers of legislation and it's not the supreme Court. Obviously this "Case Law" was improperly applied to the Constitution. But I believe this "Case Law" was the beginning for inserting the supreme Court's rulings of "thought" into the written "Common Law" allowing for a perceived in "Thought Only" change in the law. When in actuality the written law still stands intact as written in the Library of Congress's Registry of Laws. Now, how many judicial cases have been ruled on using a flawed decision based on flawed "Case Law". As for Case Law, which has the weight of Law, the Written Law or Case Law? Again the Written Contract has the weight of Law. "Case Law" is determined by the "Written Common Law". The thought of case law I believe came from the English Court system. "We the People" didn't like it then and "We the People" don't like it now and I will continue too show WHY!

In this portion of my writings I will examine two recent lawsuits by the Federal Government with supreme Court rulings. I don't like imposing myself into the judicial system because I am associating with people that have acquired an arrogance created by their incorrect education regarding the "Constitution". Their standing in society and government which have created a self righteous never wrong individual. I am not a lawyer and take pride in the fact of not being a lawyer. The law profession is the only profession where a lawyer is needed to create a contract to ensure the lawyer being hired delivers the services promised without additional payments beyond what had been agreed upon verbally or already paid for. You would think you could trust a lawyer but a lawyer is the one person who should be the least trusted in society, get the promised services in a signed contract. It is this attitude in government that allows an individual to overlook the basics upon which their profession must abide by to come to the conclusions they see as correct in their mind. It is not what is in their mind that determines if the ruling is correct. It is what is written in the "Constitution" and written in "Common Law" that determines if their ruling is correct and nothing else.

What I am putting forth is my opinion based on the facts in the "Constitution" as I see them. There are two types of thoughts when addressing "Common Law" when it is legislated or when it is ruled on. The hard facts that are what I consider as "tangible", things that can be touched, seen, heard, smelled, measured, etc. such as rivers, lakes, streams, standing water, mud puddles, gases, property, borders, pollution, etc. These things will rarely change, they are what they are unless Mother Nature changes them. Then there are the "intangible" things that can't be touched, seen, heard, smelled, measured, etc. such as Freedom, human rights, race rights, gender rights, reproduction rights, religious rights, right to life rights, animal rights in regards to being humane, etc. These may change with science (science itself can't make the change, legislation is the change) which may or may not change societies opinion. These are much harder to legislate and rule on. The one thing that binds these two thoughts of tangible and intangible together is the "Constitution" and what it allows.

There are 4 levels of law in the "Constitution" with "Articles & Amendments" that are equal in power. These are the Supreme Law of the Land in our Country and can only be changed through the legislative processes of the "Constitution" requiring a minimum of 38 States. Next is "Common Law" which are laws legislatively passed based on the country's needs guided by the "Constitutional Articles and Amendments" and must not be in conflict thereof. Next are executive orders which must conform to the "Constitutional Articles & Amendments" and the "Common Law" for which the executive order was issued under. The lowest form of law is Regulations issued by a committee appointed by the President with the power of an executive order. Any regulation of this committee must still follow the "Constitutional Articles and Amendments" and the "Common Law" for which the committee was formed under by the President and his executive order. Congress must decide on funding for any additional cost in regards to the committee or the executive order. Congress has the choice to fund one, both or neither as described in our Constitution.

The latest history of the supreme Court's decisions (5 of 9 opinions minimum) in regards to "the People's Rights" and "the States' Rights" and the "Constitution" has favored the Federal Government with unconstitutional rulings. Does its ruling go against the "Constitution"? The fact that the supreme Court has no legislative power and can only concur or not concur on the common law under the "Constitution" its ruling of "thought" has no weight when applied outside these procedures of the Constitution which are the checks and balances for the Court. The justices over the years have just failed to see this basic aspect of the "Constitution" in their infinite wisdom. The Courts continually rely on "Case Law" for its decisions/rulings but if the "Case Law" is flawed then the Courts are continually building this "Case Law" on Flawed Law. I will show how the supreme Court has violated both the checks and balances written in the "Constitution" by the Founding Fathers.

When the supreme Court makes a ruling brought to the court with a lawsuit by the President on a E.P.A. regulation on the governing of bodies of water (how lakes, rivers and streams within our nations boundaries may be used for navigation, etc.) are already controlled under a United States legislated "common law". Their ruling changed the intent and expanded the reaches of that legislated common law thus changing the wording only through "thought". It now includes, "through thought" only, water runoff, holding ponds, private ponds, standing water or mud puddles on "We the People's" private property without the "People" being represented in the process. But as I pointed out earlier the reality is the "common law" still stands intact as written in the Library of Congress.

This same scenario is being used to regulate so called "greenhouse / carbon dioxide" gases. The correct process is through the legislative branches with Congress which are the governing rules of the "Constitution" written out by the Founding Fathers. Also both the water regulation law and the law that allows for certain gases to be regulated stands intact as written. In both cases you will not find puddles, etc. or carbon dioxide in the original laws allowing them to be regulated by the E.P.A.

So I must be for pollution. Absolutely not! I am for the proper procedures of government to achieve the needs of government and the needs of "We the People". The reason this lawsuit was brought by Barack Obama was he would not work with the "People's" representatives in government. So the supreme Court obliged the President of the Federal Government with a unlawful, unconstitutional ruling that bypassed the complete legislative procedures of government. Were the original common laws "constitutional"? Yes! At this point the Court should have told the liberal left President he had to go to Congress to achieve the change of the "Common Law".

This would have ensured the "people" were represented if or when a new "Common Law" is legislated and voted on. What the liberal left supreme Court did was unconstitutionally violate "We the People's" procedures of the Constitution using its ruling as a "thought" of perception of "Common Law". The supreme Court would not have dared to strike down either law as unconstitutional because the Federal Government would have lost control over all the waterways and the right to regulate any gases causing it to still have to return to Congress for new legislation. So the unconstitutional ruling was the only way to achieve the wants of a liberal left President and a liberal left supreme Court.

Now lets return to the definition of the word "Ambiguous" which is "having more than one possible meaning". Lets use the word applying it to government. Seventy Five percent of government passes a common law stating one thing. The law is challenged not on its "Constitutionality" but on what is not in the law. One law not having water runoff, mud puddles, etc. in the law. The other law for not having carbon dioxide in it. When ruling on "Constitutionality" normally it's for something written within the common law that may or may not cause it to be seen as unconstitutional. When the supreme Court takes a lawsuit for something not written in the common law it does so not attempting to judge the law's "Constitutionality". The original laws were "Constitutional" to begin with or the Court would have deemed them "unconstitutional" and struck them down according to "We the People's" Constitutional procedures.

With the supreme Court's ruling it only allows these items to be added to the rules and regulations of the E.P.A. being only a agency of government. The actual written "Common Law" regarding each lawsuit still stands as written in the Library of Congress's Registry of Laws. This is because the supreme Court can't legislate laws with any of its rulings, if it could it would have changed the written words of the law in the registry.

Now when applying these new "Rules and Regulations" of the E.P.A. to the actual still intact written "Common Law" in the Library of Congress the E.P.A.'s rules and regulations must still abide by the written "Common Laws" on the Registry of Laws and they DON'T. So the actions of the President, the supreme Court and the E.P.A.

are all ***UNCONSTITUTIONAL*** actions because they are still not following the Written RULE OF LAW!!

With these unconstitutional acts of government, government itself has created a "Ambiguous" situation in government. A intact written law of government Stored for obvious Reasons in Congress' Library of Congress versus a supreme Court decision/ruling of "Thought" that is *NOT* contained in any Legislated Written Common Law in the Registry of Law in the Library of Congress. So under the unconstitutional system of government we are using now, "We the People" have the "Thought" of Law overruling the Written Law. I thought our Nation was a Nation founded on the *"THOUGHT of WRITTEN LAW"*? The Founding Fathers had the same "Thought" when Writing our Constitution.

The Republican Party has the same "Thought" of Government when using the terms "the supreme Court can't legislate law" and "executive orders must follow the written law". They just lacked the needed knowledge of how our Constitution directs government to function in the proper format. You never heard these two terms used by the Democrat Party, the Progressive Liberal Left, Barack Obama or anyone within his administration.

The Liberal Left Democrats and those of the Obama Administration do not possess the same "Thought" in Government. A Supreme Ruler *IS* their "Thought" of Government.

Of the two Political Parties, which one has attempted to rule by the written laws of "We the People's" Constitution? Which one has done everything within its power too and has circumvented "We the People's" Constitution? Which now truly believes in "We the People's" Constitution? The answers would be the Republican Party for Questions one and three! The Democrat Party is the answer for question two!

The constitutional guidelines for a ruling or decision on "Common Law" are the following;

1). Being one of four equal branches of government, the supreme Court can only rule on the entire "Common Law" based on Constitutionality with a vote which is a concurring or non-concurring vote only. The supreme Court's ruling or decision is only used to explain the Court's vote on the "Common Law".

2). Any supreme Court ruling or decision beyond the concurring or non-concurring vote on the "Common Law" is Un-Constitutional because it creates Ambiguity within the government branches.

3). The *House of Representatives* and the *Senate House* when forming *Congress* are the Legislators and *Guardians of All Laws*, being *Stored at the Library of Congress* in the *Registry of Laws* as *Designated by the United States Constitution*.

The Founding Fathers even formed a structure of government that leaves a paper trail not allowing for Un-Constitutional actions over our Legislated Laws. No stupidity in that action! The supreme Court has brought this situation upon itself by not following the Historical Process of supreme Court decisions or ruling striking down the law as UN-Constitutional. Allowing the topic to return to the legislative branches and if needed re-legislated by "We the People"'s" Representatives instead of nine non-elected people in black robes. This is the Historical Process designated by the Founding Fathers' Written Words of the U.S. Constitution.

Before the liberal left attack these three rules with stupidity let me point out that these rules also work and are the same rules in a three branch government system. If that is what you still perceive our system of government to be, just replace the "four" with a "three".

What is offered here is not coming from "We the People's" lawyers, justices, politicians, president or "We the People's" government which has more lawyers in it than needed. It is coming from "We the People's" Constitution helped by a citizen that is just one of many being "We the People".

The Constitution consists of three separate types of major powers; Article I: The Legislative powers, the power to write laws, distributed between two branches of government. Article II: The Executive powers, the power to implement the written law of government given to one branch of government. Article III: The Judicial power, the power to ensure the rights of the people are not violated under the written laws of the "Constitution" by the other three branches when laws are written and implemented. None of these powers given in the "Constitution" were meant to overlap or allowed to intermingle by the written words of the Constitution.

It is the supreme Courts job to uphold the "Constitution" as written which means if one branch of government oversteps its powers of the "Constitution" then it is the supreme Court's job to strike down that action as being "unconstitutional". With a President's executive order you must have an understanding as to what that order can or can't accomplish. So let's relate it to a store manager (President) hired by Human Resources (the voters) of the company of a chain of stores with the CEO being the "Constitution" and "common law", a set of rules enforced by the supreme Court. The manager's job is to run the store by the set of rules established in the "Common Law". These rules state that the store must open and close at a certain time. These rules state that the store's workforce must be adequate for the function of the store at peak sales hours to service its customers. These rules determine how many people can be hired and what hours they can work based strictly on the percentage of the labor budget (maybe 12% of sales) established by a regional manager (Congress) allowed by the CEO. Now with this power structure in place can the manager (the President) determine the store's hours being 10:00 am to 6:00 pm instead of what the Constitution states being 8:00 am to 8:00 pm? No, he must do as directed by the rules too the best of his abilities. If the store manager feels like he is short handed can he protest by moving the main workforce's hours to off peak store hours then leaving the store understaffed during peak store hours not able to service the customer? No, he must do as directed by the rules too the best of his abilities. Again, under protest, can the manager order most of the main workforce during peak store hours to the storage room in the back of the store leaving the store understaffed to service the customers? No, he must do as directed by the rules too the best of his abilities. Can the manager send the main workforce to the beach while also on the payroll clock for the day again leaving the store understaffed? No, he must do as directed by the rules too the best of his abilities.

Is this manager being picked on and how would you know if that situation were true?

You compare the numbers of his employees to that of the other stores and the sales numbers of those stores to his store. If those stores are accomplishing their goals and this manager's store has much greater sales number's then the manager is correct. But the numbers are baked into the cake. With a higher gross sales, the numbers allow for a larger store staff. But if the store's numbers are below the others then the problem is with the store and its management and staff. Are the shelves being improperly stock that reduce sales? Yes, the manager has hired a bunch of his crony friends and won't say anything or fire them which then falls on the manager. Is the merchandise being reordered properly? No, again for the same reason and again the manager's fault. Are the customers (We the People) being waited on in a prompt and effective manner? No!

If that manager had taken any of the steps I described above would he have been fired? Yes. If that manager had allowed his employees (crony friends) to slack off costing the Company money because of low sales would he and they be fired? Yes. So if the regional manager (Congress) had of brought his complaints of the manager before the supreme Court would not the court back the regional manager and warn the manager by not allowing his actions? Yes! If the store manager (President) persisted with repeated or new unconstitutional actions would he not be fired (impeached) by the regional manager (Congress) for a dereliction of his duties or actions beyond his powers as (President) store manager? Yes, because the "Constitution" states what his powers are in government, meaning what he can and can't do in the workplace. Should race, gender or age have any bearing in regards to this person being fired? Absolutely not.

This scenario is a mirror image of what has happened at our southern border that has allowed illegal immigration into Our Nation being done so unconstitutionally. It is only when politics is involved that one of the needed course of actions (impeachment) to correct the problem can be nullified by a political party and their power of (Congress's political numbers) office. The supreme Court is the other option with a challenging lawsuit of the actions to have the supreme Court correct the lawless problem. The supreme Court must have some percentage of collusion in these actions to allow these actions to continue. It is Not a flaw within the "Constitution" itself but Flawed Procedures of the Constitution that unconstitutionally allows the President to write legislation using a executive order. It is the supreme Court's job to ensure any acts of the branches follow the written laws of our Nation! Not doing so is a *UNPATRIOTIC* action of a few for their own Political gain or Ideology! Now add this to the supreme Court's actions of writing "Thought" legislation in its rulings and we now have a time bomb in government and when it goes off "WE the PEOPLE" will lose most of if not all of ***OUR FREEDOMS*** to a **GOVERNMENT** ***OUR FOUNDING FATHERS warned us*** about.

The supreme Court's only duty in regards to written "common law" and Presidential executive orders is a *yes or no regarding,"is the President's executive order following the Common Law"*. If yes, the supreme Court lets the executive order stand intact as written. If no, the supreme Court strikes down the executive order allowing the agency to return to the operating procedures it operated under before the executive order was issued.

The above issue is totally different from the I.R.S. targeting organizations not allowing them tax exempt status. This action of the I.R.S. was and is a political maneuver to block a opposing political party from having a voice in the political education of "We the People". Both parties have these organizations. This targeting began in 2010 causing a lower Republican turnout at the poles in 2012 than the Republican turnout in 2010. Thus the Un-Constitutional tactic using the power of "We the People's" Government allowed the Obama Administration to be reelected in 2012 with about a 2% margin of victory. The investigation of the I.R.S. continues.

Using marriage as an example, what voice should the government, the people and the church have to do with determining who spends the rest of their life with whom? That is a human rights issue. A choice of the people involved, not the choice or wants of others including government and the church. As a straight man I have male friends but they are not my lovers and never will be. So what I am expressing doesn't favor either ideology.

Long before government got involved with the issue of marriage, and injected itself into the business of marriage as a revenue source, the church married the people. The church's religious ideology on marriage is that marriage is between a man and a woman which sets a historical precedent for the word "marriage" and its use by the church long before the inception of this nation and government. For the government to now take over the word "marriage" which was created by the church as a union between a man and a woman and using it for a same sex marriage, is the government inserting its power of government through the supreme Court on the church? Absolutely! Government is also using its power on the individuals when government didn't and doesn't allow same gender unions. Now you ask how can I be on both sides of the fence. I'm not, the proper way for the courts to handle this situation is to rule the States' marriage laws as unconstitutional based on the laws not being inclusive to all citizens of the United States. Also including the states with same gender marriage laws using the Church's word "marriage" in anyway to perform a same gender union. This would stop the States from performing any marriage services until a law was legislated by each State that was then inclusive to all but not in conflict with the "Church". But I'm also defending the right of the church to continue with its "marriage" services with government recognition of the church's service without interruption. Also allowing the Church to exclusively retain the word "marriage" in a church service as it has been defined by the church throughout history. This means that a union of the same gender may unite under a government allowed union or whatever they designate it to be called but government can't force the church to administer the services when it conflicts with the church's historical ideology, that is a choice of the church. Also the government taking the word "marriage" for these unions is an abomination of the church's ideology and beliefs and the word "marriage" and the services the church performs is the intellectual property of the church. The word was created by the church for its religious ideology and beliefs in a church service which it has executed since the beginning of all society to unite a man and a woman. This is a logical decision with the rights of both sides being taken into account.

Now you might say I have discriminated against gays because they can't use the word "marriage". If I sided with that ideology would I not be discriminating against the union of a man and a woman and the church that ordains that union with the word "Marriage" or any other form of the word; marry, married, etc. You can't split the baby; the word "marriage" is and has been the church's baby, NOT Government's. Neither side gets everything they want nor neither side loses everything that's theirs but both sides gets what it needs and each side needs to respect the others rights to beliefs and the belief of rights. Government's involvement in marriage may be the major problem today's Society is having with marriage? When government actually endorses divorce by offering financial incentives (a lower income man can't provide) to the woman by actually getting a divorce *government actually drives up the divorce rate* and puts an end to many traditional families. If government incentives are provided at all, shouldn't they be used to keep the family together? Keep in mind *Government* has a *revenue source* off of *each Marriage* and *each Divorce* that *Government Regulates* through the local police and court system! So it spends money in divorce cases which drive up divorce rates. Is this another Ambiguous situation created by government?

Just for your information, the Constitution never once addresses the subject of marriage so anything in government not claimed by the Federal Government then belongs to the States' Government. That is another reason the supreme Court should of struck down just the law, if deemed Un-Constitutional, of the State named in the lawsuit instead of ruling for each State. Each States' Law can only be struck down as each States' Law is brought in front of the Courts not with one broad ruling. That is because one lawsuit by a person or persons against one named State has no standing with the other States. Meaning the lawsuit was against one State only not the other 49 States who were not represented in the courtroom. State sovereignty is the right of each State and the supreme Court should know and respect this fact. Also Amendment XIV does not address "equality of the people" being "equal social rights" in the Amendment. It does address "equal protection" under the law "which abridge the privileges or immunities of citizens" against laws that do so. In the Constitution there is no law regarding marriage thus there is nothing to protect "We the People" from in regards to State Law. The supreme Court has no standing on these State Laws because the Constitution lacks of a law on this subject. Thus only State Law can weigh in on this subject of "same sex unions" as it does "marriage" with Sovereignty from the Federal Government. So "We the People" are still in the same place in regards to same sex unions and again placed in this situation created by the supreme Court. So again it is a State by State issue. So either all fifty States willingly allow "same sex unions" with laws or a Amendment to the Constitution allowing "same sex unions" is needed allowing it across all fifty States.

I will say this, if the groups that are the topic of this situation jump through the proper hoops they can have this situation corrected with little resistance. I won't say what those hoops are. You need to read and understand the Constitution because the hoop is there. While doing so you may have to embrace others aspects of society and the "Constitution" that you thought you never would.

But this situation can't be used to create a law that tells the Church what it can or can't do or must do or must not do. If "We the People" want to support same sex unions, it must be done so with the proper Constitutional process of Law. Not a supreme Court ruling of "Thought" that bypasses the Constitution's processes of Law.

As for polygamy, any type of civil union will be between two people only. Also for a civil union allowing for bestiality (I do understand the Church's meaning of the word but does the Church?), if you can get a animal to say "I do" at the proper time while putting a ring on the animal's finger and it convey the meaning of a civil union to a Judge then all I can say is good luck. I can't save your Soul, that is between you and God!

The difference between the two examples is that human rights (intangible) may evolve with public opinion but legislation by the people's representatives is still what truly corrects the situation.

As far as individual's rights in business not to participate, for religious beliefs only, in a same sex union in anyway, the Free Market System will fill this need as it has done throughout the history of society. Someone will fill that need of their own Freewill for the betterment of their own financial future. So this portion of the issue can be done without violating anybody's Rights. If you don't agree with my "Thoughts" please explain Amendment I., maybe I misunderstood something where it states;

"Congress shall make no law respecting an establishment of religion, or _prohibiting the free exercise thereof_:".

So a Law can't make someone violate _Their_ <u>Faith</u> _of Their_ <u>Religion</u>, Period.

So for the Courts to force someone in business to compromise _Their Faith_ of _Their Religion_ within the confines of _Their Business_ also violates the "Constitution". As I said earlier, "each side needs to respect the others rights to beliefs and the belief of rights".

As for the "same sex Union" couple that need a Cake but may not be able to find a cooperating bakery. Just order a normal "wedding cake" and make the needed adjustments yourself. Deception is not against the Law unless there is a Law against a specific deception. Sometimes you may have to do for yourself in this world when you can't entice others including Government to do it for you and in-respect, that applies to a lot things in this world not just your situation.

With mentioning the, "same sex union vs. bakery", actual situation there is a second progression of law. The Federal law overrules State law, State law overrules County law and County law overrules City law. What entity in and of government fined the bakery over a Hundred Thousand Dollars? Does any higher level law overrule say the city law? If not, the argument then goes to the Constitution's Bill of Rights being Amendments I, VII and VIII. Also the "Go Fund Me" business discriminated against the business couple by pulling their fund raising advertisement. This action was not based on any religious beliefs!

It may seem the "Constitution" is navigating a longer distance between point A and point B. What the "Constitution" is doing is navigating the Court system around a "UN-Lawful Ditch" the Court doesn't want to drive the Law into. But the Courts seem to be aiming for those Ditches instead of avoiding them because they are not following the "Constitution".

The Constitution can't evolve in the same manner because its evolution and how it must evolve is plainly controlled by the "Constitution" through its Articles and Amendments. Rules for the process which allows or disallows common laws is the standard for governing. To deviate from the process is to deviate from the "Constitution" and to do this you might as well crumble it up and throw it away.

It is Not Amazing that a Law that has No Common Sense in it Makes No Sense. It Is Amazing that a Law that has Common Sense in it Now Makes Sense and works to the best of its ability for all citizens called "We the People".

Another example is the Affordable Care Act. The Bill was written as a tax for taxpayers not enrolling in the States' exchanges or the federal exchange. The Bill levied a $95 dollar or 1% tax of a taxpayer's income or which ever is greater on the taxpayer for the first year then going up each year after. The Senate, controlled by the Democrat Party, did not like the word "TAX" and changed it to "PENALTY" to then be scored by the Congressional Budget Office. Then the bill was passed by Congress as a "PENALTY" and sent to the President which he signed into law agreeing to execute the law as legislated.

The law was challenged in the supreme Court in regards to government being able penalize the people for not purchasing a healthcare plan. The supreme Court in the ruling stated "That the government did not have the power to penalize "the People" under the Constitution" which was correct. The word "Penalty" does not exist in the "Constitution". At that point the supreme Court should have ruled the law unconstitutional. Then the Bill should have been returned to the Senate to correct the writing (legislation) in the Bill and upon passing Congress sent again to the President to be signed into Law. What the supreme Court also said finishing the statement "but can levee a tax on "the People" under the "Constitution". The supreme Court then through "thought" changed the word "PENALTY" back to "TAX" in the already legislated law and ruled it "Constitutional" as a tax. The supreme Court again violated the Constitution of the United States with "thought" Legislation when again the actual Law still stands as written with the word "PENALTY" in the Legisled Law.

The other reason this law would be deemed unconstitutional is because of Article I. Section 7. states;

"All Bills for raising Revenue shall originate in the House of Representatives; but the Senate may propose or concur with Amendments as on other Bills".

The Bill was created in the Senate under the guidance of Harry Reid, passed to the House of Representatives too concur and sent to the President for his concurring signature. The Bill raises Revenue thus it had to originate in the House of Representatives.

Thus adding to the Federal Government's power over "the People" and "the States" because the supreme Court was willing to violate the Constitution now and in the past many times over the years in the name of the "Federal Government".

These are recent examples of both the executive and judicial branches over reach of their powers to diminish the legislative powers of the legislative branches. This in turn diminishes the power and voice of "the People" in our government which is supposed to be by "the People" and for "the People". Instead it is one elected man, the President, with the help of nine non-elected, misguided supreme Court Justices to dominate the legisled Common Laws without the powers of legislation nor the understanding of the Complete Legislative Government Process. Not the intent of the Founding Fathers.

So why are the legislative branches powers under attack from the executive and judicial branches? If the legislative branches never passed a legisled law the executive branch would not have anything in government to execute or regulate. The supreme Court would not have anything to rule on constitutionally. The attacks are a creation of a shift of power to one man, the President; something the Founding Fathers knew might happen and warned us of this possible progression over time.

Lets look at another section of the "Constitution" which might be a little tricky for some but I know it has also been misinterpreted which is "Article 1; Section 8".

"The Congress shall have Power to lay and collect Taxes, Duties, Imposts and Excises, to pay the Debts and provide for the common Defense and general Welfare of the United States; but all Duties, Imposts and Excise shall be uniform throughout the United States".

My argument here is the line "*and provide for the common Defense and general Welfare of the United States;*". Not to be confused with the Preamble, the opening statement, of "The Constitution of the United States" where it states "We the People" and just a little later it states "*promote the general Welfare*".

First of all the opening statement is part of the "Constitution" but it has no weight in regards to the "Constitution" because that paragraph doesn't fall under a body of law being a "Article" or "Amendment" of the "Constitution" so it has no weight of law. It can't be used as a guideline for government because the "Articles & Amendments" are the guidelines for government, nothing more and nothing less. I have heard many arguments in government using this phrase including some in Congress to justify "common law" welfare programs. Government officials, including many Presidents issued executive orders, using this term "promote the general Welfare". The supreme Court has even used this term in its rulings saying the phrase shows the intent of our Founding Fathers which always gets a laugh out of me! As the "Constitution" states it is not a law written into the "Constitution" by the Founding Fathers. It is an opening statement of the Founding Fathers in regards to what follows being the Laws of the Constitution, with some parts being excerpts from the "Constitution" itself. Each excerpt may or may not have been pulled from a portion of the "Constitution" and do not represent the "Article" it was pulled from because it is not the complete text of that "Article" and "Section". Also "promote the general Welfare" doesn't reappear in the "Constitutional Body of Laws" yet "provide for the common Defense" does reappear word for word. Also doesn't this phrase "promote the general Welfare" describe everything written in "Article I, Section 8" and isn't everything written in "Article I, Section 8" to "promote the general Welfare" of the "People". As far as that goes doesn't the complete "Constitution" itself "promote the general Welfare" of the "People"? Wasn't the "Constitution" wrote solely to promote a society under one united country and isn't that what the Founding Fathers meant because that is what they wrote,

"do ordain and establish this Constitution for the United States of America.",

in the Constitution's opening statement known as the Preamble. If something is taken out of context it can be twisted by GOVERNMENT to mean almost anything. So now that we are past the opening statement lets focus on the rest of the argument.

Throughout the Constitution there are words that describe people, "We the People", "Members", "People", "Electors", "No Person", "a Citizen", "Representative", "Respective Numbers", "free Persons", "Indians", "Executive Authority", "Speaker and other Officers" and these are the names for people just in "Article I" sections 1 & 2. The Founding Fathers had no problem describing people in the "Constitution" where the Founding Fathers wanted or needed them described. So lets again read the Constitutional Law line I have a argument with because many common laws have been passed with the misconception that the word "Welfare" is applied to "People". It's not, it's applied to the "United States". When using the complete line "general Welfare" means that it is in the *best interest of the United States to* **Defend Its Self**. The "general Welfare of the United States" is based upon our Sovereignty. The Definition of Sovereignty is "independence: the right to self-government without interference from outside". This now explains the first part of the sentence being "and provide for the common Defense". This also explains why worded terms describing a self defense organization or a needed element for self defense is mentioned in the Preamble and Article I no fewer than 14 times. The subject of self defense is mentioned many more times than any other subject within our "Constitution". This alone demonstrates the Founding Fathers thoughts in regards to the "general Welfare of the United States" being to protect the Union of the States and the defense of each State within that Union from invasion by a army and / or domestic violence created by a populist inside or outside our borders. If the word "welfare" was meant to apply to people a description would appear in the line of text, such as "citizen", "We the people" or even just "people" but it doesn't. What does appear just a couple of lines later is "Indian Tribes" another description for people. So do you think the Founding Fathers just forgot to put a "Welfare system in the Constitution for We the People" in 1787. If so why wasn't it included in the "Bill of Rights" of "the People" with a "Amendment" included with the other 10 written Amendments for the "People" just a few years later being 1791. Do you really think the Founding Fathers intent was to set up a "Welfare system" for able bodied people who couldn't find a job? In that time era most people had to create their own jobs with the most common job being farming to feed their families. The surplus products were sold to generate cash for the needs of that family that wasn't produced on the farm. Any family member who couldn't work was taken care of by the family not the "State" or the "federal government". Also any able bodied family member was expected to work towards a common goal of ensuring the families well-being. It was well over a century and a half later that some clever liberal lawyer politician construed the words of the Preamble as the Founding Fathers intent of wanting to do so and the supreme Court followed that interpretation with it's ruling in regards to the word "welfare". Another liberal interpretation of the Constitution to achieve something that was never intended or written by the Founding Fathers in the writing of the "Constitution".

I have now covered both aspects of the word "Welfare" in the "Constitution" and at no point does any "Article or Amendment of the Constitution" allow for a socialistic welfare system yet we have many based on unconstitutional common laws passed by government and co-supported by a supreme Court with a paragraph that isn't even a "Article or Amendment" of the Constitution.

So am I stating that no social programs should exist? No, I am stating only what the "Constitution" states which is there is no provision in the "Constitution" for the existence of a social program including a federal government funded educational program. So the argument regarding State or Federally controlled education programs should belong to the States as the "Constitution" dictates. Also every social program legislated under the pretense to "promote the general Welfare" and funded by the Federal Government is unconstitutional. I know at this point you think I am crazy and that society will collapse without them which may or may not be true. I see it as a Reset for society to renegotiate on these social programs. To get rid of the programs that don't and haven't worked at a cost of great expense or at least reel them in as for expense. The reality is all the legislation (Common Law) that allowed these programs is unconstitutional. This means society and the constitutional process of a "Constitutional" abiding government can start from scratch knowing what works and what doesn't without being handicapped by any preexisting laws to impede the process of good legislation through the constitutional process draw out in the "Constitution". To achieve this what would be needed is a Amendment allowing social programs and resulting in better social programs being a hand up and not a lifetime of benefits for able bodied people which is what the programs have become.

Just to expand on these thoughts and to put pressure on the supreme Court to correct its misbehavior and to hold it to a higher standard than the standard it has relegated itself too lets look at one more supreme Court ruling. I know for a fact its rulings doesn't follow the "Constitution" and will again prove it, beyond a opinion, that will reveal the facts and truths about the supreme Court's rulings.

I know just about everybody has heard the term "a separation of Church and State" which I believe Thomas Jefferson coined the phrase in his writings. The supreme Court also reused the phrase in a supreme Court ruling as the intent of the Founding Fathers. Again, the supreme Court goes outside of the written words of law being the "Constitution" and uses one man's thoughts for its ruling. Actually what Thomas Jefferson was saying was a "separation of government's power of law over the Church" which is what is written in the "Constitution's" "Bill of Rights" Amendment I. This ruling has been used to drive religion out of government and all things that government may fund, such as schools, sporting events (high school football), state and local government, etc. Now let's read the complete paragraph with the words within the paragraph and not by an "interpretation" of what is written.

Amendments to the Constitution of the United States also known as "the Bill of Rights" ratified effective Dec. 15th, 1791.

Amendment I: "Congress shall make no law respecting an establishment of religion, or prohibiting the free exercise thereof";

So "Congress shall make no law" is a pretty plain statement, "respecting" the definition being; "regarding: with reference to or concerning somebody or something". So this word pertains to "a establishment of religion" and continuing with the word "establishment" is "something established: something that is established as a business, institution, organization, or undertaking, I worked for this establishment for forty years". Now the word "religion"; "beliefs and worship: people's beliefs and opinions concerning the existence, nature, and worship of a deity or deities, and divine involvement in the universe and human life, an institutionalized or personal system of beliefs and practices relating to the divine". Now do I need to do the same breakdown of "or prohibiting the free exercise thereof"? I hope not! But if the supreme Court Justices need me too, I will.

So let's put forth the facts in regards to this statement and the supreme Court's ruling having to do with "the separation of Church and State".

The first fact is "Congress" has already passed legislation (a bill) with the President concurring (with his signature) to execute a law that is in conflict with the "Bill of Rights and Amendment I". It is called a "Tax Law" which the I.R.S. now uses as a threat to the "Church" if it endorses a political candidate from the Pulpit of the "Church". The I.R.S. will take the "Church's" tax exempt status away. Any tax law is unconstitutional unless the "Church" is written out of the Tax Law with a exemption written into the legislated law itself. That means any Federal, State or local government Tax Law.

The supreme Court's **_decision_** in regards to the lawsuit that created the supreme Court's phrase "a Separation of Church and State" was in violation of the First Amendment. Nowhere in the First Amendment does it state when, where or who can pray. It states nothing as to whether or not you being on government property or having a government job of any type while also being on government property that a person is not able to pray alone or with others. So how did the supreme Court come up with their "interpretation" "a separation of Church & State" that is now used at many local levels of government and by some parts of liberal society to push prayer off government grounds or government funded organizations such as schools? If the supreme Court is not legislating from the bench then how is this "interpreted decision" of law enforced if it is not part of "Amendment I" originally. The "interpreted decision" is now seen as a "Thought of Law", but is actually still not part of Amendment I after the supreme Court's ruling. The ruling didn't actually change the written "Amendment I" and all common laws that allow this situation must conform to the "Articles & Amendments" which make up the "Constitution". It is not the "Constitution" that conforms to the "supreme Court's" rulings; it is the supreme Court's rulings that must conform to the "Constitution". Now the "forces that be" are using this unconstitutional "interpreted decision" to force prayer out of government and off government grounds. This is in violation of the "Constitution" and Amendment I for what is still written in "Amendment I". It also shows how the supreme Court violated the "Constitution" and rewrote by legislative "Thought" "Amendment I" with its ruling because the supreme Court ruling has ***NO POWER over the "Constitution"***, ***ABSOLUTELY NONE***.

The supreme Court's judicial power only extends to Decisions made over Common Law with the "Peoples Constitution" as the Guideline for which the supreme Court must follow word for word. The "Constitution" itself is untouchable by the supreme Court, the President or either legislative branches of the Federal Government by themselves or together.

There is a pathway drawn out in the "Constitution" to change the "Articles" and "Amendments" of the "Constitution" through the legislative process which is a two thirds vote of Congress and a three quarters ratification vote by the States will enable the changes to the "Constitution" or by a three quarters ratification vote of the fifty States alone without Congress or any other entity of the Federal Government as described in Article V of "We the People's" Constitution.

When a issue arises such as the issue of a "Welfare Program" that is not in the Wording of the "Constitution" and the supreme Court rules with so-called constitutional intent it does so without *the power of the "Peoples Constitution". Complete Legislation of Government as designated by the "Constitution" is the only path to a Constitutional law. The American People are not ruled over by a **PRESIDENT, HOUSE OF REPRESENTATIVES, SENATE or supreme COURT.** The American People are ruled over by the **"PEOPLE'S CONSTITUTION".** It is **OUR** Document that **OUR** branches of government **MUST** govern **"WE the PEOPLE"** by as drawn out by **OUR FOUNDING FATHERS AND AGREED UPON BY THE STATES THAT FORMED OUR UNION OF THE STATES OF AMERICA.**

It was done this way with slavery in 1865 in regards to the "13th & 14th Amendment" and in regards to the "15th Amendment" giving "Black men" the right to vote in 1870. The last time the Constitution was amended is with the 27th Amendment in 1992. So where was the supreme Court with it's rulings on the parts of the "Constitution" that allowed slavery and negated the "Black's" citizenship. Because the people were seen as property and not as citizens in the "Articles" of the "Constitution" itself and did not allow the supreme Court to rule in regards to human rights. The supreme Court of that time in history understood the process of the "Constitution" and that the "Articles and Amendments" are "the supreme Law of the Land". The supreme Court administers these laws based on what is written in the "Constitution". Something some of the later and current supreme Court did not and does not understand resulting in "unconstitutional rulings" by the supreme Court.

Quick question, did Amendments 13, 14 & 15 change the "Articles of the Constitution"? Yes they did! For all practical purposes they removed the wording in the "Articles" that allowed the situation and inserted the wording under Amendments 13, 14 and 15 not allowing this situation to continue while also allowing for the Black Man's vote. If all the stars aligned again could everything accomplished with these Amendments be reversed following the Constitution?Absolutely! Could the supreme Court stop it? Absolutely not! Could it be done to the White race this time? Absolutely! Will it ever happen again? I don't believe so, our society has moved well beyond that point. Society just needs to move beyond history because history will always exist.

With the supreme Court's ruling with the phrase "the separation of Church & State" change the wording in the "Bill of Rights, Amendment I"? "**Nope**, *I just looked it up and all the words are still the same*"! That is the supreme Court legislating from the bench and now being caught at it because the legislative powers belong to the House of Representatives and the Senate with the "Complete Legislative Government Procedure" as the proper format for Governing. It is a government and the courts not abiding by the "Constitution" and the processes thereof that have created the problems "We the People" face as a Nation. The judicial power belongs to the supreme Court but nowhere in the "Constitution" is there a process for the supreme Court to make changes to the "Articles and Amendments which are the Constitution" or "Common Law" which makes their rulings completely unconstitutional. That is also why I disagree with their rulings regarding common laws as I pointed out above, if they don't understand the powers of "Articles and Amendments" what makes you think the supreme Court will uphold any common law it doesn't agree with and not change it unconstitutionally! Again the supreme Court has no legislative power to write or change even a legislatively written and passed common law. The supreme Court can rule on common law (not on an Article or Amendment in an attempt to change it) to be unconstitutional, using the words of the "Constitution" nullifying the common law if allowed. If it doesn't rule the common law unconstitutional then the "Common Law" stands intact as is. I am not sure at what point in the history of the supreme Court that it first decided to not strike down a "Common Law" and then use its explanation of what was wrong with the "Common Law", if anything, and insert their explanation into the "Common Law" to alter the law thus "Thought" legislating from the judicial bench.

As for the "Bill of Rights" and what is truly written in "Amendment I". "Congress shall make no law respecting an establishment of religion", I think that means "NO LAW" which means no tax laws, no restrictions with election participation laws whether in the Church or off church grounds. Any laws regarding the Churches are unconstitutional under the "Bill of Rights: the 1st Amendment". This also shows how the supreme Court's ruling using the term "Separation of Church and State" is completely wrong because what the Constitution actually states is "Government can not restrict the rights of Religion or the Church and in fact Religion and Churches can be involved in all aspects of government because there is nothing in the Constitution that restricts that right". Now for all of you including the supreme Court that don't like what the "Bill of Rights: Amendment I" says, change it through the process of the "Constitution" and the wording will change, not by some liberal interpretation of "Thought" by the supreme Court that is a farce under the "Constitution" and has no weight in regards to the "Constitution" and Constitutional law. If it did the wording in the "Constitution" or "Common Law" would have changed with the supreme Court's ruling.

Bonus time, the executive order that allowed the E.P.A. to regulate carbon dioxide because of a supreme Court ruling also allows for tax revenue to be collected. It also is unconstitutional because a executive order cannot be used to collect Taxes. I guess the supreme Court also missed that portion of the executive order. Are there any Justices left in America who can do their job without injecting politics into the job? Maybe a new Amendment stating; "A Separation of Politics and State". Can't separate something when it shares the same brain.

THE PRESIDENT

The President of the United States of America is elected every 4 years by an electoral college from each state and the District of Columbia. The Founding Fathers had their least amount of faith in this government office. Most of the Founding Fathers did not trust the power of government being in the hands of one man. Thus the veto overrule of the President by a 2/3 vote of Congress which is the backbone of the "Constitution".

Contrary to popular belief the "President" has no legislative power given to him in the "Constitution". When considering a bill for law the decision that is being made is whether or not the "President" wants to execute the law as written. With his signature he may sign the bill into law, at that point the "President's" job is to faithfully execute the law as written. If the "President" decides not to execute the bill (veto) as written he will pass the bill back to the House from which it originated. The "President" may include with the bill a list of ideas that would persuade him to execute the law under his administration. Congress may write into the bill all, any or none of the ideas on the list. If Congress includes all the ideas chances are the "President" will sign the bill into law. If Congress uses a combination of the listed ideas, without using all the ideas, then the "President" may again sign or not sign it into law. Congress at any point during this process may kill the bill because they may not want to change the bill as written. Congress' 2nd option is to pass the bill with a 2/3 vote of each house then causing the bill to become written law without the President's signature. At this point the "President's" job is to execute this law and can not deviate from that path for any reason. The "President's" personal view on this law must take a backseat to the "Constitution's" directive to faithfully execute all laws to the best of his ability which is his Oath of Office. Until the "Law" is changed thru the Legislative Process the "Constitution" protects for the execution of all written "Laws" under the Oath of Office.

The "President's" Oath of Office is as follows;

"I do solemnly swear (or affirm) that I will faithfully execute the Office of President of the United States, and will to the best of my Ability, preserve, protect and defend the Constitution of the United States".

This Oath of Office also protects any and all laws passed by all previous Congresses and Presidents. Now if you notice the capital "A" for "Ability" in the middle of the sentence was used by the Founding Fathers to stress to a "President" that his Ability must have a high standard. Only a non-patriotic individual could interrupt it any other way. I say this because in Article II. Section. 3 of the "Constitution" it states

"he shall take Care that the Laws be faithfully executed, and shall Commission all the Officers of the United States".

Again notice the capital "C" used for "Care" and capital "L" for "Laws" in the middle of a sentence to stress the same point. This sentence is also combined with his appointed Commissioners or Dept. Heads meaning it is the "President's" responsibility (accountability to the "Constitution" and "We the People") to ensure that his appointed Officers are also taking "Care" to execute the written "Laws". It also means the "President" "shall take Care" that his Officers are not violating the written "Laws" within the Officer's appointed Office such as the Internal Revenue Service, the Environmental Protection Agency, the Dept. of Alcohol, Tobacco & Firearms, the Dept. of Justice, etc. The Founding Fathers wrote this into the "Constitution" in such a way to make the "President" accountable for his appointed Officers. The accountability of a "President" upon notification of a violation of written "Law" by his "Officer" must under his Oath of Office and the "Constitution" investigate for the best interest of the country the possible violation of "Law or Laws". The Founding Fathers through the powers of the "Constitution" gives the "President" the full power of the "U.S. Department of Justice" to execute the "Laws" protected by the "Constitution".

All elected government Officials, Military and any Presidential appointee for Office, once being confirmed, must also take this Oath of Office being;

"I do solemnly swear (or Affirm) that I will support and defend the Constitution of the United States against all enemies, foreign and domestic; that I will bear true faith and allegiance to the same; that I take this obligation freely, without any mental reservation or purpose of evasion; and that I will well and faithfully discharge the duties of the office on which I am about to enter. So help me God".

Do you really believe Eric Holder under the guidance of Barack Obama has upheld all the laws of our Nation? If not, was a mental reservation and purpose of evasion why and how they circumvented the law which violates their oath of offices? Absolutely Yes!

The U.S. Attorney General is an appointed office by the "President". This office requires the Oath of Office in the paragraph above as do all Officers in government. In both Oaths what each Official is swearing or affirming to are the written "Laws" contained within the

"Constitution" and "All Laws that followed the Constitution". The Oath is not to another person, country, political party, any group or ideology. As a person under these Oaths you can only have a loyalty to this country, the "Constitution" and the processes thereof. It is when a government official wanders outside the parameters of the "Constitution" and has a greater loyalty to something other than the "Constitution" that undermines written "Laws" and will divide a Nation. The reason for the division are again the same reasons I just wrote about because not to follow the rules can achieve their wanted results quicker than having to go through the processes drawn out in the "Constitution". A liberal saying that encompasses this thought process is "Does the end justify the means?" which is referenced in chapter 2, 1st paragraph in Saul D. Alinsky's book "Rules For Radicals".

The President controls all appointed Officers only within the boundaries of the "Constitution". To wander outside the boundaries of the "Constitution" requires the cooperation of other high ranking individuals within government to also disregard their Oath of Offices in the name of something they see as a greater good. The only way to their goal in this process is to violate the rights of others by not following the processes of the "Constitution" which is the glue to our society, a Nation of laws.

A Presidential executive order was designed as a tool for the "President" to enhance the execution of an existing written law. With a law the President can issue a executive order, without a law to attach the executive order too the executive order is no longer a order but is legislation that changes the law it effects. The Founding Fathers never intended for these executive orders to be used to allow a written law to become dysfunctional or overruled. If a "President" uses a executive order to pull a large number of border security off a border moving them 200 miles from the border to a inland location leaving less protection for our border, does this violate the written law to protect our borders? What if another country's uniformed army crosses our border? What about another country's army that is not wearing uniforms? If the "President" doesn't call up the military to confront either foreign army, does it violate written law? The answer to all three questions is yes but to what degree? Treason, Bribery, or other high Crimes and Misdemeanors. Not calling up the military to confront an invading uniformed or non-uniformed army is Treason. Now expanding on this situation. If what is passing illegally over our border are non-uniformed terrorists or crime gangs inflicting chaos on U.S. citizens does this change the crime? No! Now if the terrorists or criminals are crossing with illegal immigrates on the same unprotected border does this change the crime? No! Now, again if illegal immigration is putting U.S. citizens in harms way on a daily bases and the situation continues daily does this change the crime? No! The written "Law" protected by the "Constitution" requires the protection of the borders and the U.S. citizens on or near the borders by not allowing the illegal crossings in the first place. So if all the scenarios but the first are Treason then the first scenario of pulling border security allowing a open border must be a high Crime or Misdemeanors because it was the first step in allowing the situation to happen. The "take Care" clause of the Constitution being

Article II. Section 3. States "he (the President) shall take Care that the Laws be faithfully executed, and shall Commission all the Officers of the United States".

The reason executive orders must enhance the law is that anything less is not enacting the law, it is now not acting on the law. With this now non-action (not enforcing the border) people are allowed in that continue criminal acts upon the citizens of the nation. If the President perpetuated these actions with his executive order then he has assisted in allowing the continued criminal acts. Thus the President assisted in a criminal act. If it happens once has the President assisted? No. If it happens 50 times? Maybe No. If it happens 500 times? 5000 times? 50,000 times? At some reasonable point the answer has to become "Yes". What is that reasonable point? If your daughter happened to have been raped and then killed by a illegal immigrant but it was only this one time would you still say no to the first assisted criminal act? If you knew that person walked right across the border, no problems, do you still say no? How about if the illegal was assisted by our own government agencies then turned loose allowing the illegal to go and do as he pleases and their please was to rape & kill your daughter, how about then? How about every crime committed by a illegal that caused a death? May be now? So at What Point?

Article. IV. Section. 4. states "The United States shall guarantee to every State in this Union a Republican Form of Government, and shall protect each of them against Invasion; and on Application of the Legislature, or of the Executive (when the Legislature cannot be convened), against domestic Violence".

Before the 9/11 attacks on the twin towers I sometimes played golf at a local Naval base where the course was on the base but open for public play. In about 2010 or 2011 public play at the course was stopped because the Navy stopped admitting civilians onto the base. You can't play if you can't get to the course. Now if our own military bases feel that their own security is at risk based on the people entering the country then is not the public's security at risk based off the same reason? Our country has had two military installations attacked, both attacks were from people that had been cleared to enter the base and one was a actual member of the Armed Forces. I had played this course since age 14, during college while playing on the college golf team I played with two of its base Commanders over the years and worked at the course on some weekends when not playing a college tournament. If a local military base can't vet American civilians for going on base what makes you think the government can vet non-citizens for letting people into our country. Military bases are what a terrorist might label a hard target but what they mostly attack around the world are what are called soft targets meaning CIVILIANS. So are WE the WORM on the HOOK? Government always has protection yet Democrats want civilians to give up their guns in the name of safety. Who's Safety? The tell all signs of a dysfunctional "Law", "Agency", "President" or "executive order" is when the same terrors are happening in the interior of the Nation by the same immigrates illegally crossing the same border. Barack Obama's handling of the Southern border is an impeachable offense. It is the fact that Barack as our first Black President has been given extreme leniency because of his skin color and his position in our Government and effect how Barack and America are perceived in Future History. This is REVERSE RACISM and PRIVILEGE allowing Barack not to follow the written Laws of the "Constitution", privileged by RACE which is RACISM. This makes Barack Obama our first Black Democrat President a RACIST along with a number of White Racist Democrat Presidents of America's past history.

Government may pass bad "Laws" but regardless of that fact it is still a "Law" under the protection of the "Constitution" whether Barack agrees with the law or not. A bad "Law" must still go through the legislative process of government to be changed with the "Will of the People". Most failures of a "Law" are created by the overreach of a law, under enforcement of a law or an ideology by the people who wrote or are charged to carry out the "Law". All written "Laws" must be executed by the "President", his "Officers" and anyone under that "Officer" with an expected high standard so the "Laws" are guaranteed to have the utmost intent in regards to enforcement.

The President must execute the written "Law" as written without delay. With the passing of the "Affordable Care Act" the written "Law" has been altered and delayed through the "President's" appointed "Officers" and his executive orders. To delay a portion of a "Law" the "President" endorsed beyond the written date of enactment is not within the "President's" powers. When allowed to do this it sets a dangerous precedent for a "President" not to enact any "Law" the "President" chooses until after he has left office. Now using this same precedent a incoming "President" may also postpone enacting the same written "Law" thus making the "Legislated Law" UN-enforceable until its enactment by a cooperating "President". This situation can also be used to overrule Congress that may have just overruled a President's veto with a 2/3 vote. The President not electing to enforce this law has now overruled Congress which was never a process of the Constitution. Also the altering of a "Law" from its original intent sets the same dangerous precedent by allowing a "President" to choose how he wants to carry out the intent of the "Law" which is not within his powers. What is within his power is how he wants to execute the "Law" by the enforcement of the "Law". Again, the "President has NO Legislative Powers given to him through the powers of the Constitution". The intent of a "Law" is legislated through the "Constitutional process" not the executive or judicial branches of government. The difference between intent of the "Law" and the enforcement of the "Law" is that the enforcement of a "Law" must be executed in a manner that is not in conflict with the "Legislated Law". For a "President" not to follow these guidelines is a "President" being disrespectful of all past "Presidents" and "Congresses" which abided by the guidelines directed by our "Constitution" during their service to our Nation and "We the People".

When the intent of a "Law" is arbitrarily changed, society can't have any expectation of government to fairly and justly apply any "Law" fairly and justly to any citizen, group of citizens, organizations, businesses, corporations or political groups because it is done so based on the aspect of which political side you may support. Now we no longer have a equitable form of law. This ever changing ability to change the written "Law" destabilizes a Nation of "Laws". It now gives our Nation a Supreme Ruler elected every four years with a limit of two terms. Now with a constantly changing system of "Law" how long is it before the election of a "President" is circumvented to retain "One Supreme Ruler" or "Political Party" with no future elections? To say this can't happen in our Nation is nothing more than to deny the lessons that history should have taught us. From the fall of Rome to Hitler's gain of power through his political party over the Democratic government of Germany along with many other examples. This is what the Founding Fathers warned us about in their writings before, during and after the writing of our "Constitution".

CONGRESS

Congress is made up of two independent of each other branches being the Senate and the House of Representatives. The one power in which both branches are given in the "Constitution" is the legislative powers of government. Each branch must convene with the other to be able to use these legislative powers in government because "Congress" is the only place each branch is vested to use their legislative powers.

Barack Obama uses a political phrase "a do nothing congress" to try to gain a political advantage using the perception created by his own parties politics. First of all there is no such thing as a "do nothing congress". When both political parties refuse to compromise because they will not move beyond their political views that is not doing nothing. For one party to have to move completely to the other side's political views to pass any legislation is no longer a compromise. This situation is not a "do nothing congress", it is a "deadlocked congress". Sometimes doing nothing on an issue is doing everything available to you to represent the people who voted you into office. The Founding Fathers thought on this subject was "passing no laws was better than passing bad laws" thus the two separate legislative branches of equal legislative powers selected by two very different methods, one branch being elected & one branch being appointed by the States Legislature of the original "Constitution".

These legislative branches' product being "legislated laws" have historically been under attack by the other two branches being the Presidents and the supreme Courts of past & present times. When Congress' laws are changed by a Presidential executive order or a supreme Court rulings which no longer allow the law to function as designed then the law is being illegally not enforced or changed. An executive order can only enhance the ability to enforce the law, not vice versus.

The Peoples Representatives of Congress (50% of power) is made up of the two most powerful branches in our form of government when they decide to join forces with a 2/3's majority vote. Under the "Constitution" these two branches are the only two of the four branches that legislate under the "Constitution" and not only allow them to combine their powers but encourage it. It is only Congress that stands between the form of government drawn out in the "Constitution" and a President becoming something more than a President, a Ruler. The only way for Congress to ensure their enduring power is it must first function with this knowledge. Even with separate views their powers must not be allowed to be eroded as a whole. Even with division Congress must up hold all past laws regardless of their ability to pass future legislation during their terms. Each house is the voice of the people, past and present, elected by all the people of all parties. The President is elected by one party. As a country built on law it will fail when laws are ignored and the process (laws that dictate the process) of government are abused. It is the power of the "Constitution" and Congress that is the power of the people that allows for our freedoms, not a President and sometimes not a supreme Court. When these branches of our government fail the People it is our home States that must take up the cause.

THE ORIGIN OF POLITICAL PARTIES

Trying to trace the political parties from the beginning of our country to today's parties is no easy task. The names of the parties may have changed but their motives and ideologies still remain the same to a degree. So it is the motives and ideologies that must be traced through history in trying to track the political parties. The two most prevalent ideologies around the time of the writing of the Constitution was the subjects of federalism and slavery. After the War of Independence the two subjects were numerously mentioned in the years leading up to the signing of the Constitution. The imminent subject of the time was federalism because the forming of the nation hinged on the forming of the government for the nation and the agreement needed between the States to form this nation. The subject had to be faced by those involved and a compromise had to be met to reach a deal or our nation as we know it today would not exist. The subject of federalism can be used to trace the political parties to a large extent for the first six Presidents. The issue of slavery also was a subject of this time period but could not be abolished with the writing of the Constitution because of its entrenchment in the many societies of the colonies involved. If the ending of slavery at this period of time had of been used as a condition for the forming of a nation our nation never would have been formed as we know it because the support needed didn't exist at this time.

During the writing of the Constitution there were two per say political parties but more like ideologies than parties being the Federalist and the Anti-Federalist. The Federalist, just like Democrats historically believed in a large central government with more power of government thus more power in the Presidential office and less power of the States. The Anti-Federalist just like Republicans historically believed in a smaller central government with less power of government allowing for the States and the people to have more say in government. The system of political parties was new to our government and things were more figured out on the fly than through planned thought thus the early political party confusion with parties forming as quickly as they died out.

George Washington was our first President and is described as a Independent in our history books. Yet to be a Independent there must be other political parties to be independent of so his affiliation should be described as more of a "No or None" affiliation than a Independent because no political parties truly existed with his election. I believe Washington had more on his plate than being worried about a political party. Also as the only President to get every electoral vote during his elections shows there was no political party that opposed his Presidency.

Washington's Vice President was John Adams and both were seen historically as federalists but to establish a new federal government as they did you would have to be viewed as a federalist in doing so. You can't go from zero government to a working government without promoting and expanding government thus the perception of federalism. So I am not sure how much of a federalist these men can be credited with, certainly nothing like what our government of today resembles with its centralized power of the federal government that runs almost ever aspect of our lives. I truly believe if any Founding Father saw what has and is happening to the government they formed would be in shock and dismay. John Adams did list the Federalist Party as his Political Party during his second term as Vice President under Washington and during his four year term as our second President. But he completely opposed slavery which fits with the Republican ideology.

The next four Presidents in our history are credited by many as Democrats and others as neither Democrat or Republican. Rarely are they portrayed in history as Republican but their political party is listed as Democratic-Republican. Yet it was Thomas Jefferson and James Madison that formed the Democratic-Republican Party.

Thomas Jefferson, our third President, and James Madison, our forth President, were the best of friends. Both shared the same political views in regards to the federal government, they were Anti-Federalist.

Now to be a Anti-Federalist in a time of a very limited government you really had to be worried about the powers of government. This is a Republican view point or ideology not a Democrat view point or ideology. Both did own slaves inherited with the family farms but both openly opposed slavery.

James Monroe of the Democratic-Republican Party was the fifth President of the United States. Monroe was the last president who was a Founding Father of the United States and the last president from the Virginia dynasty and the Republican Ideology Generation. After studying law under Thomas Jefferson from 1780 to 1783, he served as a delegate in the Continental Congress. As an anti-federalist delegate to the Virginia convention that considered ratification of the United States Constitution, Monroe opposed ratification, claiming it gave too much power to the central government.

John Quincy Adams was a member of the Federalist, Democratic-Republican, National Republican, and later Anti-Masonic and then Whig Parties. John Quincy was elected to the Massachusetts State Senate & later elected by Federalist state legislature as a Federalist to the United States Senate, where he served from 1803 until 1808. As a senator, he supported some of the Republican measures which included Thomas Jefferson's Embargo Act and also the Louisiana Purchase. History states he was the only Federalist in both houses to actually support the Louisiana Purchase. This independence in his support made him unpopular, especially to Federalists and also faced opposition from the Democrats. John Quincy Adams moved to the National Republican Party but finished his political career in the Whig Party.

Now regarding these four presidents if you had to pick between Democrat, neither or Republican for there party affiliation how could you say they weren't of the Republican Ideology thus Republican. But amazingly enough many of the academia left claim them as Democrat or being neither as to not credit their Republican ideology to today's Republican Party for its existence.

With this part of political history the waters of politics get a little muddy. The parties are again moving in different directions with the Democratic-Republican party splitting. With the forming of our government the topic of Federalism has been moved to the dormant list of political ideologies and has been replaced by the now relevant political topic of slavery. With the nation formed under our Constitution this topic seemed as if it could be approached without a cost to this newly formed nation. This topic had always been on the minds of many of the Founding Fathers long before the signing and ratifying of Our Nation's Constitution.

What is happening with the political parties is the dissolving of the Democratic-Republican party with the first spin-off having already been in progress with the newly formed Democrat Party whose beliefs were Federalist and pro-slavery. The Whig Party following close behind were still Anti-Federalist but are also pro-slavery. The group that was left reformed as the new Republican Party that were still Anti-Federalist BUT Anti-Slavery. The Republican Party was the smallest of the three groups and had to rebuild its following to compete against the two much larger Democrat and Whig Parties.

This sets up the next seven Presidents and the parties they belong too in the history of our country. Our seventh President was Andrew Jackson, our Nation's first Democrat President, our eighth President was Martin Van Buren, also a Democrat. Our ninth President was William Henry Harrison, our Nation's first Whig Party President. Our tenth President was John Tyler, a Whig when first elected as Vice President upon Harrison's death assumed the Presidency. He had numerous conflicts with the Whig Party leading to his expulsion from the Party and becoming our truly first Independent President. Tyler sided with the Pro-Slavery Democrats of the Southern States in the Civil War. Our Nation's eleventh President was James Knox Polk, a Democrat, our twelfth President was Zachery Taylor, a Whig who died early in Office which installed the Vice President as our thirteenth President being Millard Fillmore also a Whig & our last Whig President. Our fourteenth and fifteenth were Franklin Pierce & James Buchanan, both Democrat.

Now this gets us pretty much to the current political parties of the Republican & Democrat Parties of today. The Democrat ideology of the time being a Federalist (big government) and pro-slavery with the Republican ideology of the time being Anti-Federalist (limited government) and Anti-Slavery. With the election of two term and the first Republican President being Abraham Lincoln. Within weeks of his election the Democrat pro-slavery States of the South succeeded from the Union of the States. President Lincoln stayed the course in the midst of possibly losing the Civil War and fought the battle for all the right reasons being a Man's Freedom can not be determined by another man or government without any social cause (crime) in losing that Freedom.

With the winning of the Civil War by the Republican controlled Union of the Northern States this allowed for the freedom of All the Black Race within the borders of this Nation. This newly found Freedom turned out not to be as free as many thought it would be for the Black Race including the White Republican people who had sought and fought for their Freedom.

The Democrat Party of the Southern States even after being readmitted to the Union of the States worked relentlessly to take the newly gained Rights and Freedoms away from the Black Race in the Southern States. With organizations such as the KKK aka. the Ku Klux Klan, these men rode the night air on horseback intimidating the Black Race and their communities in a attempt to drive them from their homes and land. There were pockets of these same racist white Democrats in the Northern States. Just like there were pockets of Anti-slavery white Republicans in the Southern States that smuggled Blacks to the Free Northern States in what was called the Underground Railroad. This type of warfare continued for the next hundred years or so in the Democrat controlled Southern States. The tactics may have changed such as Segregation and Voting violations against the Blacks but the sentiment of the Southern Democrats always remained the same towards Blacks during this hundred years or so time period.

It really wasn't until the early 1960's that things begin to change for the Black Race in regards to how they were treated by the Democrat Party. With the election of two back to back very moderate Democrats being our 35th & 36th Presidents being John F. Kennedy & Lyndon B. Johnson. Policies were enacted that finally went after the Southern Democrat States' Jim Crow style state laws that were enacted to control the Black Race to some extent. The extent being removing the acts of intimidation at voting polls and voter registration sites. A affirmative action policy was enacted which helped create a fairer job market & more stable work place for minorities but the policies were more directed at the Black Race instead of all races. The Affirmative action policies helped lead the Nation towards the educational desegregation policies of the very early 1970's which were not enacted with legislation but a 1971 ruling of the supreme Court. These Court instructed actions were enforced under the Presidency of Richard M. Nixon our 37th President and a Republican. This supreme Court instructed action was strictly enforced by this Republican President instead of watering down the implantation actions so the ruling would have little effect. This would have been no different than what Barack Obama has done with our border and the illegal immigration situation of today.

Now we have gotten to a point where we need to talk about the rules of Nature, Human Nature and how it affects human events and sometimes causes the lack of a event or lack of needed action.

In negotiations, when a meeting is required, be careful who or what is sent to the meeting. When negotiating the viciousness of a dog towards a cat you don't meet with that vicious dog if you are the cat, unless of course the cat is a lion then the dog had better take the same advice. If a far left liberal needs their mind changed on a political issue they happen to be wrong on you don't send a right conservative tea party member too change that mind, it will only end in a argument.

Example; How can you argue for illegal immigration and then complain about low wages when it is those extra (5 million or many more for starters) illegal immigrants (that you want here) competing for today's limited number of jobs that allow for lower wages to be paid because of the competition for that job especially a lower wage job. The liberal's answer "raise the minimum wage to $15 a hour". The Conservative's reply "that causes inflation, when you artificially raise the labor rate all prices then go up, it is all relative" and so on, it happened when fuel prices went up. It will never end, I could go through the complete argument by myself for both sides because it is always the same argument I have heard a thousand times and I understand why there is only one possible answer! You can't teach economics to someone that doesn't truly understand economics to change their flawed beliefs of economics. Are you laughing yet! The answer to this economics' question is "the best quality product at the lowest price ensures survival of the business" and there are no other options or answers, period. So if you want all of the fast food businesses to go out of business raise the labor rate of every store to $15 a hour and people will brown bag their lunch because they can no longer afford the fast food prices and everyone in the fast food business is now UNEMPLOYED creating a much larger unemployed work force now fighting over even fewer jobs!!! A continuous downward spiral. If you want a better job get a skill (building a hamburger is not a skill, I do it all the time at home it's called grilling out and I can do it for about half the price for a better product, homemade fries included) or a better education allowing for a better paying job. OK, we will finish this economics class in a later chapter back to the subject.

Again If you need a liberal Democrat's mind changed you don't send a conservative Republican. Now back to the two moderate Democrat Presidents being Kennedy and Johnson. It had to be these two right men for the job at the right time in history that began the end to the Black Races plight in this country. Two moderate Democrats beginning the end to the Southern Racists Democrats activities that they had used against the Black Race for the last 100 years. This movement was better accepted by Racists Southern Democrats because it was coming not from a Republican President but two Democrat Presidents that now made it palatable for them at this time in history. It may never have happened under a Republican President just because of human nature, too many people died. The scarring of the Civil War ran too deep for too many years for it to happen under a Republican President. Both Kennedy and Johnson saw it as the right time to end the nonsense for our Nation and once put in motion it was no longer seen as that much of a political agenda even under Nixon. Politically they could have paid a price but there is no evidence of that since Johnson was reelected for a second term and this situation was not associated with Mr. Kennedy's assassination.

With this point being made lets go back to the Democrat-Republican Party at the beginning of our Nation. Thomas Jefferson as historically noted owned many slaves but all were inherited (20 to 40 estimated by history). His father's death in 1757 with Thomas being just age 14 caused the estate to be handled by others until 1764 with Thomas' 21st birth day. Even though he was a slave owner he also was a avid lifelong Anti-Slavery supporter. Thomas married

23 year old Martha Wayles Skelton in 1772 at age 33. The following year being 1773 Martha's father died and she inherited his estate, land holding, debt & 135 slaves (again estimated by history). History states he only set a small number of his slaves free in his lifetime. Thomas had many tutors in his younger years and attended William & Mary College at 16 years of age but much of his adult learning was through the thousands of books he collected and read. Thomas Jefferson was a truly educated man by others and of his own accord. Martha died in 1782 and before her death she made Thomas promise her he would not remarry as to where her children would not be raised by another woman, he kept his promise and never remarried dying in 1826. In 1807 Thomas drafted & signed a bill into law that banned the importation of slaves into the United States. Thomas Jefferson is historically know as the architect of our Declaration of Independence. Thomas had many more accomplishments than what I have written here you should spend one day of your decades of life and read about the actual man instead of hearing things on the street and then deeming them to be true because someone said it was, that includes myself and what I have written.

Learn and Verify, do not allow yourself to be indoctrinated, the more available sources the better and yet only one source may be the only truth available depending on the facts that are offered for that truth. Lies can be offered by anyone, remember these "You can keep your doctor if you like your doctor" and "You can keep your health insurance plan if you like your health insurance plan". When you accept something as the truth and repeat it to others you are putting your credibility in the hands of that person you got the information from. The written word carries more weight than the spoken word but actions carry more weight than any & all words.

Belief in the Bible is a leap of Faith, belief of History is also a leap of Faith because they are both one and the same. How far back in history can you go before history itself becomes skewed in its detailed information?

After Martha's passing it is said Thomas had a long term relationship resulting in a number of children with Sarah "Sally" Hemings being one of his slaves. I am sure some racist white and black people have also used the term "rape" in describing this non-historically documented relationship in their conversations of the topic.

History has not confirmed or debunked the relationship statement, the "rape" statement I have heard come from a few very liberal left, I include it only because it has been thrown against the wall enough times that many have heard it and a few in society has allowed it to stick in their point of view by repeating it. What motivations may be behind their repeated opinion? Politics? Racism? Hey it could be true but history has not confirmed that Thomas Jefferson fathered Sarah "Sally" Hemings youngest child which was the only DNA match. That test only showed that 25 other Jefferson males could have also been the father including Thomas' younger brother Randolph who was 12 years younger. All these relatives were in the close proximity of Thomas' home everyday of the week. Why in history is Thomas Jefferson attacked for his owning of slaves yet 10 out of our first 12 Presidents owned slaves and history depicts some as terribly cruel owners. The only two Presidents that didn't own slaves were the father and son of the Adams family. During Sally's life she never confirmed the accusation of rape or the fathers of her children. It wasn't until after her death that the accusation of fatherhood (not Rape) was made by one of her sons. So I'm done with this subject until someone can prove the correctness of History on this subject because I can't and don't have the need too!

Now what I am about to talk about is something that may be hard for some to read and I absolutely mean no disrespect to anyone but too tell history as I see it, it must be said. Remember we are talking about the mid 1700's, you couldn't go to the unemployed office to see what jobs were available and government didn't issue EBT cards that could be spent at a local grocery store if you were hungry. There was a very limited school system so education to most was unattainable unless you self educated by reading books. Also just because you have a library card (or a high school education) doesn't mean you can read.

If you are a white person imagine being both a white person & a black person of the same gender that you are today in the year 1764 at age 21. If you are a black person imagine being both a black person & a white person of the same gender that you are today in the year 1764 at age 21. Understand that Thomas & Martha had six children and of the six only two survived to adulthood and this was a family of means but by no means rich. That is why there were big families back then if all the children managed to survive to adulthood. If you didn't have a lot of children you might not have any make it to adulthood.

What is a bad Dictator or King? One that treats their subjects unfairly, one that treats their self far better than their common subjects, one that rules with a iron fist with no compassion, One that doesn't care for their Kingdom, which is the people, thus doesn't care for their subjects.

What is a Good Dictator or King? One that treats their people fairly, one that may work along side their people even if in a supervisory manner to ensure that the lifesaving work is done efficiently making this work easier for all, one that may reward good work thus rewarding a good producer which produces more taking up the slack for the older who may not be able to work as fast or at all due to their age, one that cares for their people with compassion including the old, one that cares for their Kingdom thus cares for their people.

What is a indentured servant? At this point in history they were predominately white. One who through a contract borrows money, for a purpose, in a agreement to work off the loan over a period of time sometimes being as long as 10 years. During this period of time if all your work is focused, because of the contract with the loaner, on repaying the loan then how do you have time to take care of yourself or your family with food and shelter? You can't, there is no available time too do so. It does no good for the loaner if you die weeks into the contract because the loaner loses their investment. So the agreement also must include shelter, food, clothes, etc. which are needed necessities too continue life and the more you provide to the contract holder (the loaner) the more the contract holder should be able to provide for you and yours.

What is a slave? It is a person who has been taken against their will by a person, group of people or a society to either be kept or resold as a commodity for forcibly provided labor. The definition of Slavery is color blind for a reason because all races since the beginning of time have been slaves at one time or another in one place or another. In America and then in the United States slavery was a accepted practice in all the states at one time. At this point in history it was seen as the Black Race because the majority of slaves were Black.

Again, what is a slave? Could you not take a small portion of the bad Dictator or King paragraph and then most of the indentured servant paragraph excluding the 10 year contract making it possibly a lifetime contract if not freed before death. The one thing that does standout above either of the other paragraphs is the definition of slavery being "against their will". That portion of history was not committed by (I use this term loosely) Americans because history can not say for sure no American was or wasn't on any of the merchant ships from lower Europe being Portugal and Spain. Also history shows a pirate fleet sailed off the coast of upper Africa (Libya) around the areas of Mediterranean Sea.

When the first boat load of slaves arrived in our colonial port if the slaves hadn't of been bought they would have been dumped at sea on the return trip to the Mediterranean-Africa area.

To have a slave work force is not free labor, there is nothing in life that is free everything has its cost even today the air we breathe is beginning to be taxed because of our own existence. So the costs of a slave reflect that more of a indentured servant, the loan being the purchasing price. So how both were treated may be directly related to the money earned by the farm itself. Granted there is a big difference between a slave & a indentured servant, remember "against their will"! So some slave owners may have offered much better living conditions than others. Some may have offered better social conditions than others. Some may have been mean yet some may have been like relatives or good at heart or a rapist and the meanest of mean. Remember the main body of slavery lay in the Democrat Southern States so I am admitting to defending some Racist Democrats. Funny, 4,000 years ago it was just slavery with the understanding of what slavery was at that point in history. Today it is the liberal left pushing of Racism that now defines slavery in the 20th & 21st century in many social circles. My point is the definition of slavery and Racism doesn't overlap, you can have one without having the other. When it still happens today in Africa is it black on black crime? Is that Racism? Its Slavery for a profit when they are sold. It is as inhumane now as it was then and back then life was a lot more inhumane for all races. As society rises throughout history so has humanity.

Now all of that just to get here, "3/5th's a man". For those not familiar with the term it was written into the Constitution for a measurement of black population along with a measurement for a white population being 5/5th's a man too determine the number of House of Representatives assigned to a State for federal government governing.

Society states a pessimist would describe a glass of water as half empty and a optimist would describe the glass of water as half full. Is not 3/5th's over half full and much fuller if the glass was 0/5th's full otherwise known as empty. Yet when talking about the Constitution the "3/5th's a man" clause is seen in history from the pessimist view point or the glass is empty view point.

Now with the understanding of the Democratic-Republican Party formed under the beliefs of Thomas Jefferson and James Madison as Anti-Slavery politicians why would you offer additional representation to States for having non-free, non-voting slaves during and in the writing of the Constitution? Giving these States additional representation only makes the task of removing slavery from the same States that much harder. It also helped bolster the representation of the New Democrat Party and also caused the creation of the New Whig Party which ended the Democratic-Republican Party within the next couple of Presidencies to become the National Republican Party & then morphed into just the Republican Party. That one political move along with the 1807 law that stopped new slaves from coming to the United States resulted in the Anti-Slavery Democratic- Republican Party to fall from grace with the voters after the 1829 election. All this causing the Republican ideology not returning to the Office of President for 32 years until 1861 with the election of Abraham Lincoln! Why the sacrifice at that time in history when most of public opinion was against the Anti-Slavery view point. It was exactly what was needed at this time in history. So who introduced the "3/5th's a man" clause and why? The issue was important, as this population number would then be used to determine the number of seats that the state would have in the United States House of Representatives for the next ten years. It also determined what percentage of the nation's direct tax burden the people owning slaves with would have to bear. The compromise was proposed by delegates (remember the 1st name) James Wilson from Pennsylvania and Roger Sherman from Connecticut who both were from states with a small slave population. Now as a slave owner I could argue over why the government was taxing my property. If a slave was nothing more to the slave owner than a beast of burden for labor on the plantation then why aren't you taxing our other beasts of burden at the same tax rate? My slave is not a citizen and can't vote so he should not count towards my tax burden to the Federal Government. The Federal tax was levied on the people with slaves and the States reaped the rewards of the extra representatives. So the extra representatives were the enticement for the large Slavery States' governments of the Democrat South to accept the proposal with the farmers paying the price for having slaves. A win in representation for the state at no cost to the state itself, a win-win situation for state government.

History states that James Madison was the "Father of our Constitution". He was again anti-slavery along with John Adams (the only view point they shared also the reason for the end of the Federalist Party) were very vocal against slavery during the writing of the Constitution at the Constitutional Convention. Of the 13 original States the 1790 census showed Virginia as the largest slave State with 292,627 slaves being 39% of a total pop. of 747,550; South Carolina - 104,094 - 42% of 247,073; Maryland - 103,036 - 32% of 319,728; North Carolina - 100,783 - 26% of 395,005; Georgia - 29,264 - 35% of 82,548; New York - 21,193 - 6% of 340,241; New Jersey - 11,423 - 6% of 184,139; Delaware - 8,887 - 15% of 59,096; Pennsylvania - 3,707 - 0.8% of 433,611; Connecticut - 2,648 - 1% of 237,655; Rhode Island - 958 - 1% of 69,112; New Hampshire - 157 - 0.1% of 141,899; Massachusetts - 0 - 0% of 378,556.

If our government of today wants to get rid of something in society it deems as "bad or sinful" such as cigarettes what does it do? It Taxes it as much as possible! So a Southern Democrat slave owner should have wanted from a tax stand point the clause to read at the most 1/5th a man. The Republican Anti-Slavery politicians of the North wanted 5/5th's a man which was false and a calculated bluff. So a compromise was 3/5th's a man. Why as the Southern Democrat Slavery States would you agree to that? A true compromise would have been "½ a man". This deal could have easily blown up in the face of the Republican Anti-Slavery Party with the importation of more slaves to the Southern States. But the deal had three points to it like a triangle and no matter how you spin it still has one negative and two positives. The negative was the extra representatives the Southern Democrat Slavery States would get. The two positives was the extra cost added to each and every slave which might cause a burden forcing some slave owners to maybe set some slaves free or at least not buy any more because of the added cost. The second positive point is that the life of a slave now has a value (no value 0/5th's to 3/5th's a man) to the Southern Democrat Slavery States which might then pass some protective laws protecting the States' interest of the slave's value towards the States' representatives.

The Second problem for the Northern Anti-Slavery Republican States and the Democratic-Republican Party with the agreement was truly limiting the expansion of Slavery. This couldn't happen until they captured the White House with the Office of the Presidency. Once this was done with our third President being Thomas Jefferson two things had to be done. First would have been stopping the importation of slaves to the United States through legislation. Second acquire territories for future States too dilute the extra votes of the Southern Slavery States that the "3/5th's a man" had given them. Unfortunately it did not happen in that order because as a new incoming President Jefferson had little support for the legislation needed to stop the slave trade into the Nation. So the plan was reversed with the Louisiana purchase for $15 million dollars in 1803 about 2 years into his first term as President. This set the tone for his reelection taking the Oath of Office March 4th, 1805 for his second term. In 1807, congress passed the Act Prohibiting Importation of Slaves, which Jefferson signed into law January 1, 1808. It was the attempted annexation of Florida for $2 million that lost some support for Jefferson, although the Democratic-Republican Party had all four Presidents over the next 28 years.

These four Presidents with their Anti-Slavery stance is what caused the creation of the Democrat Party that opposed their views with a Pro-slavery agenda. This pro-slavery political decision was not made from the stand point of right or wrong but from the point of how to get elected and put the NEW pro-slavery Democrat Party in power. This new pro-slavery Democrat Party has managed to stay relevant even after the abolishment of Slavery by President Lincoln under the New and current Republican Party. The Democrat Party has achieved this by corrupting the vote of the Black Race. It did so by intimidating the Black Race for the next 100 years in the Southern States' voting polls and within Black Race communities themselves. The Liberal Left Academia began rewriting points of history to cover

STEVEN KING

the Racist Democrat's tracks in history with our public school history books starting somewhere in the 1930's after the great depression. These ideas (Civil War - North vs. South, Confederacy vs. the Union was titled this way to de-emphasize the Democrats role in 175 years in history) were and are still being taught in our schools today. This style of teaching is called indoctrination and has been used throughout many governmental (Germany just being one) societies in the history of the world.

The turning of the Democrat party from a party that tried to control the Black Race and their vote by suppressing the Black Race in the Southern States changed it tactics with the election of what seemed to be a moderate pair of Democrat Presidents being Kennedy & Johnson.

Definition of Indoctrinate; cause to believe something: to teach somebody a belief, doctrine, or ideology thoroughly and systematically, especially with the goal of discouraging independent thought or the acceptance of other opinions.

The liberal left academia has of recent times used the teacher unions within each and every school system that may be liberally controlled to push these indoctrinated thoughts of our history on us and our children leading them to the liberal side of our society thus the liberal party of the Democrats. Others use the Unions as a protective shield to protect their jobs when the teacher can't teach the needed curriculum to the students. This also works for the liberal thought of indoctrination because a dumb-ed down student is easier to indoctrinate into liberal social issues such as global cooling, global warming, climate change or the liberal pushing of marijuana in the confused way it is being pushed on society and our children. Other teachers use the Unions for protection to reduce the actual teaching hours spent in school offering them now a more cushy job more like a Federal employee job. Then some are just caught in the middle and don't like it but know they can't change the system by themselves.

Dwight D. Eisenhower our 34th President, a Republican; created the Department of Health, Education and Welfare in 1953 which replaced a earlier government system. In 1979, a separate Department

82

of Education was created by Jimmy Carter our 39th President, a Democrat; from this department, and HEW was ended and renamed as the Department of Health & Human (Welfare) Services which implemented Obamacare in 2014. This shows how our educational system has been fought over by the different political parties to control the thought of the "People" through government education.

The housing services of government are encompassed with two government entities being Federal Housing Administration created by the National Housing Act of 1934 by our 32nd President being Franklin D. Roosevelt, a Democrat, and the Dept. of Housing and Urban Development created by Lyndon B. Johnson in 1966 as part of his "Great Society" program. Many programs were merged into this HUD program and these programs again intended to help the poorer working people to achieve a dream was the actual beginning of the great government giveaways for future Democrat administrations.

As I said in another chapter of my book that finding the legislation that authorized the banks zero down home financing was not my goal and this statement I attributed to just memory. If I am not mistaken the legislation was passed under our 42nd President Bill Clinton, a Democrat, that allowed for the banks to act as they did creating a needed bailout by the Tax Payer.

That brings us to today and the most Liberal Left President who uses these programs to buy a alliance of some of the people. Not only is he buying the American vote he is buying the future vote of anyone the President Barack "Barry" Hussein Obama II can sneak into the country under his unconstitutional powers of government.

Many of the Black Race have aligned themselves with the same democrat political party that for about 175 years did everything in its power to hold the black man down in society. The Black Congressional Caucus through its own "Name" should have all Black Congressional members in the Caucus but there is not one Republican Black Race member being male or female. So isn't the Caucus really the Black *Democrat* Congressional Caucus! They use your vote to line their pockets just like the African Tribes captured your ancestors and sold them to the shipping fleets of the Mediterranean Sea. Who then sailed to America and sold them into slavery. If what I said isn't true how do you explain today's current situation with the 276 Black Race girls being sold into the SEX SLAVERY BLACK MARKET TRADE.

Also why is it referred to historically as a BLACK MARKT? Where do you think that phrase came from? From History!

Now with our first Black President why is nothing being done about something the Black Race sees as so despicable in our history? Why is the resistance by the Democrat Party and the Black Race to these actions not anymore than Michelle Obama's holding up of a sign with the Words "# bring back our girls"? Why is it that the voice that is the loudest, longest through history and most consistent against these criminal Slave traders that of the REPUBLICAN PARTY? Because the Democrat thought on the subject is built around a Political Ideology which will constantly change over time to suit the Democrat Party's well being. The Republican thought on the subject is not built on a Political Ideology or for Political gain but on a Religious Faith (right or wrong) that "our creator (not man, government or a Political Party) created each and every human being equal" under the law thus all laws must be blind to race, gender, religion, thought and speech of OUR CITIZENS and that is why the Lady of Justice is Blind Folded.

Enjoy everything the Democrats do for your vote as you sell out the rest of your Race that you are so closely tied too in this country and around the rest of the World? Those of the Black Race need to use some critical thinking. Actions always speak louder than Words!

THE POWER OF GOVERNMENT

Who has the Power of Government? The President? Congress with its veto overrule of the President? The supreme Court? The President using his executive power to unconstitutionally bypass legislative Common Law? The supreme Court using its rulings to rewrite legislated Common Law? Is it Congress with its 2/3 vote that may amend the Constitution?

It's none of these! Congress with a 2/3 vote of yea by each House still can't amend the Constitution without ¾ of the States. The States do not need that 2/3 vote of the Federal Congress to amend the

Constitution. The States alone can amend the Constitution with ¾ of the States being in agreement on what they see fit to change under Article V of the Constitution. So the States still have the full power of the Constitution to change our Government regardless of the Federal Government in Washington D.C.

It's time the States start spanking the hands of the children in our Federal Government. The States by creating Amendments to the Constitution that should make the children of the Federal Government behave with accountability & responsibility to the Union of the States and their Citizens. Which States will rise to the occasion to represent its Citizens? The States can save the Union or let the Federal Government keep putting this Nation in such massive Debt that the States will have no other choice but to leave the Union. A State will not keep sending its Citizens' Tax Dollars to be dispensed by a irresponsible Federal Government and other irresponsible States that have amassed a Debt that can no longer be funded to stay afloat. It is LIBERAL SPENDING that has amassed a 20 Trillion Dollar Debt. Decisions are hard but the results of not making the responsible decisions are much harder. **The Time is Now**!

Again, when talking about the Founding Fathers and the people involved in the writing of the Constitution there were two main groups, the Federalists and the Anti-Federalists. The reason I state that the Anti-Federalists won the situation is by what is actually written in the Constitution. The States alone are the only entity in government that have complete control of the Constitution. It was the States that wrote the Constitution and it's the States that retain the full power over the Constitution through Article V of the Constitution.

With the information I have offered you to this point in my writings can you tell me what type of federal government we have? A Representative Republic or a majority roles Representative Democracy? To answer this age old question, We are Both. We are a two tier government with the 1st or upper tier being the Representative States of "We the People" controlling the "supreme laws of the land" being the "Constitution" which may alter or change the "Constitution" with Amendments by a 3/4 majority concurring vote of the Representative States. This form of governing is a 3/4 majority rules Representative Democracy. The 2nd or lower tier of our government which passes and enacts all federal "Common

Laws", which are bound to follow the worded guidelines of the "Constitution's Articles and Amendments", through "We the People's" elected Representatives. This form of governing is a Representative Republic. The "Constitution" also has wording in the document that forms a parallel element of the 2nd or lower tier Representative Republic government. The "Constitution" states that anything not addressed by the "Constitution" then belongs to each individual State to address as the "State" sees fit with State "Common" Laws on these issues. Contrary to popular belief the federal common law does not trump State common law. They both have equal protection of our Constitution because each, being federal or State common law, addresses different aspects of governing. Thus it is one, being federal or State, that may write a law that overlaps into the rights of the other that creates conflict in the law. This conflict is settled with the Constitution and which governing body has the right to write that law under our Constitution. Meaning that the federal government can't write a law that the State has the power over that subject as described in our Constitution. This form of State governing has both aspects of a majority rules Representative Democracy, being the States Rights to have the People decide a State's issue at the ballot box with a majority vote of the People, and a Representative Republic within its governing ability as described in the "Bill of Rights", Amendment X of our Constitution. This now explains why, in the original writing of our "Constitution", the Founding Fathers designated the Senate to be elected by each States' Legislature. So the Sovereign Rights of each State, being anything not addressed by our "Constitution", would be protected and defended by the Senate within our system of government and these Rights would remain with each individual State. So our Founding Fathers tried to give us the best of both types of governing. Yet we ignore and circumvent both while **NOT** understanding the words or processes of either!

With this new understanding lets examine the current situation involving the supreme Court's gay marriage decision and the jailing of Kentucky resident Kim Davis, a registered Democrat, by a Kentucky Judge. Again, show me where in the "Constitution" the word "marriage" appears? It doesn't! It was actually meant to be handled by the Church as it had been historically done but laws were passed that circumvented the Church's sole power of marriages.

But because "marriage" was not mentioned in any form the State or States own the power to oversee and write its own laws regarding marriage as stated by our "Constitution". So the supreme Court has no Constitutional law to base its decision. Kentucky's State Law passed in 1998 that banned same sex marriage is the only law that addresses "marriage" for that State. What it does state in the "Constitution" under Article III last paragraph of Section 2 is as follows;

"The Trial of all Crimes, except in Cases of Impeach; shall be by Jury; and such Trial shall be held in the State where the said Crimes shall have been committed; but when not committed within any State, the Trial shall be at such Place or Places as the Congress may by Law have directed."

The "Constitution" never addresses the subject of "Murder" so is it legal? No, each State has its own laws in regards to this matter that define the action and its punishments. Although Amendment VIII does allow the supreme Court to rule on some aspects of criminal law but how murder is defined is not one of them. Thus each State may have different laws on the subject of "murder" as each State also has different laws on the subject of "marriage." Now the supreme Court has no "Constitutional Law" with which to rule, with the only Laws in regards to either subject being the States' Laws. Also if Mrs. Davis violated a law of the United States or the State of Kentucky why was she not arrested, allowed bail and allowed a trial by Jury as the "Constitution" states? Because the Kentucky Judge had no Law, Only a unconstitutional ruling (opinion) of the supreme Court to base his opinion on, thus she was arrested under a court order "agreeing liberal opinion of the supreme Court" being his only option because she had not violated any written "Constitutional or State Law". But what about Amendment XIV where it states; "nor shall any State deprive any person of life, liberty or property"? Well lets looks at the Amendment as the supreme Court should have and has done many times in the past with "Intent of the Law" to get a decision the Court desires. Now lets talk intent of the Amendment as described by our history, instead of a opinion. Amendment XIII gave the Black Slaves their Freedom. Amendment XV gave the Black race the right to vote. So I am pretty sure Amendment XIV was passed trying to stop Southern Democrats from violating the rights of the Black race following the Civil War.

Amendment XIV begins with the words "All persons" which makes the term "all races inclusive" with the rest of the sentence pertaining to "Citizenship". The second sentence where it states "which shall abridge the privileges or immunities of citizens" is also directed at Race Rights. The word "privileges" is another word for "Liberties" and both your "privileges and Liberties" are defined by our laws. Your "immunities" are also defined by our laws. The words "life, liberty, or property" are also directed at Race Rights. All Races having the same Right to Life defined by our law, same Liberties defined by our law and same Property Rights again defined by our laws. The last part being "equal protection of the laws" means all races shall be "Protected" by our Laws. These same words are also used in Amendment V when describing our criminal justice system and they are directed only at that system which is the subject or topic of that Amendment. Without the Rule of Law the word "Liberty" means you have the right to do whatever you want! Do you now have the Right to "Kill" someone? Do you now have the Right to "Marry" someone? Both answers are yes! With the Rule of Law the States define what is a justified "Killing" and the States also define what is a justified "Marriage"! The notion that Amendment XIV was written to support same sex unions or marriages is nothing more than a unconstitutional agenda of the supreme Court.

So each and every word separately or together was the wording used to accomplish the task of ending Race violations. So not a word separately or together within Amendment XIV was used or meant to be used to alter the word, the definition or the right of the States to govern "Marriages" within any State's border.

Why is it that my argument, opinion or thought process supports Kentucky's right as a State to define "Marriage" as between a man and a woman yet my same thoughts also defend the right of same sex "Unions" in any State such as California that has a law allowing it? Could it be because the "Constitution" supports my thought or did I get my Thought from our "Constitution". When reading the words of our Constitution you can't take a word or a phrase or one sentence to determine the whole body of a law without weighing what you took against the complete text of the law. That is especially true when using a Amendment written after the Bill of Rights because each Amendment after the X Amendment had a specific purpose in our history for which the Amendment was written as I pointed out Amendments XIII, XIV and XV were written for "Race Rights" only. Complete "Liberty" allows you to do what ever you want being a good or bad desired act in society. "Laws" supposedly restrict the bad acts and should allow or promote good acts of society. When the supreme Court uses the word "Liberty" for a decision or ruling it does so without using society's imposed laws of the States or our Constitution. The word "Liberty" when used in its complete context restricts nothing and allows anything in society, that is a lawless society thus the reason we are a "Nation of Laws" that define and rightfully restrict our Liberties and are Not a "Nation of judicial Opinions". When using "Liberty", the supreme Court is actually using Liberty in its complete context that allows anything in society the Court sees fit for or not fit for society. Also why is it a Liberal Democrat can violate your rights and your State's rights using a word "Liberty" or a phrase "equal protection under the law"? Why is it they use the words out of context to violate a majority of the People's Rights given to them by our Constitution? As a Liberal you are allowed to do anything that society lets you get away with. "Equal protection" means exactly what it states, that everyone no matter what race or gender will receive that protection as written "under a law". Now will anyone including the supreme Court please show me a Constitutional law that addresses Gender Orientation! There is not one but there are State Laws that support both views with their Constitutional definitions of "Marriage". So a liberal Democrat would rather violate your rights, your State's "majority rules" rights (Kentucky being one State) and the Constitution while nobody from the other side of the issue is attacking California's or any other State's Right to Define the word "Marriage" as it sees fit. Now does this make the Liberal Democrat Party the "Hippo Critical and Unconstitutional Political Party"? I would say so! What happened to "We the People" and a government "by the People, for the People and of the People" and the processes of governing drawn out in our Constitution? Remember the "ambiguous argument" of law and "Thought of Law", welcome to a unconstitutional ambiguous Judicial system of the supreme Court and one unconstitutional judge's ruling of Kentucky. Where in the Constitution does "Opinion law trump Written Law" even if it's the supreme Court's "Opinion". Where is the supreme Court in regards to

Amendment VIII and Mrs. Davis being jailed and held without being arrested or a Trial set for a violation of a written law, is this not cruel and unusual punishment being inflicted. Also Amendment I States;

"Congress shall make no law respecting an establishment of religion, or prohibiting the free exercise thereof; or abridging the freedom of speech, or of the press; or the right of the people peaceably to assemble, and to petition the Government for a redress of grievances."

Thus what is stated is that **_No_** Law can be passed "for" or "against" a religion or prohibiting the free exercise thereof, meaning no law in regards to government or the public or private sectors of society because free exercise of religion can not be limited by government to the front or back door of the Church, faith goes with each person of faith into society. It may roam in society as long as it doesn't violate the written Articles and Amendments of the "Constitution" or the "Common Laws" allowed by the "Constitution". Understanding this concept of the Founding Fathers and America's First Congress granted by the Power of the States, anyone in government may practice the free exercise of religion within government but must do so without violating the duties or the time required in accomplishing those duties for witch the individual was hired. In other words religion can't be used for the reason you didn't get your work done, "I was praying all day". Can you pray during your break, absolutely. Do I have to be off government property? No. How about when on public property? No. How about in the private sector. Only if you have permission of the land or business owner and again if in the work place it must not interfere with the work place. The business owner always has the right to let you go if you are not doing your job. Can I demand a business owner to do something that conflicts with their faith? Yes, you can demand it but they don't have to comply and once asked to leave their property you risk arrest if you don't because you are now trespassing. How can that be? Because as the Constitution states government can not pass any laws allowing or prohibiting any of the actions I described above and the only way to alter this scenario is to change Amendment I of the Constitution. This change would also have to include a change relinquishing the "States' Power" over the definition of "Marriage" for

States to have to recognize "same gender" marriages. The supreme Court can't make any of these changes because the Court has NO power over "We the People's Constitution". Also read the rest of Amendment I and you will understand what else government can't pass any laws against. With this new understanding of Amendment I we can now move to Amendment II which states;

"A well regulated Militia, being necessary to the security of a free State, the right of the people to keep and bear Arms, shall not be infringed."

What Amendment II states is a organized Militia of a State or of "We the People's" citizens of a State or a combination if needed, being necessary to the security of "We the Peoples" free State, the right of the people to keep and bear Arms, shall **_NOT_** be infringed (another term for NO Law) by any Federal, State, Local or City law which would not allow that free State to properly defend itself against all comers including any rogue government of another country or our own. Also notice it says "the right of the people" and not the right of the Militia. Now you may be alarmed thinking that "How do you keep guns out of the hands of criminals"? In the old days when capital punishment was seen as the same punishment the victim received, by being murdered, the gun was forever removed from the criminals hand with their death. Now you state that "Capital Punishment has been ruled by the supreme Court as cruel and unusual". No, it did not. The Court used Amendment VIII, to circumvent the States' right of what could be used, to determine what can't be used to put a criminal to death. So the Court in its ruling, but also along with some States, have now left society only one viable option. If a gun is used in the direct commission of a crime being a murder, robbery or any crime in which a gun was used to perpetrate that crime, Life in Prison will keep a gun out of that criminal's hands, because they abused the right of having and using a gun. The States will have to initiate so new laws to define crime when a gun is involved. But owning a gun and leaving it at home while committing a crime is actually a responsible act of the criminal. You don't need a gun to kill someone. Your children's baseball or softball bat will accomplish the job, but the right to prosecute and punish still falls to the State. If the State wants to keep that bat, knife, hammer, etc. out of that individual's hands it has the same options. If the State releases that individual at any point or time of their sentence, it is now government and government alone that has put a weapon back into the hands of a individual not trusted to walk among society as government has done and is still doing with untrusted, with other's lives, criminals. This also allows "We the People" a choice to protect themselves and others within a society's congested city or the wilderness of Alaska. If you want to see the crime rate plummet let the criminal know that not only the intended victim might be armed but 5 out of the 10 people in the area are probably armed. Have anyone ever seen or read about a gun show being robbed or anyone at a gun show being targeted for a crime? When government chooses not to protect us, protect our Constitutional Rights or the "Constitution" itself, "We the People's Constitution" not only allows but endorses "We the People" to be the protector of all that was mentioned. If government has become a Un-Constitutional Mob, then the Un-Constitutional Mob can not be "We the People" because ultimately "We the People" are the defender of our "Constitution".

So not only are the People's Legislative branches of the People's government under attack, the People's States' Laws, "We the People's Constitution" and "We the People" are also under attack by the executive and judicial branches that has 1 person elected by "the People". With the supreme Court's gay ruling creating a new law, brought on by a minority of society (not a President), this supreme Court ruling is only supported by 25% of the Total Legislative Government Voting Process meaning no representation of "We the People" and not supported by "We the People's Constitution". This is not the process our Founding Fathers envisioned and it is not the process written out in our "Constitution".

IN OUR FOUNDING FATHERS' WORDS; LOVE, HUMOR, CULTURE AND DECEIT

Now with a little English lesson I will reveal the branches of our government and show that the House of Representatives and Senate are NOT combined under the *Descriptive Phrase* "Legislative

Branch". When using this *Descriptive Phrase* being executive branch, legislative branch & judicial branch it implies three branches of government.

"Again when you are told over and over something you begin to believe it and at some point you accept it as the Truth. There is a difference between being told and being taught. "Being told is INDOCTRINATION into a certain way of thinking without any supporting facts, being TAUGHT is backing the curriculum with FACTS that support the SUBJECT allowing the TRUTH to be seen"!

The words that describe & name our branches of government in the Constitution are the following in order of appearance: Congress, Senate, House of Representatives, Representatives, Senators, each House, neither House, a President of the United States of America, Vice President, President, one supreme Court, that House, the other House, both Houses and those are all the words.

I now will use the English language to bring reality to the forefront of my writings.

Article II, Section 1. of the Constitution states "The executive Power shall be vested in a President of the United States of America".

The subject of the sentence is the "President", not the "executive Power" or "executive branch" which is not even in the sentence. This is the simplest laid out sentence of the three.

Article III, Section 1. of the Constitution states "The judicial Power of the United States, shall be vested in one supreme Court, and in such inferior Courts as the Congress may from time to time ordain and establish".

The subject of the sentence is the "supreme Court", not the "judicial Power", the "judicial branch" which again is not in the sentence, the United States or anything after the words "supreme Court". This sentence is the second most complicated sentence of the three due to the commas.

Article I, Section 1. of the Constitution states "All legislative powers herein granted shall be vested in a Congress of the United States, which shall consist of a Senate and House of Representatives".

The subject of the sentence is the "Senate and House of Representatives", not the "legislative powers", "legislative branch"; again not in the sentence, or "Congress". Now notice in Article II and III the word "power" is used in the singular tense for the "President" and the "supreme Court" branches of government. If the "s" was used to show the numerous powers of the word "legislative" then the word "powers" would have been used in all three sentences because all three words being executive, legislative and judicial have numerous powers. Also in the English language an adjective is in front of the word it describes so "legislative" describes the word "powers"; the word "powers" does not describe the word "legislative". The "s" is there or not there for a singular or plural purpose only, to identify the subject or subjects of the sentences. There is also a possession of the powers issue meaning that the subject or subjects of the sentences are the possessors of the "power" or "powers". Who has the executive power? The President. Who has the judicial power? The supreme Court. Who has the legislative powers? The Senate and House of Representatives. In Article I the word used is "powers" and the tense is plural meaning the subject of the sentence must also be plural. The word "Congress" is not plural so the subjects of the sentence are the "Senate and House of Representatives" which now names our *FOUR* branches of Government in the Words of our Founding Fathers in our Constitution.

If the subject of the sentence was meant to be "Congress" then the Founding Fathers would have used the word "power" as they did in Article II and III. Meaning both the "Senate and House of Representatives" would fall under the single government legislative branch of "Congress" then being a 3 branch system. With the *Descriptive Phrase* being executive, legislative and judicial branches with the actual names of the three branches being the President, Congress and supreme Court.

The legislative powers herein granted are actually granted by the wording of the "Constitution" to the Senate and House of Representatives, as the executive and judicial powers are the President and supreme Court, and they do not lose these powers to

"Congress". They bring these powers with them when they convene to form "Congress" because under the "Constitution" the only place in government the Senate and House of Representatives are vested to use their legislative powers is when convened as "Congress".

If a single letter being the "s" in this sentence can change the complete structure of that sentence that then changes the complete structure of a government from three to four branches. Then this example makes my argument complete as to why the supreme Court's rulings using intent or changing the written word is the rewriting of legislation.

The fact that we are a four branch system may not be appealing too some people and to achieve a lesser three branch system only requires removing the letter "s" from the word "powers" in Article I. Section I. This now makes Congress a single legislative branch as described by our history. Removing Congress's veto overrule power of our President's veto will create a three branch system. But is still not mathematical correct because again the President's power of 33.333...percent is still twice the power of the Senate's 16.666...percent. This indicates that the President would not need the Senate's approval for all appointments in government including those to the supreme Court. The Founding Fathers' intellect towards government was so much more advanced in many ways than any following Generational Societies of people in the past or present have to offer as to the workings of government. Their working knowledge of the document being more than lacking. If today's society was given the same task of forming our government what would they form considering society doesn't understand our government as it exists today. The Generational Societies since the "Constitution" was written have only managed to skew the document's Intent, Procedures and its Checks and Balances but we haven't yet lost the original recipe for governing, WE just don't use it and the We the People allow this to continue.

With the sentences broken down as I have done, reenforces my thoughts on how the powers of government's branches must be and remain separated. This point is made with the possession of the powers statements. Thus a executive order can not alter the written intent of a legislated law. That is why the Founding Fathers advise the President to take _Care_ when implementing a written law as in not to change its intent.

In regards to the one supreme Court inserting their court rulings into a legislated law. That insertion changes the written legislated intent of the law. With the Court adding Carbon Dioxide to a list of a already legislated law of chemicals that the President can regulate is adding the chemical legislatively using a power the supreme Court does not possess. The supreme Court was right in that the President can regulate Carbon Dioxide but only after the legislative branches grant him that right through a legislated law. Thus the liberal supreme Court should of denied the law suit directing the President back to Congress to make his case to Congress for a possibly future legislated law in regards to Carbon Dioxide. This reenforces my thoughts that the supreme Court can only dismiss a law suit or strike down the entire law as unconstitutional with the support of the _written words_ of our "Constitution".

The Founding Fathers' writings of the first sentence of Articles II and III of the "Constitution" are mostly straight forward sentences. So why the change in the sentence format for the first sentence of Article I too facilitate a deception? The deception being the difference of a four branch government being drawn out in a straight forward sentence and a four branch government being hidden in a sentence to give a visual illusion in the sentence of a three branch government with two bodies forming under the word "Congress".

I will address these questions and will do so from four different perspectives. The first perspective will be from the view point of a loving father who teaches his children the proper way to do something that will improve their lives. The second perspective will be from a loving father pulling a prank on his children then sitting back and laughing as they try to figure it out. The third will be on a serious note with the perspective being from the view of a Freemason. The fourth will be from an even more serious position being the actual writing of the "Constitution" and the conflict that most probably existed during the writing.

The Founding Fathers really didn't care if you understood the "Constitution". Their intentions were that you followed their instructions in the "Constitution". Like the Father of a household instructing his children on how to perform a task. It isn't important for the children to understand why the task is performed in a certain way. It is only important that the task is done in the manner directed so you get the outcome expected. So like a father to his children the goal is to teach the process so the child will get the same outcome each time. It's not until the child grows up and deviates from the process a few times, thinking they can improve the process, that he realizes the outcome is not the same. At that point the child has grown up because they realize something is wrong causing the outcome or product of their labors to be flawed. The important thing is that you can return to the correct process because you were taught the correct process. In our case the Founding Fathers wrote down the recipe and we still don't understand it. We have changed something we didn't understand and are wondering why the people don't like the taste of the product. We also haven't matured enough to realize we have deviated or changed the process or recipe which is causing the product, the laws of government, to taste bad.

As a Father some of the most memorable times may be the pranks you pull on your children. The best pranks are the ones that require a thought process to figure the prank out. At times there is nothing funnier than to watch your child or children strive to come to an answer or result. The Founding Fathers from these first two perspectives are no different than the loving father of a good family. For over two hundred years the Founding Fathers have sat back laughing knowing we have had no idea what they wrote and we haven't realized what we have done in the changes made to the processes of the "Constitution". I've raised a bunch of idiots is their current thought.

The Founding Fathers having emigrated mostly from Great Britain brought a Culture with them when coming to the "New World". One of the cultures brought was that of the Freemasons, a charitable secret society. The signs and symbols of the group are located throughout history in many different countries including our own. The symbols are on our money and many of the monuments in the areas of Washington D.C. Some of the monuments are themselves symbols. There may still be more secrets left behind. A number of the Founding Fathers were Freemasons so it is not beyond the realm of reality that the wording of Article I could have come from the thoughts of the Freemason's secretive society.

Now for the Deceit. During the writing of the "Constitution" the Founding Fathers had to have discussed the form of government they wanted. You can not form a government without a discussion of this topic. There were 40 people who signed the "Constitution" but many of them are not recognized as a Founding Father but just one of the people who signed the Constitution. So who or whom actually wrote the document, who or whom contributed and to what extent? Our history names these people and actually narrows it down to the two people whose handwriting matches that of the original document. But I am sure the document was written out and then copied to the official document being the Constitution as we know it. There was a split in the group with one group feeling more comfortable with a three branch system and their understanding of that system. There definitely was a group that wanted a four branch government because that is what is written into the "Constitution". The three branch group may not have felt comfortable endorsing an untried four branch government but did they actually know there was a actual conflict? Like wise the four branch group didn't want to form a type of government that had failed in past history and did they express this thought to the larger group? Each group knew they had to have the support of the others to form this nation. I believe the group endorsing the four branch government supplied the wording for all three sentences and, at the least, the sentence for Article I. The Veto overrule of the President and Article V giving the power of the Constitution solely to the States was most likely supported by all given the history of the previous types of governments. They gave the illusion of giving into the three branch group while all the time knowingly writing a mathematically correct four branch government into the "Constitution". This was a very devious act and showed an intellect beyond that of the others because the sentence in Article I is not the determining factor of a three or four branch government. The determining factor is the veto overrule of the President by Congress. The four branch government group did not have to write that sentence as they did to get the outcome they wanted as long as the veto overrule was included in the "Constitution" which was their wanted process of government. This also tells me the same group had to have drawn out a power schematic showing the need for two separate legislative bodies to be able to overrule the President mathematically with the powers of the legislative branches. Otherwise they would not of wrote the sentence out as it was done to make everything correct in the writing of the "Constitution" which was important to them. This also shows their need for honesty because it was there for the reading, you just have to be able to understand the true words of the sentence. Not being able to do so is not their fault.

My conclusion is that both groups got exactly what they thought they were getting which lead to the "Constitution" being signed by all the members of the delegation. Now I will leave you with three names that I believe if it was a slight of hand deception would have been the only three in a position to understand and complete the deception being Thomas Jefferson, James Madison and James Wilson. Jefferson & Madison were the best of friends, both Anti-Federalists that developed the idea of inserting certain details into the writings of the Constitution. Madison had the position in the delegation to be and was very influential in the Constitutional Convention, history has portrayed him as the "Father of Our Constitution". In my opinion Madison along with James Wilson used their influence to help ensure the Veto overrule of the President and Article V were written into the Constitution as they were written. Again the Veto overrule of the President is the deciding factor for the needed four branches of government for the system to work mathematically. The insertion of Article V into the Constitution ensured the States retained the true power over the Constitution therefore holding the TRUE POWER of Our Government. James Wilson, also a Anti-Federalist, was a person that has been overlooked in history but was a partner with Thomas Jefferson and James Madison in this plan. Wilson was seen as being on the same intellectual level as Jefferson and Madison. He addressed the Constitutional Convention a 168 times. James Wilson was appointed to the Committee of Detail which wrote the final draft of the Constitution. This appointment virtually guaranteed a Anti-Federalist supervision of the writing of the Constitution. James Wilson then was able to ensure Article V was written as it was giving the ultimate governmental power of the Constitution to the States. It also allowed him to insert the sentence as written "All legislative Powers" in Article I. Section I. into the Constitution giving the document the mathematical balance needed to make the document correct in every aspect for Congress' veto overrule power of the President.

But then again maybe the complete delegation was aware of what was written? A question our history may never truly answer.

The final point I would like to make in regards to the writing of the Constitution and our Founding Fathers. The *Writers* of the *Constitution* had *No Problem Emphasizing* a *Word* by *Capitalizing* the *Leading Letter* of the *Word* at *Any Location* in a *Sentence* to *Stress* a *Point* as *I Pointed* out earlier *In My Writings*. Now moving 180 degrees in the opposite direction why would they use a lower case leading letter on words then again Capitalizing the following word when the first lower case word is so important as to be a branch of our government?

Article I. Section I. "All legislative Powers" ; Article II. Section I. "All executive Power" and Article III. Section I. "All judicial Power of the United States, shall be vested in one supreme Court, and in such inferior Courts as the Congress may from time to time ordain and establish. The Judges, both of the supreme and inferior Courts, shall hold their Offices during good Behaviour, and shall, at stated Times, receive for their Services, a Compensation, which shall not be diminished during their Continuance in Office."

Is it the fact the writers were *De-Emphasizing* these words to illustrate the fact that each word is a adjective for the word's "Powers" and "Power" defining what type of Power it is. Thus Emphasizing it's Not a branch or the Name of our government branches as I explained earlier in my writings! Also notice the misspelled word "Behaviour", it's not misspelled, that is the Canadian, United Kingdom form of the word that is being used, possibly known as Old English.

With this said you are probably wondering why I wrote out the complete first paragraph of Article III. Section I. It's because the same rule applies when talking about the *De-Emphasizing* of *Descriptive Words* know as *Adjectives* which describes the word that follows it and not to be confused as the name as so stated by the English Language. Now if you will notice the word "supreme" is _NOT_ capitalized anywhere in the Constitution. The Founding Fathers had no problem Capitalizing the words "President, Vice President, House of Representatives or Senate" or any other word needing Capitalization to show respect for a position or a people throughout the document. The Founding Fathers didn't disrespect the Court because they Capitalized the word "Court". Also in the middle of the paragraph it states "The Judges, both of the supreme and inferior Courts," which is just another example. The Founding Fathers even moved the word "supreme" away from the word "Courts" to again _Emphasize_ the word as a _Adjective_ and not the name. If the sentence was written as our 228 years of Constitutionally understood history dictates it might read "both the inferior Courts and supreme Court" or some similar wording. This means the Founding Fathers understood this concept of the English Language and tried their best to relay that message to the readers in their writings of the document. We as a Society do not understand this _Rule of the English Language_ thus the Court truly was not given a name in the Constitution as were none of the inferior Courts. All the inferior Courts were named as they were established such as the Sixth and Ninth District Courts. The one supreme Court wasn't ever named after its establishment in our government. The sentence only states that our nation may only have one supreme Court and nothing else. The Example words that would interchange with "supreme" being; highest, ultimate, deciding, greatest, last, top, upper, most powerful, etc. Court (of / in) the Land, But again that would _Not_ be the Court's name.

This aspect of the Founding Fathers not naming the supreme Court in the Constitution also gives extreme plausibility to the Deceit portion of my writings. If the whole Delegation of the Constitutional Convention understood that the Court needed to be named then surely with the first time newly elected government, the officials thereof would have named the supreme Court. Doing it before handling any of the items mentioned in Article I. Section 8. so as government would be properly established before any government business takes place. BUT they didn't because they did NOT Know or Truly Understand these Words of Our Constitution as Written, or maybe they simply didn't read what they were signing as was the case with Obamacare. Now the supreme Court Justices not only know and understand these words of the Constitution but can even be bold enough to interpret these same *Written Words* for their rulings. How can you read between the lines when you can't even read and understand the lines? Try crawling first before you decide to walk or even run! Now I can make a couple of suggestions to name our one supreme Court, how about the National Court, the Nation's Court. Maybe something a little more accurate being The Progressively Unconstitutional Liberal Court, Oops those are adjectives and I can't use them to name the Court, lucky you. How about naming it for Barack Obama's Presidency and also since I discovered the fact in honor of me calling it the King's Court. But in reality I would like to stick to our history as it unfolded over time and not rewrite history as liberal's have done. Keeping the Founding Fathers' descriptive adjective word being **_supreme_** using it as Written with the small "s" by our Founding Fathers. A reminder to our educated society that maybe we are just not as smart as we think we are! Try on the word "humility" and see how it fits.

Again to the supreme Court and the Present & Future Presidents, the respect of the Court & Office hinges on the respect You give OUR Constitution and the actual words contained in this irreplaceable Document. The Court's and Office's respect now hinges on the Court's & Office's Actions and "WE the People" are now truly paying attention. "I Told you these Men, Our Founding Fathers, were much Smarter than what Today's Society has to offer". So who should really be judging who?

As an after thought the Founding Fathers were deceptive while being truthful, 228 years later our politicians are claiming to be truthful while being deceptive (lying), aka Barack Obama, Liberal Left Democrats with the healthcare law as just one example among many. Who are the better men or women of government? The Founding Fathers!

What has created this? The advancement of society? A growing narcissist society? Lies for profits? How about some uninformed just being misled. Others being uninformed believers (INDOCTRINATED) that are now the misleading because they were misled. Others being the leader's that knowingly mislead to finance their careers and lifestyles being people of just bad character pushing a bad agenda for profit! Could it be as simple as that, the ladder of _LIBERALISM_?

I had read these sentences many, many times in the Constitution looking for answers. It wasn't until I quit reading the sentences and started comparing the sentences that the language jumped out of the sentence allowing me to understand the sentences' structure. This was the last portion I needed being the Founding Fathers' own words telling us our Four Branches of Government. This along with the procedural portion being the government shutdown and the mathematical equation in regards to the Veto Overrule gave me every needed aspect of the "Constitution" to prove my beliefs on the subject of the number of branches of our government. This also shows beyond a shadow of a doubt that the Anti-Federalists Founding Fathers won the battle over the Federalist Founding Fathers with the use of "**_open for the eye to see Deceit_**" (otherwise known as a superior Intellect) with a hidden four branch government that dilutes the power of the President. The Intellect and knowledge of the English Language of and by these three men (Jefferson, Madison and Wilson) was so far above the others and all the following academic history based minds of our history it allowed them to keep this aspect of history hidden for about 228 years. The statement about Deceit is only true, I believe I have proved it is, if the Federalist Founding Fathers thought they were getting a three branch government in our Constitution?

Unlike other people offering wisdom to the masses I want to be perfectly clear that I have laid out the facts to the best of my abilities in regards to Our Constitution. I did this in the attempt to let the individual weigh the facts and make their own decision. This is my attempt not too _INDOCTRANATE BUT TO EDUCATE_ the _INDIVIDUAL_ because I have _TOLD_ you nothing but have _TAUGHT_ you everything using as many of the _FACTS_ I could offer allowing you to see the _TRUTH_ as I SEE IT. Now the Decision is Yours and any argument against my teachings is Yours to Make but must be made with Facts & Truths! In a Debate on this Subject I will be the Toughest Opponent You will Ever Meet!

Also when someone or a group has nothing of value to say they usually shout it out in a attempt too drown out the _TRUTH_! When you can't win a debate you dominate by not allowing a conversation of debate, *LIBERALISM 101*.

With what I have written brings up numerous other questions in regards to the Federalist Papers. I may explore that avenue at a later point but again my writings on government are limited to the Constitution and the processes thereof written out.

Quickly, let's discuss the Liberal Left's Powers of Academia and how simple people should not question their knowledge or motives. As a simple man (not a Constitutional Lawyer or Professor) in their academic world would I have to attend a college to obtain a degree in History or the Constitution before I would be accredited by the Academic World to seek a position (Professor) to teach? Would I be denied this opportunity because my writings are from the right side being the Conservative side of the political spectrum. Yet, none of them know what I know or teach what I have taught so what is the purpose of studying in their system when the knowledge they are passing on to society is incorrect. Now should the Liberal Left's College Academia have to come to me to be accredited to teach a Constitutional Course? If I applied as a Professor to teach these same College Courses where would my accreditation come from, a college that doesn't teach a correct curriculum? Should I take a class under Barack Obama to pass his knowledge of the "Constitution" on to others? Who corrects this catch 22 scenario, my money is on the Liberal Left's Powers of Academia to steal my intellectual property for their gains in the name of our political left Liberal Democrats educational system. My response to them, three words, *EXPENSIVE LAW SUIT*! I wonder what colleges of the Liberal Left Academia taught the Founding Fathers who wrote the "Constitution" about the Constitution and the Proper Separation of Powers so the Founding Fathers would have the knowledge to write it. Beware! Be Aware when being Taught, another catch 22 scenario! Indoctrination vs. Teaching; Indoctrination teaches an agenda, a True Teaching allows for the Truth. It is your own intellect that allows you to see if you are being *TAUGHT* or being *INDOCTRINATED*.

CHECKS AND BALANCES OF THE CONSTITUTION

The very first checks and balances of the "Constitution" and I hate to sound like I'm kicking a dead horse but it is the separation of powers in the "Constitution". The intermingling of powers being the executive, legislative and judicial amongst the branches is directly written as taboo in the "Constitution". It states this fact in the first sentences of "Articles I, II, and III". The President through the issuance of an executive order can't be in conflict of the legislative "Common Law" and the "Words" of that common law. The President in conjunction with the "Common Law" when issuing an executive order that is in conflict with the common law has over stepped his "Constitutional" power. The President then being in conflict of the "Common Law" with his executive order sues through the supreme Court. The court makes a ruling on something that is first not in the writing of the "Common Law". It then with its ruling allows the President's appointed committee of the agency involved to write "RULES" and "REGULATIONS" that are still in direct conflict with the "Common Law". It's in direct conflict because the supreme Court ruling never changes a "Constitutional Article or Amendment" or the wording of the original legislated "Common Law" because it takes legislation to make those changes. Again I take a stand that any law of which the supreme Court's ruling allowing something to occur while the "Wording" of the legislated "Common Law" still doesn't allow the action their ruling is in direct conflict of the "Constitution". That is why the supreme Court's ruling can only have one of two results in regards to "Common Law". It can rule the "Common Law" unconstitutional based only on an "Article or Amendment" of the "Constitution" or it must dismiss the lawsuit, there is no third option. To rule the "Common Law" unconstitutional removes the law from the registry of laws in the Library of Congress. A supreme Court ruling where it didn't dismiss the lawsuit or strike down the "Common Law" in its entirety will result in supreme Court legislation yet the written "Common Law" still stands word for word in the registry of laws. So who is in violation of the "Constitution"? A person who violates a ruling of the supreme Court but doesn't violate a written "Common Law" or the judicial system that prosecutes a person based on a ruling of the supreme Court that never changed the writing of the "Common Law". This also proves that any ruling beyond a dismissal or a strike down of the law in its entirety is unconstitutional. The law being struck down, if unconstitutional, in its entirety is crucial because removing or adding a word, sentence or paragraph, etc. can and will alter the intent of the written legislated "Common Law". If struck down and sent back with the supreme Court's ruling as to why it's in conflict with the "Constitution" to the legislative houses it first removes the law from the books. This allows the legislative branches to rewrite the "Common Law" to meet the requirements of the "Constitution" with "We the People" represented in the process of legislation as is the intent of the "Constitution".

The other checks and balances are the President (25% of power) and the Senate (25% of power) concurring on government appointments and other needed "concurring" processes. The House of Representatives being the only branch that can initiate legislation for raising revenue. The House of Representatives and the Senate are the check and balance of each other along with the Presidents veto. The veto overrule of a President's veto by 2/3rd's of Congress is the ultimate check and balance of the President by the legislative branches.

All of the above mentioned are the Founding Fathers' checks and balances in regards to legislation written in the Constitution. There are many other checks and balances dealing with other topics but these are the checks & balances dealing with legislated "Common Law".

The Veto Overrule relinquishes the power of one branch of government being one man, the President, and offers the power of government with a 2/3 vote of "Yea" from each House as the Founding Fathers' designated in the "Constitution". Thus passing the power of government onto 2 branches of government that are the

House of Representatives and the Senate being 535 elected officials that represent "WE the People". Article V of the Constitution does the same, it relinquishes government's power with 2/3's of the States to call a Convention and then 3/4 of the States to pass a Amendment. It also relinquishes the power of the Federal government to as many as fifty State governments to as few as thirty eight State governments. It also relinquishes power of a smaller group of people to a larger group of people each and every time.

It is this power of the "Constitution" that must be enacted by the States to return our government back to the hands of "We the People" if the Federal Government refuses to act on its abuses of the "Constitution" in the People's Redress of Grievances of the People's Federal Government. If the States don't take up the cause then "We the People" must to retain our Country.

BRANCHES BEYOND THE FOUR

Before revealing that there are four branches, people always talked about the fourth branch being the people or the news media. My opinion on this is that since the House of Representatives and Senate must come together to form Congress and how Congress reacts together effects this country in many ways. Congress would be the fifth branch in theory only, not in reality.

The sixth, seventh and eighth branch is a toss up between the "People", the Federal Reserve and the news media. The reason for the toss up is today the people elect a President based on traits that do not have anything to do with the elected Office. How cool he or she is, how well spoken, how good looking they or their spouse may be, what musical instruments they play, skin color, gender, etc. These ways of electing a President continually make our nation weaker as a whole because "the People" are not getting the true abilities of a qualified individual. If the people would look to experience, character, what they say not how they say it, being well spoken makes no difference if their ideas of government are flawed. Read between the spoken lines, are they lying to get your vote, previous actions speak louder than words. Also vet all News Media, do not let them elect your chosen President just because it is who they want for President.

Our best Presidents were past Governors. How that state performed under that person is a good indication of the performance "We the People" will get from he or she as a President. If he or she can't run one State how can you expect them to run our country with fifty states? An added advantage to electing a governor over a senator or a Representative or anyone in a Federal Government position is a Governor has not been assimilated into the Washington D.C. Environment. I am not ruling out someone for not being a Governor, just giving that aspect and person much more credibility for a potential President. If "We the People" would follow this guideline then we would easily become the sixth branch and maybe more. The People can control how Congress reacts in government by electing like minded people to both branches that would work together. Thus the People have now controlled Congress with their vote moving the People's power to fifth on this list. If Congress enacts laws that promotes the Citizen People as a whole and not others outside that realm being special interest groups that just want legislation directed at and for a smaller group.

The Federal Reserve can impact the economic well-being of this nation. It can print money (quantitative easing) at any rate it deems fit which then devalues the money already in circulation. The buying power of money a individual has already earned and is in their bank account, almost like a tax and if enough is printed it can cause a monetary collapse of the dollar. It also controls interest rates which affect all types of monetary loans and savings, without banks paying a true rate it drives investors into another entity to earn a dividend on their cash with one outlet being the "Stock Market". Unfortunately the common citizens make nothing on their smaller savings while the better off make a larger return on their investment in the Market. But the Stock Market is also an educated gamble of that investment.

Today the media is as divided as liberals and conservatives are divided. MSNBC, NBC, ABC, CBS, CNN and NPR all trend to the liberal side of reporting or lack thereof with some news stories. FOX trends to the conservative side but tries to present both view points.

All media can have their view points but should describe it to the audience as such and not imply it as fact. When the truth is altered for that view point then you have misleading information or an event not being reported on at all. To truly be an informed voter and viewer all aspects of a candidate or topic need to be vetted. The vetting falls to the individual to dig through the information for the true facts. When this doesn't happen there seems to be more disinformation thrown at the audience and if it sticks then it can be perceived as the truth to some citizens if repeated enough times (used to push a agenda) by the different medias backing or opposing a government administration or agenda thereof. By not vetting news outlets and government itself for truths or falsehoods then you are allowing them to influence your thoughts. They then are herding you to the voting booth to vote your mind which was corrupted by their beliefs or agendas which may or may not be correct in reality.

THE EVOLUTION OF AMERICA

I know many people, IE. the liberal left, like to discount how events evolved and talk about the bad things that have happened under the controls of our government. They tend to bend the truth, quote half truths and at points and times that are favorable to them forget the government party affiliated with the atrocities. This is especially true if it's the party they support and they will twist the facts in an attempt to blame others stressing the fact they are never wrong and never on the wrong side of history.

Let's begin with Christopher Columbus and the discovery of America. History may or may not show that Columbus was the first European to set foot on America. Historically in the year 986 Bjarni Herjólfsson, also from Iceland and Norway, is said to have been blown off course and claims he had seen but not making land fall on the Continent of North America. Also writings indicate a Viking, Leif Eriksson, may have landed here almost 500 yrs. earlier than Columbus after hearing the Bjarni story of the land sighting. It is also said Eriksson picked up two unnamed shipwrecked European survivors from the Continent that is used to establish that they were the first Europeans to set foot on North America. Leif Eriksson is said to have set up 3 or 4 settlements in North America. One settlement was thought to be as far south as Boston Massachusetts. The Norse people of Norway are accustom to a harsh inhospitable winter environment which is common for not only Norway but also Iceland and Greenland.

So now let's ask some questions about the information. Considering that some of these settlement's climate were no harsher than where the Norse people had come from and in the case of the Boston area being not near as harsh, these people had experience setting up settlements in even harsher conditions. Why did these settlements fail and why isn't there a record of these failures? Just seems odd that some two hundred years later there are a couple of books in regards to the beginning of the settlements but no mention as to how or when they failed. A record of the earlier beginning but nothing recorded about the later failed settlements. All I can say is odd because I don't know and seems like nobody else including the people who describe these settlements know either. Many times what is know in history is the event that caused the end, rarely is the beginning documented with no knowledge of the ending event. There are mentions of hostilities between the indigenous people and the Norse settlers so were they wiped out by those indigenous people and why? Why did they give up trying to settle North America? So documentation is a little lacking in my opinion. If a engraving on a rock is the determining factor, I believe you can carbon date a rock but can a engraving be carbon dated?

As for Christopher Columbus and his discovery of North America, if you read about the four voyages he made all four were to the Caribbean Islands, Central and South America. Look at the trade winds coming off Spain and North Africa blowing west by southwest right towards what he discovered which is not North America. Considering that he sailed for the Queen of Spain from Spain and Portugal and Spaniards settled the exact areas Columbus was determined to have sailed. I would have to say this description was pretty accurate. So his true claim to Discovery is Central & South America.

Were people there? Most likely, BUT there were people where Leif Eriksson was suppose to have discovered and settled also. Seems funny that the same people who have worked so hard to discredit Columbus with the discovery of North America do not use the same argument for Eriksson. Even funnier is the fact that Christopher Columbus' own notes as to where he had been never puts him on North American ground. So who screwed this part of history up? Would it be the same people who imply he discovered North America? Why is this thought of discovery pushed so hard in our N. American culture? Is it Government History Books, many of which are written by our historians or/and anyone else? Maybe history professors? Juan Ponce de León did sail to and claim what is known to us as the state of Florida for the Spanish Crown. In regards to Columbus his discovery of North America which he never did is then discredited for something he personally never took credit for, according to his ships logs. This is a monumental flaw of history as we were taught it. His search for knowledge includes where his voyage lead him. The fact that the America's land mass was much larger than what may or may not have been documented at that time only means he had no idea of where he was once he got there. Only that a land mass existed west of the European continent. Also the fact that SCIENTISTS (our highly educated never wrong populous of society) insisted the world was flat. With this understanding to sail west from the continent of Europe may lead to your own demise. Then doing so is offering your *life* for society in the attempt to gain knowledge created by discovery of which a society will benefit.

The North American explorers from England were John Cabot who first came to N. America in the year 1497 claiming the whole east coast. Sir Frances Drake in 1582 had his ship sank and most his crew killed in a Spanish American port. Upon his return from England with a newer more powerful ship he began plundering many Spanish merchant ships. This lead to the 1588 Spanish armada being lost in a storm in an attempted confrontation with the British fleet. This event left the North American continent wide open for future British settlements. Henry Hudson then followed in the year 1610 allowing the Hudson Bay to be named after him.

The other asinine part of this argument is you can't discovery something when there are people who are already there. This is definitely an overpaid overly liberal educated professor who makes it his or her duty to pass this idiocy of thought on to our children.

First of all at this period of time the three most technically advanced countries were Spain, England and France. Also all discoveries first begin with a search for knowledge. A discovery must be documented for history to be passed down in history. It's kind of like the tree falling and it making or not making a sound. A philosophy not always dealing with fact, just because you aren't there to hear the tree fall it does still make a sound. Ask your friend who cut it down when you were not there. Sometimes a philosophical topic is as stupid as the person that teaches it. The truth is that what transpired was a search for knowledge. Were the indigenous populations of the America's canoeing to the continents of Europe or Asia in search of the same knowledge. No, they were busy just trying to survive. There society was many centuries behind in knowledge of the world and universe and were not interested with the questions of the world or universe. So it was the European populous that discovered them not vice versus. It is the search for knowledge that determines what is discovered and who or whom discovered it. It can be discovered by a person in the name of a society.

Just to prove my point lets put this into perspective and move the concept of discovery into our current time in history. The search for knowledge of space began with Russia placing a man in orbit at great personal risk to this man. Did Russia discovery anything? Yes, Knowledge! America's continued exploration of space by man or woman climaxed for a period of time with the moon landings. Each flight that has lifted mankind's foot off the ground has an element of personal risk to achieve discovery and knowledge of space for society. Upon the first moon landing did we or did we not as a Nation claim the moon in the name of the United States of America by placing a flag on it. If there had of been some type of life there, knowing it or not, do you really think we would not have still claimed it. Now has ownership been determined?

Let's progress a little farther into future space travels. Say we travel across the universe finding a planet that can sustain life as we know it. It's 10 times the size of earth which is over populated at this point in time. But this planet also has a population of man, as we know man to be. It numbers 5,000 inhabitants which have very little technology say along the lines of the indigenous American Indian of the 1500's in America. Do you really think we as a society would by-pass this planet saying "oops, there are people already here lets keep looking" and move on. Then once we established a settlement to move people there we would then allow an inferior people to rule us or deny us entry or upon entry would we try to assimilate them into our culture and way of life. And if they fought us to the last man would or would not history repeat itself as to what happened with the American Indian?

Let's do a vice versus situation where the technologies of another life form are far in advance of ours. Our planet is over populated, their planet is over populated. They discover our planet and we are seen by them as an inferior life form. They decide to wipe us out to inhabit our planet in the name of their society and they achieve their goal. At that point our freedom, society, property, history and lives are gone. We then become a blip in the history of a fitter form of life.

The only differences in these events are water or space and ships or spaceships. Questions we need to ask. In every situation, including America's history, who discovered what and who? Who had claim to the territory and who claimed the territory? Why did the indigenous people lose their claim to the land? Why were they assimilated into the populous if possible? If not why not? In each situation who now has claim to the territory? Do the spoils go to the victor? Do you truly own what you can't defend? Do you own it only when you can defend it?

I have no need to answer these questions and your answers depend on your understanding of self preservation of a person or society that will allow you to understand the history of our world. Just like the animal world only the fittest survive. A liberal will quote Darwin's theory of evolution only in the attempt to discredit Religion. The phrase "only the fittest survive" is also in Darwin's theory of evolution but liberals will never agree with that theory because it is not humane in their eyes but it doesn't change the fact. So as I have pointed out repeatedly they pick and choose what information they repeat as to the point they are trying to make. Even if it is out of context, a half truth or a all out lie. Their thought is just listen to them, do as they say, live as they say, they will take care of everything and their world will be complete regardless of what you think, want or need. Liberals function in this world but want to live in a perfect society imagined in their minds. That society will never exist because what they imagine and what is actual reality, there is only one view point that reflect the laws or rules of nature. Their view points are not the reflection of Nature's laws.

Quickly I will point out other atrocities of the Democrat party that they have through history tried to make others being the current Republican Party and America as a whole bear the burden of weight for the historical event.

1). Andrew Jackson, 1829-1837, Democrat; Martin Van Buren, 1837-1841, Democrat - Indian Removal Act., moved 5 tribes - Cherokee, Chickasaw, Choctaw, Creek and Seminole tribes from eastern states of Florida, Alabama, Georgia, Tennessee, N. Carolina and Mississippi with the forced march to Oklahoma in which thousands died during this march. Some indigenous Indians chose to stay and assimilate into the populous as citizens of the United States. Unknown to many Americans is the fact that many blacks were also included in this march. Too this day many indigenous American Indians refuse to carry the $20 dollar bill because of the President's picture on the bill.

2). James K. Polk, 1845-1849, Democrat - The Mexican-American War starts in 1846 and ends in 1848 with the Treaty of Guadalupe-Hidalgo. The war was brought on by the country of Texas being brought in as a State in 1845. The Treaty afterward bought other territories west of Texas that included pretty much everything to the Pacific Ocean at a cost of $18.5 Million dollars to the United States.

The Liberal Left of the Democrat Party use Their Political Correctness Police to express their views on how the Indians were treated in America. Yet it was the hand of their party that created the plight of the Indian Tribes. So why do they blame America as a whole and never the Liberal Democrat Party. A Liberal will never admit being in the wrong, so they like to spread the blame amongst everybody! History reveals this time after time.

The Liberal Left of the Democrat Party use Their Political Correctness Police to express their views on how Mexico lost land to America. They twist facts to imply we stole the land. Yet again, this situation was handled by a Liberal Democrat President which did of sorts create a forced sale. But Mexico also needed the money in its fight with Spain to remain Independent of that country. But again America as a whole is blamed by the Liberal Democrat P.C. Police for this situation and again the Liberal Democrat Party spreads the blame instead of acknowledging its own fault's and flaws of its Political Policies created by the Liberal Left Democrat Party.

The last is a example of the Liberal Left Democrats not addressing a issue of society being slavery. Why would a party ignore for eight years the prominent issue of the time in a society? Because they are happy with the status quo, the way things are! The Liberal Democrats voting base were the slave owners of the south, they can't get rid of their voters livelihood and win a election. Ignore it and it will go away, meaning the power of the Democrat party is more important than the Freedom of a Race of People.

3). Franklin Pierce, 1853-1857, Democrat - President during the beginning of the "Slavery" debate.

4). James Buchanan, 1857- March 4th, 1861, Democrat - President during the "Slavery" issue and President leading up to the American Civil War which began about 5 weeks after his 4 year term in office came to an end. The Civil War was April 12th, 1861 to May 9th, 1865.

The First Republican President of the United States was of a newly formed party called the Republican Party & the President was Abraham Lincoln. Lincoln ran his election bid for President on the campaign stance of all people have the right of their freedom granted by "God" not "government". With his election win over the Democrat candidate this issue of "Freedom" is what caused the splitting of the States, the Civil War, The War of the States, The North vs. The South.

5). Abraham Lincoln, March 4th, 1861-April 15th, 1865, Republican, National Union - Guided the Union troops to victory allowing the retention of the "Southern States" to keep the Union of States intact that were formed under the "Constitution". Also guided the 13th Amendment through Congress which freed the Slaves and abolished Slavery.

History portrays the Civil War as a fight between the Northern States and the Southern States. Looking back in history is there any other war that was fought based strictly on geography? The Cold War, East vs. West or was it the ideology of Americanism vs. Communism which was a class taught in high schools in the 70's. Wars are fought because of political differences in ideologies between two countries. The Civil War of the United States wasn't a North vs. South war but a war of ideologies between the establishment Democrat Party and the up and coming Republican Party over a human rights issue. The Republican controlled States against the Democrat controlled States. The Republican Northern States against the Democrat Southern States. That is how the term "DIXIECRAT" became a word in the Dictionary along with the POLITICAL PARTY of the 1948 elections known as the "DIXIECRAT PARTY" whose political platform was based on RACIST views. The Republican Party grew out of a number of Northern States pushing the Democrat Party politically out of these same Northern States. The Democrat Party's strong hold after this happening was the Southern States thus the Civil War between the Republican Party of the Northern States and the Democrat Party of the Southern States. After the Civil War, what spread to the Southern States in the next 100 years was the ideology of human rights of the Republican Party. This Republican ideology infiltrated the Southern States with a greater awareness in the 1960's and 1970's in the Southern States which were still controlled politically by the Democrat Party. These two decades where Democrats lost control of Southern Politics to the Republican Party and Ideology of "The Free Man". Thus the KKK was an organization of White Racist DEMOCRATS!

With the Civil War the Republican Party had virtually broken the back of the Democrat Party in all the Northern States. Proof being that from 1861 with the election of Abraham Lincoln to Herbert Hoover leaving office in 1933 only three Democrat Presidents was elected for a total of sixteen years in office while the Republican Presidents numbered twelve holding the Presidency for fifty two years not including Lincoln's second Presidency. So it took the Democrat Party sixty eight years before they had two different Democrat Presidents elected back to back in 1933 and again in 1945. Since the 1970's the Southern States have embraced the Republican ideology of human rights and also became a strong hold of the Republican Party. The Democrat Party reestablished itself mainly in a couple of Northeastern States that never succeeded from the Union of the States that stayed Democrat after the Civil War and the proof is the 1864 re-election of Abraham Lincoln (National Union Party) who carried twenty two of twenty five states. The states Lincoln lost being New Jersey, Delaware and Kentucky. The eleven Democrat Southern States of Va., N.C., S.C., Ga., Tenn., Ala., Miss., Ark., La., TX. and Fla. were not allowed to vote in the 1864 Presidential election because of their secession from the Union of the States being the United States of America.

Now how does a supreme Court ruling in regards to "voter suppression" rule against Republican controlled Southern States when the actual acts of voter suppression were committed under the Politically Democrat controlled Southern States of an earlier time period? Seems to me the supreme Court is punishing the Republican Party of the 90's to the 2010's (for wanting a fair election of citizen voters only) for the deeds committed by the Democrat Party. The Democrat Party has no problem with this falsehood in history and has used it to their advantage to re-establish their party. The Democrat Party has used the misguided rulings of the supreme Court (based on geography only) as a Demonizing element (lies) of the Republican Party of today. The Democrat Party including Barack Obama and Eric Holder have even today used this falsehood in history to demonize the Republican Party as racists while the demons that committed the atrocities were in their own Democrat Party of a earlier period. The New Black Panther Party (Democrat supporters) in Philadelphia, Pa. had members with weapons at a 2008 voting pole within that city. They went un-prosecuted by the newly elected Democrat President Barack Hussein Obama and his newly appointed U.S. Attorney General, a Democrat, Eric Holder. If it walks like a duck and quacks like a duck it's probably a duck. How did our history get so mixed up? Could the Liberally Progressive Democrat controlled academia in our school systems have any bearing on how history has been rewritten and portrayed?

The 13th Amendment was passed January 31, 1865 with a Senate vote of 31 Republican, 2 Democrat, 1 Unionist & 4 Unconditional Unionist votes of "Yea"; 5 Democrats & 1 Unionist votes of "Nay" with 3 Democrat, 2 Unionist & 1 Unconditional Unionist not voting.

The House of Representatives passed on 84 Republican, 14 Democrat, 2 Independent Republican, 3 Unionist, 16 Unconditional Unionist votes of "Yea"; 50 Democrat & 2 Unionist votes of "Nay" with 8 Democrat & 4 Unionist not voting and then sent to the states for ratification.

    6). Andrew Johnson, 1865-1869, Democrat - National Union - Independent - The only Vice President and President that belonged to three different political parties during his terms as Vice President and President. The National Union Party was an attempt by both Lincoln and Johnson to further the healing of the country after the Civil War. Johnson was a Democrat but ran for Vice President with President Lincoln under the National Union Party. With Lincoln's assassination just five weeks into his second term Johnson assumed the Presidential responsibilities not under the Democrat or National Union Parties because his views did not agree with the Democrat party and there now was little support for a National Union Party. Johnson finished his term as a Replacement President as an Independent. Thus making Andrew Johnson our Second Independent Party President.

Under Johnson's Presidency the 14th Amendment was passed to clear up what some Democrat states and Democrat people were doing to still violate the rights of Blacks. This should have already been settled with the passing of the 13th Amendment. The 14th and 15th Amendment was passed by the Northern Republican States without a single Democrat vote in support of passing the Amendments.

Considering the Democrat vote against the 13, 14 & 15 Amendments I see the Liberal Democrat's Political hands all over the 13th Amendment in an attempt to circumvent the Amendment to deny the rights of the Black American people. The passing of the 14th Amendment was another attempt by Republicans to close any loop holes regarding slavery and the Black man's citizenship. Also the 15th Amendment was passed giving Black men the right to vote.

The 15th Amendment allowing Black men to vote was passed February 26, 1869 with a Senate vote of 39 Republican votes of "Yea"; 8 Democrat & 5 Republican votes of "Nay" and with 13 Republican & 1 Democrat not voting. The House of Representatives had already passed the amendment on February 25, 1869 with 143 Republican & 1 Conservative Republican votes of "Yea"; 39 Democrat, 3Republican, 1 Independent Republican and 1 Conservative votes of "Nay" and with 26 Republican, 8 Democrat and 1 Independent Republican not voting.

7). Franklin D. Roosevelt, 1933-1945, Democrat - On Dec 7, 1941 the Japanese attack on Pearl Harbor lead to the internment of Japanese citizens in camps as a National security issue. This was the only time in American history American citizens were rounded up and put into security based internment camps. Many of these Japanese citizens had lost all personal property permanently other than a few personal items during this period of time. This action was allowed under the alien and Sedition Act of 1798 signed into law by John Adams our second President and a Federalist Party member which very soon became the Democrat Party.

Let's look at the 19th Amendment of the Constitution which allows women the right to vote. The President at the time, Mar. 1913 to Mar. 1921, was Woodrow Wilson who was a Democrat. I will go to a government web-site for some information, which is "Our Documents.gov", about President Wilson.

By 1916, almost all of the major suffrage organizations were united behind the goal of a constitutional amendment. When New York adopted woman suffrage in 1917 and President Wilson opposed it but then changed his position to support an amendment in 1918, the political balance began to shift.

On May 21, 1919, the House of Representatives passed the amendment, and two weeks later, the Senate followed. When Tennessee became the 36th state to ratify the amendment on August 18, 1920, the amendment passed its final hurdle of obtaining the agreement of three-fourths of the states. Secretary of State Bainbridge Colby certified the ratification on August 26, 1920, changing the face of the American electorate forever.

After reading the above information what you should notice is that President Woodrow Wilson conveniently changed his political view in 1918 towards the 19th Amendment. Was it a true conscientious decision or a politically motivated move considering that an Amendment is legislation that a President's signature is not required or needed to become a law of the Constitution? In other words if it failed with or without his support no big deal but if it passed without his so called support he would lose that voting block of all women for the Democrat Party for future elections.

Now let's look at the actual United States Senate vote on Constitutional Amendment 19.

The Vote in Detail.
The roll call on the amendment follows:

FOR ADOPTION - 56.
Republicans - 36.
Capper, Cummins, Curtis, Edge, Elkins, Fall, Fernald, France, Frelinghuysen, Gronna, Hale, Harding, Johnson, (Cal.,) Jones, (Wash.,) Kellogg, Kenyon, Kayes, La Follette, Lenroot, McCormick, McCumber, McNaty, Nelson, New, Newberry, Norris, Page, Phipps, Poindexter, Sherman, Smoot, Spencer, Sterling, Sutherland, Warren, Watson.

Democrats - 20.
Ashurst, Chamberlain, Culberson, Harris, Henderson, Jones, (N. M.,) Kenrick, Kirby, McKellar, Myers, Nugent, Phelan, Pittman, Ransdell, Shepard, Smith, (Ariz.,) Stanley, Thomas, Walsh, (Mass.,) Walsh, (Mon.)

AGAINST ADOPTION - 25.

Republicans - 8.

Borah, Brandegee, Dillingham, Knox, Lodge, McLean, Moses, Wadsworth.

Democrats - 17.

Bankhead, Beckham, Dial, Fletcher, Gay, Harrison, Hitchcock, Overman, Reed, Simmons, Smith, (Md.,) Smith, (S. C.,) Swanson, Trammell, Underwood, Williams, Wolcott.

Paired.

Ball and King, for, with Shields, against: Calder and Townsend, for, with Penrose, against; Gerry and Johnson of South Dakota, for, with Martin, against; Gore and Colt, for, with Pomerone, against.

Absent and Not Paired.

Owen, Robinson, and Smith of Georgia. The vote came after four hours of debate, during which Democratic Senators opposed to the amendment filibustered to prevent a roll call until their absent Senators could be protected by pairs. They gave up the effort finally as futile.

Changes Defeated.

Before the final vote was taken Senator Underwood, a Democrat of the State of Alabama, called for a vote on his amendment to submit the suffrage amendment to Constitutional conventions of the various States, instead of to the Legislatures, for ratification. This was defeated by a vote of 45 against to 28 in favor.

Senator Gay, a Democrat of the State of Louisiana, offered an amendment proposing enforcement of the suffrage amendment by the States, instead of by the Federal Government. Senator Gay said that from a survey of the States he could predict that thirteen States would not ratify the amendment, enough to block it. His amendment was defeated, 62 to 19.

Now as you can see the main obstacle in the U.S. Senate of the 19th Amendment was the Democrat Party with the main supporters of the 19th Amendment being the Republican Party. It also helps to illustrate the Political Democrat's power concentrated in the Southern States with Senators Underwood and Gay. It also illustrates the point I made in regards to the rebuilding of the Democrat Party in the north after the Civil War. The first Democrat President elected after the war was Grover Cleveland then Governor of New York State, next to the State of New Jersey, elected twice but not concurrently. The second Democrat President was Woodrow Wilson who was the Governor of New Jersey and as I pointed out New Jersey being one of the three Democrat Northern States in the 1864 Presidential election that supported a potential Democrat President. Southern Republicans have pointed out over the years that Blacks were treated worse in some areas of the North, would that be concentrations of Democrats in politically controlled Democrat States of the North? Such as the State where the Jim Crow comedic Character that degraded Blacks was created and promoted in entertainment being what then would of been considered Broadway in New York City as a example?

With what government documents that are available I tried to get the House of Representatives vote breakdown but the best I could do was the total vote which one government document had it 304 to 89 for passing and another had it 304 to 90. So without the vote breakdown no conclusion can be made in aspects of the House vote.

The reason for this understanding of the 19th amendment vote is that our current President has used the phrase "A war on women" as a tool to pry the woman's vote away from the Republican Party using birth control as the subject. As a physically conservative man with a number of libertarian views I can't justify partial birth abortions. I see them as murder and late term abortions that inflict pain on an unborn child without there being a true medical need for the mother. As for abortions that do not meet the standards I just mentioned above and contraceptives if it works for you it is none of my business. But if I have to pay for your abortion or contraceptives in anyway which is yours and your sex partner's responsibility or your abortion for not using a contraceptive then you make it my business because of the financial standpoint. I won't judge you if you won't take money out of my wallet for something I am not responsible for monetarily. I have a child I am raising and should not have her do without while assisting you in your sex life or the abortion of your child in regards to your choices regarding your sex life. A child is not a cold or the flu, it is not something you catch or a disease you acquire it is a responsible or irresponsible choice in life also depending on your other choices in life being good or bad.

But after getting off the subject which would you rather have, me not paying for your responsibilities in life or the Democrats not allowing you to vote which is a right in a citizen's life regardless of race or gender?

Just for your information the Constitution gives the election rights to the individual States to carry out. At no point in the Constitution does it deny the right to vote to anyone based on any physical trait including color or gender, a indentured servant or a slave. That is until they screwed the pooch writing the XV Amendment which now designated a specific gender.

With these Liberal Democrat Presidents you should be able to see a historical pattern of human rights violations all against minority races and even gender. In every instance of the above violations the liberal left Democrats have at a later point in history used these same violations against America as a whole to demonize America for its intolerance. Yet it was their own intolerance of their own Political Party and power of the Presidential Office that created these situations. It also is the liberal left Democrat Party that has failed to accept any accountability for their political agenda of any period of time in our country's history.

Today's recent violations are with social programs designed and intended to help the neediest of our population. Anyone on a permanent social program should be truly disabled or to have reached an age beyond that of having the ability to work. Again it is the liberal left Democrat's newest playbook to keep it relevant in the political world, violating the rights of some to promote the wants (not needs) of others. Now using these programs to buy loyalty to their political party. They have expanded these programs well beyond their intended purpose to accomplish this loyalty to their party. Also with the influx of illegal immigrants to bolster the Democratic Party on Election Day they are also allowed onto these programs which stresses government resources and society beyond its breaking point. Basically it is the Democrats answer to the Republican's ideology that freed the Black race, "you freed them now we will GIVE them a little something from government that again buys their souls and votes and they will greet us with open arms because we know them, we raised them on our farms". Meaning we again own them at the ballot box which will get our party back too it's rightfully lofty position in government". So the next Liberal Left Democrat President in the history of American atrocities list will be:

8). Barack Hussein Obama II, 2008-2016, a very liberal left Democrat who created America's first credit rating down grade. Created a situation with our southern border allowing about five million more illegal immigrants to cross our southern border. Snatched defeat from the jaws of victory in regards to Iraq. Lied to the American People when criticizing the previous President's $4.9 Trillion in debt then amassing about $9.9 Trillion of debt by the end of his terms. Lied to the America People about his healthcare program's cost and what the people could keep of their healthcare plans being their doctors and the plans themselves to pass the program into law. Didn't enforce a Red Line that he laid down in Syria over the killing of its citizens with chemical weapons. Barack has made the 1% richer while making the 99% poorer. There are many more examples of his bad behavior which has created bad governing.

The biggest problem Barack will leave the American People is the debt. At $10.4 Trillion when Bush left office the debt was at about 66% of Gross Domestic Product being about $16 Trillion. Barack will leave us with our debt being about 117% of the GDP with a jobless stagnant economy. This gives our country three reasonable options. One, pay down our debt with the money government already receives from the GDP. But government can't borrow so it must have a balanced budget. Two, expand the GDP so government has more available money using it towards our debt. But government must still balance the budget so that the extra money can be applied to the debt. Three is a combination of both options.

Now the Liberal Left will offer a fourth option being raise taxes. That is always a Liberal's solution, collect everyone's money if you can then throw money at the problem until it goes away. The result is the problem never goes away. Government throws money at everything to fix it. The money goes away but the problems remain. If this solution worked we would not be in debt. God knows Government has thrown money at all failing aspects of Government without any positive results including education. History confirms my statement.

When the day comes that we can't pay our debts what will our creditors want as payment? California, Texas, maybe Florida, New York or Alaska, maybe a whole region of our country? And if we don't have the money to defend ourselves who will come to our defense? If our enemies know we can't defend ourselves will they now see this as the time for action?

If you loan money to what you believe is a friend and that person then doesn't repay you, you just realized they weren't a friend. When you borrow money from your enemies and don't repay it, it just gives your enemies another reason to want to kick your ass!

No possibility of something like this ever happening right, I mean we own this country right? Survival of the fittest, Baby! Fittest Government, Military, Private Sector and Citizens. If you can't defend it, it's only yours until someone else wants it or claims it. A Good Book or a Bad Ending in the U.S. Of A.'s History?

The above fictional story is just a thought of what may happen in the not too distant future under the leadership of Liberal Left Democrats. But the provable True atrocity of the Obama Presidency is listed in a later chapter just keep reading.

UNIONS

The first unions of past years were by the people and for the people pretty much like the Constitution but just like the Constitution the unions have morphed into something not foreseen by the original people who came up with the concept. These men never would have used their concept to cause other people not to be able to work by not belonging to their union. Just like the Founding Fathers the people who came up with the concept to protect the ordinary man would be rolling over in their graves as to how liberals have used their concept as a weapon against their fellow man of the labor force. The whole concept was to protect the worker from the rich factory owner who hired mob style enforcers to fight the common man in his efforts for better working conditions, hours and pay. It doesn't protect the worker from the union which is what the unseen forces of the union have turned it into, a mob style shakedown of the worker and the employer.

In the beginning the labor force of a factory saw their power to protect the individual or the group as a whole was better served when they acted as a whole. These were poor common men, there were no monthly union dues. They did together what needed to be done whether it was for the benefit of one man or all the men. In Contrast the same men would not have stood behind a man who continually didn't pull their weight or put the others in harms way by not doing his job correctly. Does this sound like the Unions of today? I think not!

Today's unions have no problem protecting the Good, the Bad and the Ugly whether it be a worker that pays union dues or a union worker that has nothing to do with the workplace. It is today's unions that collect monthly dues even if there is no conflict or needed goal. It is Today's unions that spend the worker's money on aspects other than what the worker's need or want. It is Today's worker's union that has been infiltrated by mob figures and practices of the mob including shakedowns, payoffs and intimidation. Does the name Jimmy Hoffa ring a bell. It is today's unions that use these same mob style tactics trying to infiltrate other types of businesses to extort concessions from the businesses in the name of the workers who haven't even contacted a union.

Today's unions didn't like the supreme Court's ruling that someone doesn't have to pay dues to work in a union Plant. The union's argument is that the individual receives the same benefits it negotiated for the paying union workers. The individual's argument was that the dues were being spent on other things outside of the workers themselves. These expenses were not endorsed by a number of the worker's who the union also represented and collected dues from to make political contributions IE. the Liberal Democrat Party. The Liberal Democrat Party doesn't support the decision either because it's about the money to both the union and the liberal Democrat Party.

The union itself is not suppose to be a political party. It's main and only concern should be the workers of the plant or industry from which it originates. The workers don't benefit from any political donations but the union does so the union has now become a political party financed by the worker's dues. That's the biggest difference where as they used to be one and the same and are not anymore. That's the true conflict between people who don't like Today's unions but still respect the worker's Unions of yesteryear. Today's Union is a mob style business and yesteryear's Union was totally by and for the working people.

With this understanding lets question the automobile and steel industries. Did the demand for automobiles go down? Did the supply of iron ore or coke for steel making go away? No, what went away was "Economic Feasibility" due to the high price of Union labor and the demands of the Union that priced each out of the market's of the United States and the World. When the golden goose can't lay golden eggs fast enough for the Unions and Liberal Government, they kill the Goose or it flies somewhere else forever!

POLITICS, POLLUTION, CLIMATE CHANGE, EPA AND ECONOMY

The liberal left agenda is pushing climate change as weapon to be used against fossil fuels. Their agenda is only to increase the power of their organization or organizations around them that support their views. Building on one organization builds both organizations such as was done in cooperation with the unions. This political party is pushing a topic being climate change with the only cause being Carbon Dioxide levels as a way to alter our sources of power. To gain a man-made advantage in pricing to make their product being green energy competitive by raising the cost of using fossil fuels.

The liberal left Democrats constantly vilify corporations and big business for numerous reasons. One is also using the "tax rate" argument when no tax is paid on billions of dollars earned. The corporation General Electric has avoided (paid no taxes in 2010) paying a fair tax rate for years through the tax credit or tax deductions allowed and legislated by government. General Electrics quarterly (every 3 months) income (after all expenses and taxes) averages 3.46 Billion Dollars for the years of 2012 and 2013. The Taxes paid during this same period averages 397.5 Million Dollars quarterly meaning the taxable percentage rate average is 11.488% and 1.8% from 2002 to 2012. Yet Democrats lead by Harry Reid vilified Mitt Romney in the 2012 elections of not paying taxes when his percentage rate paid was 14.7% average on about 21 Million Dollars average each year for the 2010 & 2011 tax returns. The President gladly displayed G.E. as a member of the product producers of their "Green Energy" initiative, code word for "agenda". Why? You don't vilify someone that you are working with because one's prosperity depends on the others prosperity. The CEO of G.E. is Jeffrey R. Immelt who holds 1,962,577 million shares of G.E. as of March 3rd, 2014. In February 2009, Immelt was appointed as a member to the President's Economic Recovery Advisory Board to provide the President and his administration with advice and counsel in fixing America's economic downturn. On January 21, 2011, President Obama announced Immelt's appointment as chairman of his outside panel of economic advisers, succeeding former Federal Reserve chairman Paul Volcker. It sure looks like its fine for G.E. not to pay its fair share of taxes. Just wanting to make one connection of the hundreds of different connections involved in this "Green Movement".

Global warming was also a topic of the 60's and 70's. Its focus was placed on man-made building materials that retain heat commonly used in the home and commercial building markets. They have replaced earlier natural materials used for the same purposes. These products also emerged out of the industrial age and can be tracked directly with the one degree temperature increase the globe has seen in the last 100 years. The sayings "like a cat on a hot tin roof" and "it's so hot you can fry an egg on the sidewalk" are literal sayings because in each case the meaning is true. Heat retaining man-made materials used in today's types of construction are asphalt for roads and parking lots, sometimes concrete for interstate highways and all local sidewalks. Roofing materials include tar shingles, flat tar and paper style roofs, tin and metal roofs, even some tile type roofs, again all heat retaining materials. This movement was ignored at the time because the problem was not as prevalent as it is today but that doesn't mean the theory wasn't correct or doesn't have a causing percentage of the effect. When it rains on a hot summer day you get steam from every asphalt road. That is the transfer of heat from the road to the water bringing the water to a point in temperature to produce steam. This will continue until the asphalt's temperature falls below the point to produce steam. So its beginning temperature must have been well above that of the surrounding natural substances for this process to happen for an extended period of time. After the rain has stopped what is the first thing to dry out? The hotter asphalt road! The science, "the rule", of heat transfer is that the hotter material will warm the surrounding environment's atmosphere causing the warmer air to rise and cooler air replaces the warmer air then the process continually repeats itself until the hotter material reaches the cooler temperature of the surrounding environment then the process stops. This process continues for the duration of the source of heat being the sun continually heating the material. Now multiply this by every square foot of roads, sidewalks, parking lots, roofs around the world and you can see the effect that these materials have on our environment. There is absolutely no scientific argument that can be made against this scientifically proven effect. Now as civilization grows the use of these materials grow with it.

The liberal left Democrats including Barack Obama say the science is settled on Climate Change, blaming the rise in temperature on a convenient atmospheric gas being Carbon Dioxide. Their only argument is that the Carbon Dioxide generated by fossil fuel burning power plants is the one and only cause (except for cow herds) for the temperature rise. Their argument includes the rise of the amounts of Carbon Dioxide in the atmosphere which has moved from just below .03% to almost .04% (less than 1%) of the atmosphere since the industrial revolution. But wasn't the industrial revolution that helped cause the population explosion in the world.

My scientific phrase "Carbon Dioxide Consumption Balance" is the explanation and one very important cure for this problem. As Carbon Dioxide consuming vegetation is removed (killed) from the environment for expanded construction being civilization. It creates a negative loss to the environment's ability to remove carbon dioxide from the atmosphere. So reducing the amount of carbon dioxide emitted by man will never meet the needs to correct the problem because of the continued loss of carbon dioxide consuming plant life. When you lower one, carbon dioxide consumption being plant life, you then must lower the other, carbon dioxide output, to achieve an artificial balance. If civilization's growth is left unchecked it will eventually eradicate enough plant life that the "Carbon Dioxide Consumption Balance" will move to a negative balance. This means that enough vegetation has been removed from nature that nature itself can no longer achieve the needed consumption to keep Carbon Dioxide levels at the lower levels science has recorded in earlier times in our history. Thus today's rise in Carbon Dioxide levels.

So the real solution to lower carbon dioxide over the globe is to increase nature's consumption ability with proper amounts of plant life or proper plant life that consumes more Carbon Dioxide. That replacement plant life must consume carbon dioxide at the greatest rates possible to compensate for the natural area of vegetation lost which delivered a specific rate of carbon dioxide consumption to achieve a "Carbon Dioxide Consumption Balance". To implement such a program you must identify the plant life that consumes the most amounts of carbon dioxide as being the preferred replacement plants. Then you must determine the consumption rate of carbon dioxide for most other plants to calculate the consumption lost when removing natural vegetation for civilizations expansion. Ultimately it will be the population that the earth can support, with man's true knowledge of the problem in offering help that will determine the population allowed on the planet earth. The immediate goal is to combat "global warming, climate change" which is to replant lost vegetation using my "Carbon Dioxide Consumption Balance Adjustment" equation to try and achieve a neutral (nothing lost is the minimum result) consumption of carbon dioxide for the area before and after construction. This is the only way to keep expanding civilization without removing nature's filtering capacities of Carbon Dioxide.

The Government's own agencies promote a carbon dioxide consumption negative balance. The Dept. of Forestry when clearing an old forest growth for new pines for paper products. The spacing of newly planted pines creates a negative carbon dioxide impact. The controlled burns to kill undergrowth are two fold, 1; it again creates a negative carbon dioxide impact, 2; the carbon dioxide given off by the burn contributes to the added carbon dioxide in the atmosphere.

The Government's Dept. of Agriculture pays farmers not to plant fields to help control the pricing of food products. This ensuring a higher cost and a larger profit margin. But some selected farmers that are lucky enough to be chosen for a no plant field make the same profit without any of the work. With food prices' going up seems there would be more fields being planted to slow that increase. When a large portion of corn crops was designated for ethanol production in gasoline commonsense says that would increase the need for planted fields of corn but the price of corn just went up instead. That just increased the price of livestock feed which increased the price of meat products. So what has government accomplished? A negative carbon dioxide consumption balance, higher corn prices which drives up the price of ethanol, livestock feed and meat products. With the higher cost of ethanol our cost of gasoline with ethanol in it has increased. The use of a 10% ethanol gasoline mix was supposed to decrease our crude oil consumption by 10%. Many people argue that using that 10% mix reduces their fuel mileage by the same 10%. Thus, if true, the consumer is paying for something of which they get zero return from the product. I know for a fact that ethanol reduces cylinder head temperatures in a combustible engine and can allow for more added timing adding to a horsepower increase. This same effect can be obtained with windshield washer fluid (ethanol based) being measurably injected into a fuel system. Does it decrease the burn temperature of the fuel lowering cylinder head temps which in theory would lower horsepower and fuel mileage or does it just act as a cooling agent for the surrounding cylinder components allowing for greater horsepower which should not affect the actual burn process? My opinion is the latter but I won't disagree with the first opinion because the actual tune of the engine can create that mileage lost effect.

Lately I have heard moisture as another reason for temperature rates rising. I again disagree, moisture absolutely controls temperatures but not all in the fashion they describe. Climate Change is a natural progression of nature. The Middle East has one of the largest if not the largest oil supplies in the world. Oil is a fossil fuel created by past plant and animal life. This means that the Middle East must have been covered with a large amount of plant and life to have these oil deposits. The Middle East has been a desert for how many millions of years? This desert situation existed long before cars, fossil fuel power plants or man had any impact on the earth. So what happened? The natural event of climate change. This natural event is evident with any desert environment that has large oil deposits such as Texas and southwest North America. With a desert environment comes low humidity which determines rainfall. It is this lack of humidity that causes extreme temperatures in a desert, hot in the day and cold at night depending on seasons. In the summer humidity helps to disperse heat. In the winter it helps to retain heat.

The equator is the closest place to the sun at sea level on earth. At the equator the amount of sunlight is 12 hrs. a day with no change of season but in the southern & northern hemispheres which oppose each other for the yearly seasons, when one is summer the other is winter. This area around the globe should be the hottest place on earth due to its shorter distance from the sun at sea level. The average temperature is 86 degrees during the day and 73 degrees at night because it's the humidity that helps to regulate temperatures, not allowing for temperature extremes. It is also humidity that determines rain fall. The most pristine forests are at the equator, the rain forest of South America and the monsoon season of South East Asia forests. Even Africa at the equator has lush forests in the Congo as the only continent that developed chimpanzees and gorillas. Under this scenario it sounds like higher humidity is a correction and not a cause of higher temperatures.

Of course there are the many ocean currents and thousands of wind currents that also affect our climates. The wind currents tend to follow ocean currents when over ocean water. They both tend to move cold air &water from the pole areas to the equator and vice versus acting like a pump as a mechanism to help regulate temperatures.

The biggest question yet to be answered is this; if it's 39 degrees outside on a winter day and upon entering your home it is 90 degrees with no smoke or fire what do you do to correct the situation? Open the doors and windows? No, you check the source of the heat being the home's heater thermostat and its temperature setting. The NASA scientists have unknown answers to many questions about our sun, our source of heat and light. The sun is the center of our universe and feeds life onto planet earth. What we know about the sun is very little. First the temperatures of the sun are all estimated. When estimating something there is always a margin of error, a percentage above or below the estimate that the estimate may move but not moving outside the parameters of what is allowed. The temperatures and information I am using is right out of the NASA web-site on the sun's temperatures.

The sun's core temperature is about 27 million degrees Fahrenheit. Moving outward the convective zone's temperature drops below 3.5 million degrees Fahrenheit. At the sun's surface, the Photosphere, the temperature is about 10,000 degrees Fahrenheit. Above the photosphere, temperature increases with altitude, reaching as high as 3.5 million degrees Fahrenheit. The source of coronal heating has been a scientific mystery for more than 50 years. The science on heat transfer is that the farther you move from a heat source the lower the measurement of heat. The first aspect as they stated not understood is how coronal temperatures increase at a farther distance from the heat source. The one question overlooked by NASA is the fact that the Photosphere at 10k degrees is sandwiched between two layers both with temperatures around 3.5 million degrees. How does this layer remain at 10k degrees, 350 times less in temperature? I am not even throwing in additional temperatures for solar flares which also seem to be written off because of a lack of knowledge.

Another aspect of heat is the fuel source of which the heat is generated. When a fire begins it normally starts small, grows to a high point and how long it maintains that high point depends on the fuel source and its characteristics. Once the fuel source begins to exhaust itself the fire reduces in size and heat and at some point it goes out. My question is what stage is our sun in using the above scenario? Is it growing, maintaining or reducing? We know at some point it will burn out. Again scientists have no idea because that question is not even addressed. With what we know on temperatures a 2.5% or 5% margin swing from above average to a below average is a 5% or 10% move from the high temperature to the low temperature and this could very well be a long term pattern of the sun, a natural fluctuation in temperature of the sun. This 5% or 10% swing could easily account for a 1 degree or more rise in temperature over the last 100 years. As little as a 1% swing being 2% move of temperature from low to high would account for the 1 degree increase of temperature.

The liberal left Democrat administration including the President have studied this climate change topic and again their view as the cause is fossil fuels used to generate power at our power plants which emit Carbon Dioxide, o' yeah, cows breathing and farting, is credited for this problem. Under this thought process the almost extermination of the Buffalo herds in the west should be seen as a good thing. One fact is true if all Carbon Dioxide generating animal life dies then all Carbon Dioxide consuming plant life dies. One cannot exist without the other. But you can't expect animal life (includes man) to grow while man decreases plant life and not have a effect on Carbon Dioxide amounts.

As someone who has been hired to do a particular job if you deviate from that task it may cost you your job. As a scientist assigned to do a job that person may still face the same obstacles which may then interfere with research and where they may want to go with the research. If 100 scientists are hired to study climate change and the effects of Carbon Dioxide on the atmosphere then you have a limited study on a topic. The study is limited by the employer on what and how the study is conducted. If it was a true study then they should be able to answer all the questions from the material above but they can't. To have a conclusion based on limited facts is a study that will always point at the same conclusion because of the limited facts. The design of the study will also only lead you in that predetermined direction for an answer. Ultimately the employer knew the conclusion before the study even began which is a convenient answer for pushing an agenda. A true scientific endeavor say for a certain type of adhesive or glue may never achieve the product desired but in a true search you may unintentionally develop a glue that is used for "Sticky Notes" of which 3M made many millions of dollars on a product by accident. True story.

The industrial revolution brought products to our society that improved our quality of life. What society didn't understand at the time was what was being released into the environment. These pollutants were mostly a byproduct of manufacturing. The Great Lakes were polluted by these same unnoticed byproducts while noticeable trash was being disposed of in its bodies of water. Today the Great Lakes have recovered to some point but the pollutants still exist in the lake's bottom sediments, covered over time. We know the pollutants are there but is it feasible to dredge all the lakes to remove as much of the pollutants as possible? No, because 100% of the pollutants will never be recovered and to remix them into the waters will have a worse outcome to the lakes. One of the toxic-ants found even today in the Great Lakes is Mercury.

The Environmental Protection Agency (EPA) among many things is charged with regulating dangerous elements from entering the environment. The EPA began its work on Dec. 2nd, 1970 and was formed under the Richard Nixon administration. The EPA sets rules and enforces the rules thru regulations that restrict the use or gives directives on how to handle toxic material while in use and for disposal or recycling.

There are four levels of laws or rules within the form of our Federal government. "Articles" in the "Constitution" written by the Founding Fathers. "Amendments" written into the "Constitution" by following administrations of Presidents and Congresses. "Laws" passed by following administrations of Presidents and Congresses which are not part of the "Constitution" but are protected by the powers of the "Constitution".

"Executive Orders" issued by a President. These orders were meant to be used by the President to enhance the enforcement (not rewrite Law) of existing laws, as intended by the Founding Fathers in the writing of the "Constitution". The last is a rule, "Regulations" which I have gone to the government web site. Bing "government regulations" go to "Laws and Regulations | USA.gov." and I have insert it for you word for word.

"Regulations are issued by federal agencies, boards, or commissions. They explain how the agency intends to carry out a law". "The Rule making Process"
"Federal regulations are created through a process known as rule making".
"By law, federal agencies must consult the public when creating, modifying, or deleting rules in the Code of Federal Regulations.

This is an annual publication that lists the official and complete text of federal agency regulations".

"Once an agency decides that a regulation needs to be added, changed, or deleted, it typically publishes a proposed rule in the Federal Register to ask the public for comments".

"After the agency considers public feedback and makes changes where appropriate, it then publishes a final rule in the Federal Register with a specific date for when the rule will become effective and enforceable".

"When the agency issues a final rule for comment, it must describe and respond to the public comments it received".

Get Involved and Learn More
Find Proposed Rules and Notices
Comment on Regulations
Learn More About the Process of Creating Regulations

Articles and Amendments are the same in strength of power in our government because they are part of the "Constitution" and are difficult to change for a reason. A "Law" is the next step down in level of power. It is much easier to add a "Law" or change a "Law" but the powers that be need the support of "Congress" and a "President" all elected representatives of "We the People" to add or change a law. A "Regulation" is not a law and does not need to go through the same process. It is controlled and written by people the "President" has appointed to a federal agency, board or commission. Thus "President (I have a pen and a phone) Obama" has a very strong say (executive order) as to what is written in "Regulations". The "supreme Court" ruled that the E.P.A. which added Carbon Dioxide and Methane to the list of pollutes has "the right to regulate" these gases even though these gases were never included in the original written "Law" because they were not seen as a pollutant by our "Elected Officials". This is how the Obama administration plans on implementing their "Green Renewable Energy" agenda allowing the Democrat party to rake in millions personally and for the party with backdoor deals that are already in progress.

One of the 1st things implemented by the Barack Obama administration was the removal from retail outlets of incandescent light bulbs in the United States. The reasoning was that Compact Florescent Lighting bulbs use less energy makes sense on that aspect. The aspect that makes no sense is the fact that all CFL bulbs contain a small amount of mercury. The EPA by law is the government agency appointed to regulate this dangerous element. On the packaging of CFL bulbs, that I have seen (Lights of America), the warning label is on the back and so small I needed a magnifying glass (actually two, the 2nd being twice as big) to read the web-site any answers to any questions I may have. The web-site is www. lamprecycle.org. Anything dealing with energy savings on the package are at a minimum 4 times larger with no problem to read. The EPA has control over the size and placement of the warning label. I will now make a liberal ruling on the intent of this action just like the supreme Court does, "seems to me the EPA doesn't see a problem with the product or how it's disposed of so they don't need to enforce mercury as a pollutant anymore because it is no longer a problem and we justify this not by what is written but by all the effort needed to get the proper information". Just thought I would throw a liberal interpretation of written law into the conversation. The fact is the warning label is on the product but on the back, the size is very undersized, the information is unattainable if you don't have internet. There is a phone # 1-800-321-8100 or maybe 6100, I called it (8100), it's to a "Lights of America" receptionist recording, I didn't stay on the phone to see if help was available for a disposal question. The web-site "lamp recycle" does offer info on recycling CFL bulbs and Lowe's & Home Depot are two sites but I have never noticed signs in the stores. But if you aren't looking for how to dispose of the bulbs then you won't see it, I guarantee you. Some other things listed for recycling are lithium-ion and nickel-cadmium batteries. With the effort I just put forth how many CFL bulbs and batteries do you think go into the landfill dumps by unknowing or uncaring consumers? Most internet sites stress the low amount of mercury in these bulbs. When added up as to what maybe going into the dumps around the country that amount adds up quickly. That amount eventually gets into the environment and the water and that shows history has a tendency to repeat itself even with the EPA in charge. It does so because it is now a political issue of a political agenda being reducing power consumption to reduce carbon dioxide emissions which is nothing more than camouflage for the "Green Energy" movement. At least LED lighting is just around the corner, hopefully the price will come down and CFL bulbs will disappear. F.Y.I. I am including information directly from the EPA.gov site to see for yourself if the EPA has met it's own standards? My conclusion; trading one pollutant being a reduction in carbon dioxide for a possible increase in another pollutant being mercury is just a tradeoff of immeasurable outcomes.

1. Economics – The value of the materials to be recycled must be greater than the cost of recycling. In situations where this is not the case, laws and incentives (taxpayer money) can be effective in increasing recycling rates.
2. Technology – Products that are designed with recycling in mind will be easier to disassemble and re-process.
3. Societal – Programs will be more effective when the public is aware of the benefits of recycling and the collection and recycling infrastructure is accessible and well publicized.

The reason for the effort put forth above is that government and the EPA don't always have the best interest of the people in mind of this country or of any country because pollution doesn't abide by territorial boundaries. Looking at #1, what is the value of keeping mercury out of the environment? Do the EPA's own insights allow for keeping it out of the environment? #2, If there has been very little information or effort put forth about how to recycle CFL bulbs then can you really expect it to happen even by the people who do care? The EPA can't down play it by the little amount of mercury in each CFL bulb being 2 to 3 mg. of mercury.

The agency of the EPA with its use of carbon dioxide as an excuse is being used by the administration to push "Green Renewable Energy" over fossil fuels. Green energy as we know it is much more expensive (.22 cents a KWH) and much less reliable than fossil fuels (.04 cents a KWH). So if you can't compete price wise what do you do? If you have the ability to use the power of government you use that power to raise the price or even shutdown fossil fueled electricity generating power plants to make yourself artificially competitive. If you don't like gasoline powered cars how do you get rid of them?

You put a requirement on them they will never meet such as making them get 150 or 200 miles to the gallon within say two years. Then 100% of all gasoline car manufacturing and use within this country will cease and electric cars will be the norm for those who can afford them and afford to recharge them.

The definition of green energy is "anything that has a renewable source, a never ending source to supply energy". To begin with most of the devices used for green energy do not meet the requirements for green energy unless you have a liberal interpretation of the definition. Wind and solar energy do not meet the requirement of "a never ending source to supply energy". Wind generates zero power when the wind is not blowing or not blowing enough and solar stops providing power everyday with darkness or is greatly reduced with bad weather. So each have an end to the source to supply energy which doesn't meet the standards for the definition. The first part of the definition pertains to things that can be grown, harvested, replanted or re-grown. Most of these products by design are meant to provide energy thru the process of burning or combustion and also have limits. The limits are that it must be produced in enough quantity to supply the demand for energy. If using the same land that is used to produce our food supply then an increased production of one means a lower production of the other. This equation doesn't account for a growing population which requires more land to provide a food source. The second problem is the liberal left democrat's liberal interpretation of "Green Energy" which implies that it is an environmentally safe source of energy which is not true. If the source of energy requires burning or combustion then one of the gases produced is "Carbon Dioxide" being the same gas the EPA is using to eliminate our fossil fuel powered electrical generating plants.

In 2010, Germany was seen as the country to model your country after in regards to "Green Renewable Energy" allowing Germany to be known as "the world's first major renewable energy economy". The problem with green energy is that the powers that be are reporting numbers that enhance the allure of green energy without showing the shortcomings of green energy. The numbers I will be using are the numbers for the years 2005 through 2012 released by Germany's agency of Federal Ministry for Environment, Nature Conservation and Nuclear Safety. 1990 is only a reference, a starting point; no #'s of that year are charted or used in the percentages of which I have inserted.

When you are told over and over something you begin to believe it and at some point you accept it as the Truth. There is a difference between being told and being taught. "Being told is INDOCTRINATION into a certain way of thinking without any supporting facts, being TAUGHT is backing the curriculum with FACTS that support the SUBJECT allowing the TRUTH to be seen"!

	[MW]		[GWh]		[GWh]			[GWh]		[GWh]	
	Installed share		Hydro power		Wind energy			Biomass		Biogenic	
	Capacity	%		%	onshore-offshore		%	mostly wood	%	of waste	%
1990	4,069		15,580		71			221		1,213	0
2005	28,122		19,576		27,229			10,978		3,047	
2006	31,883	+13.39	20,042	+2.4	30,710		+12.80	14,841	+35.20	3,844	+26.16
2007	35,479	+11.26	21,169	+5.6	39,713		+29.31	19,760	+33.30	4,521	+17.61
2008	39,597	+11.60	20,446	-3.5	40,574		+2.18	22,872	+15.80	4,659	+3.10
2009	46,584	+17.65	19,036	-6.9	38,602	38	-4.78	25,989	+13.43	4,352	-6.60
2010	55,742	+19.65	20,95	+9.9	37,619	174	-2.19	29,085	+11.92	4,781	+9.86
2011	65,843	+17.95	17,674	-15.7	48,315	568	+29.34	31,920	+9.72	5,000	+4.60
2012	76,017	+15.55	21,200	+20.0	45,325	675	-5.89	35,950	+12.63	4,900	-2.00
Changed %	170.3%	107.05		+11.8	69.0%		+60.77	227.5%	132.00	60.8%	52.73
Avg.	21.29%	13.38		2.36%	8.63%		7.60%	28.44%	16.50%	7.60%	6.60%

	[GWh]		[GWh]	[GWh]		[GWh]	
	Photovoltaics (solar) %		Geothermal energy	Total electricity generation %		Share of gross [%] consumption % electricity	
1990	0.6		0.0	17,086		3.1.	
2005	1,282		0.2	62,112		10.1	
2006	2,220	+ 73.20	0.4	71,657	+ 15.360	11.6	+14.90 %
2007	3,075	+ 38.50	0.4	88,238	+ 23.140	14.3	+23.30 %
2008	4,420	+ 43.74	17.6	92,989	+ 5.384	15.1	+ 5.60 %
2009	6,583	+ 48.94	18.8	94,618	+ 1.752	16.4	+ 8.70 %
2010	11,683	+ 77.47	27.7	104,372	+ 10.310	17.1	+ 4.30 %
2011	19,340	+ 65.54	18.8	123,519	+ 18.345	20.5	+20.00 %
2012	28,000	+ 44.78	25.4	136,075	+ 10.165	22.9	+11.75 %
Changed %	2084%	392.17		119.08%	84.456	126.7%	88.55
Avg.	260.50%	49.02%		14.89%	10.56%	15.84%	11.07%

My contribution to this chart is all the percentages to the right of each category that have a plus or minus for a gain or loss in yearly contribution of electricity. At the bottom of each column to help breakdown the numbers into workable information using only the 2005 and 2012 numbers for a truer total of Gigawatt Hours gained over the eight years. The Avg. number at the very bottom of each column is the average percentage gained yearly over the eight years rounded to the nearest hundredth.

At the top left is the column for yearly installed Megawatt construction. All the other columns are the source and the Gigawatt hour generated for each year. The bottom right two columns is the total electricity generated by all these Renewable energy sources and the percentages of the total energy Renewable's offered towards Germany's total energy consumption.

People if you are reading this I hope you bought my book because this has been a lot of work in research and set up.

If you noticed I didn't finish the numbers on Hydro power because the numbers fluctuate indicating no new construction and the fluctuation is probably created by rainfall amounts. Also the Geothermal numbers are minimal and won't affect the topic but both totals are included in the end total figures.

My intention is to show the energy returns verses installed capacities is a losing situation. Don't get me wrong, if you live somewhere off the grid like Alaska anyway to generate power is worth its weight in gold. Our military dabbled in solar energy back in the 50's and early 60's and it was deemed inefficient then unless like I said you are off the grid. If it worked the military would be using it.

The first thing I would like to point out regarding the chart is that Germany has been building these Renewable Green energy sources for twenty two years and the average return on energy since 2005 is 11.07 percent. So about 89 percent of its energy still comes from non-renewable non-green sources.

Now look at wind energy, out of the eight years three years the production of power fell off. Proof that if the wind doesn't blow you don't generate as much energy. As for Offshore wind generation, the dumbest thing that can be done is build a metal windmill in a solution that is the second must corrosive after battery acid, meaning perpetual replacement and/or constant repairs. If it's not working it is not generating energy.

When looking at the Solar energy numbers the one thing that can be taken from them is that Germany has been building massive numbers of Solar farms. Yet, even in 2012 the energy return was only 22.9 percent for all Renewable Green energy. Now for the kick in the butt lets move on to the next paragraph.

The biggest point needing to be addressed is that in Germany Biomass is made up of mostly "Wood". Wood is a fuel source for burning to generate heat to generate power and carbon dioxide is a byproduct of this process, so it is not Green Energy. It is renewable but just like wind or solar but nature determines its next time of availability, it also has a negative Carbon Dioxide Consumption Balance as I earlier explained. In 2005 Biomass accounted for 17.67% of all green energy generated, in 2012 it accounted for 26.42% of all green energy generated. Now lets back the Biomass number out of the 2012 green energy number for "Share of gross energy electricity [%] consumption" being the 22.9%. Also Germany stated that it had great weather for solar power production in 2012. Now the true percentage for 2012's renewable energy is 16.85% even after all the solar construction that occurred in 2010, 2011 and 2012. That means Germany has only 83.15% left in infrastructure to meet a 100% goal of renewable energy, except for that statement is not true.

The sources for "Green Renewable Energy" as we know them are solar, wind and hydro. Hydro-power is limited to the available moving water that can be used for generating power and then there are fluctuations in what is generated but it is a variable continuous source unless the water source stops completely for what ever reason. The sources must be never ending of which solar & wind are not that type of power source. So on days with little sunlight and little wind you have little power. The nights with little wind you also have less power than that little power. No wind means no power. In actuality no one can say at what percentage of "Green Renewable Energy" infrastructure a country has to have to become energy independent because the sources are not constant. One source must be able to generate enough energy to cover the percentages of what another source was producing before that source's production percentage fell because of a lack of wind or sunlight. If you have three or four days of clouds with little wind how do you cover that percentage of energy production lost with no available alternate production of energy? Now how much of a overbuild must be built to actually achieve "Green Renewable Energy" independence? 200% to achieve 100%; 300%, 500% or 5000% to achieve 100%? A 100% will never be achieved with solar or wind because nature doesn't offer constantly perfect conditions to achieve this situation. Also what is the cost to meet this unattainable goal? Thus the reason for Germany's Biomass as a stop gap as a more constant power supply and these power plants have very little differences except the demolition of a forest than our coal fired power plants.

One more point is you can't take a power source immediately offline or bring it immediately online to the power grid because it causes power drops or surges, this reeks havoc on a power grid. Also a power company can't afford to have a running power plant on standby on a day to day situation just to supply a limited amount of energy that doesn't cover its operating costs. But it can't be taken offline because it might be needed tomorrow. It is a catch 22 situation of which there is no answer being created by the notion that wind and solar are a true never ending source of energy. These are the problems of which Germany is experiencing, unreliable power sources. Germany's power cost is the highest on the European continent with it being .18 cents per KWh in 2000 increasing to .38 cents per KWh in 2013. If "Green Renewable Energy" was a cheaper power source then why the increase while the building of solar energy sources from 2005 to 2012 had a 2084% increase in power generation? Germany's power availability predictions by 2050 are based on cutting the total energy consumption by 20% from 2008 to 2020 and 50% less by 2050. How do you accomplish this if you want or have a growing manufacturing, economy and/or population?

The green energy people also like to use Germany as a successful example of meeting power demands for the first 6 months of each year, or so they say, but the power met is not near as high for the rest of the year. Germany in relation to the U.S.-Canadian border sits a little above the 47th Latitude and heat is not the problem in summertime. Therefore air conditioning in the homes and businesses is nonexistent along with other electrical appliances they do without. So the electricity demand is almost nonexistent during summer and winter is where the demand is high. Another aspect of solar is that when the panel is covered with snow it won't work until the snow has melted or been removed. The panels can be tilted so most of the snow might slide off but then the angle of the panel is not correct for optimum utilization of sunlight ensuring its efficiency. Not to mention that you have put $40,000 dollars of equipment on your roof and in the home which your insurance company now must insure against damages due to high winds, hail and fire. Also additional costs to replace the homes roof due to equipment removal and re-installation which also figures into insurance costs. Also anything that generates heat creates hot spots in the environment thus also increasing temperature in the atmosphere.

Fortunately for Germany it has reversed its current path by experiencing the same examples I have described. A Forbes Magazine online article on 12/30/13 titled "Germany's Energy Goes Kaput, Threatening Economic Stability" reported this and I will take quotes directly from the article. "The latest report predicts that the renewable energy surcharge added to every consumer's electricity bill will increase from 5.3 cents to between 6.2 and 6.5 cents per kilowatt hour — a 20-percent price hike". "These prices have taken their toll upon the middle class, creating chaotic supply challenges and have directly contributed to nationwide job losses. Massive subsidies for renewable energy are harming the economy, imposing significant regressive costs on poor and working class energy consumers". "In an unexpected move, Germany approved its first coal-fired power plant in eight years, which is now up and running. The German energy company Steag says its 725-megawatt coal plant is just the beginning of coal's German comeback, as the country has actually approved a total of ten new hard-coal plants. These facilities are scheduled to come online in the next two years, boosting the country's coal capacity by 33 percent". "Unlike America, Europe has not been able to transition to natural gas, thereby leaving countries like Germany suddenly facing an enormous energy deficit, which experts and pundits alike suddenly agree cannot be replaced by renewables, such as wind or solar". "Unlike environmentalists in America who seem driven to squash any further development of hydrocarbons, Germans have been far more practical, suggesting that ultimately environmental goals must take a backseat to the economy". Spain, the second largest "Green

Renewable Energy" country is experiencing the same problems. The environmentalists in America if not the Liberal Left Democrats are in support of the Liberal Left Democrat's movement. Some are using the movement to line their pockets with over priced electricity being sold to the public as "Green Renewable Energy" because they are investors or owners of such systems. But when government subsidizes a private enterprise, that enterprise has a diminished exposure to failure and exposes the taxpayer to that cost of failure and the cost of the product.

Government wouldn't endorse one type of business over another would it? Yes it will and yes it has in the past. When railroads were expanding to the west as tracks crossed over rivers they weren't required with a height requirement. This limited the freight that could be moved by riverboats which had been the norm long before trains existed. If you remember some of the old photos of steamboats with their smokestacks folded over it was caused by the clearance needed to pass under a railroad crossing. This was done to put limits on one type business while giving the other an advantage because they were in competition with each other to move freight. Government's elected officials will line their pockets by aligning with a certain business that is willing to donate to the official or officials legally or illegally. This also repeated itself when railroads began to compete against each other, also with airline travel as it emerged after WWII.

What about pollution from the coal fired plants? A coal fired energy plant with no emission controls emits 100% of its byproducts. A coal fired energy plant with all the known emission controls emits just 2% of the previous byproducts. If the administration focused as much on technology for coal fired plants as it does to get rid of the plants there would be even greater reductions. But that doesn't fit this administration's political party's agenda to enrich themselves.

Of the three non-fossil fuel energy producers solar is by far the dirtiest and least reliable. I have pointed out its reliability problems. Now I will address its pollution contributions.

Solyndra, a bankrupt solar energy company, claimed to have produced enough solar panels to supply 100,000 homes with solar energy. One chemical among many used in the process of making panels is cadmium. This chemical with others creates a solution which becomes sludge after the manufacturing process of lining solar tubes. Solyndra created 12.5 million pounds of this sludge, that's 125 lbs. per home. Solyndra and Abound solar along with many more Green Renewable Energy companies left behind portions of this pollution at their manufacturing and warehouse sites to be cleaned up at the taxpayer's expense.

The bigger slap to the taxpayer's face is the fact that taxpayers funded these companies' loans that were guaranteed by agencies of the U.S. government. As of 2010 it had made loans on behalf of the Dept. of Energy for $2.9 billion. Solyndra made up about 20% of that amount. Prior to the Treasury's loan, the firm had done nine rounds of private financing and filed for an IPO which was subsequently withdrawn. Two of Solyndra's largest investors are Argonaut Ventures I, L.L.C. and the GKFF Investment Company, LLC. Both firms are represented on the Solyndra board of directors by Steven R. Mitchell. Both are investment vehicles of the George Kaiser Family Foundation of Tulsa, Oklahoma. George Kaiser was a bundler for President Barack Obama in the 2008 election. Mr. Kaiser visited the White House 16 of the 20 times that Solyndra investors or management visited there. According to White House visitor logs, between March 12, 2009, and April 14, 2011, Solyndra officials and investors made no fewer than 20 trips to the West Wing. In the week before the administration awarded Solyndra with the first-ever alternative energy loan guarantee on March 20, four separate visits were logged. George Kaiser, who has in the past been labeled a major Solyndra investor as well as an Obama donor, made three visits to the White House on March 12, 2009, and one on March 13. Kaiser has denied any direct involvement in the Solyndra deal and through a statement from his foundation said he "did not participate in any discussions with the U.S. government regarding the loan." George Kaiser alleges that he didn't discuss Solyndra with any White House officials but his investment groups were hot for Solyndra. Solyndra's IPO filing show the amount of funding Kaiser's investment businesses gave Solyndra. Over 9 rounds of financing it invested approximately $337 million, or 48% of all equity raised for the business. Although Kaiser, through Argonaut and GKFF Investment Company, LLC, did not participate in the initial two private financing rounds. They dominated the following funding rounds and were the major venture capital investors in the firm.

Another name in this mix of people that I mentioned is that of Steven R. Mitchell which was a former director of SolarReserve

LLC before Solyndra. On Sept. 28, 2011 the U.S. Energy Secretary Steven Chu announced the Department finalized a $737 million loan guarantee (what is the taxpayer's take lower or higher power rates?) to Tonopah Solar Energy, LLC to develop the Crescent Dunes Solar Energy Project. The solar project, sponsored by SolarReserve, LLC, is a 110 megawatt (by whose numbers? Not Germany's) concentrating solar power tower (a very hot hotspot in the environment) generating facility with molten salt as the primary heat transfer and storage medium. It will be the first of its kind in the United States (but not in Germany) and the tallest (great it's taller) molten salt tower in the world. Located 14 miles northwest of Tonopah, Nevada on land (how much for the lease?) leased (public free graze land) from the Bureau of Land Management, the company anticipates the facility will fund 600 construction jobs (Keystone pipe line; 20k to 30k jobs, 50 permanent jobs, funded by private enterprise) and 45 permanent jobs. The Crescent Dunes Solar Energy facility is expected to avoid nearly 290,000 metric tons of carbon dioxide annually (by who's number's on emissions) and produce enough electricity to power over (at what cost and is it continual?) 43,000 homes.

Beginning in 2005-2006 a land deal made by Senate Democratic Leader Harry Reid caused him later to collect a $1.1 million on a Las Vegas land deal even though he hadn't personally owned the property for over three years. Reid did not disclose to Congress an earlier sale in which he transferred his land (paid $400,000 for property) to a company created by a friend and took a financial stake in that company that netted him $700,000 in profit. The deal was engineered by Jay Brown, a longtime friend and former casino lawyer whose name surfaced in a major political bribery trial. Coyote Springs Valley is a real estate development with as many as 159,000 home sites, stores, service facilities and golf courses. I wonder how many of these homes contributed to the housing collapse of 2008? The deal appears to have come about because of legislative actions that Reid took regarding Coyote Springs without any disclosure to Congress. Reid put a lot of effort into a allowing a developer Harvey Whittemore to build a housing project on Coyote Springs an hour outside Las Vegas. Harry Reid and his sons received tens of thousands in campaign donations from that developer, Whittemore contributed $45,000 to Reid and his PAC also gave the DSCC $20,000. Reid's son Josh got $5,000 for his unsuccessful campaign for city council, his other son Rory got $5,000 for his successful effort in becoming a county commissioner on the Clark County Board of Commissioners.

The standoff in Laughlin, Nevada of Clarke County wasn't about a tortoise or a rancher's failure to pay grazing fees. It was about the State's Senator and Senate Majority Leader enriching himself and his family at the public's expense. The tortoise wasn't of concern when Harry Reid worked with Bureau of Land Management to literally change the boundaries of the tortoise's habitat to accommodate the development of his top donor, Harvey Whittemore. In 2013, Whittemore, 59, who headed a billion-dollar real estate company, was found guilty by a federal jury on three counts tied to nearly $150,000 illegally (Coyote Springs) funneled to Reid's re-election campaign in 2007. Not associated with this case but Harry Reid was caught in March of 2014 with illegal use of campaign funds and was forced to return the campaign money funneled to his granddaughter through her jewelry business.

Neil Kornze, 35, worked as a senior policy adviser on land-use issues in Reid's office from 2003 to 2011. Joining the Bureau of Land Management as director on April 8th, 2014 with his appointment by the President and confirmed by Harry Reid's controlled Senate. China's ENN Energy Group wants to build what would be America's largest solar energy complex in Laughlin, Nevada where Rory Reid (Harry's son) formerly chaired the county commission. Rory is currently a lawyer with the firm of Lionel Sawyer & Collins and is representing ENN Energy Group. Harry Reid recruited the company during a 2011 trip to China and is using his political influence with his office's power on behalf of the project in Nevada.

This is exactly what I pointed out earlier that happened in America's history. If Renewable Energy doesn't work for Germany what makes you think it will have a different outcome in America? Certain politicians in the Liberal Left Democrat party don't care if the product delivers a lower cost of power or even enough power to the public and it's businesses. Once they have made their money through backdoor deals in the name of "Green Renewable Energy" they can afford the increased power prices, a small price to pay for the riches their elected offices bring to them.

This is how the Obama administration plans on implementing their "Green Renewable Energy" agenda allowing the Democrat party to rake in millions personally and for the party with backdoor deals that are already in progress. Government corruption at it's finest.

In the economy section of my writings I stated I would include how pollution affects our economy and has a bearing on our job market. Our job market competes with other job markets around the world. The lower cost of labor around the world puts our market at a disadvantage but the cost to ship the product into this country offsets that labor cost to some point. The Free Trade Agreements we have with other countries allowed for this situation but another aspect also contributes to this situation. When you add this cost to the other countries cost of doing business it helps tremendously in equaling out that balance and we don't violate the free trade agreements that caused us to lose our manufacturing to other countries. By not violating the free trade agreements as consumers (we are the largest consumer market of the world) we still get the cheaper products that are a natural product of their country (say bananas) and they get ours (say corn). But by imposing this mandate on manufacturing in the other countries it equals out the cost of production allowing products to again be built in our country. What is this miracle idea? Since pollution knows no borders require the countries to meet the same pollution regulations and disposal or recycling standards of the byproducts of manufacturing that we have to meet for a foreign country to import their manufactured product into this country. If the country doesn't meet the same standards for that product then it can't be imported into our country. If the product is important to us then it will be built here by our people on a safer environmental basis.

This also makes sense in dealing with countries like China with coal plants that have no emissions controls on them. What is the purpose of exporting our jobs to a country that can dispose of the chemical byproducts as they see fit while our country has at least some regulations to try and protect the environment. Ask your government officials that same question because that is exactly what the Free Trade Agreements did, help pollute the world and put America out of the manufacturing business.

Here is the part where I may be going off the deep end, it may defy logic as we know it too some point but not in theory and I can't say it would work but I won't say it will not work. Just like "Green Renewable Energy" it sounds good but doesn't fit the description.

In the Ingalls' Shipyard there is a piece of machinery that punches out round metal filler plates for closing up access holes. This piece of machinery built in the 40's ran continually once an electrically started rotational motion of speed was achieved. It ran a full 8 hr. or longer shift without further electrical assistance. It accomplished this through a series of counter weights.

Sir Isaac Newton's laws of motion, 1; an object at rest will remain at rest unless acted on by an unbalanced force. An object in motion continues in motion with the same speed and in the same direction unless acted upon by an unbalanced force. This law is often called "the law of inertia". This means that there is a natural tendency of objects to keep on doing what they're doing. All objects resist changes in their state of motion. In the absence of an unbalanced counter force, an object in motion will maintain its state of motion. "There are forces of nature that will stop an object being gravity and friction". 2; Acceleration is produced when a force acts on a mass. The greater the mass (of the object being accelerated) the greater the amount of force needed to accelerate the object.

Everyone subconsciously knows the Second Law. Everyone knows that heavier objects require more force to move the same distance than lighter objects. "But this also means that once a larger object is set in motion the force to stop it must be greater depending on how fast you want to stop it or if you want to stop it at all. So the force to keep it moving becomes less as the object speeds up and begins to maintain a certain speed. To increase speed you must increase force, to maintain speed you must maintain force but at a lesser amount than is used to accelerate, to slow the speed you must reduce the force".

3; For every action there is an equal and opposite re-action. This means that for every force there is a force that is equal in size, but opposite in direction. That is to say that whenever an object pushes another object it gets pushed back in the opposite direction equally hard. "This also means that a larger object can push or pull a smaller object to the point of the larger object losing all it's stored energy unless acted upon by an energy source to replenish or maintain its stored energy".

Thus using the law of inertia, the law of mass, the law of force exerted and the law of equal and opposite re-action we now have the keys for perpetual motion with a littler force to maintain that motion. This is the key to a true consistently available "Green Renewable Energy" source.

The law of inertia is the spinning of an object. The law of mass is a larger mass driving a smaller mass of resistance. The law of force is the energy needed to maintain the speed of the larger object while driving the smaller mass of resistance. The law of an equal and opposite re-action is nature's forces plus the smaller mass of resistance, a generator. Now we have an equation for an electric magnetic power generating plant.

A balanced larger (using the Inertia of mass) mass, say a metal wheel design, spinning magnetic object with low friction bearings (the initial start up may need to be something other than electric magnetic, diesel engines) driven by a computerized electric magnetic (a force) pulse in a push-pull scenario which upon achieving the needed speed (less force, less power needs) to power a smaller (equal and opposite re-action) resistance, a generator (the greater the mass the greater capability, the more weight to the outside of a spinning mass the greater capability) gradually brought online to generate much more power than what is exerted on the mass to maintain it's speed thus hopefully a continuous power source that is not dependent on nature or emits a byproduct other than electricity.

A possibility of having multiple masses (more manageable in size or weight) brought online in sequence using one to start the other in motion, then two to start the third, etc. then bring the generator online. There are many possibilities to achieve this outcome. Now that is the sci-fi portion, I just had to throw it out there.

OVER POPULATION

The number one predator of the world is man. Man has no true predators other than man itself. Man of earlier times and even in some of today's non-industrialized nations had large families because of the death rate due to disease. Today's medical advances have altered that death rate allowing many more children to reach adulthood. This has created a population boom thru out many parts of the world. This boom happens mainly in mild climate areas of the world because of the resources needed for cooling and heating are less and resources themselves tend to be more abundant. The world will never see a population boom in areas of extreme cold or heat unless there are resources to combat the extreme temperatures. A country's or continent's resources become strained under these population boom conditions. Food and energy resources are the first to be impacted under these conditions. These two resources are closely related because a form of energy allows for a greater food output and a greater food output is needed to support a greater population.

The continent of Africa is a prime example of establishing a greater population before establishing the means to support that population. Portions of the continent have continually fought against famine, a energy shortage and political instability. Political instability also detracts from the efforts to deliver food and energy to the masses that might allow them the opportunity to achieve self sufficiency. Also a lack of knowledge (education) of the basic aspects of farming. Throughout time Africa has been a continent of hunters and gathers that relies on nature in its most basic form to support its populous. Nature without the help of man will only support a populous of a certain size, once beyond that certain size a downward spiral of animal life and then followed by human life must and will occur. This statement is not my statement but an understanding of the rules or laws of nature. These rules or laws are not dictated by man. Man can only manipulate the numbers with a correct understanding of the problem only to a certain point of population. An incorrect understanding will cost lives.

The world lead by the United States (Exceptionalism) has tried for the last 50 years to fight these obstacles facing this continent at a cost of their own resources. This effort has been a failing effort for a few reasons but the main reason being self responsibility of the society itself. The only way to accommodate a larger population is with individual responsibility, people that produce versus able bodied people that are consumers only. As a non-productive population grows the responsibilities shift to fewer and fewer people until it reaches a point that the responsible can no longer produce enough to support the non-productive irresponsibility population. Do you see any reflection of America in this mirrored image?

America has fought two wars of about the same length on poverty, one in our own country and the other being in Africa not including disasters that may have caused short term famines around the world. The short term famines have went away because of personal responsibility of the areas populous to again stand on its own two feet. The two wars have failed and continue to fail because the cultures have become over reliant on the assistance. Not wanting or not knowing how to be self sufficient or for that fact moving up the ladder to more (a lack of improvement) of a self sufficiency.

The world for many reasons will only handle a certain amount of population. Without technology it will be less, with technology it will be more, without (self sufficient) self responsibility it will be less, with self responsibility (self sufficient) it will be even more. Each stage of these scenarios must have a buffer of excess affordable food products to offset natural world disasters and droughts. It also must account for man-made disasters of wars and conflicts. It also has to address the effects of radical rebellions and radical governments which are a constant in many third world countries. To achieve a productive society you must have a civilized society.

Population density has an effect on all of nature and all the animals thereof. Even when not seen as a food source the encroachment on nature by man takes a toll on wildlife. Major urban cities have decimated the wildlife that occupied the land before man congregated in the area. Only wildlife that can adapt to man's encroachment occupies the cities of man such as New York City. The wildlife (insects, rats, mice) that adapt by living off the waste generated by the populous do so by concealment and are not normally seen as a food source. The other species being birds including pigeons that are seen as a nuisance. Birds of prey that fly above societies encroachment, nesting out of reach of the normal populous while preying on the wildlife environment man has now created. Very seldom will you see an animal of a size that doesn't allow it to hide from man.

As you move from urban to more rural areas the normal wildlife of nature begins to return even though the conflict between man and nature still exists just not to the same extent. The ever expanding construction in rural areas continually reduces habitat and as I also pointed out reduces natures filtering capacity of carbon dioxide of which liberals identify as a greenhouse gas. True science has yet to agree on this point but science and common sense must agree on the reduction of carbon dioxide filtering capacity being reduced with man's continued encroachment on nature.

The countries of China and India account for 36.5% of the world's population as of Nov. 4th, 2013 with their combined total being just over 2.6 Billion people. China has recognized this problem and has adopted a policy to combat their over population problem. The United States and the United Nations have condemned China's policy of one male child only per couple based on human freedoms, not based on sound science and commonsense but human emotions. I on the other hand agree on the purpose just not the means being the "one male child only per couple" concept. This concept is misguided because it will result in social unrest among future generations of only males unable to have wives based strictly on the ratio of men to women created by the policy. So the proper policy would be one child per couple regardless of gender. China's true reason for the male baby policy is to ensure a male fighting force if or when needed in the case of conflict or war. Remember what is yours is only yours if you can defend it, if you can't it's theirs. This also includes the female population of a nation. For those who may say I am off my rocker, four words "Chinese Gang Sex Trafficking". Who's off their rocker now? You have no true insight to the realities of the world or nature's true power over the people of the world.

Nature will dictate man's outcome on this planet. Man will only have a say in the outcome when man realizes nature's laws are the dominant force on the planet. Man has the ability and is in the process of reducing nature's presence. It is the amount of reduction that will dictate man's presence on earth.

If man's designed economic civilized society fails just to the point that energy is no longer available, too expensive (drives up prices, a downward spiral on who eats) or hard to get (supply and demand, higher prices) man can no longer produce enough food (without energy assistance) to support the people of the world.

To some it may sound like I should be promoting solar and wind energy. I can't support something that doesn't work. Wasting money by implementing a system that man doesn't have control of the input (start & stop) much less the output unless the rhythmic re-occurrence in nature is constant enough to produce the needed power which hasn't happened. Storage of the necessary power is just more pollutants needed to construct a storage (batteries, how many would be necessary? Would we ever have enough?) system. That's why I challenge the laws of physics in regards to assisted perpetual motion. I believe today's technology might have the ability to achieve this power source of smaller input versus larger output of energy.

IMMIGRATION

I am so tired of the saying "our immigration system is broken". The system is not broken; our laws are being broken by the people allowed into this country, people over staying their visas and by illegal border crossings. They are also being broken by the liberal left Obama administration by not following the immigration laws for border protection and deportations. The Liberal Left use the term "This nation was built on immigration" is politicizing the issue because the reality is "This nation was built on Legal immigration" and illegal immigration will destroy the very fabric of our nation. This is the same tactics (visas) used by the 9/11 Middle East terrorists to gain entry to this nation under the Clinton presidency. Barack Obama now wants to do a blanket amnesty for a estimate 11 or 12 million illegal aliens not even knowing who these people are and 90% of them haven't even shown up for their immigration hearings. He says he has the power to do it through an executive order. Let's go to the "Constitution" and read what it says about immigration and who in government has the power over immigration law.

Article I, section 8. To establish a uniform Rule of Naturalization

Article I, Section 9. States "The Migration or Importation of such Persons as any of the States now existing shall think proper to admit, shall not be prohibited by the Congress prior to the Year one thousand eight hundred and eight, but a Tax or duty may be imposed on such Importation, not exceeding ten dollars for each person".

What it states is that the existing 13 States can admit or keep out anyone the State sees fit and Congress shall have no say other than a optional maximum $10.00 Tax or duty on each person and it must happen this way until the year 1808. After 1808 all immigration legislation will be written by Congress and proceed through the normal process of government to become law. So now the actual legislated law comes into effect. A Presidents executive order can do many things to make the system work better but it can't bypass the written law making the law null & void or to decrease it's authority as law. It must create a better situation for which the law or laws to work in a more effective capacity. Our system uses passports, visas and green cards. Politicians want to use the expense of rounding up the millions of people as a reason for giving amnesty to illegal immigrants. We as a Nation have already done this once and under this system our Nation will continue to accept any and all who can sneak across the border with an open border policy. Self deportation is the only fair answer for American Citizens.

There are two ways to obtain this goal. The first option is to have exit or renew dates on all passports, visas and green cards. If this date has expired then all employers, schools and colleges, landlords, hotels, motels and real estate rental companies must deny employment and services along with notifying local police. The local police would be mandated to confiscate all vehicles of illegal immigrants for safety (no driver's license, insurance or appropriate papers) concerns. Illegal's may have their vehicles returned upon having their paper work extended with no more than 10 days to leave the country. Illegal's are responsible for all storage fees; anything not claimed within 30 days goes to auction. Upon a second offense no property shall be returned by local authorities and sold at auction for local tax coffers to offset expenses. Any local or state government, school or college not following these procedures shall have highway funding and school funding withheld until verified compliance. This puts an end to sanctuary cities. Employers must verify citizenship or shall incur a tax penalty of $5,000 per illegal person for first offense, $10,000 per illegal person and a 3 month suspension of their business license with the second offense. All legal visitors shall be posted on a government web-site for verification of status. All illegal persons caught twice or once with any type of forged papers shall do 60 days of hard labor in the county jail with all properties confiscated not to be returned and sold at auction for local tax coffers. The illegal aligns allowed to stay would be anyone with a U.S. college degree or in college at this time would be issued a student visa to finish school. All others (excusing no others) would be forced to self deport with their belonging or deported by our government without their belongings to cover expenses. All immigration must go through our legislated immigration system of laws.

The second option would be a voter I.D. - citizenship card for legal residents/citizens. Possession of this card allows the person all the normal aspects of American society; to vote, employment, enrollment at schools and colleges, availability to rentals, etc. Without the card a person must produce one of the other three entry identifications, again all rules and tax penalties apply from above and those allowed to stay would be the same. I personally like the second option better it kills two birds with one stone, illegal immigration and illegal voting. The other aspect that must be changed is anchor babies. So a child born in this country must be of American Citizen Parents to get recognized as an American Citizen. Just because you are in the country legally or illegally makes absolutely no difference, you are still not recognized as an American Citizen. It's bad enough that the taxpayers have to pay the medical bills racked up by some legal visitors much less women who are pregnant when they crossed the border knowing their intentions when doing so. The liberal left Democrats have stated it will take 10 or 15 years before illegal's would be able to vote yet they are already voting in areas of the country, so that's another lie.

Allowing illegal immigration undermines legal immigration, puts citizen's lives in unnecessary risky situations and is not the proper building block for national growth of a population. A country without border enforcement is no longer a country. I also believe this is the first step to a world with open borders which is no different than leaving your front door open in a bad neighbor hood or high crime area. This type situation only leads to the draining of tax dollars from local, state and national coffers with cost of social programs becoming available to the illegal immigrants. The cost on society to educate the minors will be astronomical because of the language barriers. It will also impact the quality of education to minor American children of public schools which is already in question. Both political parties allowing this to happen in a time of high unemployment and lower wages is an attack on the citizens of America and their standard of living. An increasing population adds to the disparity of the middle class in a jobless market. The rich get richer by using the competition (when jobs aren't plentiful) for jobs to drive down the pay wage. When jobs are plentiful the wage paid most go up to ensure the employer has a workforce for his business.

Liberal Democrats have used the immigration issue to bolster their voter roles to ensure their continued election to office. Yet this tactic creates more competition among the voters for jobs causing a higher unemployed voter numbers and wages stagnate. The Democrats then bring out the wage topic to present to the voter as them being on the side of the voter. Yet a raise in the minimum wage during a time of recession creates inflation (the cost of doing business) to the businesses that employ the under educated, under experienced people. At that time the business must make a choice to either layoff however many minimum wage employees to get back to the same labor cost it had before or increase prices to cover the additional labor cost of a higher minimum wage or a combination thereof. What has more of an influence on this decision by a small business owner is how the other small business owner's handle this same dilemma. If one chooses to layoff employees keeping its prices the same and another of the same type business chooses to raise prices then the first business has gained a decided advantage over the second business. So the safe decision for both businesses is to layoff employees which means lost jobs to the economy. Obviously not the solution to grow an economy and create jobs. It also makes a percentage of the poor poorer because they are now unemployed.

The second impact of illegal (un-controlled immigration) immigration is that the self imported labor force whose standard of living from where they came from is lower. Any wage increase from their original origin that they came from is a huge bump in their earning abilities especially if the immigrant sends the money home where he still actually lives. This scenario allows many of the immigrants to push American workers out of the trade they may have worked for years. This example is the Home Builder's Association which has hired this illegal workforce to build our homes in this country. This illegal workforce has undercut the prices for the contracted aspects of home building such as concrete, brick laying, framing, roofing, painting, landscaping and lawn management. Each time they are pushing out American workers with the builder's profit margin going up because the price of their homes they have built haven't come down with the savings the builder incurred. A prime example of the wealthy getting wealthier off the demise of the American worker and consumer.

The third impact of illegal immigration is the hundreds of billions of dollars sent south of our border each week by these immigrants. The Liberal Democrats have no problems making big corporations into villains for keeping their money they earned in other countries in overseas banks because the price of bring it home is overly high, the highest in the developed world. So let's put this in perspective, the Liberal Democrats are against law abiding corporations keeping their money over seas but promote and encourage illegal (violators of all aspects of our laws) immigrants to come take American jobs and send that money out of the country. The Liberal Democrats claim these are the jobs Americans won't do, well who built all the American homes before this illegal workforce flooded our country? AMERICANS OF ALL RACES! The Liberal Democrats encourage AMERICAN dollars leaving our COUNTRY going south of our borders to countries that supply a black market drug trade that also drains hundreds of billions of dollars out of America and the American economy. If they were truly American they wouldn't go south of the border every time we have an economic downturn and reappear when American jobs are available for them to steal from American Citizens.

The Muslim/Islam attack on France is the perfect example of what happens when a country's leaders allow a large influx of people into the country. As the leaders of France said "we can't follow all 5 million". If our government doesn't know who they are or their motives they are just serving up American Citizens on a plate of death. It may not be thousands at a time but if it is someone close to you then it really doesn't matter does it!

The main problem with the Progressive Liberal Democrat's Agenda is that it makes very little sense other than allowing Liberal Democrats to stay in their elected positions. The Liberal Democrats policies are in direct conflict with their own Liberal Democrat's solutions. It's like watching a dog chasing its tail, there is no solution once it is caught. It only entertains the people who are watching. Voters need to quit watching the dog chase it's tail, it only offers a laugh not a solution.

As for me and how the liberal left Democrats may want to label me. I'm for all races of AMERICANS and against ANY RACE that may want to come here ILLEGALLY! I THINK THAT'S CALLED BEING PATRIOTIC TO MY FELLOW AMERICAN!!

LIBERAL LEFT DEMOCRATS SHOULD TRY IT ON FOR SIZE JUST ONE TIME!!

As for the ***LIBERAL LEFT DEMOCRATS*** who want illegal immigration of any race to compete with *AMERICAN'S* for *AMERICAN JOBS* within our own BORDERS, I think that's called being ***UNPATRIOTIC*** to your ***FELLOW*** ***AMERICANS*** and their ***FAMILIES*** !!

ASSIMILATING INTO AMERICA

It is absolutely critical that an incoming population assimilate into the American culture. Assimilation includes many of our basic beliefs of freedom and human rights, free enterprise, laws, culture, language, education, religious freedom and our belief to export any of these to foreign lands that violate basic freedoms and human rights. Many times basic freedoms, human rights and religious freedom (right to be free of a religion without persecution) are violated through a religious belief, dictator or elitist government that denies what I just listed. Assimilation doesn't mean giving up all your beliefs, it means understanding that if your basic beliefs are in conflict with ours and your not willing to give them up to come here why are you leaving the area that your beliefs are accepted and are the norm? If your answer is for economic reasons then my next question to you is this "might it be those beliefs you are not willing to give up are the direct cause of the economic situation of the area you are wanting to leave!" It is not America's responsibility to assimilate to your culture, beliefs, laws or language but in us allowing you to come here that makes it your responsibility (your agreement to us) to assimilate to our culture, beliefs, laws and language.

Assimilation is like a road trip to somewhere you have never been. You know where you are and you know where you want to end up, you have a road map and directions given to you by us on how to get there. You leave your home (country) walk to the car (a means of transport, airplane or ship) and drive using the given directions. Once outside the city limits (in America) you deviate from the map and directions we have given you to reach our desired location for you, your assimilation to our culture, beliefs, laws and language. Thus never reaching that location because the effort was never given to reach that destination. If in reality this had been a true trip to a destination you didn't want to go you never would have left your home. So your true intentions was to come here not caring about our culture, beliefs, laws or with the intent to learn our language. Thus undermining our basic beliefs of a common culture of our Nation which is what binds the people of our Nation. It keeps us moving as one towards a common goal of a better society. It is for this reason I question your motives for coming here and the right for you to stay. Having pockets of different societies (cultures, beliefs, laws and languages) is reverting back to a time of the many different tribes that ultimately and continually fought each other for supremacy. It doesn't support a civilized society as is the case with today's Iraq with three different entities that can't come together and have fought for 2,000 years because they have never been one society.

As a nation of many diverse people of different originating cultures, we celebrate many cultures throughout the world and do so gladly. We celebrate many more other culture's holidays than the rest of the world celebrates just one of ours. That is a telling truth. But our nationally recognized holidays are and should remain strictly

American unless we are ready to admit we have been overrun by a foreign nation's illegal populous. This type of illegal immigration is a direct threat to the foundation of this country. If the same people had army uniforms on would we still allow them to enter unabated without any idea of who they are and their purpose for being here? Look at what happened to Crimea and the eastern Ukraine with non-uniformed soldiers entering their country. On the internet "Google" "U.S. soccer team booed" and you can see the result of illegal immigration and that is just the beginning. I can understand a emigrate from Mexico cheering the Mexican soccer team. What I can't understand is people coming to America to better their lives and booing the American soccer team in disrespect on our American soil of Los Angles, Calif. It wasn't just a few; it was a stadium of tens of thousands.

I just lied to you I do understand why this happened I just wrote about it. I would tell you the truth but like Jack Nicholson said in the movie "A Few Good Men" "You can't handle the truth". I just hope the sight of your blood or your spouse's or any of your children's or grandchild's blood doesn't upset you because many of these illegal immigrants are not here because they like you. They are here for your money, your property if presented to them. Most do not have any type of allegiance to our country. They will not fight for you but they will fight against you if the opportunity presents itself that they feel like they could win. Revenge is best when served up cold for an act committed not by our government but by our people, Americans, in the Alamo era some 180 yrs. ago that stole Texas from Mexico.

The true history is in 1820 American Moses Austin was granted a large tract of land in what is now Texas by the Mexican government. Moses died but his son, Stephen F. Austin continued with the Mexican authorized planned American settlements. The Mexican government wanted the settlers to act as a buffer between the Tejano residents of Mexico and the marauding Comanche tribes. The Anglo settlers settled where there was decent farmland and trade connections with American Louisiana. So they settled farther east not creating as much of a buffer as expected by the Mexican government. In 1829, as a result of the large influx of American immigrants, the Anglos outnumbered native Spanish speakers in the Texas territory of Mexico. The Mexican government decided to reinstate the property tax and increase tariffs on American shipped goods. The settlers and many Mexican businessmen rejected the demands leading to Mexico closing Texas to additional immigration but illegal immigration continued. The American settlers were upset when the Mexican government changed from a Constitutional government to a dictator form of government, López de Santa Anna, and its direction and agreements changed towards the new land owners of Mexico. There was an uprising by the land owners which lead to Texas being a new Country, Republic of Texas - Mar. 2, 1836 to February 19, 1846. The Republic claimed borders that included all of the present US state of Texas as well as parts of present-day Oklahoma, Kansas, Colorado, Wyoming, and New Mexico based upon the Treaties of Velasco between the newly created Texas Republic and Mexico. The eastern boundary with the United States was defined by the Adams-Onís Treaty between the United States and Spain in 1819. Its southern and western-most boundary with Mexico was under dispute throughout the entire existence of the Republic of Texas. Texas claiming the boundary as the Rio Grande and Mexico claiming the boundary as the Nueces River. This dispute would later become a trigger for the Mexican–American War from 1846 to 1848 between Mexico and the United States after the annexation of Texas by the United States on December 29, 1845. James K. Polk, a Democrat, served as the 17th Speaker of the House of Representatives (1835–1839) and Governor of Tennessee (1839–1841). Polk was the surprise candidate for President in 1844, defeating Henry Clay of the rival Whig Party (later becoming the Republican Party) by promising to invade and annex the Republic of Texas. The Whig Party had come out publicly against the annex at that time. The Treaty of Guadalupe Hidalgo specified Mexican Cession of the territories of Alta California and New Mexico to the United States in exchange for $15 million. In addition, the United States assumed $3.25 million of debt owed by the Mexican government to U.S. citizens. Mexico accepted the loss of Texas and thereafter cited the Rio Grande as its national border. The Republic of Texas became the 28th state in 1849 at the request of the Republic of Texas.

Read about this era of time not only in regards to the Mexican-American conflict but also the Presidents. It is this period in history that the newly formed Democratic-Republican Party split to later form our present day parties. As for today's situation almost the same thing is happening just in reverse. What is missing is the trigger to begin the violence. So I guess you are saying I'm some type of phobic, Mexican phobic, Latino phobic, if we are going to label people you yourself should try on Historic phobic and Reality phobic. The Obama administration wants you to believe our immigration system is broken and it is, the laws were broken by past administrations and the current administration. Barack who is just perpetrating another of his many lies during his terms in office to prop up the Democrat voting population to help ensure the Liberal Left Democrats retain future political power.

There is no way an illegal alien who doesn't speak English or Spanish (many below the border of Mexico speak different dialects of Portuguese) can provide for themselves without the ability to communicate in English or Spanish, even in the Spanish speaking populous of this country. Why is American TV broadcasting providers allowed to offer Spanish only channels circumventing the need of immigrants to learn English to watch television? It should be used as a tool to promote the English language. Many entering the U.S. are women with young children. If an American single mom can't support their family (although I do know a few hard working non college degree women that do without any government support) without government support, the reality is 99% of illegal immigrants will be supported totally by government. What party encouraged them to come, what party used government allowing them to stay, what party wants to buy their vote with a government support check? DEMOCRATS! You will not see a true Republican encourage lifetime handouts of taxpayer money. A hand up that gets that individual into the workforce and paying taxes is a true Republican's only option. This takes cooperation of the individual to want something better in their lives. When given by Democrats everything they need for basic life (except a lifetime dream) but not everything they want it takes most of the motivation away to obtain their dreams. That motivation is what is needed to become a productive American citizen. It is replaced by taking under the table jobs to supplement their government given income. So what is offered by Democrats is a menial life that replaces the motivation needed to obtain a lifetime dream.

Martin Luther King stated "I have a Dream". Under Liberal Democrat guidance Martin Luther King never would of seen that "Dream" come true. Under Democrat guidance that "Dream" was ended. Under Democrat guidance Martin Luther King's "Dream" and Life was ended.

The funny thing about the liberal left Democrats is they now believe in buying themselves into office, for their own gains of riches, is the way to keep the power of government. What their lack of insight doesn't allow them to see is when government goes away because it can no longer fund itself there will be no power of government to protect them. The starving mobs "will of the mob" wanting their heads on a stick not allowing them to enjoy their illegally gotten gains.

A NATIONAL DEBT OF $18 TRILLION DOLLARS AND CONTINUALLY GROWING IS NOT SOMETHING THAT IS ENDLESS ASK THE PEOPLE OF GREECE.

AMERICA'S EXCEPTIONALISM

What is Exceptionalism? What defines Exceptionalism? Do you know or understand this word? If you do then you know it doesn't actually exist in the Dictionary. So it is a philosophy of the word "Exceptional". Exceptional is an adjective that is used to describe; outstanding: having or showing intelligence, ability well above average. Barack Obama described all countries as "exceptional" but if all countries were exceptional would that not then be the norm and no country would standout among the others so actually at that point no countries would be exceptional. If you don't understand the word "exceptional" how can you understand the philosophy of Exceptional-ism?

Any country can be exceptional in an aspect of one, two or a few things; some countries are not exceptional at anything. The difference between exceptional at a few things and Exceptional-ism is to be also as good if not better at the same few things and being the best at all the others beyond those few. Let me put it in terms that Barack Obama should understand, "he has exceptional ball handling skills", and the difference, "the Exceptional-ism of his game". Meaning not only does he have matching ball handling skills but all the other aspects of the game including all the physical abilities and mental abilities that will allow him to be the greatest player ever! I.E. Wilt Chamberlain, Larry Bird, Michael Jordan and still to be proven LeBron James. Both players have exceptional ball handling skills, but only one player has the total package. That is the difference Mr. President.

What are the exceptional things America has done in its continuous drive of Exceptional-ism? First, it is the people that make the government of the country not the country's government that makes the people. Good people in government makes for good government, bad people in government make for bad government. If you are waiting on the country or government to make you exceptional you will die being far less than your desires. It is society that sets up the rules of government that allow you or limit you to some extent of the chance to be exceptional but ultimately it is you that carries that responsibility. The "Constitution" is what has allowed past Americans to be exceptional because it dictates how our government is suppose to work. It dictates the freedoms you are allowed to follow your dreams of Exceptional-ism when a child. As an adult during that time of physical and mental growth hopefully you found a couple of things you are exceptional at and if not you either keep looking or settle with what you have found during the journey of life.

The first exceptional thing was a paper written by a few old men that some people question their knowledge in doing so. I hope you guessed the "Constitution" and the Founding Fathers. The "some people" are the ones of questionable knowledge and motives.

Now where, when or who to start with, that's the hardest question, there are so many people so I will only hit the very high points. If I was ranking the people that contributed the most it starts with the people whose inventions allowed others to also achieve their dreams of Exceptional-ism. So my number one draft pick Behind all the people that fought or died for our continued Independence and Freedom is Thomas Edison. Mr. Edison holds 1,093 U.S. patents plus many in the United Kingdom, France and Germany. His inventions allowed others to achieve exceptional status in their own specialized fields is first and foremost the harnessing of electricity for mass power distribution. Just some of his other inventions include the first practical light bulb, sound recordings (the phonograph) and motion pictures. One of Thomas' first adult jobs was with the Western Union. He worked at night allowing him time to work on another of his inventions the lead-acid battery. This eventually led to his firing from that job causing him to focus on his true talent of inventions. What a blessing for the WORLD'S SOCIETY.

Just these few inventions have allowed others to achieve exceptional status in specialized industries such as the movie and music industries, all manufacturing industries that use electricity, all artificial lighting, anything that uses or in history has used a lead-acid battery either to start or run on, the harnessing of electricity allowed Alexander Graham Bell the opportunity to develop the modern telephone.

The Wright Brothers who some dispute the history as them being first in flight. I won't enter that argument because I'm not sure it can be proven either way? Their understanding of aerodynamic lift and aerodynamic propulsion with propellers far outpaced their competition. But their breakthrough invention of 3 axis control for flight controls was crucial and is still used today in all modern fixed wing flight including the modern day fly-by-wire systems. It was these accomplishments that allowed them to be verified as the first to achieve controlled, powered and sustained heavier-than-air human flight, on December 17, 1903.

Henry Ford with the assembly line technique of mass production. Why was this essential to the development of the world? Instead of having a number of groups of a few people building something from beginning to end. It allowed each worker to focus on a smaller task perfecting that task with accuracy and speed thus accelerating production. The second key factor to the assembly line approach was uniformed parts without variations allowing direct bolt on parts without the need to be fitted. You now have the essentials for an assembly line technique for mass production. Mass production maximized profits allowing for higher employee pay and a product produced at a lesser cost allowing that product to be sold at a lesser cost making it more affordable to all the people. This technique has spread to all facets of manufacturing allowing all different types of products to become affordable and available to the masses of people. So in reality this technique has raised the standard of living all over the world.

The jet and rocket engines developed by Germany for the war cause of WWII. Scientists were grabbed from Germany by two nations involved in the war, the Soviet Union and the United States. Each nation worked on the advancement of these inventions with the U.S.S.R. being first in orbit while the U.S.A. was the first and only country to land on the moon with repeated moon landings.

There were so many people involved in the development of this next invention that no one person or company can be accredited with the modern product. The computer which allowed man to land on the moon. Then improved by multiple companies being reduced in size and costs while increasing it's processing power but still allowing them to be feasible for the average American home. Now they are as small as a cell phone.

The U.S.A. developed and owns the Internet, a connecting system for all computers in the world. These last two have allowed uncountable new businesses to come to life around the world. Barack Obama wants to give this intellectual property of the U.S.A. away to the rest of the world. Why? The internet is already available to any and all countries of the world. What purpose does it accomplish to give it away, and by the "Constitution" I'm not sure he or his executive branch has the power to give this type of intellectual property of the U.S.A. away. Would it not be a national security issue to get rid of the Internet? It seems the President uses this term for protecting things of far less value and importance.

America's Military is and should be second to none. It is this Military might that allows our freedom and freedoms of others around the world in present day and the past 100 years. It was this might that decided two World Wars. It is not that our citizen troops of the Army are Exceptional. It is not that the citizen formed Navy and Marines are Exceptional or not that the citizen formed Air Force is Exceptional. It is the fact that each of these when combined into a Military force for self defense makes it achieve the philosophical reaches of Exceptional-ism. Divided they are Exceptional; together they achieve Exceptional-ism, the total package for self defense.

America's military is continuously coming to the aid of any Nation that has experienced a natural disaster or medical emergency with our expertise in handling those types of emergencies. Where would the world be if our charitable help didn't exist?

There are many aspects of our society that are exceptional and when combined under one nation, OUR nation achieves Exceptional-ism because we do everything better as a whole and do more for others than anyone.

Why is individual Exceptional-ism so important to be recognized and nurtured? Because when society recognizes this trait of accomplishment or talent it should reward the individual with acknowledgement. This lets the individual know they may be on the right path to finding what they may be good at in adolescents. This then may transfer to adulthood allowing the individual to advance on this same path into a successful career. It is political correctness that throws a monkey wrench into the gears of life. The idea that everyone should be rewarded the same even though their talents are no where equal in regards to the subject they are competing in with each other. This action does a disservice to both individuals. For the talented one it may cause the individual to question his abilities because the rewards are the same for everyone. For the individual that is lacking in talent in regards to a subject it may cause this individual to continue on this same path of rewarded failure. This unjust reward system may cause this same individual to continue along this same path of failure instead of moving on to find what the individual is actually talented at which then may transfer to adulthood and a rewarding career.

Michael Jordan advanced this career and life through basketball yet he retired early to play baseball. His talents would not and did not transfer to baseball so he moved on. His next attempt was at golf. Michael wanted to be the next Tiger Woods before Tiger ever had come on the scene of pro golf. Again his athletic talents would not transfer from basketball to golf. This journey for enlightenment led Michael back to the sport he showed his Exceptional-ism in which is basketball and again won NBA titles upon his return. Even today his talents (knowledge and insights) for basketball advance his career and the others around him which advances his life and their lives.

Could you imagine if Michael had the political correctness police rewarding him for his golfing abilities of which he was maybe a 4 to 8 stroke handicapped player. Fortunately there is such a thing as a scorecard in golf that Michael understood as being the guideline for a measurement of talent in that sport. If the political LIBERAL LEFT DEMOCRAT'S correctness police had their way even that scorecard would not exist revealing a lack of insight into the reality of the real world.

This example is a real life account of success, failure and success and the individual's understanding of competition and its relationship to real life. Only the Liberal Left Politically Correct Police can live in a world of fantasy where everybody should be rewarded for a lack of incentive, talent and results. This sounds more like the Liberal Left (definitely political) Obama Administration.

EDUCATION

America's educational system has been infiltrated by the liberal movements promoted by some of our upper educational colleges. Teaching liberal ideas versus teaching basic educational core tools such as reading, writing, math, science, history, etc. The liberal unions have been and are an increasing presence in the classrooms. Their power within the school system is there to protect bad teachers, working conditions and the teacher's right to teach the liberal curriculum they see fit to teach. Why? Because the liberal union supports the Liberal Democrat Party thus a educational factory for future generations of liberal thoughts with all the entities supporting each other as one. Creating a less educated individual more likely to need the Unions and the Democrat Party's handouts to survive in a overly competitive world for jobs.

Liberals act as if they support higher education but that higher education they support must be a higher liberal education for them to agree on what or how it is taught. It is amazing that Liberals will point at the separation of Church and State to drive Christian teaching and values out of our schools then start teaching Muslim / Islamic values and find a way to justify it, as if it's OK! Are they now recruiting for OUR ENEMIES?

Howard Dean recently came out saying Scott Walker's lack of a college degree (one semester short) brings into question if he is qualified to be our next President. Howard Dean being one of those liberal left Democrats has no idea of what he said and little understanding of knowledge or education. True knowledge is learned through trial and error, failure and success. What is learned then can be taught in a educational system. At one time there were no colleges or schools which means no teachers for a formal educational system, so everyone must have been stupid. So if society had no accredited teachers how was a educational system formed? The passing on of learned knowledge from generation to generation. These type of teachers were generational teachers and without them a college accredited teacher would not of been taught anything because the knowledge would of been lost if not passed on to the next generation. Something liberal teaching has intentionally stopped to meet their purposes. With Howard Dean's thoughts on a college education that means every person with a college degree must be a Einstein or a Edison and we all know this surely isn't true. What is true is the fact that if this so called college education degree passes on incorrect knowledge to support a political agenda then the knowledge is normally false and useless. Now our next generation of children are less educated and filled with false and useless information. Now what I have brought into the discussion is Howard Dean's own formal education or what was his indoctrination into a illogical liberal thought process. That's why he wasn't elected as our President! Also there are, by far, more law degrees in our government structure than any other degree, how has that worked out for our Nation? Besides it's not what you were taught that makes the difference it is what you learned!

Liberals point to Asia as a guideline for higher learning. On this point I totally agree. The problem is what the liberals are using as a learning guideline they are not following the guidelines thereof to get to that point of learning. A typical school day in China depends on what part of China you are in. In Southern China, they go 5 days a week from 7:00 am - 6:00 pm. In Northern China they go to school 7 days a week from 6:00 am - 5:00 pm. Their teachers are very strict about them being on time. The liberal school day in an American High School is (our local high school) from 9:15 to 3:15 with a half hour lunch which leaves five and a half hours. Then there are six class changes with 5 minutes to do so for half hour total time now we have a five hour school day. This now creates six, fifty minute classes. Now do you really think Liberal Democrats supported by a Liberal Union that supports a Liberal School System has the educational welfare of the children in mind with these classroom hours? Also their attitude towards homework or lack thereof is nothing more than reducing the teachers work load to fit the liberally bloated model of a Liberal Government. Resulting in a high paid under producing form of government of which we have all become accustom too.

This liberal thinking towards education is the pattern that has created a present and future downward spiral of our educational system. Each generation teaches the following generation, a dumbing down of one or two generation's of future teachers with overly reduced hours has created this effect.

One solution maybe, a common sense solution, is that most parents work from 8 am to 5 pm so make school hours from 7:30 am to 5:30 pm so blue collar working parents know where their kids should be and who they are with instead of on our streets without supervision. Liberals will say I want our teachers to now be babysitters. No! I want them to teach and quit treating our kids as babies allowing teachers to believe they are babysitting then allowing teachers not to teach.

The last few years the conversation has been about America's children's failing grades. The grades are failing because of the lack of hours in school. What was the liberal's solution, in some states such as Georgia it was for teachers to cheat on state's tests. In some cases teachers actually took the tests for the students or gave out the answers. Before that it was lowering the numerical number that represents a grade. When I was in high school 94 to a 100 was an A, today it is 90 to a 100. This does nothing more than cover for a Liberal School System that is intentionally sacrificing our children's education for their reduced time at work lifestyle.

Putting it in perspective they work 10 months (includes 1 wk. after and 1 wk. before the kids come back from summer vacation, 10 weeks) out of a year, have a 5 day work week, have a 8:45 to 3:30 give or take a few minutes work day (less homework means less after hours work for teachers). Each teacher has a planning period each working day so they teach 5 classes a day with 50 minutes off. They have all Federal Holidays off, 2 weeks off at Christmas and New Years. Teacher planning days and teacher workshops are really what? Depends on what the teacher does with it. The children and taxpayers deserve more for their education and tax dollars.

The educational system was America's only social program that worked. The idea was an innovative idea of America that put America at the forefront of educational learning in the world. Even today not all nations have a required curriculum of learning but some of the ones that do, China, are clearly passing us. Even this social program is not beyond the hands of the Liberal thinking of Liberal Democrats that will turn it into another arm of the Democrat Party. What party does the Liberal Teacher Unions support with teacher's union dues? The Liberal Left Democrat Party.

Try mentioning extending the teaching workday to just 8 hrs. for teachers. Many of the teachers with the union's support won't allow it but their pay must reflect more of the true hours spent teaching. So changes must be made to increase the hours our children are educated. Maybe reducing summer vacation time to four or five weeks to a more year round system. Maybe also reducing Christmas to 1 wk. Maybe also extending the school day with a second shift of teachers. These are just ideas to a real problem that we must face as a society. As a society we must maximize this time of learning for our children, not minimize the time as the system has done.

My intentions are not to vilify all teachers. The teachers that understand my mostly conservative writings also understand they are not the target of my thoughts. It was teachers from my past that allow me to understand the situations that our nation faces in the future. Unfortunately most those teachers of my past do not exist in today's future, you are the only ones left to help sort out this mess of identifying problems and solutions.

One last statement "is our educational system better today with Religious morals being removed by Government"? Was it a better educational system with the morale's of Religion (not one particular religion) were invoked upon the educational system allowing children to conform too a respectful classroom of learning"?

RELIGION AND SCIENCE

The belief in religion is a soul searching journey of life. Your views may change as your life evolves through your time on earth. If your life never changes with the knowledge acquired during a life time, mistakes made by you and others, your views also may never change because you where never held accountable for your mistakes. Being accountable for your mistakes is one of the learning processes of life.

The problem I have with the church and it's teachings of religion is the same thing I just pointed out, it won't evolve with its knowledge gained through its life time. When science and religion clash because scientific facts do not support the religious story of the Bible they do so only because the church allows it by not evolving with the knowledge. The church has a problem with the concept of the evolution of man. The religious story of God creating earth in six days and the seventh was a day of rest. Now isn't this story line mimicked in our society itself with the creation of the "week" in a calendar month? The Bible never defines the length of God's day and science can't. When relating life times to a dog or a cat man has determined that 7 years for each animal equals one year for a human. So with either animal being 10 human years old its life expectancy in relation to humans makes that animal about 70 animal years old. Since faith will never die God will never die so now put a length of time on God's day? You can't. So the day of rest could be the time for the earth to cool or the time needed for earth to generate vegetation to support God's intended life forms. Like the chicken or the egg, the same type question is which came first the vegetation or the seeds. Considering no form of life as science knows it could survive the earth's formation where did those first life forms come from? God, Space, other planets? Evolution starts at the beginning of a life form's life; evolution does not create that beginning life form. Science can't truly answer that question and science may never.

Science has exposed facts not acknowledged by religion or the church. A part of earth's history not documented by the human hand of religion such as dinosaurs and early man. It is the earlier forms of man that originated the science of the "theory of evolution" even though a link is missing in man's evolution it seems pretty clear. Religion itself allowed these facts to be used against its teachings by not acknowledging the scientific facts as they came to the forefront of reality. It wasn't "science" that discredited some parts of religion. It was people (none believer's of faith) that used the science in an attempt to discredit religion. If religion had of embraced the science the science never could have been used as a weapon against it. When you combine the two thoughts, science doesn't alter or disprove any words of the Bible and the Bible doesn't alter the findings of science.

The history of man is documented in three ways. The writings or drawings of early man before a common language existed, the writings of man in the Bible guided by God's hand of a faith based religion and what science has discovered through time.

The Bible states that Adam & Eve were the first man and woman which lived in the Garden of Eden. Science with its theory of evolution actually backs up this fact because at some point of human evolution the first modern man and woman had to come into existence. Was Adam & Eve the first modern man and woman? If not why not? There is no scientific evidence that can disprove the Religious Faith's claim of Adam & Eve. It might disprove the religious faith's assumption that Adam & Eve were the first man and woman species but it definitely doesn't disprove that Adam & Eve were the first modern man & woman. With human evolution the stages of man's physical progressions also includes a scientific missing link that ties early man with modern day man. So again I ask the same question about Adam & Eve being the first modern man & woman in the Garden of Eden, Why Not!

In a section regarding pollution & climate change I pointed out that the area of which the Garden of Eden is said to have existed had to be a lush rain forest type of terrain for the existence of its oil reserves of today. It's kind of funny to see non-faith believers trying to use science to disprove a faith based believer and vice-versus when in actuality they both support each other, science and religion, when using the larger picture of what is known.

So what you actually have is non-faith believers using science to attack faith based believers and faith based believers denying science in an attempt to defend their faith. In reality they are both wrong in their opposing thoughts regarding Faith and Science.

As for the church not embracing this line of thought it just excludes some people who want a soul searching faith but have a conflict with the church's non-evolving knowledge of the world. Even Science of today has acknowledged a new particle in an atom as "God's" particle.

Another aspect of society used against the church is "war". "There have been more people killed over religion than anything else" is a well known saying among non-faith believers. It is used to diminish the very basics of which religion was established. Long before there were "governments" to rule society it was the church that established the rules of which society lived under to make it civilized. Now that "governments" have replaced the "Church" as the rule maker for a civilized society there hasn't been a religious war in how many centuries until today's Religious war again in the Middle East. Also during this transformation from a church to a state ruled society there was a period of history when the State and the Church rode side by side into battle but today they see each other as foes at least in America. With governments as civilized societies' rule makers have wars diminished? No, just the faces have changed from that of the Head of the Church to a Country's leader of the establishments that now go to war being governments. As a society do we blame governments as we do religion? Maybe, but the actual culprit is mankind itself because it is the common link between the two forms of a organized civilized society in man's history.

With mankind identified as the face of war, what creates or causes a war? A dispute? A dispute over territory, trade, wants, needs, greed, power and even today still religion. Yet all these traits are attributed to all humans. Keep in mind religion is a belief and can be hijacked for a cause by humans as also can government. How does mankind avoid war? It all depends on the participants. It only takes one to cause a fight unlike the false saying "it takes two to fight" "it only takes one not to fight that may get their ass beat". There is no cure for war just like there is no cure for the traits attributed to humans that may be the cause of most wars. War is constantly around each and every one of us whether it is actually happening or not. It is a natural aspect of nature, the war for life even if it is between a lion and an antelope. It truly is nothing personal in the animal kingdom but it can be in the kingdom of humans. There is no cure, these traits will be with man as long as man exists but it makes us feel better when we put the blame on something other than ourselves. Too contrary belief there is such a thing as a just war. It's no different than someone stopping a bully from picking on a kid that can't defend himself from that bully. A neighborhood society that knows it has a bully within its ranks that then offers that bully a weapon such as a gun is no different than the world allowing a bully Country to achieve Nuclear Weapons, someone's going to get shot. The idea should be too take any and all weapons away from the bully. Japan voluntarily disarmed after WWII and for the next 70 years Japan has been an up standing citizen of the world but the sovereignty of that Nation was guaranteed by the U.S. under a signed treaty.

Is Religion a bad thing in society? If it is then so is government. It was the way a civilized society was organized under the Church rules of religious laws to govern society in earlier civilizations before the invention of governments. What were the rules implemented by the "Church" to govern society? In the Christian Faith it is the

Ten Commandments.

1. Do not worship other gods. : This works as long as there are not different religions with different ideologies of religion which then creates conflict.
2. Do not worship idols. : The same problem exists as mentioned above except worshipping a actual idol had been replaced by "a larger power" being "God" as the bases for religion.
3. Do not misuse God's name. : Don't take "God's" name in vein. Even better don't cuss. Learn to hold a conversation without these unnecessary words.

4. Keep the Sabbath holy. : Live each day as the Sabbath, not doing so makes the individual a hypocrite of their faith and the life they pretend to lead. The Sabbath day is Sunday, the day of the week to focus on your religious beliefs in a religious setting.

The first four Commandments deal with the thought of "Religious Faith" or beliefs. To have beliefs of these first four Commandments makes the next six Commandments much easier for society to follow.

5. Honor your father and mother. : Honor them with your respect. Respect their views and thoughts. Respect the fact they have decades of knowledge and history they are more than willing to share with you, it is you that must be willing to hear them whether you agree with them or not at that time. All knowledge doesn't come just from a book, life's experiences also accumulates knowledge.

6. Do not murder. : If I have to explain this to you, you probably aren't reading this anyway.

7. Do not commit adultery. : Stay loyal to your spouse and family, nurture them first not others.

8. Do not steal. : Everyone should know the basic meaning of these three words but it also goes beyond that basic meaning. To accept payment for something that was misrepresented. A service that was not delivered to your best abilities then the price negotiated is also stealing.

9. Do not lie. : All of society hinges on these three words. A society of liars is a society that can't trust the person next to them. Half truths are also lies because the truth is still being concealed. In a society that offers truths all can be trusted.

10. Do not covet. : Do not want or desire another person's spouse, family or possessions. Making any effort in doing so only reduces the time allowed for you to earn your own possessions, needs or wants. Don't even spend the time for admiration. Use this time to earn the heart of your own soul mate which will lead to the family you desire if correctly nurtured.

Now as you see is there really anything sinister in these religious 10 Commandments. Even an Atheist (a non-believer of faith) can't condemn the last 6 Commandments and wouldn't condemn the first four if they truly understood the purpose of early religion. Yet the Commandments have been forcibly removed from government buildings because of an unconstitutional Liberal supreme Court ruling brought in front of the court by a group representing a smaller portion of the population being Atheist. Let them hang a rebuttal to the Commandments or the Religious Faith. To condemn religion for the problems of the world you also have to condemn government because the problems haven't changed with what rules society. Moving from a "Church" ruled society to a "Government" ruled society has probably degraded society even more with the government's removal of religion from mainstream government. The supreme Court has no problem using their misinterpreted beliefs of the Founding Fathers intentions on one subject but won't quote the Founding Fathers known intentions regarding religion which are written directly into the "Constitution" and remain there today. It seems to me that some of the most immoral people are many of our elected Representatives and employees of government. Louis Lerner of the IRS pleading the fifth not to incriminate herself by testifying about what went on in the "peoples" government. Veterans Administration officials taking bonuses while denying the country's wounded warriors proper access to the medical system built specifically to service our veterans. Seems like the VA has served its officials better than the military personnel that protected them and apparently government allows it. Do you think religion would allow this to happen? If it was a religiously funded and run hospital for veterans would it happen? History states absolutely not! So there are aspects of the Church that can accomplish a task that government can't no matter how much money government throws at the task. Why? Because there are very little morals in the government workplace. I hope that's not surprising! So now how does government instill morals in a society it governs? It can't! It can't legislate morality but it will fine, jail and place you on probation to raise funds for government in the name of not following laws for what government sees as immoral for an unlimited source of funds. Funny what the government does or doesn't see as immoral. If it did, people in government would lose their jobs and some would go to jail but government DOESN'T! Congratulations, Government has now achieved the supreme Court's wishes of a separation of Church and State, a separation or removal of morality and replacing it with immorality.

Science has moved outside the atmosphere of our planet to explore other planets within our galaxy. Science is now looking outside our galaxy at other galaxies and seeing the enormous extent of space's reach. Science has now identified one particular particle within an atom that science states life would not exist without it. Science has named this particle the "GOD" particle. Science was once used to denounce "Religion" allowing our government that sees it as a threat to its power to remove the moralities of Religion from our society of schools and government having now degraded our society outside government.

Sadly, Liberal Left Democrats using Government with the Atheist movement have used science to damage our society to a point society itself may never recover. The funny part is now science has come full circle and many scientists have embraced the fact that the odds are so astronomical against the galaxies forming as they have without some type of *DIVINE INTERVENTION* which is a form of Religious Faith.

Do you really think the Liberal Left Democrats will correct the damage they have created? Have they ever corrected anything they have caused in History? No! The only time the Liberal Left will act is doing so using society as a whole being blamed for the atrocities committed and not themselves for the atrocities. When payment comes due, again society pays the bill not the culprit being the Liberal Left. The Liberal Left have never been held accountable for their actions throughout the history of our Nation.

The perfect example of this is the Darren Wilson shooting of Michael Brown in Ferguson, Missouri. A false narrative being "Hands Up, Don't Shoot" was begun by Dorian Johnson and quickly (same day) picked up by the Liberal Left Democrats of Congress lead by the Black Congressional Caucus, the President Barack Obama, the U.S. Attorney General Eric Holder and the Liberal Left Media including racist liberal Al "cocaine dealing" Sharpton. So the civil unrest between the time of the shooting and the release of the investigation of the shooting that disproved the narrative was driven by the Liberal Left.

What was the cost to society? A portion of Ferguson burnt to the ground lead by Louis Head, a violent felon, being Michael's stepfather. A number of these businesses were Black owned and allowed to be burnt by Democrat Liberal Governor Jay Nixon who did not allow the Ferguson police to intervene. Two Police Officers, neither being white, killed in New York City by a Black man. Another assaulted both by a Black man and another two officers shot in Ferguson by a Black man.

Who pays for this? Society! Definitely not the Liberal Left who pushed and endorsed these actions in the name of civil disobedience! What was civil?

The Republican Party is the base for Christianity in this Nation. The Democrat Party is the base for some Christians but also houses agnostic, atheist, Muslin or Islam believers. Agnostic and atheist are not a religious belief because their thoughts only focuses on what others should not believe. So what are the differences between Christianity and Islam?

Christianity is dictated by the Bible which states to go forth and bring willing people into the Faith. It also states for those unwilling to enter the Faith to still treat them with kindness, with the understanding that the Christian "God" will pass judgment when entering the Afterlife.

Islam is dictated by the Koran which states to go forth and bring the unwilling people into the Faith. It also states for the people of the faith to pass judgment on the unwilling by inflicting death upon them. With this totally opposite view of Faith, doesn't it then through reasoning, show that Allah has no "self" power on earth and very little in the Afterlife. Allah's only power is to offer up seventy two virgins when you do what "Allah" is unable to do for himself. If he has no power on earth and very little in Afterlife does it not bring into question his actual Existence? Should not "Allah" himself stand in judgment of non-believers to demonstrate his powers as the Christian "God" does? To do this, demonstrates his equal power of earth and Afterlife as "God" retains. Not doing this shows Allah's lesser power than "God", on earth and in the Afterlife. Also if there is no Christian God then Allah will stand in judgment of all and he will then reward his followers with a long life and seventy two virgins in Afterlife while dealing with non-believers also in the Afterlife.

POLITICAL VIEWS ON GOVERNMENT

I will begin with my own political positions and classification in the political theory of government. I classify myself first as a conservative with a subculture of libertarianism meaning I am a conservative libertarian. I am not Republican because the parties' party line at times does not reflect most of my views. With only two parties in our political system you must side with the one that supports your most important views that you have with a balancing act when choosing. Anytime a third party emerges it does so at the cost of the party it emerged from thus virtually handing the election to the opposite party of which you have even less shared views. So this option is not truly an option because of the history of the results. To start I will define the word "Conservative" Politically by the dictionary;

1. reluctant to accept change: in favor of preserving the status quo and traditional values and customs, and against abrupt change. 2. Cautious and on low side: cautiously moderate and therefore often less than the final outcome.

The problem is the word "conservative" can be applied to the Democrat Party when Democrats were in favor of preserving the status quo and traditional values and customs, and against abrupt change when the Democrats fought for keeping Slavery.

With that said this means that the Republican Party were liberals for wanting change in regards to the abolishment of Slavery.

So both terms are relative as to what is being discussed. You can be either depending on the topic.

To me this is confusing when being applied to my beliefs in government. So I will define the word with my thoughts;

1. Reluctant to accept change that has no purpose or makes the situation worse. Change must be controlled to achieve the wanted outcome. Change is inevitable, nothing remains the same. It is how the "Change" is controlled that determines your destination being the results of the change.

2. Physically Conservative: being that in giving an estimate the actual cost will be no more and should be actually less than the estimated cost.

3. Physically Conservative Spending: not spending money just because it is there to be spent. When spending money using it only for the things needed to accommodate for the needs or tasks. Ensuring that the money spent accomplishes the task for which it was spent. Having accountable oversight of the needs or tasks to ensure that the goals of both are met. Only individuals can ensure a greater effectiveness, more money only ensures greater waste. Anything that doesn't meet these standards is a failed process and wasted money on my part.

Amazingly government rarely accomplishes any of its tasks and the results are most times failures because these standards are not in place to assure success.

What is the longest war America has ever fought? The 50 year long war on poverty. The welfare programs instituted in America have been a miserable failure because more people are now enrolled in the failing programs than ever before. Clearly once in the program there are few ways out not only for the parents but for the children of the family. When raised in that environment it is the environment from which a child learns to operate for its future earnings. To change this ever circular motion of this repeatedly failing system it is the system that must be changed. To just throw more money at it is a statement that the program works but it has always been under funded. It also states it has been under funded for the last 50 years and when money is allocated it is never enough. If using only funding as an excuse for failure of a program then any war, Korea or Vietnam, which we failed to win was caused by under funding, not policy or tactics. Again it is the program or system that is failing because about $20 trillion dollars has been spent on the programs since their inception. This government program has consumed more tax revenue than any other dept. or program of government but has had the least effectiveness.

The educational system is the most successful government program, for fighting poverty, even in the condition the educational system is in today. The education system has lifted more people out of poverty than all other welfare programs combined. The problem with the education system is that children are not required to graduate. When there the time tends to be wasted by many individual children and the friends they drag into that same mind set.

So the answer might be to tie the welfare system to the educational system meaning welfare money for child attendance, participation in class and grades. Placing this responsibility on the parents to ensure attendance, enhance participation which should result in better grades. The parent also will have a responsibility to see that their children get their homework done and may assist in doing so because grades also affect welfare payments. This also may help a parent that probably also missed some adolescent education. These efforts are no different for this family than it is for all other families with children in school. This will also create a responsibility between parent and child and if a multiple child family will create a responsibility among and to younger siblings. Now tie teachers and guidance counselors to parents with students' performance and tie welfare counselors to teachers and parents to ensure a proper learning atmosphere at home.

For anyone to oppose any type of change of a welfare program obviously is accustom to, promotes and accepts failure. Of course this is the government we are talking about and it has gladly accepted failure on many topics.

Let's define "Liberal" Politically by the dictionary; 1. broad-minded: tolerant of different views and standards of behavior in others. 2. progressive politically or socially: favoring gradual reform, especially political reforms that extend democracy, distribute wealth more evenly, and protect the personal freedom of the individual. 3. generous: freely giving money, time, or some other asset. 4. not literal: not limited to the literal meaning in translation or interpretation a liberal interpretation of the rules. 5. culturally oriented: concerned with general cultural matters and broadening of the mind rather than professional or technical study.

The first definition, is a Liberal Democrat tolerant of religion? I say no, they may be tolerant of the Muslim religion which is not tolerant of the Christian religion so that intolerance is fought thru a d-fact-o-force including atheists. Are they tolerant in standards of behavior? Again no, they are empathetic to minorities unless that minority doesn't back their political views. In the case of a black individual man they are referred to as "Uncle Tom", a reference to the "slavery era" of an earlier time to diminish their message to others of their kind or race. Number 2; Do Democrats favor reform? No, anytime a government program is talked about to help ensure an effective outcome they don't want to touch it, Democrats don't back any type of personal responsibility of the recipients of the program thus the program and the recipient's situation remains the same. How about political reforms that extend democracy to other nations? No, domestically they won't support minorities having a different view that doesn't support their political agenda. Overseas, they will not support any type of action to deliver democracy to a society oppressed by government. Do they distribute wealth; definitely, they have no problem taking from the responsible individual and giving to the individual who won't accept or doesn't want any responsibility for themselves, their lives or their families. Do they protect personal freedoms? No, they didn't protect any of the individuals mentioned above except for individuals not wanting responsibility for themselves. Number 3; do they freely give money and time? Yes and no, they freely give other people's money thru government as the solution for failed government programs that constantly stay "failing". Of their personal money the contributions to humanitarian causes tend to be much less, unless the contribution is for a political cause they favor. This sounds exactly like Bill and Hillary Clinton and the Clinton Foundation, what happened to the money collected for Haiti after the earthquake? Where did it go? As for time it is also mostly distributed in the same proportion and for the same reason. Number 4; not limited to the literal meaning in translation or interpretation a liberal interpretation of the rules. If the rules are ever changing by the translation or interpretation what is the purpose of having written law in the first place. An oppressed society constantly has a changing (to fit government's needs) rule of law to oppress its citizens. Number 5; concerned with general cultural matters and broadening of the mind rather than professional or technical study. How can any government program be successful when general cultural matters and broadening of the mind overrule the needs of professional and technical talent needed to implement a government service? This is the exact reason the Affordable Care Act web-site didn't work on roll-out and cost close to a Billion tax payer dollars. It still doesn't work just like the healthcare law. Crony Capitalism at its best. If Facebook had to have that same amount of money to build its web-page or web-site the company would not exist today. This also explains what is happening to our school system and our children's education.

Lets define "Democrat"; supporter of democracy: somebody who believes in or supports democracy or the democratic system of government.

If you want to see Democrat democracy or a democratic system ran by Democrats then "Google or Bing" "DNC (Democrat National Convention) vote on God" on your computer. That is Democrats at their best when in public. With a verbal vote a suspension of the Rules to adopt "God" to the DNC platform meaning "God" was not in the platform. Three verbal votes clearly evenly divided yet the woman said "you got to let them do what they want to do" and clearly a predetermined decision was made. So was it Democratic? Obviously Not! Was it a Democrat vote? Obviously Yes! Imagine what you get when they are not in the public eye, maybe that same predetermined decision made for everyone by a few. Also did you hear the Governor's speech and How Barack Obama acknowledged "God" by saying he recognizes Jerusalem as the capital of Israel. The statement meant nothing on the subject of recognizing and installing "God" into the DNC platform. It was saying something while actually saying nothing, he never acknowledged "God" or a Christian Faith. Were the people who claimed he was a Muslim in 2008 before he was elected correct and was his campaign based on lies? He spoke about Bush taking out the citizen's credit card and driving up the debt to be put on the shoulder's of our children yet he doubled our nation's debt.

Was he lying then? You can have only so many excuses for so many lies, at some point you have to acknowledge it was a lie, deception so a politician could get elected as President.

Another point I want to make is that the "Liberal Left Democrats" which were in power of our government have modeled their views and actions on a book called "Rules For RADICALS" by Saul D. Alinsky. This man is a walking contradiction of himself and all he talks about. One example is he says his religion is Jewish yet he also claims to be agnostic, What? My conclusion about "Liberal Left Democrats" is the phrase itself is a Oxymoron, thus it's policies are the same and rarely perpetuate people to a higher standard of living unless it's their (Al Gore) members or financiers' (George Soros or Warren Buffet) of their political party.

Lets now define Libertarian; 1. advocate of individual responsibility: somebody who believes in the doctrine of free will. 2. advocate of individual freedom: somebody who believes in the principle that people should have complete freedom of thought and action. Now everyone knows you can't have total freedom of your actions but you should of the actions that don't directly affect others monetarily, property wise or personally. The word "directly" must be used here because if the word "indirectly" is used you can tie any action of one person to having some type of effect on others thus outlawing all actions of any individual on this basis.

What is the second longest war America has fought? The war on drugs. The war on drugs began in the late 60's and early 70's on many different types of recreational drugs. Our government system has determined what is safe and what is not safe for many decades under the Food & Drug Agency. It is amazing some of the things that are seen as safe by this agency. A warning label on the product or a disclaimer on a TV commercial, mandated by government, allows many products continued profitability. Image a product that battles the symptoms of hay fever but one of the side effects of the product is possible heart attack and death. Sounds like the suffering of hay fever may be a better alternative than a heart attack or possible death. My point is the government endorsing a product that can cause a worse outcome than the illness itself is not a safe remedy, but this rationale is not used in government decisions regarding marijuana.

Prohibition began on January 16th, 1920 when the 18th Amendment to the "Constitution" came into effect causing the production, sales, possession and consumption of alcoholic products illegal within the U.S. borders. This war on alcohol was also a war on a recreational drug. Prohibition created a black market for bootleggers, smugglers and speakeasies. It also accounted for numerous arrests, convictions and jail sentences. A prominent past Democrat President's family made a fortune smuggling alcohol from Canada into the United States. The organizations formed during this time period by the President's father were also used to drive the election campaign of his son during a later time period. In 1933 the 21st Amendment ended prohibition even through local laws enacted during prohibition and still allowed after prohibition caused some type of prohibition until as late as 1966.

Government has demonized marijuana at its earliest time of appearance as a recreational drug by conducting false studies with false health advisories and flat out lies. Imagine the government as not being totally truthful, not hard to do is it. Here is were I have a huge problem with the Republican Party. It endorses personal responsibility on many issues yet it doesn't allow for personal responsibility on most issues, one being the recreational drug issue. To me this waters down the issue to a position of what it only allows in its own eyes. My position on marijuana is no different than alcohol. Both are used commonly in today's society but what are brought to the forefront are the failures of certain people and blaming marijuana usage as the only culprit for their failure. News Flash, I will bet you these same people not under the influence of anything still fall on the failure side of the teeter-totter. Government never acknowledges the successful people of society who use for recreational use and contribute billions to government in the form of taxes. Worse is the fact that people are treated differently in the government court system due to their standing in society. It also creates a situation with the working class that is not on an equal level with upper management with drug tests. Not to mention qualified people caught by laws are now listed with a criminal record being blackballed by the employment world of which contain people using the same drug. Again this type of prohibition

188

has created a black market and all the problems associated with it as it did alcohol.

As a country we transfer billions of dollars every year to Mexico for black market marijuana. The Mexican government promotes this black market because it is seen as an income for the country. As a tourist of Mexico, say on a fresh water fishing trip, you will see marijuana being grown around most fresh water lakes. Our government knows this is happening but does nothing to get rid of the source. That makes our government culpable in the black market. To arrest our citizens for something our government has just as much responsibility for just creates a failed policy and unfair system of government. This money could easily stay in this country while freeing up border patrol to concentrate on border protection by decriminalizing marijuana and setting society acceptable rules to accommodate for this move. Such needed laws is not using in public or in the presence of minors, just because you belong to a nudist colony doesn't give you the right to go nude in public or in the presence of minors. No driving under the influence, minimum age of 21, just commonsense rules of society already in place for alcohol. If grown it must be protected against theft by the public, this is to help keep it out of the hands of minors or the grower losing their crop to theft. Once the demand is met here the black market disappears along with many of the problems government has created on this subject and the money stays within our borders. Now we have created a personal responsibility situation and you then punish for the lack of personal responsibility as is done with alcohol. What about the increased potency of today's Marijuana? That is being done through the process of altering the conditions for growing the plant not actually altering the plant. I don't see it any differently than wine coolers, wine, beer, alcohol, grain alcohol and moonshine which all have different levels of alcohol. I have seen people who are drunk not able to walk but I have never seen someone who is stoned (the term used by smokers) not able to walk. Also an alcohol overdose (alcohol poisoning) will kill as there is no such thing with marijuana. In reality marijuana is a safer recreational drug with fewer illnesses attributed to it than alcohol. Also normally a greater potency just means less used to achieve the same level of relaxation much as alcohol is used by someone not wanting to get drunk. The marijuana movement does itself no favors by having smoke-ins in public. It is something that should be done in a more private setting away from children and others as to not draw attention. Sex is a beautiful thing but you don't do it in public square at noon time. Also using tax dollars (EBT cards) for purchases justly raises concerns among people about the topic which wouldn't be there if, again, personal responsibility was in the forefront of the movement. Unfortunately personal responsibility is not at the forefront of any subjects our government discusses. The movement for marijuana is on the Liberal Democrat side of politics thus the reason for how the movement is actually being opposed by many in society.

What about the other more dangerous drugs such as cocaine and heroin. My opinion is these are much more dangerous with the reason being they have been altered from their original state by man. Coca leaves have been used by the indigenous population of Peru for many generations but cocaine, a man made product of the coca leaf, is exported under a black market system from the same South American countries. So how do we stop these products from entering America? A black market system will never go away as long as demand exists. Only the incoming supply can be altered and the cost to control supply is determined by resources needed to achieve the goal. The needed resources is determined by a few factors, the biggest being the area of needed control. For South America that area would be at the Panama Canal. Having a much smaller force for a much smaller area is cost effective and goal effective to drastically reduce the flow of cocaine while protecting the canal and controlling immigration from South America. Heroin is manufactured from the Opium plant grown in the eastern regions of the Middle East. Its production (not cultivation) in Mexico has raised six fold from 2007 to 2011 and placing Mexico as the second largest opium producer in the world. This shows beyond a shadow of a doubt that Mexico has become a narcotic manufacturing and exporting government state with its main customer being America. Our choices as a country is to clean up Mexico as was done in Colombia or increase our southern border security to stop these products and illegal immigration. A combination of these suggestions is also a possibility being cleaning up Mexico and protecting its southern border from smuggling of illegal drugs and illegal immigration.

Ignoring a failed policy only leads to greater problems or a continuing waste of resources on a situation that government has little effectiveness to be able to change. Thus our country's expendable resources continues to shrink and at some point a deficit is created. As long as you continue with the deficit causing policies your yearly debt will continue to grow, it has no choice. Again throwing money at a problem will not create change; only a changed policy in this situation will effect a social change of personal responsibility of actions. Government can't govern on all morality issues; it can only jail the citizens for noncompliance which is just another expense that punishes the Tax Payer.

POLITICAL CORRECTNESS

I constantly hear the conservative media imply there is a group of people that push Political Correctness. Sure there is a group their called the Liberal Left Democrats that use the topic of Political Correctness to push their Agendas.

Take one of their favorites being the larger percentage of Blacks in our jails. Crime is not on the streets of which the rich live. Crime gets progressively worse as you move down the income ladder, so logically the most crime is on the streets of the poor neighborhoods. The crime is driven by the desire to survive or move up the economic ladder depending on the individuals situation. Stealing food is not the desire to move up the economic ladder but a survival instinct of being hungry. The sale of drugs on a street corner of a poor neighborhood may be one or the other or a combination of both. Both these situations of hunger and drug dealing can be attributed to many things. A true mental illness, bad life decisions, a lack of education, a lack of job opportunities, a lack of desire to follow the correct path for continued economic success. Instead always looking for short cuts that lead to the certain later down fall of that individual.

Even education is not the total answer to the problem because if every individual in this country had a College Education then everyone would be employed which would not be true. There is no difference in that situation and nobody having a College Education but everybody having a High School Education. As was a past generation, because if the jobs don't exist then everyone can't be employed. But it is Education or a "God given talent" that has separated the masses on the economic ladder. It is also Education that allows Our Nation and other Nations to create and maintain the high number of jobs we do have that supply the rest of the worlds needs. It is when we price ourselves out of a certain market of production or services to the rest of the World and even with supplying ourselves that we lose jobs to the less educated parts of the World. These people have a much lower standard of living thus a much lower pay rate. Now the only way to create new jobs is through innovations of new technologies which require an educated Society to deliver these technologies.

So what does political correctness have to do with what I just wrote about? Basically it is a competition between the people within one country and then another competition between the Nation's People and the rest of the World. When the Liberal Left Democrats bring its thoughts of Political Correctness into our Government and Society it does so wanting to bring a end too the competition among the people. Such as rewarding all who compete in a certain competition with the same prize no matter where they finished. It doesn't reward the effort of the winner anymore than it rewards the effort of the loser which is a confusing message to send to a young child. The message being the individual doesn't have to put forth the effect to be a winner. This is not a life lesson that needs to be taught. By following this taught ideology people will never reach their true potential because the effort to do so has been taught out of them. This is the basic life lesson learned and promoted by Communism and Socialism. The lesson is that government controls where and how far your own life may take you and not yourself because the Desire & Freedom is gone that allows it. It is now a conditioning by the Liberal Left Democrats that creates a learned condition (Pavlov's Law) for non-achievement. Once this learned condition grabs hold of a society it's at this point society falls from the world market. This helps too create a stagnate society of falling incomes and less job opportunities because the Nation's inability to compete in a Technology Driven World Wide Market. The fact that every time the minimum wage is raised it is just making it that much harder to compete with other nations for manufacturing that requires less education but a need to learn a job that is just more of a repetitive type job.

This conditioning that I speak about is what is being used by the Liberal Left Democrats on minorities such as our Black Race or for that fact Any Race that is in the lower income of society. When government offers benefits above and beyond the basic necessities of basic life then it is conditioning each and everyone receiving those benefits. The condition is that of a learned non-desire of achievement that doesn't allow those to learn how too earn what they want in their own life instead of what government gives them. As government fails ($18 Trillion Dollars in Debt) those government scraps being put on their plate becomes less and less and at some point may be very little as it is in a true Communist or Socialist Country.

This downward spiral has only been accelerated by our designed too under achieve, Union and Democrat Liberal Left controlled Educational System with one example being the length of the school teaching day, the graduation rate and allowed dropout rate. Why do you need an education if government is going to take care of all your NEEDS and WANTS?

FREEDOM OF SPEECH

The Politically Correct Liberal Left of the Democrat Party use words, sometimes redefining them as a means to stir political and civil unrest. Civil unrest helps to drive liberalism. Liberalism assists in the creation of violence. Thus that is why liberalism is Violent, and advances the fastest under a violent society.

The other aspect of liberalism is the fact it is used to mobilize the youngest and least educated in the world of reality. How can you voice your opinion about jobs or wages when you never had either. The reality of the real world is you are being used by the Liberal Baiting Powers of the Democrat Party. They have no problem risking your Future, your Freedom, Your LIFE for their Goals. And when attacking, you tend to attack the same society from which you come. They just tend to be the older now wiser of your society. So is it now racism for which you protest or is it age-ism because that is who you attack being a older generation like your Mother and Father. Yet the older generation of Liberals are the same ones that also have never grown up and they issue orders they won't follow themselves being rioting. So they just stand on the sidelines cheering you on! As a younger adult you still don't like being told "no", "don't do it" do you? Is "YES" that alluring? Fact is "No" is the most unused or misused word in our society.

Speech cannot be regulated in a free society and there is no middle ground so the only alternative is Speech must be free thus the term "free speech". The Founding Fathers knew that to regulate any type of speech would require a power of government that our Founding Fathers never intended for government to possess. This "thought" of our Founding Fathers was their first realization that government could not control every aspect of life without becoming a dictatorship within a Democratic Representative Government. Now there is a fine line between a majority Democratic Representative Government and a dictatorship. It is the Constitution that protects the minorities from certain types of oppression of the majority, speech being one. It is not the majority of people that upsets the majority of people when free speech is abrasive, it is normally the minority that upsets the majority. As to who is who makes little difference but who is right on a subject offering a true look into the future outcome of a idea is the only goal. Now debate is essential to produce the pro's & con's of a idea then allowing to see its future impact based on reasonable thoughts. This process is essential for what ideas to act on and those that need to be discarded & then history decides the outcome of societies choices. Thus free speech is essential to a society that is based on the ideas of the people, the people's government and a free market or free enterprise system.

What government can't protect society from is Stupidity or a Liar's Free Speech. Yell "Fire" in a theater causing a mass exodus or riot type exit of the people and you may be charged with in-sighting a riot if caught. Now did government protect you from that form of stupid or a liar's Free Speech? No, it didn't and no it won't ever. What government does is put a penalty or cost to the individual for doing that type of Free Speech. Can it stop it? No, government can't stop liar's within government but with a cost or penalty to the individual that yelled "fire" it has now made a attempt to regulate Free Speech. Is this wrong? Remember it is normally the minority that upsets the majority. The minority is the person who yelled "Fire", the majority are the people who fled the theater. If all of the majority had of yelled "Fire" at that one minority do you think the person would have ran out of the theater while watching no one else move? No, the act of the minority was to see if they could get everyone to leave the theater, because of a possible threat to themselves being fire, as a reaction to a joke for whatever reason.

So is a atheist who yells Stupid Free Speech words at Faith based believers a act to get a reaction that may cause a conflict? Yes it is to get a reaction but No, if there is no immediate threat to themselves so reacting with anything other than words is inappropriate. Yet it is almost always the activist (the minority) that infringes on the rights of others with violence when responding in kind. It is only obstruction that ends a debate before the truth may be revealed to the masses.

As you were reading that last paragraph were the Faith based believers in your mind "Christian"? In our U.S. society atheists only attack Christians so it is a condition created by the power of the minority society. Why do they not attack the other religions like the Islam believers? Because the atheist and Islam believers are on the same liberal side of the Democrat party which opposes the Faith based believers that are the base for the Republican party being affiliated with Christianity, defeating one helps defeat the other.

Why can some criticize Christianity yet the same people oppose any criticism of the Islam Faith? Now enters the Liberal Political Correctness Police of the Democrat party to obscure the lines of what is allowed and what is not as they see it, what words can be used by whom and when. Can society use the word "Nigger or Negro"? How about "Cracker"? "Wigger"? or "Whigger"?

Society is what creates speech, each and every word was created by someone in society. The dictionary was not brought down from the mountain with Moses along with the Ten Commandments. So now was the word "Nigger" a intentional slant of that time period or just a word created by someone of that time period to identify a Black man who may or may not be a slave. The word "Negro" was also created by someone supposedly as a non-offensive alternative to the word "Nigger" yet the definition of the word "Nigger" has never changed. Now society has not only created a word with a meaning but now has later condemned that same word and replaced it with a more Politically Correct word created by someone to appease others. If "Negro" truly appeased others why has society moved on to other words in succession as "Colored", "Black" and "African American". Each time with the older word being labeled as offensive and the new word or now phrase being deemed politically correct (as not to offend) by some unseen force or a smaller portion of society. If this was true why haven't such organizations as "The United Negro College Fund" also had its name changed due to societies demand? Remember, the liberal political correctness Democrat party decides what words can be used by whom, when & where. Has society truly found possibly two words that do not offend and are accepted by the Race the words are intended to identify. When identifying a White person in America only two words come to mind being "White" or "Caucasian". So what about "European American"? This term was never used because of the many different cultures of White Europeans and the fact that anyone moving to this country does so accepting the principles on which this country was formed, built and has evolved into as a Nation of free citizens. Now the term "African American" is offensive to me because it implies a percentage of each, African & American, to all Blacks. So what percentage of American are they? Born, raised and hopefully educated in what once was the greatest educational system in the world. To me it is what is instilled in the person towards our nation that determines the American percentage not the color of their skin.

Now lets explore the words "Cracker" & "Wigger" remembering that today's society has expanded the meaning of one word in the way it is used and created one word along with its meaning or definition. The word "Cracker" has been and is still used to describe a food form. The word in the "Nigger, Negro, Colored, Black and African American" society is now used as a intended offensive slur towards Whites because a Cracker is white unless of course it is a wheat cracker then it has a form of color and no longer white! So with this understanding is a mixed race person say Barack Obama now referred to as a "wheat cracker" by the same society? I doubt it because a word used for racist activities will only be used by haters against others. That same society sees Barack as one of their own based strictly on having some amount of color to his skin. Now this term "Cracker" as we all should know, also came up through history as the White man who cracked the whip on the slaves but the crack of the whip actually began in Africa when Africans were taken into society as slaves by all Races including their own Race. Don't believe my statement, look into the history of the "Bullwhip", its origins are from the country of Spain. Brought to Central and South America when the Spaniards settled in that section of the Americas. So were the Spaniards involved in the Slave Trade? Absolutely. Any possibility their ships were loaded with "Trade Goods" including Slaves and once they were dropped off in North America other goods were then delivered to Central and South America then picking up goods and returning with them to Spain. So along with the Bullwhip they might of introduced slavery to North America. What is their race considered to be African, Middle Eastern, European being White, Latino? I think Latino is their race classification is it not? How do you think Latino's along with the Spanish language got to Central and South America? So even today's society being Black or White has now created a new meaning for a food form with no actual understanding of were the term came from being the Crack of a Whip. So where is the liberal political correctness police of the Democrat party to make this adjustment?

Now for societies word "Wigger" which is not in the dictionary but is used by both Races to describe a White person who aspires to be of Black culture by say just wanting to be a Rapper in the Rap Music culture. Notice that I used the word "culture" and not "business". If it were a business would a Black skin be a requirement as is seen in today's Black society to be a proven thug Rap artist? Apparently if you weren't brought up in the culture of the Black thug neighborhood with the experiences that it created you can't Rap as a musical form. Eminem also known as Marshall Bruce Mathers III fought against this racist form of Black culture oppression against him even though he came from the same "hood" and faced the same obstacles as other Black Rappers except for the fact he also faced Black Racism from the Black society that controlled and promoted the industry. Sounds just like the racism of earlier sports in America just a different industry. So is the term "Wigger" racist or neutral?

Maybe it Depends on who and how the person wants to be perceived by others that may or may not be offended by the term, so is it racist or not?

"Whigger" is a term again not in the dictionary but was predominantly used in the early 1840's through the 1850's. The word its self is a combination of the word "Whig" and the word "Nigger". It was used as a intended slur by the Democrat party for the opposing political party that opposed slavery of the Black people. The political party was known as the"Whig" party which became the Republican Party with the election of Abraham Lincoln who set the Black Race free.

Imagine that, the Liberal Political Correctness Democrat Party as the first to use the common word "Nigger" used at that time in history to describe the Black Race as part of a Racist Word that its intent was to demean the Political Party that supports Freedom for all people. What made it seem a derogatory word for the Political Whig Party? Because Democrats viewed the Black Race as a inferior race to the White Race thus demeaning the Whig Party with a newly created word that grouped that political party with a inferior race in a attempt to give that party the illusion of a inferior political party all seen through the racist eyes of then mostly Southern Democrat slave owners.

So which is more of a threat to free speech, the individual that yells "fire" in a packed theater or a Political Party that creates rioting fires by continually stirring the Race Pot to untruthfully promote itself and its agendas. Its agenda is not the people of all Races who are citizens of this nation but the elected people of their own political party to remain in power at any and all costs to all of society.

The Liberal left would like to take away any words they deem inappropriate at anytime. What's next, what we are allowed to talk about, how much time should be spent discussing a topic. The Liberal Left can keep their hands off my dictionary and my free speech.

With that said, I would like to leave you with the words to a very balanced Thug Rap song that talks about their culture, race, criminal thoughts, sex and society's financial cost.

"Cracker Nigger Thugs, they want more than my hugs, I got game, I give them their names, baby daddies tonight, unless they decide to fight" its much better with music and accompanying background gun fire!

Their only words, people. Designed in a era of time being present or past history for a purpose of communication between people. But when putting the words together it shows a failure of society. A failure of these people in society. Some may have money but do they have morals?

You can't ask someone to "pass the crackers" if society had never given it the name of "Cracker" in the first place. There is not a word in the dictionary that has created our history. Society creates and records history accurately or not. Society creates words along with its definition. Society also changes definitions of words making the word something it was never intended to be thus society can now scold others like a middle school hall monitor for using the word in a nation of free speech. The use of certain words being allowed in certain sub-societies while being disallowed in other sub-societies is not in fairness and not Free speech. If society wants a word not used in society it must not be used in all aspects of society! You can't create a privileged society by what words they are allowed to use in society and then disallowing these words in another. Thus government or society can't regulate "speech". That is why your Mother tried to teach you the basics of the real world when she said "Sticks and stones may break my bones but words will never hurt me" but you, as a child, teen, young adult and adult are still not listening! I wonder what causes that!

GOVERNMENT HAS BECOME A HIGH-END WELFARE SYSTEM

The free market system determines wages and salaries beyond what the Federal Government determines as minimum wage. The Federal government is the only entity that determines its own wages. Unfortunately it also determines what the taxpayer receives as a work ethic from each and every government employee, also known as work accomplished for pay received. If the same standards were applied to free market jobs employers would go out of business because the product of many government employees is far less than their counter parts in the free market system.

Take the Veterans Administration's doctors they average seeing 2 to 3 patients a day and in the free market doctors average about 8 or 9 a day. The output of V.A. doctors is 2/3 or 66% less than what is accomplished in the free market. There are about 16,000 lawyers (average pay just under $99,000) in the employment of the IRS alone with the total employed being 93,337 and 91,082 are full time permanent according to 2009 numbers. There are 2,748,978 civilian federal employees in the United States as of January 2009. This is according to the Federal Employment Statistics published by the U.S. Office of Personnel Management. Employees with security agencies (CIA, NSA, etc) as well as the National Imagery and Mapping Agency not included in this number. The percentage of civilian federal employees that work in the executive branch of government is 97.6%. The 2,748,978 also doesn't include civilian retirees, military or military retirees, contractors or the added employees caused by the implementation of Obamacare.

I tried to see how many people are employed in the Federal Trade Commission which is in charge of the Do-Not-Call list. I have called this agency at 1-888-382-1222 no less than 20 times to report abusers of the list with phone numbers and if I could of talked to a person I had business names. Have I gotten a call back? No. Have I stopped receiving unwanted sales and robo calls? No. Now when the Federal Trade Commission was appointed to handle the Do-Not-Call list do you think the agency's budget was increased to accomplish this task given to them? I am sure it was. Are taxpayers receiving the promised services of the law and the agency that enforces that law? No.

The newspaper's headlines at one point of time was filled with the V.A. scandals of alternate waiting lists and appointments being canceled so that managers can receive thousands of dollars each in good performance bonuses. Yet the product they are offering doesn't reflect the pay or the added bonuses. This is nothing more than government employees stealing from the American taxpayer and continuing that theft with retirement payments and benefits.

It's bad enough that government jobs out pace free market jobs with pay, benefits, holidays, vacation time and a government funded retirement instead of a 401k plan that may or may not be there in a free market job. The reality of government is taxpayers probably receive .25 to .30 cents on each taxpayer dollar spent for the services any government agency provides. The rest is lost in low productivity and not needed positions of government thus showing up is the only requirement for a high end Welfare system. Today my understanding is they don't even have to show up to get paid! What a Job!

THE NATIONAL DEBT IS A BORDERLINE PONZI SCHEME

What is a Ponzi Scheme? Bernie Madoff was arrested and convicted for running a financial Ponzi scheme. Ponzi schemes are not that complex, they rely on an individual or group of individuals to coordinate the fraud. This individual or individuals convince numerous victims to invest in a legitimate fund with promises of large returns on investment. The new investor's money is then used to pay smaller dividends to previous investors and any additional money (there is always additional money because the individuals determine who and how much gets paid out) goes into the pockets of the individual or individuals. To keep perpetuating this fraud they must have an infinite number of unknowing willing investors.

The Federal Government sells U.S. Savings Bonds (financial investment) which earn an interest and at maturity of the bond can be cashed out. The government also borrows money (financial loan) from other nations to fund government for a certain period of time. Part of that financial loan (borrowed money) is used to pay the minimum interest payments (rarely any money is paid on the principal of the loan) of previous financial loans (borrowed money from other countries) and to buy back matured U.S. Savings Bonds. The additional money pocketed is used to pay dividends or what also may be seen as salaries of government workers, social program checks or welfare programs, needed infrastructure, etc.

What is the difference other than one is an individual and one is our government? When the government continually borrows money to fund it's budget while paying minimum interest payments on our loans isn't that a Ponzi Scheme?

The only way for government to end this Ponzi Scheme is to balance the yearly budget allowing government to run on money that is not borrowed. If government continues its historical policy of borrowing it perpetuates the Ponzi scheme putting our nation in a worse position to be able to recover.

As Bernie Madoff found out a Ponzi Scheme cost his family everything he stole leaving them with nothing and he went to prison by the powers of the U.S. Government. Who will prosecute the U.S. Government for the Ponzi Scheme it is running? The answer is the World's (other nations) investors when they quit loaning money to fund our government causing a financial U.S. Crisis. At a debt of $18 Trillion Dollars and a government budget that is around $1 Trillion Dollars a year larger than what is generated in taxes the future gets closer every year.

It is no wonder why the government is coming up with such imaginative ways to levy taxes on our society. The latest being the taking of pictures in our own national parks. Commercial photographers will have to buy a yearly permit at a cost of $1500.00 dollars or face a $1000.00 dollar fine. I wonder what the cost will be for an individual to take pictures of our national parks, oops, I meant the Federal Governments National Parks. In 10 years from now it might cost you $100.00 just to get into our parks.

Again, what is the difference between an extreme right ideology & an extreme left ideology of government? Going to the extreme right means having no form of government which creates anarchy. Going to the extreme left means more government and government control of the people with a ever increasing debt to fund that larger government which collapses financially creating no government and also anarchy. The difference is the money owed ($18.6 Trillion Dollars) to the investors which includes other countries. All under the big government scenario of both parties!

THE LIBERAL'S DISABLED AMERICA

What I am writing about was inspired by a young man at a convenience store I talked to tonight. As I drove up on the side of the store the young man was sitting on the concrete base of a light post. He looked suspicious so I locked my doors upon leaving the car. Returning a couple of minutes later he politely asked if I could spare fifty cents for a gallon of milk which at first I thought was strange. On second thought he could be old enough to have a young family on hard times so I gave him a buck before initiating a conversation. I asked him if he had a baby to justify the buying of the milk he replied "no". I asked him how old he was he stated "nineteen" and I quickly asked him if he graduated high school, he said "yes". I asked him what he was doing in this small town of little opportunity? He stated he was here to see his family. I replied where are you from and he replied "West Texas". I asked aren't there a bunch of jobs out there and he said "yeah, there are a bunch". I then said why would you leave there not having enough money to get back? He replied, "Yeah, I'm waiting on my first Social Security check so I can get back". Now I'm puzzled as to how a 19 year old capable young man gets Social Security so I asked. He replied he was "Paranoid Schizophrenic".

Let's discuss his claims of Paranoid as described in this definition thereof; adj

1. distrustful: obsessively anxious about something, or unreasonably suspicious of other people and their thoughts or motives
2. showing characteristics of paranoia: relating to or showing the characteristics of the psychiatric disorder paranoia

During this encounter with him he never gave a sign of being Paranoid, if anyone had signs of being Paranoid it was me with my suspicions of him on the side of the building. He answered each and every question I asked without suspicion of me or my motives for the questions to his best ability that seemed not to be hindered by any mental disability or disorder. Why would he be where he was "vulnerable" on the side of the building and not out front in the light of the store if that condition truly existed?

Schizophrenic as described in this definition thereof; adj
1. of schizophrenia: relating to or resulting from schizophrenia
2. offensive term: an offensive term meaning characterized by conflicts and contradictions (insult)

Schizophrenia as described in this definition thereof; n
1. psychiatric disorder with symptoms of withdrawal into self: a severe psychiatric disorder with symptoms of emotional instability, detachment from reality, and withdrawal into the self
2. offensive term: an offensive term for a state characterized by contradictory or conflicting attitudes, behavior, or qualities (insult)

Again he had absolutely no signs of emotional instability or a detachment from reality. He never seemed out of his comfort zone during this conversation, he also acknowledged the flaws of his travel plans which showed to me his understanding of reality. That along with the fact of his understanding a government check would get him where he wanted to be was a realistic resolution to his situation. The fact that he initiated the conversation in a very normal and polite way with a tone of assertiveness without any tone of being overbearing implies a normalcy of life. This to me showed he knew how to interact with people and how to use his communication skills to get the results he desired, a little change for milk or beer? Although our drinking age is suppose to be twenty one. So again I didn't detect a withdrawal into himself. If anything his interactions with me demonstrated he had plenty of experience in dealing with others and felt comfortable doing so knowing I did not pose a threat. Ebola could be ramped in this country and I would bet money he would have shook my hand. So nowhere does he fit the description as defined in my mind.

My own personal experiences with even friends have shown the Liberal's agenda to put capable people on the disabilities' payroll. It's amazing how a disabled person can do anything they need done for themselves, putting up a fence, unloading a large generator off the bed of a truck, playing golf, riding motorcycles, rebuilding a camper, etc. These people may not be of liberal thoughts but are using the liberal thoughts of government to achieve a lifestyle free of working a normal job they are physically capable of doing.

Government can't take care of itself much less every person that it may deem as developing a physical or mental problem that might reduce their productivity but not put an end to their productivity. Even having medical stints inserted into a artery can now generate a government disability check. This type of disability system only reduces the funding for the truly disabled that have truly lost their ability to be productive on any scale.

How does a over achieving Quadriplegic hold a job and successfully fulfill the requirements of that job when a single hip replacement recipient stops an individual from returning to the classroom to teach? The answer is desire! The Quadriplegic had their right to a normal life taken away. Accomplishing the most basic aspect of human life allows them a sense of normalcy in society. This allows them to see themselves as a more normal member of society. Something that person perceived themselves to have lost at some point in their life. As for the hip replacement recipient who hasn't lost the normalcy of life or the ability to return to that life. It is that person's desire not too because the demands of a working society are more than their mental capacities allow them to handle. A government check allows the avoidance of the pressures of a working society.

These government checks for a Military (one and a half years of care and rehabilitation, discharged for medical reasons) enlistment shortened because of a car and a later motorcycle accident are unearned. While not on duty during either accident, these accidents caused a two year total time enlistment. His enlistment ended at about age twenty two. He stated to one friend he was actually AWOL from his Military Base when involved in the car accident. Both occupants were drinking and supposedly running from the police when they hit a telephone pole. After the discharge he achieved two college degrees under the G.I. Bill. Before the hip replacement his disability was thirty percent for a monthly $700.00 dollar check. This check wasn't enough to support his needs so the individual continued to work in the private sector. When his hip completely went out he was teaching at a local college while on crutches. Upon the single hip replacement at a age in his mid forties he stated right after the government paid for V.A. surgery "he never felt that good since the accidents". What encouraged this behavior to not return to work is a 100% Military disability check of $2400.00 monthly and a Social Security 100% disability check of $1050.00 monthly. This allows for the person's nightly bar attendance. The $3450.00 monthly non-taxed check is now a unearned early retirement government check. Now the rest of working society must deal with a even greater pressure to pay enough taxes to cover this situation. Now multiply this by every unearned disability check or unearned, undeserved government check of any type.

Jack Nicklaus had his left hip replaced at fifty nine years old and just 10 months later returned to the Senior PGA Tour to play Professional Golf. His desire and love of the game and the people that surround the game was his driving force to a even earlier than expected return. To this day he continues to be a productive member of society. The Golfing World continues to enjoy his Golf Course Design Construction Company with its finished courses along with his other endeavors within the Golfing World.

What is the difference between the two? The first loves himself beyond anyone or anything else. The second puts others before himself along with the things that made him who he is. He sees these things as bigger, more important than himself. Which one do you believe is happier with their lives? Is it the money that created the happiness or was the money just a byproduct of doing something he loved which also benefited society?

You might think the individual would donate some of his time at the V.A. for the veterans who were truly hurt in the service of their country while also defending his freedom. But no, because he has no ties to the V.A. or the Military or what other Servicemen might call "Brothers" beyond what is given to him by them. Yet he quotes his Military service as honorable because he signed his "name" on a contract, while never fulfilling that contract. His stories of "The Red Phone" that connected him to the "President" or "The Paper" he wrote that caused the "President" to bomb the Libyan Leaders Palace. So what he takes from all the Injured or Killed in Action Soldiers of any War, beyond their money is their Valor which he has now Stolen to advance his own self perceived image in society. Also being 100% disabled he routinely mentions his "Rock Star" status of playing in a band that plays only "hole in the wall" bars. If this is true is he truly DISABLED while drawing TWO DISABILITY CHECKS? Is the cash income reported or is he again just lying? Or is he just another problem in and of our Society itself?

LIBERAL IDEOLOGY VS. CONSERVATIVE IDEOLOGY

When joining a political party there are no qualifications to be a member of either party. A liberal can be a Republican and a conservative can be a Democrat, it's a choice that no person, group or government may make for you just like freedom of religion. How that choice is made is the political argument within yourself with possible outside influences such as parents, family, friends, the teachings by others expressing their beliefs on you, etc.

The main thoughts of the Liberal Left Democrats are larger government, complete government control which creates more confusion and ineffective government, more taxes, no religion, no choices unless allowed by government, less freedoms by design.

The main thoughts of the Conservative Right Republicans are smaller government, less government control creating less confusion and effective government, less taxes, choices in regards to religion, all choices are yours unless disallowed by reasonable laws, more freedoms for all by design.

Would you rather have a smaller government that everything it touches works as designed or a larger government that everything it touches fails as designed? With a failed government policy comes confusion and ineffectiveness of government. More government equals more taxes, less government equals less taxes. More government involvement (regulations) equals more taxes, less government involvement (regulations) equals less taxes. Now which one offers more freedoms for the people?

When the Liberal Left protest, things get destroyed and innocent people get killed but the Liberal Left always see them as heroes such as Occupy Wall Street with multiple rapes committed. This type of protest has progressed into more violent RADICAL protests (RULES FOR RADICALS) always backed by the Liberal Left. It isn't until the protests cross a line the Liberal Left helped pushed them over that they deny all wrong doing. Again the Liberal left not accepting responsibilities for their words or actions.

When our Conservative Right parents, grandparents or anyone attending a Tea Party Rally is deemed by this same Liberal Left as Crazy, Radical and Destructive is like a childhood exchange of words between two 6 year old's on a playground. How crazy, radical and destructive is paying for a permit and picking up your trash after the event is over? I sure don't want to meet a Conservative Grandma in a dark alley, could be curtains for me!

The Liberal Left always expect change to be achieved through violence, it starts non-violent but overtime always ends with violence. "What do you want?" "Dead Cops" "when do you want it?" "Now". The Liberal Left got what they wanted, two innocent Police Officers assassinated in New York City.

Liberalism comes around about every 45 years but once tasted is rejected each and every time. It comes in like a lamb and leaves with the violence of a lion. It is pushed back by Conservative thoughts and this change is brought on totally violence free. So how is it Liberalism only function's off violence and again recedes into history while Conservatism always in a non-violent movement pushes Liberalism again into history. Is it the FACT that most Liberal ideas come from the childish thoughts of an unattainable perfect society? Only a better society is attainable, a perfect society will never be reached. The reason being the portion of society that wants liberal socialism will not participate in its cost to obtain it. Its cost to them must be free of any type of investment so it must be given to them. The closest to a perfect society is a working society. Yet the foot print of Liberalism remains in our society and government through the Liberal policies that continually remain in place long after the movement has receded. Our National Debt didn't get to $18 Trillion with Conservative thoughts and policies. The Progressive Moderate Republicans along with Democrats have allowed the many Liberal Left policies to remain within our government which is what has created the "Tea Party" movement. The Tea Party's sole purpose is to force a true Republican Conservative Ideology onto the Republican Party. This Conservative Ideology in my belief is from more of a financial point and effective government point of view than a social laws point of view for our Nation.

Liberals are just like the child with the new bike that makes sure the other kids on the block know his bike is the best not knowing or taking into account it's an inferior knockoff. The Marijuana issue is the perfect example of the new bike and showing it off to everybody in the town square with public smoke ins that now have created a push back of public opinion and rightfully so. It doesn't need to be in the public domain of under age citizens, period! A more Conservative approach would do the movement itself a ton of good instead of over excessive celebration causing a penalty flag to be thrown causing a self inflicted penalty. The words best used to describe what are needed are "reasonable, responsible and thoughtful". These words unfortunately are not part of the Liberal Left Democrat's vocabulary or actions. The fact that the child's bike is a cheap knockoff is the perfect example of Obamacare aka the Affordable Care Act which was passed without the input or votes of a single Republican in either Legislative Branch of our government. A new perfect bike a new perfect law. Each touted as the most perfect product ever produced. When problems evolve with each they are deemed as minor and can be over looked because as a whole they are great. As the same problems persist and new ones come to life Liberals begin to admit that a few correctable problems may exist in the product but still make no fixes. With the bike not being fully tested or Obamacare not fully implemented because of the effects it may have on the next national vote. The Liberal takes that problem plagued bike to Dead Man's Hill. Making that ultimate test of the bike the rear wheel comes off at 50 mph sending that Liberal to the pavement enduring the wounds that create life long scars. With Obamacare Barack Obama continually stated there was nothing wrong with that rear wheel, "If you like your health insurance you can keep your health insurance, period"! and "If you like you're Doctor you can keep your Doctor, period"! Once on Dead Man's Hill at half speed, 50% of implementation, the wheels come off (losing insurance and doctor) Obamacare and throws its rider to the pavement enduring the wounds that create life long scars.

The difference between these two scenarios is that the Liberal assumed the responsibility of the test ride while the American citizens are assuming the responsibility of Obamacare. The nasty truth of liberalism is that others assume the responsibility for what Liberals bring to the table. Others have to eat it while the liberal sneaks off not accepting the criticism for the taste of the dish. Also skipping out on the responsibility that it made many citizens sick with no true healthcare system to turn too.

Liberal Left Democrats again have no problem not answering for the problems they created. They also have no problem allowing others to accept the blame that should be placed squarely on the shoulders of the Democrat Party. They also have no problem accepting credit for something they had nothing to do with or actually opposed. The falling oil & fuel prices of late 2015 created a problem for Russia. Its main export is oil thus with the falling price Russia's Ruble went into free fall. Barack Obama points to the sanctions brought upon Russia for invading the Eastern Ukraine as what caused the down turn of the ruble. But it is the falling oil prices not Barack's sanctions that are the culprit in this situation. In actuality the falling oil prices also hurts Barack Obama's Agenda for Green Energy and its movement forward. Barack never authorized the Keystone pipeline because it might lead to lower oil and gas prices also hurting that same Agenda. So Barack's own claims too anything going on with oil and fuel prices in regards to Russia's economy is nothing more than another opportunistic lie of the Liberal Left Democrat Party. Trust me, Barack would have rather seen oil prices still going up allowing him one more reason to push his Democrat Party's Agenda of Green Energy. When given rotten tomatoes make rotten tomato paste and feed it to the unaware public. There is never a new low only a lower new low to go to for Liberal Left Democrats who have lied, denied and camouflaged history by attempting to rewrite history. Democrats truly don't like religion or the thought of a God because they see themselves as God in the only religion that matters to them being the control of total power of Government. God save the Liberal Left Democrat's Souls. As rock-n-roller's Bill and Hillary Clinton sing "Get your money for Nothing and your Chicks for Free".

LEFT, RIGHT; EXTREMES AND THE ECONOMY

The liberal left for the past number of decades have branded the Republican Party as war mongers. Just to set the record straight World War I began July 28th, 1914 and ended November 11th, 1918. What is believed to have brought America into the war was the sinking of the British ocean liner "RMS Lusitania" on May 7, 1915 which carried 128 Americans. The Germans claimed it was carrying war supplies to Europe. Later reports indicated this was true, even though the United States originally denied the claim. So the government being in charge of war supplies and in charge of what, when, where and how these supplies were shipped put war supplies on a passenger cruise liner bound for England. This done during a war with a enemy submarine fleet trying to enforce a embargo of England. Also this was done after a agreement of governments, Germany & U.S., not to target passenger ships because our government guaranteed war supplies would not be shipped in this method. Yet our government lied and did subvert that agreement. Now who is responsible for the deaths of these people on that cruise liner? Our government or Germany's? It wasn't until a number of American supply ships were sunk, two years after the sinking of the Lusitania that the U.S. entered the war on April 6th, 1917. The U.S. President from March 4th, 1913 to March 4th, 1921 was Woodrow Wilson a Democrat.

World War II began in 1939 on the European Continent but the U.S. entered the war on December 7th, 1941 with the Japanese attack on Pearl Harbor in Hawaii. This attack was lead by a large fleet sailing from the mainland of Japan not unknown to U.S. Intelligence. U.S. Intelligence was already in high gear after Japan had invaded Manchuria in 1931 and then China in 1937. Also the U.S. Government had enacted an oil embargo in July of 1941. I also believe a reduction of steel shipments was also enacted earlier. These embargoes were designed to limit the war capabilities of Japan. The U.S. had two main territories in the Pacific Ocean one being Hawaii and the other being the Philippine Islands of Asia which was acquired along with Cuba, Puerto Rico & Guam from Spain in the Spanish-American war. So the U.S. presence in Asia was already seen as a threat to the region by Japan. Hawaii is a strategic point militarily for the U.S. in the Pacific Ocean especially to supply a military force in Asia. Japan and the U.S. both knew this fact. Now a territory doesn't necessarily have to become a State of America and America doesn't necessarily have to make a territory a State and on December 7th, 1941 Hawaii was a territory. The strategic placement of the Hawaiian Islands made it imperative for this territory to become a State. The immediate attack notice on Pearl Harbor was not sent to the Commanders of the base until an hour after the attack even though our government knew Japan's fleet had sailed east from Japan. So now my question is was the attack on the Hawaiian Islands a repeat of history by our government as was done in World War I? With the results being, 1) the entering of the U.S. into World War II, 2) an even greater presence of America in the Hawaiian Islands and 3) the attack illustrated to the indigenous population how vulnerable the Hawaiian Islands were even with the presence of the United States. But this fact would not have been driven home to the indigenous people if the battle had of taken place 300 miles northwest in the Pacific Ocean out of their sight. So was the attack on Pearl Harbor also a scare tactic to drive the Hawaiian Islands towards Statehood which happened in 1959? If this scenario has any plausibility did our government sacrifice almost 3,000 military lives for the chance to have Hawaii as our 50th State? The war ended for the U.S. on September 2nd, 1945 with Japan's surrender. The U.S. President from March 4th, 1933 to April 12th, 1945 was Franklin D. Roosevelt a Democrat with Harry S. Truman also a Democrat using two atomic bombs on the Japanese cities of Hiroshima and Nagasaki to end the war. With the defeat of the Japanese navy could a U.S. Naval embargo of the Japanese Islands along with air assaults have brought the war to an end with Japan? Or were the results of the two Atomic bombings more a necessity than what was necessary? Was it another Democrat atrocity? If it can be seen as a American atrocity then it can surely be seen as a atrocity committed by a Democrat President's decision.

The Korean War began on June 25th, 1950 and ended July 27th, 1953. This war was viewed as a Cold Era War involving the U.S. on one side and Russia and China on the other side. The President from April 12th, 1945 to January 20th, 1953 was Harry S. Truman a Democrat. The war actually ended 6 months later under the Republican Presidency of Dwight D. Eisenhower who held the office from January 20th, 1953 to January 20th, 1961.

The Bay of Pigs invasion of Cuba involved a U.S. - C.I.A. trained revolutionary force. The plan evolved under President Dwight D. Eisenhower, a Republican, but the plan was taken over by the next President. The invasion launched from Guatemala on April 13th, 1961 and on April 20th the invading force surrendered in failure. This may have also contributed to the following Cuban Missile Crisis of 1962 which the U.S. used a naval blockade to stop Russian ships from entering a Cuban port. The President was John F. Kennedy from January 20th, 1961 to November 22nd, 1963 a Democrat.

The Vietnam War also seen as a Cold Era War involving the same participants just a different country. The war began November 1st, 1955 but an American presence was there as early as 1950 with U.S. Advisers. The war escalated in 1961 and 1962 with the tripling of soldiers in each year and 3, 500 Marines were deployed on March 8th, 1965, to protect the U.S. Air Force bases and the ground war had begun. The war peaked in 1968 and ended for the U.S. on January 15th, 1973 with the suspension of offensive actions against North Vietnam. This war encompasses five Presidencies being Harry S. Truman (D), Dwight D. Eisenhower (R), John F. Kennedy (D), Lyndon B. Johnson was a Democrat President from November 22nd, 1963 to January 20th, 1969 and ending under Richard M. Nixon's Republican administration from January 20th, 1969 to August 9th, 1974.

The invasion of Granada began on October 25th, 1983 was a counter movement to a Soviet/Cuban backed military coup. The invasion lasted a few weeks returning the country to an elected Constitutional government. The President of this time, January 20th, 1981 to January 20th, 1989, was Ronald Reagan a Republican.

The Panama Invasion occurred from December 20th, 1989 to January 31st, 1990. It arose from a free election being deemed null and void with a dictator, Manuel Noriega, appointing himself the d-fact-o leader. The main reason for American intervention was the treaty involving the Panama Canal. The invasion restored the President elect to office. The President was Republican George H. W. Bush from 1989 to 1993.

The Persian Gulf War began August 2nd, 1990 and ended February 28th, 1991. It was created by Iraq invading Kuwait. U.S. and Coalition forces drove Iraq forces back to Bagdad in about 100 hours of military action. The United Nations Security Council Resolution 687 passed in April 1991 established formal cease-fire terms. The President was George H. W. Bush (R) from January 20th, 1989 to 1993.

The intervention in Bosnia and Herzegovina by NATO began February 1992 and ended November 1995. NATO supplied mostly U.S. air cover issuing a no fly zone for most of the conflict but did consist of U.N. Peace keepers on the ground. The President under this conflict was Bill Clinton (D) from January 20th, 1993 to 2001.

The War on Terrorism in Afghanistan began on October 7th, 2001 following the 9/11/2001 attacks on the twin towers in N.Y. City. The reason for the invasion was the terrorists training camps that trained some of the terrorists. The war was supported by the U.S. Congress and the nation of Great Britain. The terrorists credited for the attacks entered the U.S. through legal immigration methods allowed by Dept. of Immigration under the previous President being Bill Clinton (D). The President at the time of the attacks was 9 months into his 1st term. He was George W. Bush (R) January 20th, 2001 to 2009. The war continues today under the current President Barack Hussein Obama II (D) January 20th, 2009 to current date.

The Iraq war began on March 20th, 2003 under George W. Bush (R) and was justified under two main reasons. In 2002, the United Nations Security Council passed Resolution 1441 which called for Iraq to completely cooperate with UN weapon inspectors to verify that Iraq was not in possession of WMD and cruise missiles among a list of topics also included in Resolution 687. The dictator, Saddam Hussein, of Iraq had not met the terms of the United Nations Security Council Resolution 687 from the Gulf War. Saddam also did not meet the terms of Resolution 1441 by still denying U.N. inspectors free access. On December 15th, 2011 the U.S. official involvement came to an end under Barack Obama but the conflict has again erupted to destabilize the country.

Here is my problem with the liberal left and their attempt to constantly rewrite history on many different subjects to excuse themselves of any responsibility. From the information above, anyone can see that the Republican Party is no more a war monger than the Democrat Party is peaceful. I will not pick either side as good or bad because I agree with what was done by both sides, maybe sometimes not how it was done. The one thing learned by extended wars are the public will lose their support of a war lasting longer than about 4 years. A liberal left will not agree with any type of Republican aggression even if in self defense because they will not defend a Republican on any topic. Everything is political and everything is on the table to use as a weapon even if they endorsed it at the time of the decision. Politics overrules right or wrong, people being free of an oppressive government or oppressed by the same government is a right and wrong issue not a political issue. They have constantly used the "WMD's" excuse being "there were no weapons of mass destruction" cited by a U.S. led survey group that said only degraded remnants of misplaced and abandoned chemical weapons were found to constantly smear George W. Bush for being a Republican. Only a liberal left Democrat can excuse the fact that Iraq had used chemical weapons between 1983 and 1991 fifteen times killing over 40,000 people mostly Iranians & Kurds. Iraq made 5 chemical weapon attacks in 1988 alone. Now I will insert a news article from earlier this year, 2014.

MOSCOW, July 9 (RIA Novosti) – Iraqi authorities warn UN that militants from The Islamic State of Iraq and Greater Syria (ISIS) seized a former chemical weapons storage in the province of Muthanna, AP reported Wednesday.

According to the news agency, back on June 11, 2014 the militants took over the facility where over 2.5 thousand chemical rockets and warfare agents (chemical) were stored.

When the U.N. passes a Resolution to have weapons inspectors inspect a countries sovereign territory there is a reason and a purpose. Not achieving the purpose causes exactly what is happening within Iran today with a rogue nation going against U.N. sanctions to develop a nuclear bomb which puts the whole world at risk.

Now lets move on to the National Debt. Again only a liberal can run for office smearing G.W. Bush for his administration's spending then have his own administration almost double that amount and then have the nerve to come out on February 21st, 2014; Barack Obama said "the age of austerity is over". In my 54 years of life under the flag of this Nation we have never had an "age of austerity". So it was another Political lie.

On November 22, 1963 our National debt was $308.5 Billion. On September 5th, 2012 our debt hit $16 Trillion Dollars. The breakdown of the spending over this time period is this. Democrats have held the office of President for 24 years, Republicans 28 years, Democrats have spent $7.674 Trillion during that 24 years, Republicans $8.447 Trillion over 28 years, that averages out to $319.75 Billion for Democrats and $301.67 Billion for Republicans of yearly deficit added to the National debt for each party's years in office. There really isn't that much of a difference, about 6.5%, considering the amounts except for the failed social programs through the decades of the Democrats with a estimated cost of $22 trillion dollars that some part of this total is contained in every President's budget from the point the programs were enacted. The cost of the wars that both parties were involved in total, add them up it's not near $22 trillion. The numbers offered below have the actual dollar amount and the inflation calculated dollar amount. An additional $1.7 Trillion and additional two years can be added to these figures under the Democrats for Barack Obama's second term. Also any deficit reduction under Barack's term can't be attributed to either party because neither party expected the sequestered budget to kick in because both sides expected to pass a budget. For anyone who wants to bring up Bill Clinton's two terms lets talk about them. His first term with a Democrat Congress of his party had a debt of $1.122 Trillion. His second term with a Republican Congress being his political opposition his debt was $418 Billion. Bill has no problem taking the credit for something that was forced upon him by Newt Gingrich and the Republican Party. As for either side's claim of a balance budget even $418 Billion is $418 Billion short of a balanced budget. So the conclusion is we as a Nation have never had "an age of austerity" since the first deficit year sometime way, way before 1963. As a Nation we have not had a balanced budget in at least the last 70 years plus. Both political parties have done a dismal job of managing this country's debt. You can't expand government and not expand the deficit and the debt.

Congressional Research Service Report for Congress (RS22926)
Military Costs of Major U.S. Wars
(Updated to Include Appropriations Enacted Through June 30, 2008)

	Years of War Spending	Peak Year of War Spending	
	Total Military Cost of War in Millions/Billions/Trillions of Dollars	War Cost % GDP in Peak Year of War	Total Defense % GDP in Peak Year of War
American Revolution	1775-1783		
Current Year $	101 million	NA	NA
Constant FY2008$	1.825 billion		
War of 1812	1812-1815		1813
Current Year $	90 million	2.2%	2.7%
Constant FY2008$	1.177 billion		
Mexican War	1846-1849		1847
Current Year $	71 million	1.4%	1.9%
Constant FY2008$	1.801 billion		
Civil War: Union	1861-1865		1865
Current Year $	3.183 billion	11.3%	11.7%
Constant FY2008$	45.199 billion		
Civil War: Confederacy	1861-1865		
Current Year $	1.000 billion	NA	NA
Constant FY2008$	15.244 billion		
Spanish American War	1898-1899		1899
Current Year $	283 million	1.1%	1.5%
Constant FY2008$	6.848 billion		
World War I	1917-1921		1919
Current Year $	20.000 billion	13.6%	14.1%
Constant FY2008$	253.000 billion		

	Years of War Spending	Peak Year of War Spending	
	Total Military Cost of War in Millions/Billions/Trillions of Dollars	War Cost % GDP in Peak Year of War	Total Defense % GDP in Peak Year of War
World War II	1941-1945		1945
Current Year $	296.000 billion	35.8%	37.5%
Constant FY2008$	4.114 trillion		
Korea	1950-1953		1952
Current Year $	30.000 billion	4.2%	13.2%
Constant FY2008$	320.000 billion		
Vietnam	1965-1975		1968
Current Year $	111.000 billion	2.3%	9.5%
Constant FY2008$	686.000 billion		
Persian Gulf War /a/	1990-1991		1991
Current Year $	61.000 billion	0.3%	4.6%
Constant FY2008$	96.000 billion		
Iraq /b/	2003-2008		2008
Current Year $	616.000 billion	1.0%	4.2%
Constant FY2008$	648.000 billion		
Afghanistan/GWOT /b,c/	2001-2008		2007
Current Year $	159.000 billion	0.3%	4.0%
Constant FY2008$	171.000 billion		
Post-9/11 Domestic Security (Operation Noble Eagle) /b/	2001-2008		2003
Current Year $	28.000 billion	0.1%	3.7%
Constant FY2008$	33.000 billion		
Total Post-9/11--Iraq, Afghanistan/GWOT, ONE /d/	2001-2008		2008
Current Year $	809.000 billion	1.2%	4.2%
Constant FY2008$	859.000 billion		

From the above chart our Nation has spent $7,252,104,000,000.00, (7 trillion, 252 billion, 104 million) calculated with inflation figured in at 2008 rates, on all the wars since the forming of our Nation.

How is it as a Nation being only 228 years old and for the first 143 years or so its citizens managed without handouts of government? But in the last eighty five years and more like the last fifty five years our Nation has spent $22 trillion dollars on welfare for some of the people. If that money had never been spent our Nation would be $4 trillion to the good not having a debt. What results do we have to show for that $22 Trillion dollars? Every social program our Nation has is failing, plain an simple. Are we going to keep feeding each and everyone of them without attempting to improve any of them until our Nation goes broke? It might be Barack Obama's Father's Dreams but that was not the Dreams of our Founding Fathers.

There is a philosophy that drives each political party. Liberal democrats want; bigger government, more social programs, higher taxes which results in more government control of the people. Conservative Republicans want smaller government, result proven social programs, lower taxes creating a vibrant job market, which results in less government and less control of the people.

Every time government is expanded it increases the cost of government. Democrat's could create an agency that oversaw the welfare of the last animal of a species and when it died the agency would never go away. The main reason government can't be reduced in size is that once someone lands a high paying, great healthcare and sick leave, great vacation time, great holidays, great retirement, great working conditions, some positions with great bonuses and some positions don't even have to meet job demand or have any job demands are all protected by government. How can government reduce its size when government protects these jobs without ensuring a return of services by the people employed? Some government jobs are no more than government welfare just with better pay and benefits. If government tries to reduce its work force, unless it's the military, the only way it can be done is the position is not replaced after the person dies, retires or seldom quits. Before this happens a new administration comes in and it's back to the same old situation. So government never gets reduced. The only reduction that can be achieved is in the military because this part of government doesn't have the same protections as the civilian part of government. The Republican Party has never realized this while the Democrat Party has used it to their advantage to drive their agenda's, bigger government being just one.

Using this same method all social programs are expanded in the name of the poor people. Government is expanded with additional people to manage the programs. Even if a social program is deemed inefficient, ineffective or corrupt with fraud it isn't changed or done away. Democrats use the phrase "to balance the budget on the backs of the poor" to demonize Republicans when trying to do so. Using this method how can anything ever change? It won't and our debt will continue to grow because of a lack of checks and balances.

With a rising deficit and debt, without an avenue to reduce government thus reducing the cost of government the only way to try to pay for it is to raise taxes which is the path Democrats prefer. Tax the working to pay for the nonworking or poor, sometime they are one and the same because of their choices. The plan becomes higher taxes on corporations, larger businesses, smaller businesses, richer people, higher income working individuals, upper middle class, middle class and lower earning middle class. As some corporations and larger businesses are driven out of the country due to constantly rising taxes. Higher paying jobs are lost meaning more unemployed or underemployed and a drop of income. Some go out of business because they lack the revenue or size to leave. Others close because their product may not be transportable and they can no longer compete due to overhead. These situations all add to jobs lost. This pattern repeats itself until there is nothing or very little left. Each time these scenarios happen the people become more reliant on government for a hand out because there are no jobs left for a hand up.

With the loss of jobs and more people being thrown into the job market this causes wages to fall. Add in the illegal immigrants competing for existing jobs and that drives wages down further. My example; if an employer has 10 job openings and 300 people apply the employee can pay less because of the competition for the jobs, this is especially true for unskilled labor. If the employer has 10 job openings and 3 people apply with 2 saying they were offered more money down the street, what does the employer have to do? Advertise more money to fill the positions.

Democrats want to raise the Federal minimum wage to $15.00/hr. because of what I have described above to correct a problem they are creating. When an individual at a fast food business takes your $10 bill for a $5.63 order and rings it up, then you give them .13 cents and they can't count out your change, are their skills really suited for that job or deserve a $15.00/hr. minimum wage? Minimum wage is designed for unskilled labor, kids right out of high school and probably still living at home. An individual has to have a skill that is in demand to justify any additional money paid for their labor and knowledge. Each time the minimum wage is raised it pushes unskilled labor out of the market making it impossible for them to get any experience to acquire a better job with better pay. Also a $15.00/hr. minimum wage in New York City is not the same as a $15.00/hr. minimum wage in Pensacola, Florida. So a National minimum wage doesn't work on a National Level. I heard a liberal Democrat make a sarcastic statement "so we should do away with the minimum wage" when replying to a Republican statement of "so why not raise the minimum wage to $30.00/hr." I wish it had been me she directed that remark to because I would of said "Yes". That would allow more unskilled people into a work force they can't get into, it would allow them to learn skills they didn't have before. Allowing them the opportunity to move up the ladder instead of watching others from the sideline. What about the added people and a decreased wage? First the illegal immigrates would leave because of the competition for the lower paying jobs. Second, I would rather give assistance to someone who is working their way up the ladder than someone sitting on the couch at home waiting on a government check. Third, an employer didn't get to where they are by being stupid. An employer hires for a certain skill set and knows there is a cost to hiring that skill set they want or need. If anybody could do the job it would be a minimum wage job. If the employee makes the employer's investment in him a lucrative situation, not at the expense of the employer's customers, then he will be rewarded with higher pay. If the employer chooses not to pay more then he risks losing this employee to his competitor because the employee has attained a skill valued by other employers. Also, while working, school is never a bad choice if you are truly willing to commit yourself to both tasks. Just remember this, nobody and I mean nobody works for nothing for a living. On the other side of the coin nobody should make a better living for a lack of achievement or for a lesser quality of work they offer than the job requires.

As for jobs to put people to work, the government and the people can't vilify the rich for being rich. Most of the rich were not rich at some point in their lives. Alexander Graham Bell made his family a fortune with the invention of the telephone. Thomas Edison holds 1,093 patents in this country alone. Mark Zuckerberg with four other co-founders invented Facebook and is worth Twenty Five Billion Dollars himself today. Do any of these people not deserve the money they have earned through their work, their ideas and inventions that have made your lives better not including the people who may work for these companies? Don't forget that taxes are paid on all that money three different times, the company pays taxes, the individual pays taxes and the inheritance tax is 50% of a estate over One Million Dollars when that family member dies. How much more does government deserve?

Once getting past this money for a "no achievement attitude" which includes our lack of achievement government we can understand what it takes to create jobs. Over taxing the people that create jobs just causes fewer jobs and collects less revenue. If the tax rate is 0% then the revenue collected is Zero. If the tax rate is 100% the revenue collected is also Zero. Remember nobody works for nothing that also includes the job creators, being People with money or a idea or both. Have ever in your lifetime you been hired by somebody with less money than you for a full time job? Government making it harder or more expensive to start a new business reduces the number of new businesses and new jobs. So quit and start making it easier to establish a new business allowing it to grow.

The Laffer Curve shows that there is point in the Federal tax rate code that generates the most revenue because that point achieves a balance between taxes collected and private money needed for capital investment which allows for job creation. That point may vary between twenty and twenty four percent. Doing away with the tax deductions which skews the tax rates allowing bigger more profitable companies to pay less we now have a tax code that will generate the most economic growth possible. With economic growth comes jobs, with jobs comes a competition for employees, and with a competition for employees comes higher wages. This is not something new to economics. Government has a habit of doing things that are used to push an agenda which never turns out to be a good thing for society as a whole. An agenda is aimed at a certain portion of society to help but normally it actually ends up hurting more than helping. Sometimes a agenda is also used to enrich the people pushing the agenda!

The extreme far left and the extreme far right ideologies share a portion of space on the ideology chart. The extreme far right under their ideology would not have any form of government. In the other direction the extreme far left will spend government into oblivion creating a collapsed government which then is no government. One stage of the Liberal Far Left government before the collapse of government is a government with total control. An elitist few or a dictator making all the decisions. The only difference between the two situations is that one situation has no government so it creates no government debt. The extreme left leaves you with no government and a huge government debt with people looking for $18 Trillion plus of their money back. Where on the ideology chart in regards to debt do you believe we as a Nation are located, the left or the right? Where on the left / right chart do you believe the size of our government is in relationship to size and effectiveness. A bloated government of the Liberal Left or a reduced government on the right of center ideology being Republicans?

There are three stages of debt; the beginning, the middle and the end. The beginning is that first time you leave a balance on your account. The middle is the point you see the problem, make a choice to correct the problem and start paying your account down. There are two types of endings to the one "end" which is when you pay your account off. The second is you failed to see the problem when in the middle stage or ignored the problem until you started missing payments. Now because you no longer have available credit people come for their money or your (their) property. If our country's money is worthless then what option have we left them? What part of America do you think they will want? Will they settle for a part?

I truly don't see a way out of our debt. Even if we grow our economy increasing our gross domestic product that extra money will never be spent to lower our debt. Our population will not allow it, too many hands in the till. Some use the economy after WWII as an example of our debt being at a 100% of our GDP. The difference is we had in place a manufacturing system while the rest of the industrialized world's manufacturing system had been destroyed. A distinct advantage that is not so today.

The last bit of info I offer here is people pick political parties for many different reasons, rarely are all the beliefs within a party follow the party line. So when joining a political party a person may not even agree with the fundamental beliefs of a party. That's why we have had spin offs such as Liberal Left Democrats and Conservative Right Republicans. The one thing that is consistent is the liberal left is not defined by boundaries to accomplish something because of their low moral belief system. As where the conservatives are confined to the boundaries through their belief system. Why do you think the left demonizes the right when they actually follow the lead of the left in doing the same thing? It's hard to win a boxing match when you are constantly hit below the belt and when returned in favor the other wants you Disqualified. In a boxing match a referee calls the fight fairly as to what is right or wrong. In Politics the people are the referees but they don't call the fight fairly as in what is right or wrong. A call is based on politics as to which party they are registered with. To fight a dirty opponent sometimes you may have to stoop to their levels or otherwise you lose. This thought is constantly used against Republicans to shame them into not using the same tactics being used against them by Democrats. Because then you would have a more even fight.

During the 2012 election I had a bet that all the liberal mediators could not get through the debates without one liberal mediator injecting themselves into the debate. Candy Crowley of CNN news proved me correct! She sided with Barack on the subject of Benghazi and whether Barack called the attack a terrorist action or a spontaneous reaction to a video. The liberal Candy by injecting herself into the debate altered the debate which was not her job but was her purpose when she did it. A punch below the belt. Where were the Referees? My bet was with a liberal, he said that was OK and didn't honor the bet. Could you really expect anything different?

Although I have to admit the organizational skills of the far left is amazing at times. Regardless of the moralities of how they did it such as paying people to protest at McDonald's that don't even work in fast food or even have a job. The morality of this is very questionable if not a underhanded action of the labor unions backed by Liberal Left Democrats.

LIBERAL CREATIVITY

Creativity is essential to many aspects of society. Many professions require a creative mind to be successful in what they do. For a painter of natural nature very little imagination is needed except for the possible creative techniques used to get the look that helps bring that natural nature to the painter's canvas. A abstract painter may not use any creative technique to create their abstract painting because the abstract is the painting itself not the technique. A imagination of thoughts is what is needed to create a image that doesn't exist in reality.

This concept extends along all lines of creative products that surround us in our daily lives and at points may crossover from one into the other. Lets make the painter of nature a conservative and the abstract painter a liberal. Keep in mind this is not a rule because as I stated one may crossover into the other. The music business is another example, what is the most liberal types of today's music and do the artists tend to be liberal? What is the most conservative form of today's music and do the artists tend to be conservative? How about writer of science fiction and fiction both being based on fictional thoughts and non-fiction being based on facts?

As I stated one may do one of these things but not be able to crossover to do the other. One needs to enter a world of non-reality to reach the abstract thoughts to accomplish their profession and then the other doesn't because their profession doesn't deal in abstract thoughts but of those of reality. So when crossing over do all, most, a few or none ever cross back from abstract thought to the actual realities of the world. A actor or actress may refer to doing a movie as the same thing as going into a real war? Obviously they are not the same thing, not even close. One is non-reality and the other can be a life ending reality. With one, if you die it was by accident. With the other, if you die it was on purpose! It was the opposition's purpose to kill you! With enough money one may be able to create and live in a non-factual world. One of which they see themselves as always right and feel that the world would be alright if others only lived in the same fictitious world. This is the bases for the liberal left's ideology to embrace Socialism. If the poor were only allowed to live in my world.

When you are making tens of millions of dollars yearly it might be easy to get lost from reality. The world your money creates for you may be so different from blue or white collar working families. Why does some child stars find it so hard after that stardom to return to a average world when the stardom ends? Never being able to return to that way of life and never adjusting to a normal average life.

The liberal left of the academic world pushed Obama's Obamacare legislation written by Jonathan Gruber of MIT, Massachusetts Institute of Technology. They believed it was exactly what the people of our country needed. Gruber stated it would be the stupidity of the public that would allow for the passing of this taxing healthcare law. Once in place and implemented the liberal left academic world saw their own healthcare rates going up and then started to reject the law by wanting a waiver from the law. Now doesn't this actually bring the subject of the liberal left's, of the academic world's own intelligence into question? And if so, doesn't it make them also the subject of this chapter of my book? They created something never believing it would apply to their selves, so are they actually living in a life of reality.

My point is when dealing with reality only the facts of reality are the true facts. Any facts related to a non-existent reality are truly non-existent facts attached to a world that doesn't and never will exist no matter how hard you imagine it such as Socialism.

Everyone has heard the saying "which came first the chicken or the egg"? Some may not realize there is a deeper meaning to the question being if you can answer the question you can also answer the question of how life began on this planet. So it is a philosophical question that has a deeper meaning. How about the saying "If a tree falls in the forest and your not there to hear it does it make a sound?" is also a philosophical question. The difference between the two is one is a truly a philosophical question while the other is a shallow question because the answer is obviously yes, it does make a noise regardless of where you are at the time. If you have never experienced or seen a tornado does that mean it doesn't exist?

The liberal left are trying to use such sayings as "you didn't build that" when addressing businesses and the taxes they pay. But the two, who built the business and the taxes they pay, are completely separate of each other. There were businesses in this land long before there was a U.S. Government taxing them. Our government had no problem with the billions of dollars of taxes it collected off of cigarettes until they were linked with citizens health. Now cigarettes are taxed with a government "we want you out of business" sin tax that is only paid by the purchaser not the cigarette companies. Our government determines the tax rate and what deductions are allowed by each corporation, big business, small business and every individual that earns a income. So if the problem exists it is a problem that government itself has created and controlled from day one. So why is it the liberal left say "you didn't build that business" when they did while paying taxes doing it. Now if the product they are selling to the public is not faulty why is government wanting to tax them with a much higher sin tax table? The liberal left must see businesses as sinful. The true fact is the People's tax money built government and all of Washington D.C. and much of the surrounding area including each and every house of the Federal employees. It is our tax money that paid for everything including those homes. This is the same type of liberal statement because those peoples homes were paid for by the work they did under a agreement with our government. Isn't that what business did, so the liberal left is using the "you didn't build that" to vilify all businesses for political gain by dividing the people. Business owners vs. the people that don't own a business. A fair tax rate with fair deductions and a responsible government is all that is needed. Once the tax rate and deductions are changed to a easier system where the 1040EZ tax form is actually easy will make our government responsible with each and every dollar spent? No, because government spending was never addressed. Until it is, government will always want more money because the only way the money consuming beast continues to live is with more money.

Have you heard "Businesses don't create jobs"? That is a liberal left new saying to combat the saying "government doesn't create jobs" which are both wrong. Government does create jobs, each time government expands government it creates jobs and if government expanded to paying for all jobs that is Socialism. If businesses didn't create jobs there would be no jobs because government would go broke with its own inefficiency. Some people say demand for something creates jobs and without demand you can't create jobs. I say really. Has anyone ever bought a single rock? Is there a demand that I can sell you a single rock? Yet there was one man who made a small fortune selling PET ROCKS! Imagine a business that creates its own demand, Facebook, all sports, a "book" alone, my "book", a kite, etc. There are products invented everyday that are not seen to be in demand until the invention itself created the demand because the invention offered something that wasn't there before. If the pet rock had never been a "invention" would you miss it? How about Facebook? You can't miss something that you never knew existed! So it is the invention that creates the demand. It is only a copy or a modification of a previous invention that needs a demand such as a land line telephone that transformed into a cell phone. I don't miss cell phones, never had one, I had no demand for it, same with Facebook but not true with televised sports. We are all captured by a product and the demand never existed before the invention. So the reality that surrounds us is one of our own making.

TODAY'S LIBERALISM IS A DEVELOPMENTAL ISSUE

Childhood development encompasses many aspects of human thought and life. Child development encounters many stages of life with the first being communication which mainly is a basic understanding of speech and language. This is not as much taught to the child as it is experienced by the child in the household. So how the child talks and the words the child uses is a reflection of the household the child was raised. From this point the lessons of right and wrong within the family household is taught. To correct a child for using a word deemed inappropriate at this stage is not the fault of the child but the household of which the parents control. Correcting the child is the result. Correcting the Parents is the Correction and Cause for the child ever learning an inappropriate word.

This is the main reason society can't have an appropriate conversation on hard issues because inappropriate language and personal attacks on the individual (Don't kill the Messenger) are seen as a defense instead of countering with ideas and thoughts. If there is a lack of countering ideas and thoughts then liberals attack with basic inappropriate language or insults to get away from or change the subject or topic, the basic fight or flee of human nature. If it were an actual fight that inflicted bodily damage human nature dictates fight or flee with the winner fighting and the loser fleeing. In conversation a liberal is allowed to stay in the fight until they see the flaws of their ideas or thoughts. At this point instead of admitting their flawed thoughts they flee to change the subject or attack allowing them to continue the fight without admitting to their flawed thoughts. So they see it as a victory because they stayed in the fight, bobbing and weaving with no bodily consequences. This directly relates to a child of the first few grades of school that might bring a bad word or language home. Upon using it in the household he or she is corrected through conversation but without admitting this thought "the child still sees that language as acceptable among his or her friends" at school. Once caught at school by a teacher and the parents are notified is there another conversation or a get their attention spanking? You know you have reached the mental capacity of a liberal when they act like children and abandon civil conversation.

The act of lying is a moment of liberal action. Everyone has lied at some point in their lives even if it was a little white lie to your children, husband, brother, sister or parents, etc. The difference is the after effects caused by the lie that determines the severity of the lie. The more severe the lie the more Liberal the individual is with the truth. If the lie has a true impact on your children then it probably wasn't a little white lie. If there is no impact on the children then it probably was a little white lie such as teaching your children about Christmas and Santa Claus. Is that a lie? Yes and No! How Santa Claus is presently described is a lie but it is done to excite the younger children in the household about a Spirit and certain time of the year, a time of giving, for family and friends. The commercialization of Christmas is a totally different subject so I won't go there. History shows that this came out of the European Anglo-Saxon culture of true events and has been carried down thru future generations. Liberals have no problem attacking Christmas and would take this precious fleeting moment in time away from every individual and family if they were allowed. Even though they may participant they are the Scrooge of this time because it also reflects a religious philosophy they can't stand, that of "giving".

Knowing the difference between a little white lie and a real lie is what determines who lies and who doesn't, the severity determines if it is a true lie or not. A person who repeats a lie of another person is not a liar but misinformed. If that misinformation has been shown for what it is "misinformation" and then is still repeated by the same person then they have chosen to repeat the lie thus making them liars. Lying is a choice of the individual, people are free to lie even to get elected to office unfortunately. It is your duty to know what is a lie knowing if you repeat it you also may be seen as a liar unless of course you are comfortable with being a liar. There is a saying "that some people would rather climb a pole to tell a lie than stand on the ground and tell the truth". Great examples of lies are "If you like your doctor you can keep your doctor", "If you like your healthcare policy you can keep your healthcare policy", "Not a smidgen of corruption", these lies will go down in history as some of the most severe lies of a Democrat President (Barack Obama) told to the citizenship of America to help pass a flawed Liberal Left Democrat sponsored legislative bill.

The only way to counter Liberal Left ideas or thoughts which are more of a philosophy than an actual thought process is not with philosophies but with real life facts and common sense. Liberal Left Philosophies contain very little facts, are not backed by real life historical results and virtually no common sense. To illustrate no common sense I'll use the Liberal Left's Democrat Speaker of the House of Representatives' Nancy Pelosi's own statement, "We have to pass the bill so that you can find out what is in it away from the fog of the controversy", which offers a no common sense approach because if there was a controversy isn't that the best reason to read it first. NO individual, including Nancy Pelosi, would sign a financially binding document without having read it first, to do so shows no common sense so it was nothing more than a stupid political statement bordering on a lie to push a flawed political action of the Liberal Left. Each of these lies and this statement will forever live in infamy on the internet on Youtube.com just type in the quote, Liberal lies and stupid statements forever caught on tape. Future Price, Priceless!!

Liberal policies often conflict with their own liberal policies which again demonstrate a lack of common sense of their thought process. If there is an employment problem in the country being large numbers of unemployment stepping up immigration with the numbers allowed only increases the numbers of unemployed people. It is at this point what is then being competed for is social programs monies among the unemployed or underemployed poor people. This competition for these benefits may cause others to lose or have their social assistance checks reduced or stopped to expand the money pool to help cover the additional people allowed into the country. During an economic slow down immigration numbers should be reduced to reduce the competition among people for the jobs that are available. This also relates to the minimum wage paid by employers. If there are more jobs available than people to fill these jobs then employers must compete with other employers for workers in a limited workforce. This competition among employers will cause them to raise what they pay if they want to fill the jobs available within their company. So in essence a liberal open immigration policy allowing large numbers of immigrants to enter America goes directly against the social programs designed for poorer American citizens. This same policy also goes against the same poorer American citizens having jobs available for them and keeps that pay lower if you do find that job. This same policy also affects the quality of your children's education and the money available to do so. It affects your child's ability to get college educational assistance which affects your child's ability to provide for themselves in the future.

So why would the Liberal Left Democrats have a policy that is in direct conflict with four of their other policies? It's not about you, it's not about you having a job, it's not about that job paying enough money for you to live off of and it's not about you receiving enough money from a social safety net program until you can find a job. It's about the Liberal Left Democrats paying you the least amount through social programs allowing them to spread this money out among many more non-American people, it's about your American jobs being spread out among more non-American people, it's about the low wages created because of the influx of non-Americans, it's bout the Liberal Left Democrats offering you just enough to keep you voting for them! It's about the non-Americans voting for them now and in the future! This allows the Liberal Left Democrats to keep their $174,500 a year jobs in Congress plus excessive benefits with the ability of the power of government to make much more and maintain the lifestyle they enjoy and deserve. Those staying in office keep their friends employed in upscale Washington D.C. with great government jobs while you suffer. The Liberal Left Democrat motto is "Let them eat cake" with EBT cards.

Many children don't like rules that may keep them or others safe because they are not old enough or mentally developed enough to understand the reasoning behind the rules. When taking your child to do anything there are rules they must follow to keep them and the others around them safe during this activity. If they are not old enough or developed enough mentally to follow these rules then they are not old enough or developed enough mentally to participate in the activity. Liberal Left Democrats don't like rules or laws that don't directly benefit their party. The rules and laws through the Founding Fathers eyes were meant to benefit the people as a whole not either political party. That explains their actual hatred of the "Constitution" because it limits what they can do but they continually find a way to circumvent (going around) the laws of the "Constitution". They have historically done this through history as I have pointed out. The "Constitution" protects the rights and freedoms of the people from an overly powerful form of Government. Just like a child that is not mentally developed enough the Liberal Left Democrats fail to see this because they are the children wanting to change the laws that protect the adults from the powers of government to take our rights and freedoms.

The male child romance of being an outlaw, rebel or playing army is most times practiced as a child because of what is taken in from real life of that time period as cool, imitating real life. Teens and young adults (eighteen to maybe mid twenties) while still going through this liberal stage of life are still having liberal thoughts and dreams of excessive over indulgence. The examples being dreams of being something such as a Rock star, Movie star, Billionaire Investor,

President, etc. which satisfies the dreams of having everything, money, power, women, homes, yachts, cars, etc. Also during this same time period they are being exposed to or participating in conversation on social issues while still having the outlaw, rebel and still the necessary imagination of childhood to be able to imagine things that will never evolve from imagination to reality. It is this trait that allows many of advanced age liberals to have views of anti-government, anti-rules and laws, the perfect society, one world order, free movement from country to country, etc.

The reason I say these are not realistic thoughts is because to be anti-government as a whole means to be anti-society. Without government then you have society organize into destructive groups such as mobs rule in which "only the strong survive". Being anti-government should not be confused with not agreeing with a certain law or laws that dictate society's rules. To want to bring down government because of a couple of laws or a political view is no different than "throwing the baby out with the bathwater". Because I don't like one aspect of government I will work to get rid of all government.

There is no such thing as a perfect society, it is unattainable. The best society can be is for the majority of the people without trampling on individual rights controlling society. This allows the individual to move up or down in economic society regardless of gender or race, etc.. But again, the individual's own knowledge and talents dictate this type movement in society. Nature dictates that society must be a working society with everyone having a purpose. Your knowledge and talents dictate what that purpose becomes. In nature's ant or bee societies you won't see a single individual not producing for the society of the colony.

The idea of a one world order and the free movement of people is a fallacy. Societies are formed by like minded people, you don't intentionally form or start a family with a spouse you don't like or trust and this is no different for social societies. A society forms only when people can agree on a rule of law which is our "Constitution". Society disintegrates only when people can no longer agree on that rule of law. That's why dividing a society into smaller groups with each supporting a handful of different ideas is a great way to undermine society itself. That's why assimilation is so important, adding a different sector of society say Muslims wanting Muslim law and/or Sharia law just creates division because they are in conflict with our laws. Yet they keep coming, why? To undermine our society of unclean, impure infidels, their saying not mine!

Now to the last stage of Liberal dysfunction which is where the decision is made between liberal thoughts and reality. Upon entering the workforce many have to leave much of the liberal thought process behind. It is amazing how having to pay your own way changes your outlook on reality. This is the point you realize if you have done enough in the learning years of life to support yourself in the real world. If you realize you haven't you might return to the educational system or trade school if you have the ability to learn beyond what you have already been taught. If not you may enter the workforce as a hands on learning system working your way up within a company, but a strong effort is required to be rewarded. It also may take years before your position in the company begins to reward you as where a college degree person may continually step in front of you because he/she may be seen to have more potential.

The last step in reality is forming a family and having others relaying on you, liberal thoughts don't pay the bills. Children from a family of money can hold on to liberal thoughts much longer when attending college which is generally a liberal environment depending on the college. Some of these are the educated liberals and have the best chance of staying liberal because their means (earning potential or family money) allow it. You can be anything you want as long as you have the money and/or desire to sustain that path. People at the bottom caused by their own faults or possibly in conjunction with a flawed educational system and/or both many times find themselves outside the private enterprise employment system for multiple reasons. These people find themselves more reliant on government assistance of some type for many years of their lives. It is the Liberal Government system that continually keeps them at the bottom of the social ladder without the desire of upward mobility in society. Many of these feel like society has short changed them and believe they are owed something by society, now we have the haves and have not's of society. Many may enter a life of crime to shortcut the required effort for climbing the economic ladder. Others who qualify may rely on a lifetime of government assistance.

The most horrendous of the liberal individuals are the liberally educated that don't understand the basics of economics and life itself. They have been coddled most of their lives missing the opportunity to truly develop into a responsible adult. I use the word responsible adult very loosely because they can pay all their bills for their family and they may provide jobs to others in every responsible way. It is the liberal thoughts brought to government by many of these same people that believe people are not responsible for their own lives. That is because they weren't responsible for their own lives because others were responsible for them during their informative years, sheltered from reality. They don't truly have knowledge of what it takes to have others stand on their own two feet that aren't people of means as the liberals are and still remain. It is these liberal thoughts that keep the down trodden continually down trodden with no sense of self responsibility to rise above life's obstacles.

The most devious of the liberal groups are the liberal individuals that still abide by the childhood notion that rules and laws are made to be broken. Being governed by laws that dictate the processes of government (the Constitution) is just another obstacle in their way. When they are caught doing so it is lie, deny, cover-up by party support and ignore if possible. Right or wrong never is the topic of their style of government. If you haven't noticed I have never used the word "Democratic" when describing Democrats. That is because they are the least democratic of all the parties that have existed in our nation's history. My supporting example is the 2012 Democrat National Convention, Google: DNC vote on god, does that sound DEMOCRATIC to you, they needed a 2/3 vote to carry the motion and at best got a fifty-fifty vote. But the power of a few being the leaders of the Democrat Party had already determined the outcome before the vote ever took place. Democratic, I don't think so! And they govern the same way. A few will violate your vote to get their way! A few will violate their own Parties rules about a two thirds vote to get their own way. If they will violate their own Parties rules what weight does the "Constitution" actually carry? NONE! It would be gone today if they had the say. The ends justify the means!

The most vicious and dangerous to a civilized society is the Radical Liberal individual and groups thereof. Over the years many of these groups have popped up in the history of America. Their liberal ideas that America is the cause of all wars which cause the deaths of innocent civilians during the conflict is a excuse to spread their propaganda. The conflict is used as the excuse for their violent acts many times against uninvolved civilians of their own country. Many of these groups came to existence during the Vietnam War era. Even though a Democrat administration got America involved in the war what America was trying to defend were the basic human right of freedom from a government being North Vietnam backed by China and the U.S.S.R. (Russia). The War was more of a political standoff as was fought in Korea years earlier just a change of venue with the same high cost of American soldier's lives.

These same soldiers on their return home were spit on by liberal left haters of the war. If asked of each soldier what their experience of the war was I am sure not a one would describe it as a vacation. A National Draft had been enacted meaning no soldier had a choice other than students enrolled in college. It was many of these same liberally educated students that abused our soldiers. In my case being born in 1960 it was my Father that the liberal left haters hated for being responsible enough to understand his responsibilities under the Oath, "HIS WORD", he had given long before this war began. Today many Liberal Politicians take an Oath of Office "THEIR WORD" which actually has NO MEANING WHEN DONE because their actions defy their Oath. A Liberal's words can change to suite their purpose, in other words they can lie and there is no conflict with their character as a person.

The weather underground and the black panthers were the two main groups formed during the sixties era. However the black panthers were more of a liberal black power movement than a liberal anti-war, anti-government movement in my opinion. I'll begin with the black panthers because they are not a real influence on today's liberal movement. One of the main things that caught my eye during my very little research on the subject was the name Fred Hampton. He was one of the head members, holding a few different titles in the panthers of the late 60's but he was not the typical black panther or radical liberal of violent acts from what I could find. He just didn't fit the radical activist mold. What caught my eye was the claimed fact he was shot to death by some, assassinated by others which was confirmed by a F.B.I. investigation. Not to debate the mission or guilt of the black panthers lets just say that the panthers were not a totally peaceful organization. Fred Hampton's life ended the morning of Dec. 4th, 1969. Let's look at who held national government offices and who held what offices in Chicago Ill. at the time of the Chicago Police and F.B.I. 4:00 am raid of the Monroe St. apartment that created the subsequent killings.

The President in his first year in office was Richard Nixon a Republican from Jan. 20th 1969 to Aug. 9th 1974, the U.S. Attorney General was John N. Mitchell a Republican from Jan. 21st 1969 to Mar. 1st 1972 and the Governor of Illinois was Richard Buell Ogilvie a Republican from Jan. 1969 to Jan. 1973. The four lasting elements of this situation is the fact that all the above positions in National government had been held by Democrats the previous 8 years. The Chicago position of Mayor had been Democrat from 1931 to present day (2014) with the actual mayor for this time period being long term Democrat mayor Richard J. Daley (controls police dept.) who served from 1955 to 1976 upon dying while holding office. The last long term element is the Director of the Bureau of Investigation (began in 1924) which became the F.B.I. in 1935, this person was J. Edgar Hoover who held this position from 1924 to 1972 for a total of 48 years. There are many aspects of this man's secret life and his abuse of powers of office that you should read about. Let me just describe it as "Sex, Lies and Video Tape".

I believe this continued centralization of power led to a perfect storm of government that caused the execution of Fred Hampton by the Chicago police. The previous civil unrest by the radical liberal (including the panthers) groups, acts of violence, shootouts, bombings, bank heists, etc. It was easy to be "guilty by association" at this time and a lot of unanswered unasked questions remain. All this had been set in motion by a liberal Democrat government long before the elected Republican national government of Jan. 20th 1969 had taken office.

Now let's go back to the year of 1968 and it will show why I stated that the wheels of government, controlled by a Liberal Democrat Party, had already been set in motion. The Presidents for this time period were John F. Kennedy a Democrat from Jan. 20th, 1961 to Nov. 22nd, 1963. Next was Lyndon B. Johnson a Democrat from Nov. 22nd, 1963 to Jan. 20th, 1969. The U.S. Attorney Generals were Robert F

Kennedy a Democrat from 1961 to 1964. Nicholas de B. Katzenbach a Democrat became Attorney General from 1965 to 1966 and was moved to Under Secretary of State from 1966 to 69. Ramsey Clark a Democrat became the U.S. Attorney General from 1967 to 1969. The Director of the F.B.I. was still J. Edgar Hoover. The Mayor of Memphis Tennessee was Henry Loeb a Democrat from 1960 to 1963 then again from 1968 to 1971. Henry Loeb is an interesting and suspicious individual along with J. Edgar Hoover. Henry Loeb was the Public Works commissioner in Memphis from 1956 to 1960. In 1959, he tried to organize a political "white unity" electoral ticket to oppose the increasingly organized black vote in Memphis. Loeb also opposed desegregation, declaring support for "separate but equal facilities" and describing court-ordered desegregation as "anarchy". His antagonistic acts to civil rights and labor grew more in his second term, refusing in the 1967 election to make any concessions to black union workers. He returned as Mayor after winning the election despite Memphis's black community intensive opposition to his election. The start of his 1968 term reflected the election in every way with punishments to the politically opposing unions. Loeb enacted harsher conditions on the sanitation workers which started the Memphis Sanitation Strike on Feb. 11th, 1968 when about 1300 Black sanitation workers walked off the job.

On Apr. 4th, 1968 at 6:01 pm a group of men stood outside a hotel room when one shot rang out bringing one man to the concrete of the second floor. That man was Martin Luther King, Jr. who had a Republican ideology of a Liberal Republican Agenda (equal rights). He had been to the city numerous times in support of the strike, facing off against Conservative Democrats who wanted to keep the Black race a second class race in society. If Martin Luther King, Jr. were alive today he would be referred to as an "Uncle Tom" by the Liberal Left Democrat Party based upon their actual responses to current African American Republicans. In reality it is the Black Democrat Caucus working under the same party (Democrat Party) that has throughout history persecuted the black race. It is this same Black Caucus now promoted and used by the Democrat Party as a tool to keep the race under the wing of the party. Not allowing, with the use of Democrat policies, the black race to pursue or achieve any type of life's dreams. So who are the actual Uncle Tom's?

Just a quick thought, History describes Henry Loeb as a White Conservative Racist Democrat. Shouldn't that make Martin Luther King, Jr. a Black Liberal Equal Rights Republican? Was Abraham Lincoln a White Liberal Equal Rights Republican or a White Conservative Racist Democrat? Confused? It's all relative to the understanding of history.

Another Democrat who opposed the equal rights movement of Martin Luther King, Jr. was a Political Democrat and Governor of Alabama being George Wallace. Wallace took the Oath of Office as Alabama's Governor on Jan. 14th, 1963. His political stance opposed desegregation of races in the south. He stood in the doorway of the University of Alabama in an attempt to deny two Black individuals admission. He also tried this same tactic with four Black youths at four separate elementary schools in Huntsville. His best noted speech included,

"In the name of the greatest people that have ever trod this earth, I draw the line in the dust and toss the gauntlet before the feet of tyranny, and I say segregation now, segregation tomorrow, segregation forever".

and during his losing attempt at the 1958 Democrat primary for Governor his aide Seymore Trammell recalled Wallace saying,

"Seymore, you know why I lost that governor's race? ... I was out niggered by John Patterson. And I'll tell you here and now, I will never be out niggered again". "The President (John F. Kennedy) wants us to surrender this state to Martin Luther King and his group of pro-communists who have instituted these demonstrations".

The Liberal Left Democrat Party has made that above statement come true in the reality of today's society. It was Democrats that put this man in office not Republicans and the only time in history Republican ideology is described as pro-communist. This man had no concept of equal rights, what a Republican stands for or what communism is in reality.

My last example is Woodrow Wilson a Democrat President from Mar. 1913 to Mar. 1921. Wilson continually supported segregation with such statements as

"I feel sure that this must go against the grain of the white women. Is there any reason why the white women should not have only white women working across from them on the machines?"

What he was referring too were white women working in government jobs across from Black women.

The 110 years of race turmoil known as the Jim Crow (not a actual person but a character of entertainer Thomas D. Rice born in Manhattan, N.Y.) era was basically from 1865 to 1965. The Jim Crow laws perpetuated by Democrats of that era pretty much came to a end with the passing of the Civil Rights Act of 1964 and the Voting Rights Act of 1965. Although a number of laws after 1965 were still passed to correct all the loop holes the Democrats would continually take advantage of to correct anti-racist laws of the past. This lasted into the early to mid or later 70's.

This era of time is unique in American history because of the subject of slavery and equal rights. In regards to these subjects it is the only time and only subject that Democrats are labeled as Conservatives (no or little change) and Republicans are seen as Liberal (a major change). This was created because of the major changes the Republican Party ushered in on the subject of Black Rights. I don't actually totally agree with the Conservative and Liberal political labels on these two topics because they were only switched on these two topics. The Liberal agenda "the ends justify the means" of the Democrats which dominated the control of Southern Political Offices was to do whatever it took to stop the freedom of the Black race. That being the reason for having to pass the 14th and later the 15th Amendment of the Constitution. All the laws there after were to protect the freedoms of the Black race in America from Democrats. It wasn't until the 60's that the Democrat Party realized their futile attempt in doing so was lost forever. So the Democrat Party moved from the left to more of a center positioning with Presidents Kennedy and Johnson. The Democrat Party had to make this move to stop from becoming irrelevant as a Political Party being that thirteen Republican Presidents and only five Democrat Presidents had been elected since Lincoln in 1861 to Kennedy in 1961 a 100 years later. This was the reasoning for the Republican-Democrat support of the Civil Rights Act of 1964 and the Voting Rights Act of 1965 done under a Democrat President making the Democrat Party more relevant to the voting block of America.

With all the positions of government power being held by elected Democrats how is it the party is never held accountable for the racist acts committed under their political parties' watch? How is it, Democrats can be affiliated with the deaths of minorities (multiple minority types not just one type) and then can a number of years later call the Republican party racist for not wanting to give hand outs to the poor. Republicans believe in a working America, an America of jobs. Again, the fact is Republicans don't believe in lifetime handouts to any race or gender, they believe only in a hand up to get people into the workforce to stand on their own two feet without the cane of government. How is wanting and needing American Citizens regardless of race or gender to work to support themselves and a Nation racist or sexist? A none working Nation Will Collapse, debt vs. income! If pay is the issue then 11 or 12 million illegal immigrates being given amnesty to compete with American Citizens of all races for jobs and deflating the job wages for lower wage earners is racist to all American Citizens regardless of Race. This being done again by Liberal Democrats to bolster their voting numbers to ensure their grip on government. Does this actually help any American Citizen get a job or raise their pay upon getting that job unless of course it is a Minimum Wage Job ($15.00/hr.) then you will make more but everything will cost more so it is all relevant. You're still on the bottom of the labor and wage ladder until you learn and master a skill that the masses do not possess, anyone can make a hamburger.

I got a little off topic to again show other examples of Democrat social fraud and the lies of the party perpetrated while trying to paint the Republican Party as racist.

The weathermen or weather underground committed MANY acts of violence against society in the name of wanting a peaceful world. The flaw in their thinking was the acts they perpetrated where against the side involved in the war that was protecting the freedom of the people being invaded. The weathermen also had ties with the communist party because they supported the philosophy of a communal society. So the propaganda of peace was a ploy or lie to push their real beliefs of a communal style society. The Communal Style of Societies per say involved in these wars were North Korea,

North Vietnam and China thus the weathermen's alignment against their own government which wasn't and isn't a communal style of government. Of the three nations with a per say communal style (communist) government does any of them have a higher standard of living amongst their poor compared to our poor? Do their citizens enjoy the same freedoms we do? China's recent adaptation to a more free enterprise system says tons on this topic. The liberal left's flawed ideology of a perfect society is at the root of their agenda. This continually pushed philosophy brings to them the massive riches of their desires. Just like the people who race bait have accumulated massive wealth. Also Religious leaders of mega churches that have accumulated massive wealth. Ex-Vice President Al Gore is using Climate Change to the same extent, look at his accumulated wealth since leaving office. What's his job? To push a Green Energy agenda for multibillion dollar companies. It is done for their gain not their so called beliefs or your needs, IT IS HOW THEY MAKE MONEY! PERIOD! It is this amassing of wealth that proves that each type person I mentioned uses their so called beliefs as a bridge to wealth. If they truly believed in their beliefs wouldn't they sacrifice that excess wealth for their beliefs? Is it against the law? No! Should you see it? Yes! Do you see it? Most times Not! Jesus was not a wealthy man! He did everything and gave everything that was his, including his life, to and for ALL the people. The reality of giving versus the reality of taking or the illusion of both by the people I mentioned.

This continued belief in things that won't ever become a reality because they are in direct conflict of the laws of nature and the nature of man is the child within the liberal adult never evolving beyond the child's beliefs. The lack of knowledge of life's responsibilities then are handed down to unknowing others of the populous, the searchers for answers, our children in our liberal educational system. It is this system of the liberal left that has rewritten history covering the abuses of their own party.

It is the Liberal Left that is no longer looking for answers but has determined they have all the answers that is so dangerous. It is at this point they will do anything using any means to accomplish their goal of forcing their minority beliefs on the majority of the people. Voter fraud has been one of the tools to achieve their goal of political dominance whether it is the machines at the polls, arranging for illegal's to vote, wanting more illegal's to bolster their voting rolls, multiple voting, using other family member's ballots to vote, etc. Every time one of these is exposed it favors only one political party and that is the Democrat party. This liberal party is not above stealing an election. The use of governmental powers to influence an election is also not above their present day actions with the I.R.S. and D.O.J. used to silence opposing political parties in the 2010 & 2012 elections. There is a historical pattern of the Democrat party that shows it has abused not only the minority citizens of America but every aspect of what some of our Founding Fathers wanted America to be built on being Freedom for All.

SOCIALISM, COMMUNISM VS. THE FREEDOM OF AMERICANISM

We spent about half the time rediscovering the "Constitution" and how it is suppose to work. That design of governing by our Founding Fathers is a continually giving gift from them to every past, present and future citizen of this Great Nation. The Document itself is not perfect and can not defend itself against those who see it as an obstacle to Socialism or Communism. It was not designed to promote either one of these types of ideologies of governing. It is a Document that promotes Freedoms of any and all aspects in the thoughts of life including Communism and Socialism. But on a smaller scale meaning the amount of people who want to participate in that lifestyle being less than the majority. The "Constitution" allows this within the borders of our sovereign nation but it is up to you and the others involved to support that Commune-ism, Social-ism lifestyle and not the government that the Founding Fathers designed. The liberal left want Commune-ism and Socialism but only if they can force it on the entire country. Why have the liberal communes and socialist societies of the sixties and early seventies within this country failed and no longer exist? If it were a good thing wouldn't they still be in existence? As for the real Communist or Socialist societies in the world's governments being China, N. Korea and a few others they survive by not allowing the FREEDOMS "We the People" enjoy within their borders. Those Governments take all Productive earnings and then redistribute a much lesser amount among the people which promotes a something for nothing attitude. If your going to get it anyway why strive too do a good job or complete a job in the time given. This also promotes less productivity of the population because it takes away the incentive to be productive by limited rewards for the work done. If anyone believes in a higher wage this is certainly not the way to get it. Commune-ism and Social-ism both survive by what it doesn't give you and both ideologies offer no options for increased wages because they do not reward increased productivity. The only ones rewarded are the people in control of government.

Can a free society such as America be turned into a Communism or Socialism type society without an actual change of our style of government? Absolutely, a free society must move in the path of least resistance to achieve that type of change. Any sudden change from a free enterprise system to a total Socialist, Communist system would meet great resistance of the nations Citizenship. So government must change in stages with the first stage being Socialism camouflaged with a higher tax rate of the working (productive part of society) to subsidize the nonworking or lower wage earners (nonproductive or less productive part of society). Once this has been accepted by society then a continually increasing tax rate is used to drive the redistribution of wealth. When that tax rate reaches a breaking point with businesses then the businesses shut down because of the inability to meet the cost of operations. That is why it is crucial that government maintain a reasonable tax rate to promote our ideology of government and requires government's responsibility to be as small as possible and effective as possible too allow that reasonable tax rate. Government alone with its cost of operation, deficit & debt can be used to move a society in the direction of socialism, communism. Government (Federal, State & City) and Government alone decides how much money is left in the hands of the people. Each time a new tax is implemented or a existing tax is raised that money comes out of the hands of the people causing a continuously growing smaller middle class thus a continuously growing larger poorer class. When the people no longer have any money in their hands then they must rely on government for all of life's needs. Government will pay for the minimum needs but not much more once a true Socialistic, Communistic society has been reached. It is the giveaway's that drive our debt and deficit which compound the problems like a downhill rolling snowball getting bigger & bigger. Like Ying & Yang there is a balance that must be maintained before freedom disappears and government then controls our freedoms. Money allows for our freedoms and without it you have little freedom. Our Founding Fathers' Constitution is what set up our free enterprise system and both are and have been abused with the power of government itself.

Now with a failing free enterprise system of government has the opportunity to take over a business with a taxpayer cash bailout putting the business in the hands of government happened? Absolutely! This has already happened in our history with bailout of General Motors and a number of other businesses. At this point a ideological decision must be made to either allow the business to adjust it's debt or government assuming that debt and the business. In reality that is government's choice because the power of government is in the hands of government when the "Constitution" is not followed by government. What if government had decided to keep GM from the very onset? That would have been the last step in the first step of Socialism, Communism. Instead GM was allowed to file a government overseen bankruptcy permitting it to balance its debt sheet on the back of many shareholders, retirees and other workers of related business subsidiaries GM owned. Government also took a loss of about $25 Billion Dollars of taxpayer money with the Democrat supported Unions (UAW) being the biggest winner in this situation. They are now an owner of General Motors without an investment to the company other than being an employee at the time of the event. This government overseen bankruptcy did not follow our bankruptcy laws as it was administered by the Democrat Administration of Barack Obama.

Now is any reader actually thinking about how close our Nation came to that first Socialist, Communist step? At this point your attention is on what I just mentioned. In reality the Socialistic events that have already happened and are continuing to happen are now unnoticed because they are becoming the norm in our society under a Liberal Left Democrat Agenda which is the TRUE first step towards Socialism.

With each Liberal Left Democrat President in our history we as a Nation have moved two or three steps to the left of center. Upon realizing what has happened we then move back only one or two steps back to the right. This type of movement throughout our history has moved our country much farther left than most people realize. This continued left movement has only one type of ending! Bad! We as a Nation are about $120 Trillion Dollars Left of center on the political spectrum with no effective long term plan to get that political spectrum back to center for a Nation to continue into history instead of being history.

THE RESULTS OF LIBERAL DEMOCRAT POLICIES

A liberal handout by government to fund anything that is not within reason or doesn't achieve the desired results is wasted money. Any organization funded by government being national, state or local that its goal is not reasonable or doesn't achieve its purpose is also wasted money. At this point either government de-funds the project or overhauls the project in an attempt to get the needed results. Not to do either of these means you are satisfied with the results and are willing to continue throwing money at a project even though the mathematical figures show the project isn't working. Is this not the definition of insanity?

Our national government continues with many social programs that meet these same qualifications. Most are lifetime welfare programs that were never intended to be used for a lifetime. Now anyone who wants to throw military spending into this same group has no understanding as to what I am discussing. First the military is designed to protect all citizens within or outside our borders. It is the funding that allows this to happen today and into the future. Cutting that budget only makes us more vulnerable to other countries. Identifying waste in that budget is a totally different subject. Secondly has the military protected this nation for the last 238 years including two World Wars so that spending has had the desired results of keeping our nation free. If you are not interested in freedom then that budget can be cut to zero! We then have no need for a military. The one war our nation doesn't want to lose is the one fought on our shores.

The liberal policies of many Democrat controlled states are great examples of failed liberal policies. Let's take "Start Up New York", a company can relocate there or started there and not pay property taxes, state taxes or sales taxes if that company qualifies for these tax exemptions. Why are these areas free of businesses in the first place? Could it be the fact of the Democrat's belief in higher taxes has run these companies out of the state or out of business in the first place! What is the purpose of having tax free zones while areas outside of these tax free zones have businesses that are still paying a much higher tax rate that is not in line with other states? A slightly higher tax rate can be argued for the infrastructure offered in that area but free enterprise will determine whether that higher rate is justified or not. That fact is the reason for New York's business dead zones. Now to continue with the high taxes in the state on businesses outside these No-Tax Zones only causes other businesses to consider moving to other states while the state tries to lure new businesses to the state with its 10 year No-Tax Zones. Why not keep your state tax rates more in line and retain the businesses you already have? It's just like the local cable or phone companies that lure you into a one or two year contract with a lower price then run you off with much higher than normal prices after the contract expires, absolutely no difference.

Let's now look at Detroit, Mi. as a city. The political powers that have guided this city for the last 54 years have been the Democrat Party. The city had a vibrant automobile manufacturing base that created a vibrant taxable income for the city for many years. The manufacturers being continually pressed by the unions for higher wages and better benefits pushed the manufactures to the brink on its cost of product versus profit percentage. This imbalance caused the manufacturers to move out of the country to Mexico and Canada to create a lower cost of product while maintaining its profit margin thus keeping the cost to the consumer down. So what does the Democrat party have to do with the union? The Union has financed the Democrat party since the late 40's or early 50's which then joined the two at the hip like Siamese twins. This flow of money to local and national politics allowed local and national politicians to have a blind eye or support the unions every time there were labor negotiations between the unions and manufacturers. This unbalance of political support is what lead the manufacturers to leave the country. Even if they had moved to another state, the union would have followed the cash cow. Even today the unions have no intentions of leaving the workers or businesses alone. The unions pays S.E.I.U. workers to protest in front of fast food restaurants is if it were the workers of the restaurant and that is not why the true worker's unions were established. It has become more about the union than the worker.

In present day Detroit with their tax base now gone and people leaving the city to find work the city has found it can't pay its own city pay role. The people that are still there work for far less an average wage than what it averaged before the manufactures left. In reality the policies of the Liberal Left Democrats have lowered the wages within the city promoting a rising unemployment situation among private sector jobs. Yet the local government number of employees has not decreased in numbers or income level thus a bailout by a Democrat Liberal Left Administration headed by a Liberal Left President Barack Obama at a cost to tax payers of $3 million dollars to city government. This figure doesn't include special government grants (taxpayer dollars) to the city and residents of the city that are more than a $100 million dollars with this city being $18 Billion dollars in debt at the time of it's bankruptcy. Also a bankruptcy is essentially a bailout by investors of the free enterprise private sector accepting less or getting nothing on the money owed them on investment or services rendered.

The Liberal Left City Officials of Detroit as part of the city's assets has a very extensive Art Collection valued as low as $2.5 Billion dollars to as high as $20 Billion dollars if sold at auction. They are now working towards holding onto the entire collection in the bankruptcy. One of many arguments being used is that this "Art Collection" is the "People's Art Collection". If it's truly the peoples art then sell some of it to help the people whose tax money bought it. Just the top 5 pieces of this collection is worth $252 Million on the low side and $490 Million on the high side.

1. "The Wedding Dance," Pieter Bruegel the Elder, c. 1566, oil on oak panel: $100,000,000 to $200,000,000 Million Dollars

2. Self-portrait, Vincent van Gogh, 1887, oil on artist board, mounted to wood panel: $80,000,000 to $150,000,000 Million Dollars
3. "The Window (Le Guéridon)," Henri Matisse, 1916, oil on canvas: $40,000,000 to $80,000,000 Million Dollars
4. "Dancers in the Green Room (Danseuses au Foyer; La Contrebase)," c. 1879, oil on canvas: $20,000,000 to $40,000,000 Million Dollars
5. "Gladioli," Claude Monet, c. 1876, oil on canvas: $12,000,000 to $20,000,000 Million Dollars

What the Liberal Left Democrat City Officials want is to use this art as an attraction with the admission fees going to supplement the city's retirement fund of their city workers and their own city official retirement plans. I am sure these Politician's retirement plans are much more lucrative than that of the true blue collar worker with the city. The reality is the nation's taxpayer's get to bailout a Liberally run city that has mismanaged its tax dollars allowing the city to keep its art collection to fund a city work force that the city won't cut because of the union of which the Liberal Democrats support. Then as investors the national taxpayers get to pay full price admission to see art work we bought for the city to keep. Only In Liberal America.

California is ground zero for the West Coast Liberal movement. The state has been on this liberal path for maybe more than 60 years. Yes, it's had a few republican governors but registering as a republican is no different than getting a library card. You don't have to be a republican to register republican and you don't have to be able to read to get a library card. Liberal is Liberal it doesn't matter what party you are registered to vote in.

Today's California is $132 Billion dollars in debt not including it's $80 billion dollar unfunded liability of the union's negotiated teacher pension system. This pension debt is growing by $22 million per day. As of 2010 California has had three major cities declare bankruptcy and they are City of San Bernardino, Town of Mammoth Lakes and the City of Stockton. Each of these cities has had a court's decision that allows each city to cut the worker's pensions. Each city had over promised and under funded each of these retirement pensions. The Liberal Democrat's liberally give the money away and when they run out of other people's money they take back what they over promised to pay.

Our Nation is $18 Trillion dollars in debt with $120 Trillion of unfunded liabilities with no end in site. Whose pensions are those the Federal Government will cut when insolvency is achieved, even Social Security will not be off limits at that point. In the mean time pay your taxes so that more of your tax money will go to places accustom to wasting money due to bad government decisions. This fit's the Democrat's philosophy of "reward the non-deserving and penalize the deserving" which is different than "take from the haves and give it to the have not's" because in every instance they had it before they pissed it away with liberal ideologies or agendas.

AMERICA HAS AGAIN TASTED THE LIBERAL LEFT'S RECIPE FOR GOVERNMENT. IS THE TASTE IN YOUR MOUTH A GOOD OR A BAD TASTE? GET FAMILIAR WITH THE TASTE BECAUSE THIS TIME WHAT IS LEFT ON GOVERNMENT'S PLATE IS OBAMACARE AND ALL THE REGULATIONS NEW TO OUR GOVERNMENT.

LIBERAL POLITICS IN CONFLICT WITH LIBERAL POLICIES

Having a confused government is not done by accident, it is conceived thru stupidity. A tax system that taxes everything but spends the money on other things not related to the product it taxed or the effects caused by the product which is the reason it TAXED the product. This creates what I call a "Money Puzzle". Money flying everywhere in government creating confusion and a accountant's nightmare. Not knowing what came from where thus where it goes to pay for what means every time government has a shortfall in money collected from taxes it only can see the need to raise all Taxes.

Saturday morning while waiting for college football games I was watching Neil Cavuto's show "Business". They were talking about the Federal and State gas tax and how it was shrinking due to cars getting better gas mileage and electric cars. Of course the liberal voices on the show argued for raising the Federal gas tax to fund road projects. The Conservative voices pointed to the stimulus package which most of was spent on other things than roads. Green Energy is also infrastructure as seen by the Obama Administration and that's where a lot of the stimulus money was spent with crony capitalism. The true argument was never mentioned when talking about tax revenue for roads. The true taxes collected from vehicles which are driven on our roads are not limited too just a gas tax. Government collects taxes each and every time a vehicle is sold regardless if it is new or used or how many times it is sold. Government collects a yearly tax on each and every vehicle's license plate decal for any vehicle on the roads. Government collects a tax for a license plate for any type trailer that is pulled behind a vehicle on the roads. Government collects a tax from every driver's license issued for a driver to drive on the roads. Government collects a tax for every new auto part bought to keep a vehicle on the road. Government collects a tax on parts and labor when a vehicle is fixed at an automotive repair shop. That's what government does, it collects and spends your tax money, it is government's sole purpose. Government's purpose is not to ensure your tax dollar is spent with any type of meaning of responsibility. Government collects and spends, when it collects more it spends more. Obviously a vehicle generates many more taxes than what is being spent on our roads. Government just isn't spending it on our roads. Government is wasting it in other places as government does. Larger, Bigger, More Government must be the answer along with the idiots we continually elect to local, State and Federal government. Like Nancy Pelosi would say "we need to raise the gas tax so we can see what government spends it on, beyond the fog of government"!

Now with the price of Gas down the Liberal Left Democrats reason for raising Gas Taxes goes up. Liberal Democrats whine about how to put more money into the pockets of the poor because they don't know how to do it. So when it happens and they had nothing to do with it they don't understand. Lower gas prices puts money in the pockets of every American that drives just like a raise at work would. It also means Americans might be able to drive more also raising more tax revenue being collected. Now Liberal Democrats and some Progressive Republicans want to take some of that raise back with a higher gas tax. They won't cut government but will cut American Citizens to bleed our red for their cut of the government green. Once they raise the gas tax and gas goes back up will they remove the extra tax or will Liberals & Progressives stay silent as Americans continue to bleed red? That's how Liberals & Progressives look out for Americans, silent when needed and boisterous when they should be silent. A perfect example of how government doesn't care and doesn't work for the people. Government works only for Government!

The truth is that the Free Market for Petroleum (oil and gasoline) Pricing was being manipulated by the supply side. The supply was intentionally lowered (being oil or processed gasoline) or remained the same as demand went up driving up oil and gas prices artificially because the supply was always there. This put pressure on other parts of the world's economies and when they receded with less demand (people cutting back) it finally caught up to the Petroleum Market. The pricing bubble popped causing the price to fall as the market reset to its true value based on supply and demand. This was a problem originally created by governments. If the supply side had of stayed up with the demand side keeping the price more stable then the economies of the world would of continued to grow. Instead they experienced multiple downturns directly in step with higher (energy prices) gasoline prices.

This also shows how critical it is for a energy source to be as cheap as possible so even the poor can afford it without government assistance. The true adjustment now is for the energy companies to reduce its labor costs without reducing its labor force to reflect the pay rates before the bubble began. Stabilizing (lowering) the economics of the World Markets for all items produced (food) including petroleum based asphalt allowing the current tax dollar to fund more projects. The Markets have no problem raising prices but when adjusting for lower prices can't seem to figure it out without layoffs or shutdowns. Thus continuous inflation reducing the buying power of every countries monetary money. This makes the poor poorer and moves the lower middle class from the middle to the upper poor all based on the buying power of their money. Historically this is how modern economics has operated and that is a flaw in the system of not being able to adjust properly downward for deflation, thus the economic system of government is geared only for driving inflation upwards.

With the economic turn down of 2008 one item that drove the turn down was the housing market. Banks allowing non-qualified purchasers to buy homes their income would not have allowed them to buy. What allowed this? I have not dug up the proper information in regards to legislation that allowed it but just by memory I am mostly sure the policies came under the Carter & Clinton administrations allowing for a zero investment (no down payment and all costs rolled into the loans) in the home by the purchaser. The banks advised people to buy homes they could not afford but allowed it to happen with a lower payment grace period (3 to 5 years interest only loan) that was affordable to the purchaser. The idea was to flip the home before the grace period ended making money on the sale of the home. Sounds great until the scheme collapsed and the people with no investment in the home walked away leaving very few of the loans with the banks. The banks had bundled the high risk loans and resold them to other investors or a government entity being Freddie Mac & Fannie Mae which along with the large banks got bailed out by the Tax Payers.

Well the Bush administration should of seen it coming! Maybe, Most Likely should of but what could he have done about it? If he ended the program before the crash ever happened every bleeding liberal would have blamed him for taking away housing for lower income people. When he then advised the People about the high risk it was creating every bleeding liberal would of said he was lying and just punishing the poor. Funny a liberal can out and out lie, get caught 22 times on film saying the lie and liberals will deny, make excuses or lie about the lie to the bitter end. Isn't that a character flaw? Maybe a developmental issue? Here come the liberal excuses, their defense for defending a lie. The next step is, their defense of the defense for defending a lie! I wonder how far I could take this? I thought loyalty only went so far?

Now the government programs started out as a good program for lower income people to afford a home. Great idea and a needed idea. Yet the people it was designed to help took advantage of the programs with the help of the banks. Imagine that a liberal "give you something" program taken advantage by the low income people with the help of the greedy rich that the middle income had to pay for and you wonder why the middle class income families are disappearing in the economic system. Doesn't this sound like all the give away programs that are being enacted today and are being taken advantage of again by some of the poor. But the rich aren't getting rich off of it, maybe not but the pot stores in Colorado are when EBT cards are used to pay for the drugs. With cash from a EBT card allowed to buy ANYTHING, when it was meant as a good deed by the middle class to the poor for FOOD. Now all government has to do is raise the money given through EBT cards to fund every aspect of low income people's lives. This of course takes any reasoning and ambition away for the poor to better themselves to improve their own lives. So government itself is holding the people down by removing any reason for people to accomplish a life's dream. How many children grow up dreaming of living their lives through a EBT card!

As a Conservative Libertarian I advocate the decriminalization of marijuana but these liberal idiots have done nothing for that movement but set it back. Their Liberal Acts of doing it in everybody's face while also buying it with everybody's money. How uneducated do you have to be to not understand what you are doing to the 60 year old movement you didn't start in the first place. Again a liberal with a foot hold and is in the process of pissing it away.

With a turned down economy and people needing jobs, letting others into the country only means more people need work. How are the new people going to add to the economy when they are now in the same group. Now just a larger group needing jobs?

Capitalism is where a employer pays you for your work, Socialism is where government pays you for your work, What is it when government pays you for not working? Government pays farmers for not planting a crop on a certain acreage! If we are short on corn (ethanol & livestock feed) why is it not planted? Price control. If it is in demand and supply is too small it should actual be over priced! The Farmers say corn feed is almost un-affordable, higher meat prices shows they are telling the truth!

Government is suppose to make everything it touches better, why is almost everything government touches worse? Divorces didn't start going up until government got involved. The family didn't start falling apart until government got involved. Government taxes to create a civilized society, how much more civilization can a civilized society stand?

THE TOPIC OF RACE

How does a White man talk about the topic of race without being labeled a racist by a majority of the Black community or the supporters thereof or any minority race? Do I have to be a minority to talk about minorities? Then should a minority have to be a majority to talk about majorities. Do I have to be Black or Latino to discuss Black or Latino problems and you white with a vice versus situation. The only requirement is an intelligence to point to the problems and create discussions giving options for possible solutions.

There are three ways to accomplish the task without the labeling. One is to say everything that agrees with the majority black point of view and never venture to the side of disagreement. That is the Democrat's logic when talking race, avoid a serious debate and when cornered with logic & truth label the opponent as racist. The second is too tread lightly, avoid serious topics if possible which limits the discussion, show remorse when possible for something you did not create or support and let the black community continue to play the role of victim. The third way is the I don't care if you label me way, that's your choice and I have no control over your choices so the possible labeling means nothing to me. I feel that what I have to say is more important to you than the label you may choose to give me! So is your labeling of me more important to you than what I am going to say? Will my words carry less weight for you because of the color of my skin? Those are the choices you now have to make within the consciousness of your own mind.

At 55 yrs. old in 2015 I have seen misguided racism by both White and Black races. Racism is human nature instilled in all races excluding no races of humanity. It's no different than Patriotism or being proud of the neighborhood you grew up in as a kid. It's not until your world expands beyond that neighbor that now allows you to be proud of your city or school you attended. So every Saturday during college football season there is racism between the fans of the teams that are playing, it's just not about skin color of a person. Some will say it's all a form of patriotism and I agree one hundred percent. But when it gets to race it's not longer seen as a form of patriotism it's now Racism. Being proud of your race is no different but it does box you in with a predetermined group of people based on similar skin color. This then also groups you into the **Culture** of this same group. This group is who you are until you progress into the next bigger and better group, whatever group that may be, that is of your choosing. But staying in the same group that is based on skin color never allows people to move to the next step or group. Now you are stuck in the color of your skin group where all racism develops from in all races. Our Constitution doesn't state it is one race's responsibility to pull up or support another race. It _DOES_ state that one race or portion of a race can _NOT_ impede the progress of _Any Race_. It does so through individual Freedoms. History shows the Black Race of this country were impeded from progress. The Black Race's misconception is that "the White man held the Black man down" which was never true. Our country was and still is divided almost half and half politically between Democrats and Republicans. So for the Black Race's phrase to be true it would have to read "the White man of the Democrat Party held the Black man down"!

The BIG BANG Theory, Evolution or by God's Hands, these are the ways described in science, history and religion that our world formed with societies and civilizations growing and disappearing throughout history around the world. The powers of evolution or by Gods Hands is what separated the races into groups, it wasn't a choice of any man, group or race. That is just how it happened, a predetermined outcome of nature. Where each race developed in the aspect of the world's geography is nothing more than the evolution of civilizations. Through this time of history civilizations grew with some engulfing others causing one to grow and bringing the other to an end. Sometimes during these events the populous of the losing civilization were enslaved to build the civilization of the winning populous. To the winner go the spoils of war, a law of nature. Darwin's rule of evolution, survival of the fittest, also a law of nature. These sayings are all true, from the beginning to the end of time they will never go away.

Al Sharpton who I believe makes his living off the Black race by race baiting recently stated "We were building pyramids when whites were building ......"? What he was referring to was the pyramids of Ancient Egypt. History suggests these pyramids were built using slave labor. This viewpoint has recently been challenged by Egypt's archeology chief Zahi Hawass suggesting all the workers were paid laborers even though slavery flourished in Egypt in 2500 B.C. and on that point Hawass admits. He just suggests that the pyramids weren't built with slave labor based on a handful of bodies discovered entombed within an area of a pyramid itself. So Al Sharpton is referring to Egypt's civilization and populous as being Black. I'm not interested in debating that aspect but I am sure Zahi Hawass would have no problem with that debate. My point is Al Sharpton himself through his own words has stated either the Black populous of Egypt had enslaved themselves or the other option being Blacks were enslaved by Arabs about 4,000 years before slavery was ever brought to America. Would Al like a second chance at what he was trying to bait everyone with by explaining himself with some type of truth instead of a high school pep rally?

My point is slavery has been around since the beginning of time, it was one of the spoils of war even in Africa among the Black Tribes. Even in today's time a Black Warlord (another name for a tribe leader) in Africa took 280 or so Black girls for the sex slave market. I'm not sure how many races have been enslaved but throughout the thousands of years of history I would bet no race barring none has not endured this form of inhumanity at some or multiple times in history.

Now with this said at what point in history did the Republican Party disown the Black race or at what point in history did the Black race disown the Republican Party? A Republican President and a lot of like minded Whites gave their lives for your freedom. I understand that Blacks fought in the Civil War too but that doesn't change what I just stated. Please answer the question, what did or didn't the Republican Party do that allowed Democrat's to now become your savior in society?

When mentioning Lincoln's accomplishment in regards to slavery a Liberal Democrat including Blacks will say "that was 150 years ago and things have changed". Well when discussing race that same Black Liberal Democrat will say "the white man has held the Black man down". That also ended 150 years ago so using the same logic of "time passed" shouldn't this topic be water under the bridge as the Republican accomplishments regarding the ending of slavery have become. A Liberal Democrat being Black or White will reply, "NO, it is the last 150 years of suppression that the term, the White man held the Black man down, represents". But as I have pointed out it was not Republicans, it was Democrats that held the Black man down. See that's what is so great about Liberalism owned by the Democrat Party it has no logic on every topic it might encounter. So have you answered the question yet about abandoning the Republican Party? Going back to your logic what has changed in the last 150 years? It was Democrats that held you down for that period of time since 1865. It was two racist Democrats that killed Abraham Lincoln and Martin Luther King, so again what changed?

I can't force Liberal Democrats of any color to answer this question. So I will offer a logical answer in their place. As I have pointed out it took two moderate Democrat Presidents to put a end to the Liberal Left Democrat's suppressing the Black race in society. It was this action alone that brought a lot of the Black race into the folds of its historical political enemy being the Democrat Party. Today's Liberal Left Democrats have now grasped the formula to retain the Black vote being affirmative actions directed at a certain race using welfare programs. So now votes are for sale to the political party that uses taxpayer money directed at certain races. Have these actions of the Democrat Party raised the plight of any race in America? No! There are more people in poverty now than at any point in America's history and the Black race leads the way with the most living in poverty. So the Black race have sold their votes for a minimal or negative return to its race. These actions are also putting other races into the growing poverty levels.

The two moderate Democrats being Kennedy and Johnson only helped bring to a end what Republicans had begun 100 years before and been trying to end during the last 100 years. The Republicans always had the memory of the Civil War and never wanted a situation created that might cause a second one because the cost to our country was enormous.

Throughout history there are a few factors that have determined the survivability of a society with the main factor being intelligence. It is the intelligence of a society that has distinguished that society for a moment in time of history. The number of distinguished societies of history has been tracked in history. There are more distinguished civilized societies of history in the Mediterranean Sea area than any other part of the world. Remember "civilized" is a loose term, it changes with the perceptions of man. The Bible describes and depicts the Garden of Eden as modern man's origin located somewhere in the Middle East. The origin of modern man beginning here is backed by history because technology of a society, the acquiring of knowledge, also began in the same area of the world. For this to happen what is it that humans must possess to spread the knowledge of technology? That would be intellect. The ability to understand things that others can't teach you if others have no knowledge of it. It also means the ability to learn a concept from another who has mastered that knowledge. This also must be vetted to ensure the knowledge has been mastered. If a boat builder launches a boat and it immediately sinks has the builder mastered the knowledge? No! Also with it's sinking if the builder has left with your money knowing the result before it happens was this not his AGENDA to steal your money? Vet the teacher and the information. So with this being said the advancement of a civilized society is in the hands of the people with the intellect of understanding allowing them to spread knowledge to others in their society which advances their society. Also a society which fails in this progression of events fails as a society becoming a point in time of history. There is only one alternative to the word "Beginning" and that is "Ending", everything in the middle is "continuing". Nothing that has ended has ended well otherwise it wouldn't have ended. The ending of a civilized society has always ended badly. But for any of that to happen you must have had a beginning!

That brings me to the 7 Continents of the world being Africa, Antarctica, Asia, Australia, Europe, North America and South America. We can remove Antarctica from this list because no civilization has evolved there because no civilization can survive the elements to the standards for a civilization.

Of the other six continents which continents have had a distinguished civilized society of the past or present? Which continents have offered the most amounts of technological advancements throughout history to mankind? Which continents have offered the least amount of technological advancements throughout history to mankind? Which continents continually need the most help from the rest of the world to feed and care for its people? Which continent is the least advanced as a whole when talking about the standard of living of that continent?

Now many may get upset with the "emotion of pride, self defense of race being the emotion of racism" but the obvious answer is Africa. There has been a historical disconnect between intellect, knowledge and technology and the advancements needed for a civilized society within this continent even to the present day. The two civilized societies that have existed throughout the history of the continent are Ancient Egypt and the current Nation of the Republic of South Africa. Historically the eastern end and southern side of the Mediterranean have been of Arabic descent. South Africa as a country was built by immigrants from the Dutch Netherlands and Britain. After WWII German immigrants also immigrated to the country. The Dutch originally set up a way station (a port in present day Table Bay) around 1650 A.D. for the shipping that traveled the spice trade routes from Europe to southern Asia. So now removing the Arabic civilization of Ancient Egypt and the European built civilization of South Africa you now have no civilized societies that have evolved out of the African continent and the "Black" race thereof.

At this point I am sure many of you are saying "Racist White Man". If facts and truths of history are racist then turning your head away in denial is a sign of ignorance; lack of knowledge: lack of knowledge or education; unawareness: unawareness of something, often of something important; ignorance is bliss, it is often better not to know about something unpleasant. Now have I insulted you as a "Black Person" or a person of "any color"? I haven't called you a name and I haven't implied anything. If you are thinking of any words that may replace "ignorance" look up the definitions so you can correct your thoughts. I also said you had to commit an action being "turning your head away" before the term I used would come into effect. So if you are still with me let's keep moving forward and if not that is by your choice, no others, YOUR choice being FREE to do so.

One point I would like to make in regards to slavery is that this inhumane action was a product of the views of societies throughout the history of the world with no race being immune to the inhumane actions thereof. So for how many years has slavery been on this earth? Four, five, six thousand years or almost since the beginning of any type of man, modern or pre-modern man. This Country, Our Country gained its freedom from England after the War of Independence but the actual United States Government wasn't formed until 1789 with the signing of the "Constitution". From 1789 until 1865 under our Republican President Abraham Lincoln who abolished all slavery of all races not just "Blacks" was a period of time being 76 years. Yet forms of slavery still exist today in the continent of Africa, caveman type marriages and sex slavery, that's fact. So thousands of years of slavery and it's still on going in other parts of the world and you hold our Nation and today's Republican Party responsible for the 76 years of slavery that existed in this country. I say this because of the Black Race historically backing the Democrat Party. I would have thought all races in this country would celebrate this accomplishment of abolishing slavery? But no, it has been laid at the feet of the White race of the Republican Party as the racist party. The 150 years since 1865 during "the White Man holding the Black Man down" years were created under the Democrat Party's Political Agenda to alienate the "Black Race" from the social gains of access to government. This also is laid at the feet of the White race of the Republican Party. If that isn't Political Racism what is? And unearned at that! Again would you like to answer my question that I asked earlier? At what point in history did the Republican Party abandon the "Black Race" or at what point did the "Black Race" abandon the Republican Party?

Now let's tie intellect and knowledge into our educational system while also tying the Democrat's Agenda to alienate the "Black Race" from our government's educational system.

What I am about to discuss is not just a race issue, it was in the beginning but in the last 20 years or so it has become a issue of "means" which is a disadvantage of the poor of our country.

Why did Democrats want segregation? First they didn't want to be in the presence of the Black race, it allowed for an out of sight out of mind attitude. Secondly it also allowed state or local governments to create a "less than" educational system for the "less than" second class citizen they also created. Thus a White Democrat privilege which dominated the Southern States after they had reentered the Union of the States after the Civil War.

Why do Democrats oppose charter schools and allowing children students of failing schools to move to a better school? Because an uneducated individual will tend too rely on government for future financial support and will vote for the Political Party that offers that government financial support. A better educated individual will not need or qualify for that government support thus the tie is broken between the individual and government along with the tie to the Democrat Party. That is why upper education of college's has been infiltrated with the Liberal Left's Ideology so that now the educated individual will also support the Agenda of the Liberal Left's Ideology of the Democrat Party. Remember me saying "When you are told over and over something you begin to believe it and at some point you accept it as the Truth". Thus a continuous circle of thought of the poor and the liberally educated based on a flawed educational system and the teachings thereof created and supported by Liberal Left Democrats. That's why Democrat's with the Teacher's Union's oppose extended school hours and the subjects I just pointed out. Liberal Ideology has a strangle hold on our government and government's educational system that will lead to the failure of America.

With desegregation laws implemented because of Republican Ideology the Liberal Left Democrats had to alter its game plan of educational denial to "Blacks" to an educational denial to all with its flawed Ideology of thinking and thought being imposed upon our educational system. Rarely do the Liberal teachings follow the true events of history thus a liberal rewriting of history. It's this rewriting of history that has lured the "Black Race" back onto the Voting Plantation Farms of the Liberal Democrats paid for by taxpayers to keep people (Any Race) poor with small amounts of government subsidies/welfare. Liberal Democrats have no problem using government money to secure their Political Future with any race, aka illegal Hispanics. Liberal Democrats will spread a limited pool of government money among the largest pool of potential voters as possible. Once out of government money and with the need for more will raise taxes on the working and employer's of the working. This is much easier to Democrats than creating jobs for people that might want more than a predetermined amount in a government check. This process continues until government no longer has the means to continue this process. Then that small government check to anyone receiving it ends with no jobs available to anyone that now wants or needs a job. Also remember the jobless number put forth by government is not the same as the job participation rate which is the number of true jobs available in America. You can't have a low jobless rate with a lower jobless participation rate than previous years because the true meaning is no jobs for the people. Allowing illegal immigration of large numbers during this economic period only increases people on the government subsidies / welfare programs which then shows a under lying meaning for this action beyond economics. Now a low jobless rate with a higher than the previous years job participation rate means people are working and jobs are being created. This causes wages to go up unless again government allows immigration being legal or illegal then causing wages to level out or maybe even decrease depending on the numbers allowed into the country. These immigration actions if permanent only increase the problem for citizens in regards to jobs when the country experiences its current or next economic downturn. A legal immigrate with a green card that expires may not be able to renew that card at that time due to the economic situation. If the process is done correctly by government. That's why it is called a guest worker program because it may be part-time not meaning weekly hours but amount of time the job is available to legal immigration under the green card system.

White collar college educated individual's (again of any Race) jobs are by far less impacted by this type of a green card system or illegal immigration. It is the blue collar working man that must compete with the green card system and/or illegal immigration. This increased labor force will drive the wages down in certain sectors of blue collar employment if not cause that individual to lose that job being replaced by a lower paid immigrate. Even a blue collar business owner may lose his customers to a lower bidding immigrate/

worker/business owner. When living ten people to a type of shelter your living costs are a lot less and immigrates will live like that for extended periods of time that they are here. The business owner whose sole income not only supports his family in a single home but also the people who may work for him.

Who in the Black community has lost family businesses or employment to illegal immigrate workers/ green card business owners? Again those traditional blue collar jobs of our housing and commercial building industry being brick laying, concrete work, framing being wood or steel, roofing, painting, etc. were lost by the Black and White Races to immigrates who will do it for less. The exchange rate from dollars to pesos allows this because that is where their money is sent, south of our border. As with most imported things sometimes quality suffers as the price falls.

Other jobs or businesses lost to other races (middle eastern, India & Bangladesh descent) being convenience stores. My understanding, correct me if wrong, on this topic is that these immigrate races are allowed special government backed no interest 7 year loans allowing them this opportunity to own stores. It also allows them to sell that business then again game the system with another 7 year same type loan. I have even heard of local governments waiving the cost of a beer license for these same individuals while still charging other races for that license. This is not how America works, under our Constitution, disadvantaging some while advantaging others. You can't have an equal citizenship by not having an equal citizenship. Someone whose family may have moved here a 125 years ago had to find their own way in America. During those 125 years that family most likely past down some type of wealth to its next generation. Under Barack Obama and the Liberal Left Democrats that wealth is being handed to the Hispanic Race as they enter this country illegally. One or both political parties have done and are doing the same for Middle Eastern & Indian Races (not to be confused with Native American Indians).

Of the Black Race the poor and most of the educated are constant supporters of the Democrat Party. Many of the poor quote that "not working for the white man" is more important than having a job. Yet many White people do not hold that same sentiment when working for or with (as a franchisee) a Black ran company such as "McDonalds".

Yet that same young man that won't work for the white man won't work for the Black man because it's fast food. Don Thompson is the President and CEO of McDonalds. The people who work immediately under this man are all white. All these white people must not have a racist bone in them to work under a Black man and Don Thompson must be an Uncle Tom to be in this situation according to Black Democrat leadership.

The fact is the poor uneducated Blacks can't move beyond the race issue because of a lack of education which allows the Liberal Agenda to indoctrinate them into a thought process of the Liberal Left's Political needs. In return some in the Black Race are given minimal support to obtain a non-working minimal existence that the Black Race has become accustom too since their injection into America through slavery. Even slaves got paid in some form or fashion being shelter, food and clothing. Of course the shelter, food and clothing were always the bare minimum for the slave owner to get by with. Now what is the difference between that slave owner and government that does the same thing? A government system created by Liberal Left Democrats designed to allow and promotes you to fail in their educational system, in the job market, in life. They suck the ambition from your soul with a minimal government check that you can always fall back on when you fail. A door to door salesman fails 9 out of 10 times but an optimist would say that salesman is successful one out of ten times. So it's how you take failure which determines whether or not you go to the next house. With a government check that need to go to the next house is diminished and most times extinguished leaving you at home waiting on that minimal check and Liberal Democrats waiting on your vote and you submit, which is the path of the least effort. A trait of human nature but not instilled in a human for doing nothing. The least effort is a process of intelligent thought to successfully complete a task with the least amount of effort which is being efficient in completing a task or job.

The Democrat party's greatest modern day President is John F. Kennedy. The most referenced Democrat speech in history is President Kennedy's when he said "Ask not what your country can do for you but what you can do for your country". This philosophy has been abandoned by the Liberal Left Democrat party which now embraces the exact opposite phrase being "Ask not what you can do for your country but what your country can and should do for you". This new philosophy of the Liberal Democrat party is not just extended to our country's citizens but to noncitizens entering our country illegally with tax payer dollars thus buying votes to help ensure the Democrat party stays in power with disregard to our country's true needs and debt. So in today's political Liberal Left Democrat party and the political Progressive Establishment Republican party this environment would not and could not allow John F. Kennedy to be elected as President even as a Republican because of his Conservative view. This alone shows how far to the Left the full spectrum of government has moved. The Liberal Left Democrats leading the way to the Left and the establishment Progressive Republicans following as fast as the Conservative aspect of the party allows them which has been, not by choice, significant.

The situation of today is no longer a race issue but an issue of the uneducated poor of all races in America. This situation will continue to get worse with a designed for failure educational system. The Liberal Democrat Agenda is dependent on an uneducated population and the indoctrination of the educated with Liberal thoughts and beliefs.

Did you ever answer my question about the Republican Party? You cannot save a person from himself without the person's help! Translation, No one can help you unless you are willing to help yourself. Republican translation, a hand up (to a better life) not a hand out! (that continually keeps you poor).

LOCAL POLICE AND THE JUDICIAL SYSTEM

The First thing I want to state is "If you pass enough laws, the government; being Federal, State or local, you can make everybody a law breaker or criminal to some degree.

All government employees are a reflection of the society of which they are selected from for that government position whether it is local, state or federal governments. Just because an individual is selected for a position of authority doesn't mean that this individual's character has improved or changed to a neutral position in regards to how the individual treats anyone, group or race. My numbers may not be totally correct but I believe they are very close on what I am about to state. I believe about 25% of the individuals involved with police enforcement are corrupt in some form or fashion. The level of corruption may be from a small to large form but if known about would not allow that individual to be a peace officer. I believe another 25% also know these individuals are corrupt but protect them with a unspoken code of police officers not to disclose such instances which make that same group also corrupt because of the knowledge they possess. This leaves only about 50% of a police force that are truly a officer of the law with a unbiased approach to their job and the citizens they are appointed to enforce the laws upon. These percentages may change for the better or for the worse depending on the police department that is being looked at.

As a individual if you happen to be in a place that allows or forces a officer to question your reasons for being in that certain place at that time it is how the officer treats that individual that determines the character of that officer and whether your rights are violated or not. Again, to see the true character of a man give him power. It seems like explained situations tend to illustrate these situations best so example one is three white friends, two living in their hometown and one in the military arriving home from the Philippine Islands. A fourth friend was flying into New Orleans a few days later so the three friends were going to pick that friend up at the airport. It just happened that the friend's arrival happened to coincide with Mardi Gras in February of 1980. The three friends left a few hours early to spend a couple of (2) hours to experience Bourbon Street since none of the three had ever been during this festivity. Considering that they were driving and it wasn't an overnight trip a designated driver was appointed which was an easy task because one of the three did not drink. During the drive, the friend who had come in from the Philippines gave his two friends custom pocketknives from that country. The three friends spent about two hours from 7pm to 9pm on Bourbon St. amongst a mass of drunks. One, the driver had nothing to drink, one had a beer and the other may of had two beers. On the walk of about eight blocks from Bourbon St. back to the car the three friends heard an alarm going off in front of them. They couldn't tell if the alarm was on the street they were on or one of the parallel streets to the left or right. Sure enough about a block and a half down the alarm was going off in a store and just beyond that was a black man sitting in a car. Just before the police showed he threw an empty bottle of liquor out the window breaking it on the road. Within seconds of that, a couple of police cars drive up with four officers exiting the cars. At this point, the three friends are about 50 yards beyond the store and while walking by the store had not noticed anything criminal about the alarm, thinking it was a false alarm. The police called the three friends back to the store location and had the man get out of the car also coming to the same location. The four officers, three white with the leader being black, asked a question of the early 20's black man then cut him loose while making the three friends spread them against the building. The black officer's first words to the first friend were "Do you have any weapons on you". The friend replied "no" not realizing he had the gift knife in his right rear pocket. The officer knew this when he asked the question for two reasons, one, he saw the bulge created by the knife in that rear pocket. Two, the officer went directly to that rear pocket upon hearing the "no" answer and pulled the knife out. The black officer held the knife to the right side of the friend's head and said "son, I ought to beat your ass". The officer did the same to the second friend finding nothing. When asking the same question of the third friend he replied, "yes, it's in my right rear pocket and looks exactly like the other knife". The officer then made that same friend remove his boots making sure there was nothing in them. Upon realizing they were clean, the officer threw the boots on the concrete and stomped on them. The officer was trying to get a reaction upon which they could react allowing them to violate the three friend's rights even more. Any type of reaction would have given the officers the green light. The officers cut the three friends loose keeping both knives but the officers could have done the same by investigating the false alarm first while holding all the individuals until confirmation of the false alarm. The alarm was the officer's excuse to violate these individual's rights with an illegal search and seizure. The friends went on to the airport to pick up the fourth friend. At the airport, the three friends got into a discussion with a black baggage handler who advised the three white friends of what the local police were doing to the local civilian population. Upon being picked up by these local police the people were being taken to a highway overpass and having a hardhat strapped on their heads and beaten in the head with those huge metal flashlights. Can you imagine if these three kids had of tried to defend their rights? The justice system would have violated their rights even further with jail terms.

A second example is a D.U.I stop in Marietta of Cobb County Georgia a suburb of Atlanta. An individual going to a local bar grill known as "Doc's" in Marietta on Hwy. 41. The bars parking lot is surrounded by landscaping that does not allow a driver to see the oncoming traffic at the Hwy. 41 exit until they are at the four lane Hwy. The bar grill ran nightly weekday specials for dinner that were very competitively priced especially for a single person not wanting to cook or eat fast food. This incident happened in the early 80's when the machine D.U.I. test was 0.10 to be deemed legally drunk under the law. This is advertised in all government paid for ads which ask people to be responsible when consuming any alcohol. The government also has a recommendation of one beer or one ounce of alcohol per hour depending on the weight of a person only as a guideline for safety.

This individual enters Doc's at 7:00 pm to have dinner as he had numerous times before because he lived a couple of miles north off of Windy Hill Rd. While having a complete home cooked type meal the individual had two 12 oz. Budweiser beers with his meal. Upon leaving Doc's at 9:15 pm the individual went south on Hwy. 41 to take I-285 east one exit to I-75 north to the next exit being Windy Hill rd. and right for two blocks to the Riverbend Apartments and Condo complex on the Chattahoochee River.

Where everything went wrong was at the very first light for the turn from north Hwy. 41 onto I-285 west. A white early 80's model Mazda RX-7 had pulled almost if not a fender length into the lane of Hwy. 41. The individual in his 1978 Cougar XR-7 saw the car and checked his center mirror and then right hand door mirror making sure no vehicle was there, moved to the right crossing the center-line on his right but moving back to the left to his lane for the next left hand turn onto I-285. With both those lights, the one before and the current light, being green for this individual turned left onto the I-285 east on ramp. At about half way up the ramp the lights of a police vehicle came on so the individual pulled to the right shoulder of the on ramp. The individual exited his vehicle meeting the officer at the rear of his Cougar, this was an accepted procedure at this time in law enforce unlike today where they want the individual to stay in the vehicle. The officer stated he had pulled the individual over for an illegal lane change. The individual indicated that he had no intention of changing lanes and that the move to the right was caused by the white Rx-7, which had pulled into his lane. The officer asked where the individual was going and where he had been, of course the individual answered "home and Doc's". The officer then asked if the individual had been drinking. The individual said he had two beers with diner over about a two hour period. The officer asked for the person's driver license and registration so the individual turned went to the passenger side of his car to the glove box, retrieved his vehicle registration. Closing the passenger door, he returned to the officer at the rear of his car handing the registration to the officer and beginning to pull his wallet out of his rear pants pocket only to have the officer throw him over the trunk lid of his own vehicle to cuff him. The individual asked what the officer was doing. The officer replied, "I'm arresting you for D.U.I.". The individual replied that the officer had not given him a visual test or a breathe analyzer test. The officer put this individual in his patrol car heading to the sheriff's office without locking or removing the keys from the ignition of the individual's car. Once reaching the sheriff's office 10 to 15 minutes later the individual was rushed for a breathe analyzer test before even being booked although the individual had already been arrested. The individual blew a 0.05 which is half of what was determined by law too be legally drunk which is 0.10 on the test at this point in time. At this point, the individual saw the officer's eyes lose contact with anyone else in the room knowing he had screwed up. At that point, the officer had to fall back on what the law states as officer's discretion that allows an officer to make an arrest based on an alcohol level of 0.05 to 0.09 of which the individual had never heard of this law. The officer had no choice because the arrest had already been made even though the office had never done any type of field sobriety test to make that determination.

The government pays for television advertising too bring awareness to drinking and driving and the individual's responsibility when doing so, yet the advertisement itself is false like what most of government does is false. Like also offering a guideline on how to be safer when drinking & driving being one beer or one ounce of alcohol per hour as a guide when this guideline doesn't actually meet the guideline of the law that is also never mentioned being officer's discretion in any government advertisement. So government itself will intentionally mislead a citizen allowing government to arrest that same citizen while the citizen was doing nothing more than trying to abide by the law by following the guidelines advertised by government. That sounds like government entrapment.

The individual upon release from jail retrieved his car from the impound lot and contacted a lawyer about his situation. After a face to face meeting, the lawyer indicated to the individual that the D.U.I. charge was trumped up and would not stand up in a court of law, which is exactly what this young individual wanted to hear from a much older mature lawyer. Payment was discussed with the lawyer stating that the payment was enough to represent the individual until the outcome of the charges were dealt with, so the lawyer was paid in full by check at that point.

With an attorney on the job, within a week, he learned that the State's attorney had added a charge of reckless driving to the two other charges of an illegal lane change and D.U.I. The officer's statement now was that he observed a vehicle leaving "Doc's" with its tires spinning. Now this didn't make any sense because 1) the officer would of pulled the individual over way before the point he did. 2) the charge was added by the State's attorney who wasn't there. 3) the officer would of used that reckless driving charge as a original ticket instead of the improper lane change ticket which was one of the two original tickets. 4) the vehicle wouldn't spin a tire from a stop much less a roll on it's best day and spinning a tire is not reckless driving, there is another legal term for that action. What the ticket was used for was a plea deal with the individual's attorney because being informed of the added ticket the individual pointed out these same topics to his attorney. His attorney now wanted even more money to pursue his client's innocence if going to court, which was the exact opposite of what he had earlier stated. Therefore, the truth was bargained away with the cost of the truth being more than what the client could afford knowing he had been sold out. The plea was a reckless driving ticket with no points applied too the individual's license. Was this actual justice or the protection of an officer by a State's attorney office during his first D.U.I. arrest of his career, which is what the client's attorney found out? A bungled arrest, false charges and injustice, exactly how government functions, ineffectively.

Let us keep going with one that is completely documented by the Santa Rosa County Sheriff's Department and the county courts of Santa Rosa County, Florida. The individual is Mike Brayard, who was arrested for public intoxication. Upon being booked into the Santa Rosa County Jail, he was put in a holding cell to sober up. A public intoxication charge is a misdemeanor and what Mike left the county jail with was a felony while in the protective hands of the Sheriff's office.

To start with, let us understand the meaning of "public intoxication". When an individual is publicly intoxicated, he may be a nuisance to others in the public domain but let us move beyond that aspect. The real reason to justify the arrest of a publicly intoxicated individual is that he or she is a threat to themselves or others whether it is by accident or on purpose. With the arrest the police are now suppose to be protecting the individual from himself.

So now, Mike has been put in the drunk tank because he is a threat to himself or others in the public domain, not because he had committed a crime beyond being drunk in public. However, while in that drunk tank cell where the officers are suppose to protect him from himself they charged him with a crime committed while behind bars and under the influence of alcohol. What did Mike do, he threatened to blow up the jail if they didn't let him out! Really, is that how shallow and mean an officer of the peace has become or the prosecuting State's Attorney's Office and how about the Judge. This was the closest thing to a lynching by the authorities without it happening. A true injustice committed by the whole system from beginning to end. To hold him responsible for something he said while the same entity had arrested him for being a threat to himself makes absolutely no sense, exactly how our government functions with the people we employ in government. The bigger violation of this persons rights was along with the felony another of his rights was infringed upon being his right to vote. If you pass the police officers certification, you are hired. If you pass the State Bar to become a lawyer and prosecutor, you're hired. If you have been a lawyer long enough then you may be a Judge, you're hired or elected to the Judicial Bench. No type of screening is used to filter these people other than the fact of not having a criminal record. It is amazing how once in a government position a criminal arrest or prosecution no longer becomes a legal action against them once all their friends in the system chip in to help in the situation. A system of privilege? Happens constantly across America does it not? At worse they lose their job but as a citizen you lose your job most of the time while also being prosecuted and adjudicated. This non-prosecution is nothing more than sending an individual down the road to inflict the same atrocities on others just in a different jurisdiction. Have you ever noticed how an officer when looking at an individual's record it is the arrest record he looks at and not the individual's conviction record! I thought a decision of innocent meant innocent and the arrest would then be removed from the arrest record but it's not! So a form of guilt is still attached to the individual's record regardless of guilt.

Let us go to the City of Douglasville, Georgia another suburb of Atlanta out I-20 west. With the purchase of a house in this city, two brothers moved to this town. A couple of years later with the city's implementation of a city code enforcement program with its duty to ensure the beautification of the city's resident's homes. This included citations for not keeping a home's grass cut or debris from being able to be seen from the road. It also included vehicles that are not tagged from accumulating in a front yard of a home and other rules which the city's elected officials might see as necessary for a purpose. This purpose also included ticketing parents whose children played basketball in the streets of their neighborhood with one of those portable basketball goals with the base filled with sand or water. To the south side (left side) of the brothers' home were neighbors who were in their mid to late 20's being a brother with his pregnant sister and her husband. Across the street from their house was Quincy Thomas his wife Marion and their two children Quincy Jr. (Q-J) and daughter Maya. Also to the left of the brother, sister and husband neighbors was two Douglas County Sheriff's Office Deputies with the owner of the house being one of the officers I will call DG.

The younger neighbors on the left had a problem keeping their grass cut and had gotten a couple citations on different occasions for this code violation. Quincy across the street at some point had acquired a 1969 Mustang Coupe of which he wanted to restore for his son who would be turning 16 in the next two years. The car ran, hadn't been wrecked but needed paint, carpet, tires and a few mechanical things to make the car presentable and safe as a sixteenth birthday gift for his son. The purchase of this vehicle gave the family three cars in their driveway, two in the carport with one being the Mustang and Quincy parked his vehicle in front of the Mustang in the driveway. With the forming of the code enforcement dept. it was only a couple months before the officers of that department realized that the Mustang was not tagged or insured but it wasn't being driven. After a coupled of encounters with code enforcement Quincy thought he might have to get rid of the car because of the problem it was creating. The car itself did not make the property unsightly in any form or manner. Code enforcement told him more than once to move the vehicle by either getting rid of it or moving it to the backyard or tag and insure a vehicle that wasn't being driven. Quincy did not have anyway to work on the car if moved to the backyard because it would be exposed to the weather and he would then be working in the dirt. This almost became a style of harassment by the department. What ended this was that Quincy remembered that of all the houses on this street his was the only one that had not been moved into the boundary of the city limits and was still in the county's jurisdiction thus the City of Douglasville Ga. had no jurisdiction. It would have been nice for the City of Douglasville to know their own city limits boundaries before bringing grief and the heavy hand of the city to a family they had no jurisdiction over.

This same city does a spring and fall pickup of many types of trash being cut shrubs, small trees, home appliances (washers, dryers, etc.) and home improvement debris with one being carpet. The older brother of the two brothers wanted to put down wood floors in the house replacing the carpet. He did so by cutting up four foot sections the length of the room then putting down the wood floor allowing people to walk on either the wood floor or carpet except for a six inch space between both. Each carpet section was then rolled up and stored in the basement for the next fall or spring pickup. The job was competed and all the old carpet was neatly stacked in the basement awaiting the coming pickup. The Douglas County local paper announced the week of the pickup in their paper. The youngest brother moved the carpet to the side of the road on the week of the pickup as instructed in the paper. The city's code enforcement came by and left a warning citation _IN_ the _Mailbox_ to remove the carpet from the side of the road. The younger brother called the code enforcement office in regards to the situation and was told the sanitation dept. had not sent out notices as of that date and the date had been moved back by one or two weeks. The younger brother not wanting to move the carpet back to the basement again having to move it back up in one or two weeks stacked it in his utility trailer. The trailer stayed parked to the right side of the house's driveway and was tagged so it was legal under code enforcement rules. Again code enforce put another warning citation _IN_ the _Mailbox_ warning that the carpet should not to be visible from the road. Now he could have maybe put a tarp over the trailer or put a carpet remnants for sale sign on the trailer to maybe bypass the code enforcement rules but instead hauled the carpet to the dump paying the $6.00 charge for doing so. Too him it had become more hassle than it was worth waiting on the county pickup.

About a week later the younger brother was in Quincy's carport talking to him (a black man) when a code enforcement vehicle stopped just short of his driveway across the street. Two people were in the vehicle, one being the code enforcement officer, a black woman, the brother had been dealing with in regards to the carpet situation. The driver of the vehicle was a white older man maybe in his mid 50's whom the brother had not seen before. The man got out of the vehicle and walked to the neighbor's carport door knocking on it but no one came to the door so he walked back to the car. Mike's wife was home with her newly born baby but didn't go to the door because she didn't know the person at the door. She didn't notice the code enforcement vehicle because of where it was parked and they wore their street clothes when on duty. The brother in the carport told Quincy he was going down to talk to the woman and he would be right back. Upon reaching the passenger side of the car he knelled down and began having a normal conversation with the female code officer. He expressed how his intentions weren't to drag the neighborhood down and that the city should offer a little leeway considering the confuse caused by the local paper. Yet it was the city or the sanitation dept. that released the dates to the paper. He also wanted to mention the fact that the officers were entering the citizen's mailboxes to deliver city citations, which is beyond their authority and against federal law. The White code officer was in the driver's seat writing another citation for the neighbor's grass for about the third time. Before the conversation reached the mailbox issue and without the brother or the woman having a problem with the conversation the man interrupted. The man's opening statement was disrespectful when he said, "son, my advise to you is to get your ass back up in that yard, boy". The brother being caught off guard and insulted by the statement looked the man right in the eyes replying, "fuck you". The man then said, "I'll have you arrested" with the brother replying, "that may be true but you won't get out of that car and arrest me". All of what was said by both men was in a normal tone without any type of a raised voice or inappropriate action. Everything was normal other than what was said. With that said the brother walked back across the street to Quincy's carport and told him he was about to be arrested. Quincy laughed saying "arrested for what, nothing happened". The brother then told his friend what had transpired at the vehicle. Quincy still insisted nothing would come of it. After a few more minutes the man exited the vehicle walked up the road to the mailbox opened the door and inserted the code violation citation into the mailbox. After that, he turned looking at the two men in the carport and motioned for the brother to come down to his location in the road. The brother motioned for him to come up the driveway to the men's location. The man returned to his vehicle without the vehicle leaving. For the next 5 to 10 minutes, the brother stayed in the carport talking with Quincy. He mentioned to Quincy why would I walk down there to talk to a man who has already insulted me and threatened to arrest me. During this time, the Sheriff's Deputy and his Deputy roommate across the street had started dragging portions of a tree from the backyard to the front yard curb for the now scheduled sanitation pickup. A few minutes later a City of Douglasville police officer arrived and arrested the brother strictly on the advice of the male code enforcement officer because the city officer failed to question or take a statement of anyone else in the area including the female code enforcement officer, Quincy or his wife and two children who were in the house or either of the two Sheriff's Deputies. Upon the city officer's arrival, the woman code enforcement had gotten out of the vehicle and with the cuffing of the brother, she said, "this isn't right, this has been blown all out of proportion". Once hand cuffed by the city officer the now bad ass code enforcement officer thought it was now safe to show his government given power to abuse a citizen. He came within inches of his ear to yell in his ear "fuck me, fuck you" three or four times without the city officer protecting the individual from any harm that might come from this man's actions. The officer's actions showed he knew this individual being the male code enforcement before this situation took place, another possibility of bias. The brother actually thought about head butting the man while he was taking this abuse but knew that would have made the situation worse so it remained only a thought. With the male code enforcement officer's yelling it brought the two Sheriff's Deputies from the backyard of their house to the front yard at the road to see what was going on. They identified themselves as officers to the city police officer, which is also, what probably stopped the male code enforcement officer from yelling into the suspect's ear. Now with his arrest the brother is booked and put into a city holding cell after making a phone call to his brother to have him come bail him out on a signature bond.

Once receiving a court date and appearing on that date in a city court in front of a city judge for a plea of guilt or innocents the brother asked a couple of questions. First he asked about a court appointed attorney and the judge said a court appointed was not done in a municipality court. The second question was if he could have a jury trial and again the answer was "No". This was based on the fact that the court wasn't seeking jail time and this gives the court the right to have the case heard only by a *"city paid for"* judge. Wait just a second, not seeking jail time after already having been jailed depriving that citizen of free movement and bonding out is jail time. Also when the *plaintiff is the city* is this not a conflict of interest? In my opinion how do you get justice when the decision maker (the city judge) and the plaintiff (the city) are one in the same. In this case the judge would truly have to be above board and not in the city's pocket adjudicating in the city's interest. With his two questions answered, the brother entered a plea of not guilty. What was very unusual with this plea date was that both the code enforcement officers with maybe one of their supervisors was there sitting in on the plea. They had no requirement or obligation to be there. The fact that they weren't out doing their appointed jobs was an indication of what was to come in this Kangaroo city court system. While leaving the brother caught the black female code enforcement officer in the hallway away from the other members of the code enforcement department. He stated to her that she witnessed everything, what was said and done, her testimony being truthful or not would be the true deciding factor. She had no response.

Now with a trial date set the brother went to the city prosecuting attorney and filed a motion of discovery to have all evidence released that the attorney had in regards to the case. Upon receiving the evidence folder a few days later the brother discovered that the statements (the only evidence) made by both code enforcement officers was that the suspect was in Quincy's driveway yelling at the top of his lungs, insults, for 10 to 20 minutes before the code enforcement officers called for city police. Well the brother thinking that this was such a bad lie that he would not have any problem showing the statements were false even if the female code enforcement officer lied.

The brother then went and got some court summons forms to ensure any needed witness would be at the trial to testify. The court stated that the summons could either be served by the police department at a cost of $50 dollars each or can be served by the defendant at no cost. The brother served Quincy and his wife, Mike and his wife who code enforcement put their citation in their mailbox. On trying to serve the Sheriff's Deputies, he found it a little more difficult. On finding out about the summons because they would move quickly from the car to the house and then not answer the door when knocked on. It took him a week to serve both officers and upon serving DG, he stated, "Why are you serving us we didn't hear or see anything"? The brother replied, "Exactly, now read their statements because you did hear when the code enforcement officer was yelling because that is what brought both of you to the front of your house to the road".

The brother then went to the city's personnel office for the records of both code enforcement officers. Not trusting having to walk into the lion's den of city government, he took a voice-activated tape recorder with him. Upon the request for the employee's files, which are public documents he was notified that the files would have to be redacted to ensure personal information was not released and that it might understandably be a day or two for this to happen. So he gave them his phone number to call him. Now in going there to request these files it was unexpected so no one at City Hall knew the brother was coming.

Once receiving the phone call from City Hall personnel that the files were ready, he again entered the lion's den only this time they knew he was coming. Again, with tape recorder in hand the brother went to city hall and the personnel department. Upon arrival, he was then informed that each page copied would cost $0.15 cents and looked like there were maybe 125 pages. The brother asked if he could review the papers to see what was pertinent in the files as to the case. They directed him to a meeting room at which point he sat down and started going over the material. About 10 minutes later a person stuck their head in the room checking on him. A very short conversation was held in regards to if he needed anything but the brother answered, he was fine. About a total of a half hour later, the brother had about 12 pages that were relevant to the case. On exiting the room moving to the human resources counter, he handed back all the pages except for the 12. Showing them the twelve, he handed them $2.00, got his $0.20 cents back, and headed for the door to exit city hall. At the information desk at the entrance and exit of city hall four people had gathered not including the desk person. Upon reaching the desk a man, the head of code enforcement, addressed the brother regarding the impending case. He stated how code enforcement has the power to enforce the rules of the City of Douglasville. The brother replied, "It's not the rules that created this problem it's the personnel that has created this problem". The man continued to spout that his personnel are hired to enforce these rules. Again the brother replied, "It's funny how you believe citizens should follow the rules of your department and yet your department doesn't follow Federal Law when entering the mailbox of a citizen to deliver your departments citations while also disrespecting these same citizens verbally". The man was stuck on the mailbox issue by saying his department had the right to enter a citizen's mailbox to deliver a citation with the brother each time he said it replied, "NO, you don't". It wasn't until the information desk person spoke up saying "he's right" referring to the brother. The brother looked at the woman behind the desk, said "thank you for knowing the law", and turned leaving.

What the brother had discovered in the papers was interesting in regards to one of the code enforcement officers. Lets begin with the woman, she was her churches bookkeeper and had little in regards to her job performance in the file. She had been employed with the city beginning only with the inception of the city's code enforcement department. Each time the brother had spoke with the woman she was a normal polite, not siding on the abuse of power side and not apologetic for doing her job, exactly what a public servant should be. Although she also entered mailboxes, to deliver the city's citations but had done so at the direction of the head of the code enforcement department. The same person who the brother had argued with over the same subject. So why would a religious person after swearing on the bible to tell the truth then lie? The pressure of keeping her job! Anytime a government (local, state or National) whistle blower comes to the forefront with the truth, what happens? History has continually dictated that they are degraded, punished and demoted if not forced out under the system of what we know as Government or "the good ole boys". So when and as long as this mentality exists, justice can never be obtained from the same entity that also disburses justice being government and in this case being city government.

Now for the male code enforcement officer, his file had maybe 100 pages. The brother's pages he paid for were mostly the pages regarding this person's employment with the City of Douglasville, Ga. This person began his employment with the City of Douglasville as a firefighter with the fire department. During his time with the department, he continually had problems following the orders of his superiors, which was documented numerous times in his personal file. Upon the department heads of the fire department having had enough of this man he was transferred unbelievably to the City of Douglasville City Police Department. Again, the man had the same problems with any type of authority in the City Police Department as indicated and recorded in his personal file. At this point, the person was transferred to his third City Government job being the Code Enforcement Department of the City. Now if this person's attitude was as bad with his immediate supervisors what makes anyone believe this same bad attitude couldn't be directed at a Citizen of the

City of Douglasville? The authorities within that city government knew this man's history and still protected him so he had these types of opportunities to inflict his rage or anger on unsuspecting Citizens of the City with the brother being one of them.

On court day for the prosecution, the two code enforcement officers and the lone City Police Officer showed up for court. For the defense, would you like to guess who didn't show up? If you guessed the two Douglas County Sheriff's Deputies being DG and his officer roommate you would be correct. The brother had hired a lawyer at a minimal cost of $350.00 dollars to help insure his rights were not abused in court. The understanding was the brother would do all the legwork in regards to material and witnesses for the case. Upon the realization that the two officers were not going to show the brother told the lawyer. The lawyer again going the way of the dollar told his client that if he postponed the trial he would need more money to return? Is this in the name of justice, or money? The brother now knowing both the officers were not interested in justice or the duties of their oath might also lie once on the stand so went with the witnesses that were there, being Quincy and his wife and Mike and his wife. There was also one statement added to the city's prosecutor's list of evidence which had never been turned over when the motion for discovery was filed. It was a sworn statement by the woman at city hall who had stuck her head into the room checking on the brother. In the statement, the woman had stated that the brother was disrespectful to her while there. The judge was about to admit this sworn document into evidence when the defendant brother mentioned that for the whole time in city hall he had that voice activated recorder with that conversation on it. He stated that he also would like to have it entered into evidence since the court had already read the statement in court. The judge then reversed course stating that this individual was not in court so could not be cross examined and decided then not to allow the sworn statement thus not allowing the defendant brother's tape recording into evidence so it no longer needed to be played to the court. Really? The journey of the court was never an attempt for the truth! Would you like to guess who the judge sided with in regards to the testimony and yes, the one thing that was determined in this trial was code enforcement admitting going into mailboxes to deliver citations. Was anyone arrested, fired or even disciplined? No! They also started using tape to attach citations to citizen's mailboxes and home doors. The brother got court costs, probation with probation costs for 6 months with early release upon finishing 40 hours of community service, which could only be done one eight hour day a week. The city employees found it disappointing that the brother got a medical release that allowed him to serve his community hours in Cobb County at the American Cancer Society. They were looking forward to having this person in their services for whatever reasons, I am sure we can imagine what might have been in store for him in this justice driven city.

For the next four years, the Black Code Enforcement Officer knowing she had lied and knowing the brother along with Quincy knew she lied, would hide her face while passing by the brother's home if he was in the front yard. What do you think her god of her church thinks about her actions? Only she will know the outcome. Forgiveness only comes when the truth is revealed to all unless you are Catholic.

Now you might think the brother blamed the black woman code enforcement officer. Actually, he felt sorry for her and her choice in this case. She was the closest to being a caring human being out of the group and the rest were white. She was the only person to show and feel any guilt in what had been done. In regards to the rest, nothing.

As for the two Douglas County Sheriff's Deputies, the brother got film footage of the officers throwing parties at their house located on this narrow road with no parking signs all up and down the road. Also with city police allowing the cars of fellow officers to illegally park on the road known as roller coaster road to locals and called Cindy Dr. The brother also has footage of on duty officers in sheriff's cruisers picking up people at the house and driving them to the store and back. On the deputies back deck he has film footage of what may be an officer antagonizing a 12 year old mixed race child that while shooting a BB gun was told by someone "I'll get my gun and shot you". Now you should be able to see an officer of the citizens is not always what you get, and justice is not their goal. The "good ole boy system" is alive and well in government and it's not racial but directed at the poorer citizens that may not be able or want to spend the money to fight the trumped up charges. Even doing so doesn't mean justice will be served. Seems government is the only entity that gets a fair trial because government holds the power.

With these four factual stories, there are two things in common with each and every one of these situations being an abuse of power and everyone cooperated with the law enforcement while having illegal things done to them. In the case of the three friends in New Orleans, I have heard you don't take a knife to a gunfight and you don't start a fight with the person who has the gun and your knife. Being stupid with an officer of the law will not help your present or post position regardless of the character of the officer that is arresting you. Is there a problem with the system? Absolutely. Can it be corrected if the system itself is corrected? Yes. Is this a race only problem? Absolutely not the above harassed or arrested were all white and actually, one black man was released while retaining three whites. The whites are the privileged when talking in the context of the race debate and police abuse Blacks only but as you can see that ideology carries no weight. The ones that abuse, abuse all citizens regardless of color but it's the race baiters of the Liberal Democrat Party that want to make it a Black issue only when it's not. This endangers all involved because violence is what the race baiters want, to ensure their livelihoods, their donated money lifestyles.

Let us again look at Trayvon Martin, Michael Brown & Eric Garner. I am not going into depth on any of the cases I am just going directly to the facts.

With the Trayvon Martin case, first there is no law that states someone cannot follow you for whatever reason they see fit. Second, stalking is being followed by the same person on numerous occasions not a one-time occurrence. Third, the stand your ground law had no bearing in regards to this case. The witness testified as to who was on top and who was on bottom with the top person inflicting damage on the bottom person and by the law that is self defense. The stand your ground law endorses the use of a weapon when needed to ensure your rights to stay or go somewhere you have the right to be. If the weapon had of already been pulled by George Zimmerman, Trayvon would probably still be alive today. Who attacks someone that has a gun pointed at them? Someone not in their right mind! Also if Trayvon had of just hit him in the nose, which is still assault, but had not followed that action by going down on George to inflict more punishment I believe he would still be alive today! Trayvon's bad choices ended Trayvon's life.

Next is Michael Brown, I will go back to this person's life history to make a point. His parents were divorced, which parent was granted custody by the portion of government that makes that decision? The Courts and it was the mother? She had remarried and the individual she married was not the type of person I would want around my child. Michael's friend that was with him during the last half hour of his life was a person of questionable character. His tattoos and especially the teardrop tattoos at his eye which is a gang member status symbol for having two kills of other people or gang members. As a parent of either gender if this person even tried to come around any child of mine he would be run off with my child having the understanding I will not put up with you being around that person. Now with that said do you believe that was Michael's first attempt at shoplifting or strong arm robbery? If the man in the store had of truly tried to stop Michael, what do you think would have happened to the man? Michael at 6'3" or 6'4" and 292 lbs. was not pulled into that SUV by that officer without his own willingness to enter the vehicle. His blood was inside the vehicle, his blood trailed down the road and then back again towards the officer. Six or Seven black citizens of the neighborhood testified that Michael's actions matched the forensics of the shooting scene and the officer's testimony. A so called witness, that same friend of Michael, states Michael was shot in the back but he wasn't, also stated Michael stopped raised his hands, turned and dropped to his knees but if this were true where did the blood trail come from leading back to the car and Michael's body. So this person's testimony also is not supported by the forensics of the case. Therefore, anybodies testimony that stated these same facts were not credible, and some even later admitted they never saw or was at the site of the shooting when it happened and that is perjury. The last bit of forensics not mentioned in the case is something you saw as a kid. When running and falling, depending on speed, the asphalt cherry you received were scratches from the asphalt showing the direction you were traveling when receiving the injury. Did Michael receive these types of injuries?

I'm all for police officers having camera footage and audio anytime they interact with the public, 24/7 when on the job. Michael's mistake is that he confronted the officer with violence giving the officer options under the law to achieve what the officer felt needed to be achieved to secure the officer's safety, otherwise known as officer's discretion to protect himself.

The death of Eric Garner in the Liberal Democrat City of New York was police abuse, period. Yes, he was resisting arrest but he was resisting without violence. It was the abusive maneuvers of the police that killed this man not this man's actions alone. Being arrested for selling loose cigarettes because of taxes not being collected is a poor excuse for the death of this man. Obviously, this law is aimed at the poor because you will not see a person of means selling loose cigarettes. Ann Coulter had the best saying I have heard yet, "Don't stand between a Liberal Democrat and the taxes they collect they will kill you over the tax money". So the Liberal Democrats upon passing this city law wrote into the law that this individual would be arrested instead of being ticketed for such an offense. The officers with this law are placed in a position by the Liberal Democrat lawmakers to have to make an arrest on such a low level crime. Are not Liberal Democrat law makers just as much at fault as the police officers? When you write a stupid law, it has consequences. Again I still have to fall back on the aspect of resisting the police which would of never put the police in that situation had Eric just turned around and put his hands behind his back. If you don't like Eric being arrested for selling loose cigarettes then protest at the Liberal Democrat's door step of the Mayor's office and those that passed the law because the fault is in their hands for the situation the law created.

Just to illustrate that this white person is no more racist than any blacks who are also racists, Rodney King was not being arrested and was being beaten beyond an attempt to arrest him. O.J. Simpson was NOT GUILTY because the evidence was tainted the moment the investigating officer took the blood sample to the crime scene and upon turning it into the lab the amount drawn from O.J. didn't match what was turned into the lab. Other than that I think it was probably him but beyond a shadow of a doubt. But do you really believe O.J. would of got off with a court appointed attorney? Honesty should be at the root of justice and race, politics or anything else has no place in justice it only muddies the water's of the facts that lead to the truth on which justice is applied. Without truth, justice has no meaning.

As for protesters, the Constitution gives every American that right. As for rioters, the Constitution describes you as a criminal. That is because when individuals purposely inflict suffering onto other innocent individuals you have now committed a criminal act. You have now become no better and even worse than the Rodney King officers and they went to jail and so should you, congrats.

As for the truth, race baiters, protesters, rioters and racists of all races let me leave you with a name, Miriam Carey. The 34-year-old BLACK WOMAN dental hygienist and former Brooklyn resident who was shot by White House Security while in her car and her 1 year old child in a child seat in the backseat. What happened to the investigation? Is it the fact that Blacks protesting and rioting at the house of a Black Liberal Democrat President would be a black eye for the so-called racist movement or a Black Liberal Democrat President? By these same people, not saying a word shows the true racist and sexist views of this group of people. The truth and justice is not high up on your list of morals. Remember what I am saying, there was not a word compared to the other two shootings so what is your excuse? Address the people please because in this situation all you people must know and agree with the truth because none of you have said a word or had any type of protest. The riot pushers and race baiters addressing these events and Al Sharpton, being one and the same, can't say he hasn't been to the White House. So please explain it to me, why the silence with her death? Being a white racist, sexist male, I think something stinks in regards to everyone mentioned regarding her possible misguided killing. I personally would like to hear the truth of the event of her death, was she resisting officers? Yes, she drove off at a moderate rate of speed. Did she hit an officer with her car? Not in the video footage I saw. Did she die because of a health related issue brought on by an officer's possible abusive technique? No. To me it looked like she had been boxed in by police with their vehicles and then shot while still in her car. Are they guilty? You don't know until you hear the evidence. Therefore, Washington D.C. go peacefully protest so we can all hear the evidence. No slurs, no false statements, no race issue, just a respectful protest to have all the evidence released in regards to her death because in my eyes the cat's in the other tree and your barking up the wrong trees.

A LIBERAL KING, A UN-CONSTITUTIONAL PRESIDENT

Where to begin to describe this man's two terms of office. I'll start with something that always throws people off when discussing Barack Obama and his 2 terms as President. What are the two GOOD things Barack did for our country? First with the Gulf of Mexico Deep Horizon oil spill he kept the event's litigation out of the courts with his heavy handed type of governing. This statement only includes the litigation of the event not the clean up or any other aspect of the event including the results of the litigation. My statement only suggests that the costs of the clean up and cost for any assistance to the citizens affected would have been tied up in the courts for god knows how long. So these costs would have fallen on the citizen tax payers. Ironically the ability to correct the blowout in a timely manner falls on the environmental groups that caused these wells to be built farther offshore in deeper water where man could not get to the well to fix because of the depth of the well allowing for a longer period of oil flow.

Second is the fact that Barack brought too the forefront most of the flaws of and in the Constitution. His time in office has illustrated how to circumvent portions of the Constitution using the powers of Government and his political party in doing so. He also is the first President that has used race as a cover to accomplish these actions. The fact that his skin color made it difficult if not impossible to suggest that some of his actions were unconstitutional was a privilege in itself, a privilege based on color, thus a black privilege even though he is half white. He uses his color to suit his situation. To suggest he violated the Constitution was and is deemed by the Democrat Party and the Liberal Media as a racist issue is now a political advantage of one party over another based on race and not the procedures or the written laws of the Constitution. So is this now a Black Privilege of the Presidential Office for now and anytime into the future? How far can a Black Republican Uncle Tom President go beyond the limits of the Constitution before the Democrats yell foul? Also when doing so would that also be racism when confronted by Liberal Democrats. The answer is not far because the Democrat Party already calls a Black Republican Congressman an Uncle Tom. This action is not deemed as racist by them or the Democrat citizens when in actuality it is a racist slur directed at a Black man plain and simple. The key is a Black can't be deemed racist even though they are human and it is a trait of all humans to some extent including Blacks or any other race. No human no matter what their color or political party is above the laws of nature, your not, no matter what you may believe or try to make others believe. It is only the extent of the emotion that determines where you stand and racism is racism no matter how you camouflage it and it doesn't work in just one direction of society.

With this being said I will try too do this section from as neutral of a stand point as possible limiting my thoughts to only things I can prove with facts. Any thoughts outside that realm I will not inject race into and will point out it can't be proven for certain.

I'm going to first go after the sealing of documents. As a normal person, at the expense of a lawyer and court costs, had their birth certificate and/or school records sealed? This says something about the person's motives. Does anyone reading this have their documents sealed? A majority of more than 99% would say no. My understanding is Hawaii automatically seals birth certificates, fine. That still doesn't explain high school and college records. Having a birth certificate sealed is a person's choice but under the Constitution (law) there are requirements of an individual to have a certain type of citizenship to be eligible for the Presidential election. This rule of law has been in the Constitution from the Documents inception. So a potential Presidential candidate must release the needed documents to verify his citizenship to "We the People". That means all the people not just a select few of the Democrat Party or any other political party. It is not a political argument it's the law written in the Constitution by the Founding Fathers. His choice to not or stall in releasing this needed information was used as a political weapon.

When Barack was interviewed about his attendance in Rev. Wright's Chicago Church he addressed some questions in a way that made no real sense. When asked about Rev. Wright's stance on America and the degrading things Wright had said about America in his church sermons Barack replied "I really didn't pay attention to the church services". If you are not there for the church services what are you there for? How can you spend 20 years in your family's church and then say you didn't pay attention to anything in the church for those 20 years? My god his two children were Baptized in that church.

This is what I meant by vetting a Presidential candidate. He has a college degree in the studies of the Constitution and doesn't realize or care about the requirements drawn out in the Constitution that require him to reveal his citizenship status in order to be a candidate. As for the topic of Rev. Wright's church nobody attends organized meetings on every Sunday morning over a period of 20 years and says "ah, I wasn't paying attention". Barack could of said many sensible things other than what he said like "I don't agree with everything Rev. Wright speaks about in his sermons" but he didn't he chose a white lie on a minor issue. Again if you will lie about the small stuff you will definitely lie about the things that matter such as Obamacare and "you can keep your healthcare insurance and doctor", repeated many times by Barack.

Barack when choosing a side on a issue or topic has been so wrong so many times. Occupy Wall Street vs. Tea Party, Beer Summit, Trayvon Martin vs. George Zimmerman, Michael Brown vs. the Police, Arab Spring, Iran vs. Israel, Enemies vs. Allies, Nuclear Iran vs. non-Nuclear Iran, the Russian reset, Putin, Terrorism, Iraq, releasing terrorists, releasing domestic killers, immigration, etc. where should I end? Statistically a neutral person couldn't be wrong that many times without picking one winner. So the side he chose to side with was the side driven by his agenda and not by the facts of the situations.

Another lie told by Barack was the statement he made in regards to the $4.9 Trillion spent by the previous President Bush in his two terms as President. Barack stated it was like taking America's credit card and running it up by borrowing for government. I actually agree with Barack's statement. Unfortunately Barack didn't agree with

Barack's statement and has a $7.5 Trillion dollar debt for his first six years of his two terms. Because of his first two lies I had my doubts about his statement and my doubts became reality with this being his third lie as a Presidential candidate. So was it that as a candidate Barack didn't understand the deficit and debt problem or he did but lied to get elected. Barack has used this borrowed money to repay some of the people of this country and other Nations for America's Colonial actions he has deemed as wrong. Yet in his infinite wisdom that doesn't allow him to see that these wrong actions where enacted by the same Political Party of which Barack Obama represents. Thus Redistribution or REPARATIONS for what the DEMOCRAT PARTY has done in HISTORY, NOT what AMERICA has done in HISTORY. Yes, America may have elected these Democrat Presidents but as in Barack Obama's case were they elected on their own lies during their candidacy?

Barack has been caught telling so many lies during his terms that at some point you can't trust what he is saying is the truth. So an individual goes from hearing what is believed to be the truth by this person. When vetting these same words for lies to now believing what is said are lies and having to now vet those words for any truths. That is where the old saying comes from "I know he's lying his lips are moving" because he can't be trusted with the truth. I would still like to know what Barack meant when caught on an open microphone saying to a Russian official "I'll have more leeway after my re-election". More leeway for what? It can't be a matter of National Security if the country you are saying this too has been a cold war enemy since WWII. Is there a possibility that this "leeway" was a position he could take in regards to the invasion of Crimea and the Ukraine. Not opposing the invasion with an opposing force or weapons to the invaded country's military but sending blankets and food is a red carpet invitation to Russia and Putin to proceed unabated by the West or NATO.

Liberal Left Democrats have used the rising cost of oil and gas too demonize the younger President Bush during his terms because he happened to have made some of his money in the business himself. Where was that same criticism as gas hit almost $5.00 a gallon and a barrel of oil went over $100.00 a barrel under Barack Obama? Pointing to the sanctions placed on Russia lead by Barack as the cause or anything he did is nothing more than a political reply to defend Barack. The last thing Barack wanted to see was falling oil & gas prices. Why? Because it affects his Green Agenda of Solar & Wind Power making them less able to compete in the Energy Market due to Falling Energy Prices. If he had of wanted lower oil & gas prices he would have issued more drilling permits for Federal Lands and would have allowed the Keystone Pipeline from Canada to be built which never happened. In reality a President can have little effect on the price of energy unless they limit drilling or place more taxes on the products themselves.

Barack Obama regularly falls back on his education as a "Constitutional Lawyer" using it as a tool to imply he understands the Document known as our "Constitution". His understanding of this Document is so far left of the document's true intent. Again Liberal Democrats do not like the document because it is suppose to make them operate within the confines of the written law. When going outside those confines of the written law being the "Constitution" it gives the citizens such laws as Obamacare which has been written, rewritten, and continually changed thru regulations to suit the special interest groups of the Democrat Party. Such being Labor Unions for their own gain being allowed to opt out of the original healthcare law as written avoiding the Cadillac tax on very good healthcare insurance policies. This causes other portions of the citizenship to have to pickup the costs of the law with higher premiums leaving the unions monetarily unaffected. That is why it is imperative for a President's executive orders or a committee's regulations to follow the guidelines of the written law. If truly governing for all the people Barack and Democrats would of focused on the cost of insurance, what insurance companies pay to hospitals for healthcare procedures. Compared to what medical facilities that do not accept any type of insurance charge for the same healthcare procedures and the enormous disconnect of pricing between the two. This is caused by insurance companies required procedures. The true tell-tell sign of a corrupt Presidency is one that issues Executive orders or Regulations that alters it's own laws passed during it's own control of government such as Obamacare. To my knowledge Barack Obama is the only President in the history of the United States to be sued by a group of Nuns over their own birth control or any issue to date. I thought the reasoning for the Democrats argument was for women to control their own reproductive choices. Unless of course they are Nuns. Three words "Abstinence and Faith" Barack, something you show to be lacking in your character. That is a great distinction for the history of an American President and a newly obtained low for your administration.

Abraham Lincoln was saddened by how quickly the nation divided after his election caused by his thoughts on human rights and freedom being granted by god, not man or government. Barack Obama was happy by how quickly he divided the nation into groups or otherwise he would not have done it and would not have continued doing it. The process was continued because the Liberal Left President along with Liberal Left Democrats saw it as a political advantage regardless of what it was doing to the country. Again, Political Party before country. The war on women: men vs. women, the haves and the have not's: rich vs. poor, the employed tax payers vs. the unemployed or under employed benefits recipients. A aspect he has maintained with the lack of jobs that also create low wages. Black vs. White by backing lawless acts of one race while ignoring lawless acts against the other race. Atheists vs. Religion / Christians vs. Muslims, his political party (Democrats) and him have backed atheists and Muslims over Christians. Young vs. old with the financially un-established young supporting the financially established old with the Obamacare healthcare law. Liberal vs. Conservative, Barack and Democrats referring to the Conservative House of Representatives as Terrorist when in actuality are a equal branch of government and when combined with a agreeing super majority Senate has more power in government than the President. Government vs. Civilians, the IRS targeting of civilians based upon party affiliation. Elected Democrat Government vs. Military, Democrat's in government demonizing military actions of which they approved of just years earlier, lack of attention regarding the Veterans Administration, draw down of Military levels of employment, over 4 times as many people work for government than are in the Military, over 92 times of more people are on a welfare program than are in the Military. A Sovereign America vs. a open door Liberal Democrat's endorsement of a New World Order America, illegal immigration. Allies vs. enemies, alienated our allies around the world while believing the Obama administration could bring our country into the good graces of our morally lacking enemies. Our enemies just used this perception to advance their own causes at a cost too America and our Allies.

Abraham Lincoln's intentions in his second term were to govern with a sense of unity for the nation, thus his reasoning for running as a National Union Party candidate and not a Republican. His choice as Vice-President was Andrew Johnson a Democrat also relinquishing his party's affiliation to run as a National Union Party candidate. These two men saw the needs of a Nation as a greater good than the needs of their original political parties. These two men were our first and only National Union Party President and Vice President in an attempt to heal our Nation after the Civil War. With Lincoln's assassination Johnson's move from the National Union Party to an Independent Party affiliation and not back to the Democrat Party was his attempt to continue the beliefs of the two men. Thus as I mentioned in another section Andrew Johnson being our only Independent Party President in the history of our Nation.

Barack Obama has governed with the use of division of our citizenship, brother against brother. More like what happened with the Civil War. Divide and Conquer in the name of a political party. This thought of governing is the direct opposite of how Lincoln & Johnson viewed what our Nation needed at its greatest time of need in its history. At any point in history doesn't a Nation still have "a greatest need" for that time period of history? Imagine Lincoln & Johnson using Barack's thoughts of governing during their Presidential time in office, we as a Nation would not be a Nation of 50 States.

Barack Obama's political origins came out of Chicago Illinois as a community organizer. Funny thing about the words "Community Organizer", it is such a broad term in relation too who is being organized. Is it a city block, a portion of the city, half the city, all the city, a portion of a state, half a state, all the state, a portion of a country, half a country, all the country? Barack's thoughts on "Community Organizer" are not based on any type of geography but based strictly on his political views of the Democrat Party and he has never wavered from his party's beliefs. No political party's beliefs or agenda is 100% correct but Barack has governed as if his or his party's beliefs are 100% correct despite what happens in a National Election.

A true organizer is one that brings both sides together to discuss their different views and then attempts to alter those non-truth based views through discussions. A true organizer and at this point a mediator will be non-bias recognizing both side's views and seeking compromise where compromise is appropriate and staying firm & maintaining course when not appropriate. Three men in our country's history have followed these thoughts and abided by these rules and they are Abraham Lincoln, Andrew Johnson & Martin Luther King, Jr.

The ironic aspect of these two men's lives is that Abraham Lincoln was assassinated by a Native born and raised Northerner John Wilkes Booth of Bel Air, Maryland. Martin Luther King, Jr. was assassinated by a Native born and raised Northerner James Earl Ray of Alton, Illinois. Both assassins where sympathetic to either the Democrat Party's ideology allowing and wanting slavery or the Democrat Party's ideology allowing or wanting segregation and in either case wanted a second class person or citizen.

Barack Obama's political views are right in line with previous Democrat Presidents in regards to atrocities committed throughout the history of America. His own campaign promises to end the wars in Iraq and Afghanistan along with closing the Guantanamo Bay Terrorist Prison in Cuba. These promises theoretically boxed himself into a corner with his own illogical thoughts & promises. First of all you can't end a war while the other side is still attacking you. Secondly what our country has described as a "War on Terror" is anything but a War on Terror. Terror tactics are what are being used by our opponents but the war its self is a "Religious War" on "Christianity and all other Religions including Atheism" by a large aspect of the "Muslim / Islamic Religion". A war that has been fought throughout the ages since about 600 A.D. Maybe the supreme Court can put an end to the war with a separation of "Church and War" ruling or ruling against "Religion and Atheism" outright removing both from our country. What scares me is that a true Liberal sees this as an actual solution not realizing there is a second step still needing to be taken to obtain this idiotic solution which is adopting the Muslim / Islamic religion. OOPS, isn't that what the Democrat Party wanted to do at it's Democrat National Convention with it's original political platform for the 2012 elections. It wasn't until Democrats had that

LAUGHABLE DEMOCRATIC VERBAL VOTE to reinstate GOD into their DEMOCRAT PLATFORM. Another Priceless moment caught on tape to be replayed on YOUTUBE for future generations of true AMERICANS. Google or Bing "DNC vote on GOD". Notice that the Chairman of the DNC mentions that Barack Obama recognizes Jerusalem as the Capital of Israel but nothing about the recognition of GOD by Barack Obama. It is this attitude of Barack that has allowed the deaths of thousands of Christians who Barack sees as an Invasive Religion of the Middle East. Yet Christianity was created and evolved from that same region at least 600 years before the existence of the Muslim / Islamic Religion thus Barack's and the Democrat Party's lack of support for Israel. So is Barack Hussein Obama II a closet Muslim having falsely portrayed himself as a Christian to get elected as our 44th and current President? How far will a Liberal Left Democrat Politician go as to lie to be elected to an office of our Government?

Barack Obama spent his first two years as the closest thing to a King this Country has ever had in my lifetime. Barack never had any intentions of working with anybody other than his closest fellow Democrats and his hand picked staff working towards a political game plan for his Presidency. The very first political move was to lock America's Representatives, some Democrats & all Republicans, out of the room during the writing of a Health Care Bill aka the Affordable Care Act aka OBAMACARE. With the impending vote on the bill Congress wasn't given the time to read the bill. It passed on strict party lines with NO Republican votes. This action of a King set the stage for future non-cooperation by Republicans. Barack Obama made it plainly clear that elections have consequences and with Democrats dominating both legislative houses and the office of President that this gave him the opportunity too rule as a "KING". Even the MEDIA portrayed him as a "KING" with magazine covers such as Time magazine. The cover portrayed the, for a lack of a better word, man with his head back looking down his nose at all people. KING Obama has used this same pose while knowing he was being photographed in un-staged photo opportunities. It is this part of his character that has also brought his Narcissistic traits to the forefront of his character. Adolf Hitler used this same pose during his public speeches and had the same character flaw along with others as does Barack. I believe Barack fashioned his style of speaking after Adolf Hitler because history, has and it was well deserved, portrayed Hitler as one of the most charismatic speakers ever. Barack's own arrogance is what lead too Obamacare being his only self perceived accomplishment as President. Imagine if the Democrat Party with the numbers to do almost anything had done just that by passing new immigration laws, his green agenda laws using Carbon Dioxide, etc. in those first two years. It was his own arrogance of believing he had all the time in the world because who would oppose a KING like him?

Well in 2010 his party lost control of the House of Representatives being 50% of the legislative branches. It was this single loss that ended his abilities to have legislation passed into law unchecked by a opposing political party. This brings us to the four year Whining section of his Presidency. With losing the House and his abilities to have his agenda based legislation passed he started WHINING to his base of voters that Government had been stopped by a inferior half of one third or 16.666...% part of government that is not allowing his agenda's through government. OOPS, just a bad miscalculation on his part for NOT understanding our government? But even under a 3 branch system the House of Representatives (16.66...% of power) and the Senate (16.66...% of power) are still a checks & balance of each other. Barack should of known this but would not recognize that fact because he sees it as his party controlling the Presidency and ½ of Congress still out numbering the Republican Party in control of the House of Representatives. Barack got a quick lesson on our type of government finding out he had to work with Republicans if he wanted to pass any type of legislation. KING Barack work with Republicans, he would never stoop that low as to work with the peasants of politics. Thus the next four years of **Barack Obama WHINING to the public** and his liberal base on TV about *"A DO NOTHING CONGRESS"*. He used this phrase a hundred times or more to justify his present and coming executive orders that unconstitutionally created legislated law too push his agendas. Again, he did this while also using his privilege of skin color *(RACISM)* as cover for his executive actions.

Now with KING Obama losing the House of Representatives and the Senate. My prediction for Barack is he will not change his direction or attitude because his intelligence level will not allow it.

Our KING will continue ***NOT*** to work with the Republican peasants of politics because in doing so he must give up his THRONE AS KING. His future two years as KING will encompass his character as now a *"Whiner" in Chief of America* also allowing him to gain the *THRONE AS THE KING OF WHINERS.*

Barack has ruled as President with the privilege of being Black causing a handle with care attitude, a do not offend attitude or the race word "Racist" will be used in his defense. This privilege has allowed him to rule in a different manner than any White President in past history due to his skin color instead of being judged by his actions and performance in office. If history portrays Barack Obama's Presidency in a favorable manner will that be based on his actions and performance in office or because of skin color? If history portrays Barack Obama's Presidency in an unfavorable manner will that be based on his actions and performance in office or because of skin color? Considering that academia is controlled by the Liberal Left the facts of his Presidency will not truly be portrayed but limited as historical facts have been in the past. This is a protection system of the Liberal Left to camouflage its own acts in history and present day actions by rewriting or not truly connecting the dots of history to keep the Liberal Left Democrat Party relevant so that it may retain some type of power in future government.

This is the True Liberal Left Democrat's atrocity of Barack's two terms. Barack's only option to achieve his campaign promises of ending the wars and closing Guantanamo Bay Terrorist Prison and maintaining the Democrat's Liberal Left views are the "Death by Drone" option. A true "War on Terror" would include an all of the above approach, capturing terrorists when able for needed information using interrogation methods the Liberal Left Democrat's President deems as humane and "Death by Drone" for terrorists not available for capture. Forget the lost intelligence by not capturing our opponents then having to interrogate them for the information. Forget the fact that Barack and the Liberal Left Democrat Party tried to use these Enhanced Interrogation Techniques as a lawless act against a former Republican President, Military under his guidance and the current Republican Party. The "Death by Drone" was the only option because how do you close Guantanamo Bay Prison while continually adding to its prisoner population? With each individual added it makes the task of closing it that much harder. This also explains the "No Boots on the Ground" tactic and the original pulling of troops from Iraq by undermining the "Status of Forces" agreement because that would generate Terrorist prisoners. If you kill that individual you don't add to the population allowing at some point for the facility to be closed with prisoner reduction. This also brings into question the killing of a high value target such as Osama bin Laden who could have offered massive amounts of counter intelligence. He would have also offered massive amounts of problems for the Obama administration if captured alive. Where would the administration put him after being interrogated and could you ever release the man who organized the 9/11 killings of almost 3,000 Americans? The answers are Gitmo & No, thus this would have caused the situation of never being able to close the Guantanamo Bay Terrorist Prison. If you are now never able to close Gitmo because of one terrorist what is the purpose of letting all the other dangerous terrorists go when the facility will remain open? Now with that said what was the true directive given to our troops when going after bin Laden in his compound, was the directive more to kill than capture? Considering that the shooter shot him 3 times in the face I think it's safe to say the directive was too kill. With this aspect of Barack's Agenda revealed it also gives the answer for the none pursuit of the Terrorists that attacked the United States' Consulate in Benghazi, Libya. The fact that the Liberal Left Democrats would not use the word "Terror" was their attempt too make these actions a criminal offense allowing them to be adjudicated in a criminal court then sentenced to a prison within the United States again not adding to the Terrorist prisoners at Gitmo. So the "Death by Drone" was an attempt to kill three political birds with one stone. Allowing for the Demonizing of the Republican Party for its Enhanced Interrogation Techniques and also making good on a campaign promise of closing Guantanamo Bay Terrorist Prison. Upon achieving these tasks would also achieve a Presidential legacy for Barack Obama and the Democrat Party. The "Death by Drone" wasn't just a Tactic of War against Terrorism but more of a Tactic of Political Gain at a cost of human life whether being an innocent child or an adult guilty of Terrorism. A trade off of setting some free from Guantanamo Bay while killing others in the battlefield all in the name of politics.

Are the political actions of Barack Obama an impeachable offense during his office of Presidency? The fact that the deaths were based on a Political Agenda, a campaign promise, does it raise it to a greater accountability as a War Crime? Or will **REVERSE RACISM** protect him because of the color of his skin? <u>**DEATH BY LIBERAL DEMOCRAT POLITICS, THE ENDS JUSTIFY THE MEANS!**</u>

The Liberal Left Democrat King with his taught knowledge of the Constitution and vast experience of incomplete terms in the State Legislature and as a National Senator began his Presidential term. Upon employing his beaten opponent Hillary Clinton both began to change America and the World as promised.

What is a Treaty? A Treaty is a Agreement between two or more Countries. So a Agreement between two or more Countries is a Treaty. What does "We the People's" Constitution state in regards to a Treaty; Article II Section 2, second paragraph states;

"He (the President) shall have Power, by and with the Advice and Consent of the Senate, to make Treaties, provided two thirds of the Senators present concur (agreeing with a vote);".

What does the Constitution state about a agreement? It is never mentioned within the Constitution because the Founding Fathers understood that a Treaty and a Agreement are one in the same, being two different words for the same action offering the same result. The needed two thirds concurring vote of the Senate is to ensure that the Treaty or Agreement is in the best interest of our Nation and then our Allies interests. Also, Israel, the one Nation that has the most to lose was never part of the process.

Barack "we are giving them the O-Bomb-A Bomb" Obama stated he had the power using a executive order to make a Agreement with Iran without the Senate's oversight. The Republican Controlled Progressive Congress bit on this theory and sponsored the Iran Nuclear Agreement Review Act of 2015 — sponsored by Senate Foreign Relations Chairman Bob Corker, a Tennessee Republican — ensured congressional review and oversight of the agreement. The Senate wrote the Bill, the House of Representatives concurred with a passing vote and the President happily signed it into law. But the new law now states that the Senate can only override the presidential agreement with a non-concurring two thirds vote of "nay" which is the exact opposite of what our Constitution states. This basically removes the Senate from the process of making Treaties.

How do you think the supreme Court will rule on this action if the action is questioned? Will it use the present result as a precedent in a ruling for the same action in the future? Will Israel have to act alone in its own interest of existence to now be condemned by the governments of the world including ours? Has "We the People's Constitution" been circumvented with a Un-Constitutional "Common Law"? Are the Republicans in Congress that Progressively Stupid? The answers are the Liberal supreme Court will rule with O-Bomb-A, Depends on how it affects the Liberal Agenda, with all the other answers being "Yes".

Stupidity is not the greatest problem "We the People" now face. The shredding of "We the People's" Constitution being the only Document that stands between "the People" and a dictator being a Un-Constitutional President or a Dictating Un-Constitutional Government. The Founding Fathers Intent with our Constitution is that if a President wants a Treaty with another or other Countries he must work with a preset majority of the Senate being a minimum of 67 Senators which will ensure its passing. Under Barack Obama's formula of government a Treaty Agreement will pass with the support of just 34 Senators which stops the Treaty Agreement from being struck down or stopped. Also under the Review Act of 2015 only 41 Senate votes are needed to stop the Senate from even voting on the Treaty Agreement which this vote has already occurred with all these 41 needed votes being all Democrat. Under this new Un-Constitutional form of governing, "We the People's Constitution" is no longer the supreme Law of the Land, it has been supposedly overruled with a executive order of the President and a stupidly thought out "Review Act" of Republicans in Congress not knowing or understanding the proper Argument.

With this understanding has the President and these 41 Senators preserved, protected and defended our Constitution under the "Oath of Office" that each has taken while being sworn into office? The answer is No! Is this alone a Impeachable act? Yes. It is readily known within our government that Iran offered and is still offering Battle Field supplies to our stated enemies in the Middle East, Syria being one. Our government also has proof the Iranian government finances "Terrorism" within the region. "We the People" have seen our own Citizens arrested and prosecuted for delivering financial aid and for trying to enter the war on the Syrian side thus siding against America's Interests and policies. Yet Barack Obama and these 41 Democrat Senators under their Treaty Agreement are offering $150 Billion Dollars in Financial Aid by releasing Iran's sanctioned money. Why is none of this money not being used for the refuges created by the "Terrorism" supported by Iran? These same Democrats have offered up a Nuclear Bomb to Iran, even if Iran follows these Treaty Agreement guidelines it will legally be able to achieve this goal after 12 years. So is this action of arming Iran Treason?

Now under Impeachment rules, the House of Representatives handles the Impeachment (the arrest) process. The Senate Adjudicates the verdict (guilt or innocence). With 435 members of the House of Representatives and 247 being Republican and 188 being Democrat, 41 Democrat representatives are needed to make the 288 number to start the Impeachment process in the House of Representatives. Political numbers will not allow for this action. So it is no longer a issue of right or wrong in regards to our Constitution but the Political Power to allow it.

I could blame the Constitution, but to make this process easier with lower numbers only allows for a Constitutional President to be Impeached by a possibly Un-Constitutional Congress. So the fault may belong to the politically liberal supreme Court or possibly the States for not correcting this political problem which is undermining our governing "Constitution". Ultimately it is "We the People" and our vote for a Un-Constitutional Political Party that is the problem. Now placing the blame where it belongs, on "We the People" for not supporting the Constitution or working for social and financial (deficit & debt) change through the guidelines set in our Constitution makes the downfall of the "Rule of Law", our Constitution and Nation inevitable.

Hillary Clinton's vast experience in politics is having to leave her home State to find a Liberal Left Democrat Senate seat in a State that would elect her. After one and a half terms as Senator she launched a losing Presidential run. With the defeat Hillary became Obama's first term Secretary of State and together both managed to set the Middle East on Fire and Restart the defunct Cold War.

With the explosion of violence in the Middle East comes the attack on the Benghazi U.S. Consulate. Hillary described the attack as "just some guys out for a walk". Who walks at night in a group with AK-47's and RGP Grenade Launchers. Speculation is there might have been some type of gun running from the Benghazi Consulate to the Syrian rebels in Syria. This same organization being the rebels in Syria are also ISIS in Iraq fighting against the U.S.A.

The reality is the attack on the Consulate was falsely blamed on a video called "Innocence of Muslims" by Nakoula Basseley Nakoula for political cover. Too enhance this cover-up the local government in Los Angeles California violated Nakoula's probation. Now understanding that Los Angeles is a liberal sanctuary city for illegals and normally might protect this man, they didn't! Although the reasons his probation was violated is nothing more than what illegal immigrants do while being protected from deportation by local government. Using a alias for the video is not against the law, it is called using a stage name. Also using the name for his driver's license which is against the law but illegal immigrates do it all the time in regards to their documentation in these type of cities.

Both Barack and Hillary promised the arrest of this awful man to the victim's families when their bodies were being unloaded after being returned from Benghazi. No possibility that the Liberal Left Democrat administration of Barack Obama and Hillary Clinton with phone calls to the higher ups pressured the liberal local government to arrest this man? And is this in a sense violating this man's rights to some degree while Barack and Hillary go unpunished for lying about a video and what it didn't cause for the reason of political perception.

Now discussing Bill and Hillary's philanthropy project being the Clinton Foundation. Why is it that such good people as Bill and Hillary beginning in 2007 can donate $15 million dollars to charity with $200k going to other charities and the other $14.8 million dollars being donated to "themselves" through the Clinton Foundation while taking a large tax write-off for the donations. Meanwhile their foundation only donates to the "needy" 12 cents of every dollar donated to the foundation. That means the Clinton Foundation keeps 88 cents of every dollar donated while personally collecting Millions from foreign nations for themselves and the Clinton Foundation. What happened to the money in regards to earthquake ravaged Haiti? Bill says, it depends on what the definition of "is" is. I also heard Harry Reid heard that Bill and Hillary are not paying personal taxes and not using proper procedures in regards to their foundation that allow it to remain tax exempt.

THE "WARS ON" WILL NEVER END

The War on Poverty will never end. The War on Drugs will never end. The War on Terrorism will never end. To end a war you must sign a treaty or a peace agreement. Who on the other side of these wars are going to end the Wars even with their signatures? They are all a supply and demand problem.

The War on Poverty is the supply of good jobs being less than the demand of our population. The War on Drugs is a supply of drugs to meet the demand of the people who use all drugs or a certain drug. The War on Terror is the supply of people willing to commit Terrorist acts until we meet their demands of Sharia Law and thus losing our rights and freedoms to the Religion of Islam.

With poverty you may increase job opportunities but the fact is there will always be the few who don't want a job and are willing to live in poverty in order not to work. With drugs the supply can be altered but never completely stopped and demand will still exist. With terrorism you will never cleanse the earth of deviate minds and their willingness to kill others for whatever reason, only the numbers can be reduced until the next generation is born.

With Terrorism the answer is not to isolate ourselves but to isolate the Terrorists not allowing them to export Terror to the rest of the World. To do this Terrorists must be limited as to their travel outside their Muslim countries and error on the side of caution when making travel judgments. We don't have to keep them there, we just have to not allow them to travel here. Because once here we don't know for sure their motives in being here, is it to kill us or live like us? Can anyone truly decide who is who? Our Government can't on its best day! It can't determine who has an agenda against the American People and who doesn't. We can only bury our loved ones and our fellow Americans. This is the cost of doing nothing or government allowing it to happen using Liberal Left thoughts as the reason it can't be reduced or stopped. This same logic then dictates that the American lose of life within our own borders can't be reduced or stopped because of our own Liberal Left government policies being a Open Door New World Order. This is what has happened in France and other parts of Europe. Government can't and won't protect its people when it isn't even trying.

We as a Nation can't dictate how other Nations allow certain people into their country. The problem they create by doing so is their problem. The problem we create will be the same problem when we follow in their footsteps. Then becoming our problem brought on by the stupid decision that allowed it. The Patriotic Citizens of America have a Decision to Make! Abandon the American People or Abandon the Liberal Left Ideology that has forced this situation upon America!

THE YING & YANG OF REPUBLICAN DECISIONS

I have spent all this time showing the Democratically favored rewriting of history that has been used to protect the Democrat's Political Power. So I feel obligated to point too a couple decisions of Republican Presidents that were politically motivated. What I am giving is not a character flaw but the Ying & Yang of decisions.

First will be maybe our most revered Republican President being Abraham Lincoln. His action was not taken during his terms of office but before as a trial lawyer.

Remember my pointing out that government will support one industry over another. Also how steam paddle wheel boats had to convert their smoke stacks to fold over to clear railroad bridges over waterways. The Attorney who represented the railroad was Abraham Lincoln. He won the case in the courts that penalized the shipping industry going up and down the Mississippi River transporting goods between the north and the south. The shipping industry had used the Mississippi River as a trade route long before the existence of the railroad. Abraham Lincoln had no idea that this court case would come back to haunt him during his Presidential election and winning the Presidential Office. The court case itself pitted the southern shipping companies of New Orleans against the railroad companies of the north. The court case itself was the first aspect to divide the south and the north caused by a court decision of government that created the first political rift leading to the War Between the States. To put this situation into perspective Lincoln only argued the case in the courts. The weights of the facts are that the courts that heard the case were located in the northern states of the railroad's backyard. This created a perceived bias of the court system by southern society. Abraham Lincoln's Presidency was then seen as an extension of that bias in regards to the businesses of the south. So the Civil War was not strictly an issue pertaining to Slavery but also other issues that our MAINSTREAM TAUGHT HISTORY doesn't correctly portray.

Our most respected current Republican President is Ronald Reagan. His main accomplishment in my mind was the ending of the Cold War causing the fall of the Berlin Wall which split the country of Germany between the Communist East and the Free West. How did he accomplish this? As President he increased military spending expanding the scope of the Military with Military inventions. One Military invention that history portrays as a rouse was the Star Wars project. The project itself was deemed to be much farther along than it was in reality. Its intent was to make the U.S.S.R. believe the U.S. could repel an offensive nuclear attack then retaliate ending the existence of the U.S.S.R. It also allowed the illusion of First Strike Capabilities. To pull this rouse off President Reagan had to offer the illusion that America had this capability. He did so under the cover of military spending for such items as the M-1 Abrams tank, F-117 Stealth Fighter Bomber and Stealth Technology itself. The U.S.S.R. in an attempt to keep up spent itself into oblivion and the nation collapsed under its own debt.

Now under this necessary rouse of President Reagan's and his eight years to pull off this illusion our debt grew 1.764 Trillion from 934 Billion to 2.698 Trillion. President Reagan also took us off the gold standard and backed the value of the U.S. Dollar with our Gross Domestic Product. He also stated that we as a Nation would move from a current production / manufacturing economy to a Service based economy.

Now my questions are, was coming off the gold standard a necessary evil to expand our debt by allowing available credit for the needed monetary capital. All funding the projects to maintain the illusion which caused the collapse of the U.S.S.R. ending the Cold War. This brought down the Berlin Wall without a shot being fired or a life lost. It also ended a real threat of a nuclear war. Was it money well spent? My opinion is yes but coming off the gold standard also allowed future administrations to continue that upward spending curve until we are now over 100% of GDP. All the easy money has been wasted by government. With our money backed by the gold standard our currency was based off a much smaller total wealth being gold on deposit with our government. Moving our dollar to being backed by the GDP in reality allowed our government to borrow dollars against that much larger GDP number. Those dollars being the difference between the total government wealth in gold versus the increased government wealth created by moving our dollar backing to the GDP created more money available to government. Coming off the gold standard was letting the cat out of the bag to never be put back in because our gold reserves no longer match our debt and dollars on the world market. To return to the gold standard of backing our money would devalue the dollar greatly throwing the country into a certain depression. So that option is now no longer an option without paying down our debt. And it's still not an option because our Nation can't balance its own budget much less pay down our debt to go back on the gold standard.

Now a lot of that easy money was spent on increasing our infrastructure in this country. But we have out built what we can financially maintain becoming more of a burden too keep it and more of a burden to repair or replace.

Also how come we couldn't have kept our manufacturing for as long as possible while also creating more Service type jobs?

Was President Reagan responsible for ending the Cold War? Absolutely! Was he responsible for the spending that followed his administration? Absolutely Not! Barack Obama as President has spent $7.5 Trillion of our debt, the most of any President, in his first six years of office and Ronald Reagan died in 2004. Put the responsibility where it belongs on the back of all the following administrations for spending their share of that easy money and the government attitudes that allowed it. Spend it like there is no tomorrow because there is no tomorrow if government keeps spending it. That easy money is gone forever and the bills are due!

I believe if inflation was calculated using the correct numbers for tracking, it would show this point in history as the beginning of the Inflation Up-Curve. Inflation mirroring our Spending and Debt Curve when charted. This also explains the ever growing gap in incomes of the rich and the poor that affects the size of the middle class. This would also prove that easy (no bang for the bucket) government money thrown at a free market or crony market system (Obamacare website) is one of the main drivers of inflation. Meaning every time government spends a dollar without a return (hand out vs. hand up) on value it has not only wasted that dollar but also devalues each and every dollar on the world market. Quantitative Easing under Barack Obama isn't the only way too devalue the dollar.

When reading this next section you may wonder why I included it in the Republican section and not a race section of the book? I do make my point and it is a misconception of Republicans.

As a Republican, born and raised in the South, I was raised in a period of time where there were a lot of mixed messages. I never saw myself as a racist because skin color was not a issue in the area of Florida I was raised. As a child I did see it on television. But I played football and golf with all races including Blacks. So I have included a childhood story in regards to a childhood experience.

Let me tell you a 10 yr. old boys story. It was the summer of 1970, a weekday with a blue sky, a few fluffy white clouds, a little warm with little wind but not unpleasant. He was walking, playing golf by himself and was in the fairway on the fifth hole at Eglin A.F.B. Golf Course.

He was waiting for a group of three men in front of him to clear the green. As two of the men (white men) put their clubs away in the golf cart the third (a black man) started walking down the hill to the sixth tee box. The boy hit his shot to the green and was walking with his head down starring at the ground thinking of the coming putt. There was a commotion to his left and the man who was walking had fell down and was still on the ground. The boy was just short of the green when this happened and he hurried down the hill towards the men.

He asked what happened and one man replied "he was walking down the hill, stumbled, caught himself and then just went down a step or two later". The men quickly decided the younger man would run to the clubhouse and the older would take the cart and whoever got there first would be for the best result. That left that boy there by himself.

The man was face up with no movement, if he was breathing he couldn't tell. The boy decided to push on the man's chest like he had seen on television. As he did the man made a gurgling sound which startled the boy, he quit. He wasn't sure if what he was doing was helping or hurting. He sat there watching this man, the moisture on his face, the lack of movement.

This man was a common figure at the course, known by most, liked by all that knew him too the boy's knowledge. Never in the time it took for the ambulance to get there did this boy consider the color of this man. All he knew about the man was he was a fellow golfer, a member of a club that brought great joy to the many who played there and that he needed help. The ambulance arrived later and took the man away, the boy not even knowing how long it took, it seemed like a eternity.

The boy walked to the clubhouse with his head down staring at the ground, not contemplating the next putt or the next shot. To this day the boy couldn't even tell you if he picked up his ball from the previous shot as he left the area, that really didn't matter to him. The boy knew he had sat there at the tender age of 10 years old and had watched a man die. Black, White, Red, Yellow, however society may describe you made no difference. He felt helpless.

At thirteen yrs. old his parents moved to Milton, Fl. because his father had gotten a civil service job at Whiting Field. The boy took a lot of great childhood memories with him from that golf course but he also took one he will never forget. Later at about 20 yrs. old the young man took a Red Cross course at P.J.C. so that he would never be put in that situation of helplessness again. To be able to help anybody at their greatest moment of need regardless of color, gender or anything else that may try to divide society. That 10 yr. old boy has not spoken of this but feels that in the so called divided racist society of today he needs too, its just not nearly as bad as some people make it out to be. That 10 yr. old boy was me.

The mixed messages that were offered thru maybe teachers or society itself regarding the south were directed at a few topics but one was the Southern Flag of the Civil War. As a child, society said it represented a lifestyle and heritage of the south. Remember at this point in time being the mid to late 1960's the educational system was still controlled by the Democrat Party. I also understand that after the civil war both Republicans of the North and Democrats of the South agreed that this style of teaching would be allowed in the south. It was deemed to be part of the reconciliation of the States. In today's world these teachings have just led to more unrest because of the taught ideology vs. the reality. With this one aspect not belonging to the Republicans but in reality to Democrats how many other perceived moments in history are owned by Democrats but through the "thought" of teaching are laid on the back of Republicans. The flag was and is not represented in the true aspects of our history. As children you are very impressionable and this ingraining of "thought" may not be correctable for some taught under this indoctrination style of teaching. At least the true aspect of "racism" was not taught leaving only the Democrat's Confederate Flag of the South now being defended by Non-Racist Republicans believing the Flag represents a "Lifestyle & Heritage". Democrats will not only abandon their own heritage but will try and place that same heritage on the backs of others for Political gain! Nothing is sacred but the party's power.

As a adult I defended the Southern Flag based on this learned concept. With the writing of my book I now have altered this concept in my mind knowing I was INDOCTRINATED into the subject as a child. I now understand I was taught to defend the Southern Flag of Democrats while the whole time having my faith, heart and vote in the Ideology of the Union's Stars and Stripes flag of the Republican Party.

Now who else has been INDOCTRINATED to believe that the Southern Flag represents Southern Republicans and not Northern Democrats of today's political spectrum.

The Democrat's Confederate Flag is a sign of a earlier time of oppression being the slavery of Blacks. With this understanding it should be removed from all Republican State Capitals of the South. Should it be removed from history? Absolutely not. Not knowing our true history is what has gotten us to where we are today. A confused

Nation with our history based on Democrat educational lies. My, how history changes things when the true history is applied.

This aspect has always bothered me since being a kid. Knowing that I am not a racist but having to endure the Racist Rants of Democrats because of being a Southern Republican.

RESPONSIBILITIES OF CHOICE

Our Founding Fathers in writing the Document known through our history to us as our "Constitution" is four pages of rules in governing, government's needs, procedures and Freedoms. Most people see these four different topics when reading the "Constitution" but don't understand the rules in governing, government's needs, its procedures or even the word "Freedom". The word "<u>Freedom</u>" has very little meaning without the words "<u>of Choice</u>", without choices what can you do with "<u>Freedom</u>"? When the three are combined to form the phrase "Freedom of Choice" the three alone are not complete. Your "*<u>Freedom of Choice</u>*" doesn't guarantee that your choice will be in your best interest even though you made it. If that choice you made was not in your best interest to meet your needs then that same choice will probably not be in the best interest of anyone else either. So the phrase "*<u>Freedom of Choice</u>*" is also not complete without two words being placed in front of that phrase. Can you guess what those two words are that make this phrase complete? "*<u>Responsibilities for</u>*"! Yes, "***<u>Responsibilities for Freedom of Choice</u>***" is **ACTUALLY** what the ***<u>"Constitution" guarantees you, Not Your Freedom!</u>***

Yes, your *<u>Freedom of Choice</u>* comes with *<u>Responsibilities for</u>* your Choices that affect yourself and directly affect others. If you drink and drive and have a accident that injures or kills others. Then your *<u>Freedom of Choice</u>* although not wanted (all bad choices are not wanted) doesn't relieve you of the *<u>Responsibilities for</u>* that Choice. Now your Choice because it is your Responsibility may relieve you of your <u>Freedom</u>. Also relieving you of your *<u>Freedom of Choice</u>* for a certain period of time while being incarcerated as your Responsibility to society. Also your *Freedom of Choice* say to buy a used vehicle has "*Responsibilities for*" purchasing that vehicle to ensure it is reliable. If the vehicle turns out to be unreliable then your *Freedom of Choice* was a bad Choice. Your *Responsibilities for* that purchase may not of been complete when researching or inspecting used vehicles. If you drop out of high school being a *Freedom of Choice* this Choice may have a lifetime affect. Historically, if most of your life Choices have been bad then with each Choice you have paid for that Choice with the *Responsibilities for* that Choice.

When government gets involved with the "***Responsibilities for Freedom of Choice***" what government has historically done is remove the "*Responsibilities for*" from that "*Freedom of Choice*". Leaving intact that "*Freedom of Choice*". But it wasn't the "*Responsibilities for*" that created the problem, it was your decision allowed by that "*Freedom of Choice*". The "*Responsibilities for*" are life's lessons learned for your decisions whether being good or bad, allowed by that "*Freedom of Choice*". So by government removing "*Responsibilities for*", what are actually being removed is ***Mother Nature's education of life's lessons***. Once having removed the "*Responsibilities for*", the cost also is relieved from that individual and then placed on all of Society. When Society allows this it now makes itself Responsible for all the debts incurred by any Irresponsible Individual. Those Individual's are now encouraged by government to keep making their bad life's decisions because society (everyone else) will pick up the bills.

So why does government remove the individual's "*Responsibilities for*" and not the right choice being removing the individual's "*Freedom of Choice*" once they have abused it? Because **GOVERNMENT** sees itself as the **SUPREME POWER** even **GREATER** than **NATURE ITSELF!** It has all the questions, all the answers, all the corrections. The fact is our Government itself functions in this same manner, Free of Responsibilities for its Choices in governing. So government is just passing along the only traits government knows, Irresponsibility and More Spending.

Can government remove someone's "*Freedom of Choice*"? Absolutely, Federal, State, County, City and now some neighborhoods have all taken away that "Freedom of Choice"! The funny thing about government when removing that "Freedom of Choice" it does so to the part of Society that has shown its "***Responsibilities for Freedom of Choice***". Recently the federal government has taken away the "Freedom of Choice" for Healthcare choices such as doctors and policies of the Responsible too insure the poor whom many stay poor because of their "*Freedom of Choice*" not too better their lives. Some States have also been a part of this scenario but States sometimes play a even bigger role. Lets examine 3 recent events involving State and Federal government.

Sarah Murnaghan, the 10-year-old girl dying of cystic fibrosis needed a transplant of both lungs. No child lungs were available and Federal Regulations would not allow adult lungs to be used on a child younger than 12 years old. She was expected to die before her 12th birthday. Kathleen Sebelius, was Barack Obama's "*Freedom of Choice*" pick for Secretary of the United States Department of Health and Human Services. She is better known for her failed role out of the Obamacare aka. Affordable Care Act Billion dollar plus web-site. She is also in charge of the regulations that surround the organ transplant system. Now as for Sarah, her doctor said that transplanting adult lungs into her was a viable option meaning he thought it would be successful. HHS and Kathleen Sebelius opposed such a option and were willing to let the child die with there decision. The State and Federal Courts backed HHS' decision until Sarah's parents threatened to sue. Sarah got her adult lung transplant along with another 11 yr. old boy with both being a *SUCCESS*!

About a year ago, the parents of 15-year-old Justina Pelletier brought her to the emergency room of Children's Hospital in Boston. According to local reports, doctors quickly diagnosed her with psychiatric problems. Prior to that visit, Justina had been under treatment at Tufts Medical Center, also in Boston, for a rare condition known as mitochondrial disease. A disorder where the body's cells don't produce energy, which causes chronic fatigue and severe digestive problems. That medical psychiatric misdiagnosis was the basis for the state to come in and take Justina away from her parents and the care she was receiving at Tufts Medical Center. So Justina came to Children's Hospital for a ailment, maybe or maybe not related to her mitochondrial disease. Justina walked into that hospital with a normal childhood lifestyle. After being denied her previous ongoing treatments was finally released over a year later being wheel chaired out not physically the same person when she came in.

In the last part of 2014 "Cassandra C," was diagnosed with Hodgkin's lymphoma in September. Medical experts have testified that Cassandra has an 85% chance of survival if treated with chemotherapy. Without it, doctors say, she likely will die within two years. She has been undergoing chemotherapy against her wishes for three weeks. After she missed follow-up appointments, the hospital contacted the Connecticut Department of Children and Families (DCF) out of concern that this was a situation of medical neglect. The court said that attorneys for the girl -- who is 17 and therefore still a minor -- failed to prove that she is mature enough to make her own medical decisions. The state was right in this case.

Now we have three separate cases where the State along with the court system and the Federal Government have removed the "*Freedom of Choice*" from a individual and their family (parents). In these three cases government was wrong in the first two but correct on the last case. That means that the government's own "*Responsibilities for*" its own "*Freedom of Choice*" was wrong 2/3rd's of the time and right just 1/3rd of the time. Earlier in my writings I stated that government was only right about half the time and in this situation it was even less. The actual ratio for the right decision was 1 out of 4 times or twenty five percent because in the first case there were two children saved with the adult lung to child transplants. This is not a very good ratio for a entity to be making decisions regarding people's actual lives by removing their "Freedom of Choice".

I am sure you have heard the term "a Franchise Business". When used in the Free Market Place of Business this system of businesses create a huge number of small business owners. Each business then employs a much greater number of people. But when County or City Government uses the term "Franchise" within its own county or city boundaries it has the exact opposite affect. It eliminates competition and reduces jobs by offing up its captive population to one business with negotiated rates to service a given area. Sometimes this Idea goes a step further by the government entity replacing their model of a "Franchiser" with county or city government services they themselves will now mandate to its captive customers.

Now when a county "Franchises" out a service such as Cable TV or Garbage pickup it does so by removing the "*Freedom of Choice*" of the population. But it also removes all the other businesses being the competition by putting each out of business by not being allowed to do business by that local government. The local government does this by stating it's in the best interest of the populous because the government entity will negotiate a very good price. What else does government negotiate the price of something for our best interest.

The first flaw in this plan is the only time you receive a true outlook on what it costs for the service is the very first time bids are taken. Because these bids are in competition with the other bidders for the Franchise. Anytime thereafter when negotiating rates what does the government entity's employee's know about the cost of Cable TV or Garbage pickup without being in the business itself. That government entity's official might reply we look at invoices to verify actual costs. The flaw with that is Venders offer discounts (2% to 10%) if the bill is paid by a certain date and most times that discount doesn't show up on the original invoices. Secondly actual costs can be manipulated to show greater costs thus a greater fee raise allowed by the government entity. Third, the government entity loses interest in real fee negotiations after a few years and the Franchiser never loses interest in collecting more money. So the consumer has no voice and no options (no "*Freedom of Choice*") at that point other than to do without the service if the consumer has been priced out of the service. Today's cable TV hooks you with a lower fee for the first year or two and with a expired contract raises your bill as much as 100% over the next year. With the entry of satellite TV that put too a end the monopoly by Cable TV on the PAY TV situation. So what Satellite TV has done is take local government's power to "Franchise" Cable Pay TV to one business owner and return competition to the market being DISH, DIRECT and AT&T's U-Verse. None of these signals come from the only TV cable coming off the closest telephone pole and that is what allows them to offer their service. What they have returned to the "People" is the "*Freedom of Choice*". With that Choice is the "***Responsibilities for***" that "***Freedom of Choice***" which is shopping the **PRODUCT FOR PRICE AND UNDERSTANDING THE QUALITY OF WHAT YOU PURCHASE!**

When local government itself *doesn't offer* a service but *mandates its own service's* such as Garbage, Water & Sewer making itself the "Franchiser" who ensures what the consumer is getting is the lowest price available or the best product? Local Government does because it is the ONLY PRICE available and the ONLY PRODUCT available. This self "Franchising" has become a very lucrative source of income which is collected for a SERVICE instead of a TAX. But if the SERVICE is MANDATED but not needed or over priced and the PRODUCT is less than expected are you sure it's a **SERVICE & NOT A TAX?** *NO CHOICE* means *NO FREEDOM* and who shoulder's the "*Responsibilities for*" that? Local Government or the People themselves for allowing it to happen?

With Governments own deficiencies of intellectual understanding was Government's removal of "*Responsibilities for*" Society's Wrong "*Freedom of Choice*" of life's Decisions the Right Choice? The Liberal Left making Government's Choice! When Government removes the "Freedom of Choice" it removes a little bit of our "Freedom" each and every time it happens. Free Enterprise of our Society is what allows for those choices, it is government and only government that takes them away.

With what I have pointed out what other Societies on this planet take away its citizens "FREEDOM OF CHOICE"? Relieving the individual of all "Responsibilities for" achievement which then allows Government to decide where you work, what you own if anything, until the day you die? Doesn't it sound like Communism and Socialism. It is Definitely NOT what the Founding Fathers wrote in the Document being Our "Constitution" which gives Society both the "Responsibilities for" and the "Freedom of Choice" and lets us, not government, work it out from there.

So **MOTHER NATURE'S OWN UNDERSTANDING OF MAN** is that much more *advanced* than **MAN'S OWN UNDERSTANDING OF MAN** or even **MAN'S UNDERSTANDING OF MOTHER NATURE'S LESSONS OF LIFE!** The Liberal Left should quit trying to replace the Laws of Nature with LIBERAL Government?

THE FLAWS OF THE CONSTITUTION

The flaws of the Constitution were not intended by the Founding Fathers. Their "Constitution", is an extraordinarily written document for self governing "by the People" "for the People" and "of the People". It is a document if followed by the words in it offers the guidelines needed to achieve self governing. Unfortunately a human trait to improve on something is a driving force in the human character of man. This trait is a great aspect of our society that pushed our society to achieve great accomplishments throughout the history of this nation. We have led the world as a nation since our inception as a country. It is also this same trait that is leading to a government no longer controlled by the "Constitution" and the power of the "People" allowed under the "Constitution". The first problem when trying to improve on a product is understanding the manufacturing processes and what it is suppose to accomplish as a product. Without this understanding any changes to the manufacturing process will change the product and the accomplishments of that product resulting in an unintended and not necessarily better product. The "Constitution" is a product of the Founding Fathers and we have changed it, disobeyed its words and are in the process of making it something it was never meant to be. All in the attempt to improve something we as a society lost our understanding of at some point in history. Whether it was changing the way Senators are elected or a current representative of the house stating that "terms of the House of Representatives should be a four year term". The supreme Court over the years inserting its ruling to change written laws which was never done until some point in past history. These are all man made changes whether or not the change was constitutional as I have pointed in a few cases. There are also changes to the "Constitution" which are flaws, not of their time period but of ours. Things written into the "Constitution" that applied then but not now. Such as wording in the Articles that allows elected officials to go unpunished for violations of "Common Laws" which "We the People" are prosecuted under the same laws. For Example "Article I, Section 6" a line states:

"The Senators and Representatives shall receive a Compensation for their Services, to be ascertained by Law, and paid out of the Treasury of the United States. They shall in all Cases, except Treason, Felony and Breach of the Peace, be privileged from Arrest during their Attendance at a session of their respective Houses, and in going to and returning from the same; and for any Speech or Debate in either House, they shall not be questioned in any other Place".

The portion regarding arrest was written into the "Constitution" because the elected officials rode home on horseback through what might have been a political foe's representative territory. Also when this was wrote the sessions originally only lasted a few weeks then they returned home. Neither one of these is now the case and I believe it is being used to block elected officials from facing the punishments of "Common Law" and I will give a couple clear examples.

Wesley Snipes was arrested, tried and convicted on tax evasion laws in regards to three million dollars in taxes. Charlie Rangel was accused of failing to report income from his rental of a beach side villa he owns in Punta Cana in the Dominican Republic. A three-bedroom, three-bath unit. It has rented out for as much as $1,100 per night in the busiest tourist season. He was censured in the House of Representatives as punishment.

My point is that not paying your taxes is a violation of "Common Law" and when the violation was committed he was not treated in the same manner as an ordinary citizen. His offense doesn't fall under the guidelines of "Article I, Section 6". As for the House of Representatives and the ethics committee that is the punishment for a representative of the House. As a citizen why is the "Common Law" punishment avoided? I believe he must be held accountable with both. If not that makes every elected official a privileged citizen and above the tax laws and everybody should pay their fair share as Democrats have pointed out on numerous occasions. This includes monetary punishments and punishment through the judicial system as every citizen is punished.

Another example being Martha Stewart sent to jail for insider trading with the stock market. Nancy Pelosi as speaker of the House of Representatives used the knowledge of legislation in the legislative process to purchase 5000 IPO shares of Visa (credit cards) at $44 dollars and two days later was trading for $64 dollars a share while the legislation never made it to the floor of the House for a vote. Her punishment, none it's not against the law but a sweet $100,000 dollar profit on knowledge that she controlled the outcome allowed this profit. A "Common Law" was passed later to reel in these abuses but just a little later the legislation was revisited. The law was gutted by the same Congress in a late night session all while Nancy Pelosi was in control of the House of Representatives as speaker of the House. Again an example of a privileged citizen system. Now if you have a privileged class of citizens in a society what is the rest of the citizens of that society's class stature? I would say "second class". Also a citizen of minimal financial means might be a "third class" citizen in regards to the law. These are just two things that need to be corrected through an "Amendment of the Constitution" so that Congress can't go back in the middle of the night and diminish the law so it becomes a law that enforces very little.

The last sentence of "Article I, Section 6" is very interesting in what it allows to be said on the floors of either House. With its written words it allows lies, deception, defamation of character as was done to Mitt Romney about his taxes during the 2012 Presidential campaign by Harry Reid on the Senate floor. With this situation as a citizen anything said on either house floor may or may not be the truth. I am not sure this can be corrected because the elected officials would spend their time chasing after lies instead of government business. As one citizen to another, with each not having a political agenda, investigate and vet statements said on the floor and determine its truth. Don't forget those that lied by not backing them because they will lie again.

Some may say I have an agenda or ideology which I am pushing with this book. They are absolutely right in their assumption. My agenda or ideology is to force government to follow the processes of the contract agreed upon by the "People" and the "States" being the "Constitution". I hope my voice in this section of my writings are the views of "We the People" to bring our elected officials back to reality and the same social class. "We the People" all live under the laws of the "Constitution" so let our elected officials experience the same laws that we live under daily with no exceptions.

The 5th Amendment allowing citizens not to self incriminate themselves by testifying makes complete sense when applied to the free enterprise system outside of government. The 5th Amendment makes no sense when applied to government jobs being an elected position, appointed position or an employee of government. When government goes awry "WE THE PEOPLE" need answers to correct the problems that allowed the situation to manifest in the first place. A law is no better than the people that are in a position to enforce it. If the law breaker and the enforcer of the law are on the same political side then enforcement of the laws may never happen. That is why I recommend that the 5th Amendment be altered, not covering the positions of elected, appointed or employed persons of the Federal Government excluding the military. The 5th Amendment would still cover any Federally employed individual outside the duties of their government job.

The current event regarding the Obama's administration's dealings with Iran and its nuclear proliferation with a Executive order agreement is just another example of deception to circumvent the law of the Constitution. The administration has given the perception that it has the power to sign a treaty with Iran without the Senates concurrence. What does the Constitution state?

Article II. Section 2. states "He shall have Power, by and with the Advice and Consent of the Senate, to make Treaties, provided two thirds of the Senators present concur;".

So Barack as President doesn't have the power to formulate a Treaty with Iran without the Senate, period. Well what about trade agreements? Nope, lets go to the Constitution.

Article I. section 8. States "To regulate Commerce with foreign Nations, and among the several States, and with the Indian Tribes;".

With the Senate's letter to the parties concerned being the President and his administration along with informing the Iranian government that a agreement would be none binding without Senate approval was a statement of fact. Democrats accused the writer's of the letter as traitors. When is following the "Constitution" a act of Treason? Isn't NOT following the "Constitution" a treasonous act or a impeachable act as stated in the "Constitution"?

With the Obama's administration's BLUFF being called, John Kerry stated on TV that the administration didn't have the power for a Treaty but could enter into a Executive order agreement with Iran. Is this True? No, not by the "Constitution". Executive orders can only be issued to government agencies within our government, not to other Sovereign Foreign Nations of which it carries no legal weight throughout the World.

Well the supreme Court would say he has the right as long as the other nation agrees to the agreement because the precedent has already been set with previous Presidential Trade Agreements or Treaties not voted on by Congress or the Senate. No, again the "Constitution" is the SUPREME law of the land not a supreme Court's Un-Constitutional Decision. Even if 93% of the agreements were not backed by Congress for a trade agreement or by the Senate for a Treaty that doesn't and did not REWRITE the "CONSTITUTION". What the precedent states is that the "Constitution" has been illegally circumvented 93% of the time making the agreements UN-Constitutional without a passing vote of Congress or the Senate depending on it being a Trade Agreement or a Treaty.

This again illustrates my point in regards to the REWRITING of the "Constitution" and "Common Law" by the other branches of government.

The Founding Fathers counted on the fact that the people of government would enforce the written laws no matter what political party controlled government at the time. History has repeatedly shown this as not true and justice is politically motivated by the party in charge. Especially when one party, Democrats, in its own philosophy doesn't like to abide by the rules that are set in place. Instead of changing the rules which are allowed through the rules of the "Constitution" they would rather circumvent the rules with the powers of government. Even though that path chosen is in direct conflict of the "Articles and Amendments of the Constitution" and "Common Law" that are also protected by that "Constitution".

The liberal portion of the Democrat party known as the liberal left has stated "the Constitution should be a living, breathing document". It is a living, breathing document! It just doesn't live and breathe at the pace the liberals want. The liberal left Democrat party believe the changes to the "Constitution" should be easy to make to oblige an incoming President or political party allowing them to push its agenda easier. In reality a "Constitution" easily changed will perpetually change with greater frequency to a point that no one knows truly what the laws are because of the speed of perpetual change. A civilized society of laws must have stability in regards to law. The laws shouldn't change with each and every President or political party every 2 or 4 years on a political whim. When a law is administered it should be done so in a fair and equitable way to each and every individual and this scenario will not allow that to happen. Also if the "Constitution" was that easy to change what stops a current President from becoming a permanent President. With the powers of a political party to make the changes necessary to accomplish this situation as was done in Germany before WWII with Adolf Hitler. The fact is the liberal left of the Democrat Party would love to see the "Constitution" go away. Again, Saul D. Alinsky wrote a book that is a guideline for radical thinkers called "Rules for Radicals". Liberal Left thinkers treat this book as their political "Bible". The first Rule; don't follow a law or rule you don't like or hampers the movement of your agenda. The second Rule; THERE ARE NO RULES. Radical: Radical Islam, Radical Muslims, Radical Religions, Radical Governments, Radical left, Radical Right, Radical Thinking, Radical Radicals, is there truly anything good in the concept of Radical. Radical is the point or just before the point everything is going or has gone bad and rarely turns the situation around because it is Radical actions that got you to that point in the first place. A radical action at this point is a return to the system that was abandoned before an alternate chosen path of Liberal or Radical had been taken. This every forty or forty five year recurrence of liberalism in our history has left remains of its effects for decades after the actual liberal movement has vanished from government. Government will change after each recurrence because government never actually returns to its true form after the liberal movement has vanished. We as a society have backed away from the liberal movement after sometimes a small dose and sometimes a much larger dose. We understand at that time the taste it leaves in our mouths and the mouth of government. We taste it because not enough people at that point of time in history have not tasted it to understand the ramifications of a liberal movement. Even after again tasting it and refusing to eat it and by moving away from it we still each time leave a little of it on the plate of government. It stays in some of our policies (deficit and debt), laws and the procedures of government itself like a very noticeable stain on our favorite shirt and can't get it out and won't throw it away.

The Founding Fathers knew all this when writing the "Constitution" and countered all these attacks with Checks and Balances written into the "Constitution". To not recognize these features, the Checks and Balances, thus allowing them not to be enforced leaves the "Constitution" eventually defenseless. As a society you will rue the day our society allowed this document to fail. It IS what got this nation to the forefront of the world economically and socially to achieve the greatest civilized society. To lose it, eventually everything else goes with it.

SOME CORRECTIONS OF THE CONSTITUTION

The flaws of the Constitution are the lack of ability to enforce the abuses of the "Constitution" which is then a lack of ability to protect the "Constitution". What has created and allowed these abuses is the Political aspect of politics. Politics has now replaced right or wrong in government which is a huge mistake of the people allowing this to happen among their own parties. One party can't abide by the right or wrong ideology without the other party doing the same because politics promotes more politics. A "Constitutional" abuse is now determined by politics, as to the controlling party's support or non-support of an executive order or supreme Court decision. The supreme Court no longer uses the words of the "Constitution" or that of "common law" to make a decision in regards to either. The court virtually writes its own legislation with its own decisions. So now in regards to the "Constitution" what part of government is in charge of the document's protection? The Founding Fathers assigned the supreme Court with this duty of protection but the court is now only blind folded as to the words of the document. Its decisions have now been based on politics.

Justice John Roberts wrote the decision on the Affordable Care Act. In their decision he stated that the court didn't want to make a political decision by striking down the law based on the individual mandate being a penalty. Even though a penalty is not allowed under the "Constitution", the "word" penalty doesn't exist in the "Constitution", it's not in the written words anywhere. So the supreme Court changed the "word" to tax. The first flaw in their decision is that they based their decision on politics and not the written words of the "Constitution". Under the misguided insight of today's supreme Court a correct decision would have been to strike the individual mandate from the law as unconstitutional. In doing this it would have left a law that is now financially unstable, unsustainable and dysfunctional. Knowing that the 2010 elections had changed the direction of government with the House of Representatives going from Democrat to Republican control the supreme Court knew their decision would have virtually ended the A.C.A. law. So they changed the "word" "penalty" to "Tax" letting the law stand based on political reasons.

This decision of the supreme Court makes my point in regards to the only power the supreme Court has is to rule the law "Constitutional" or "Unconstitutional" as a whole. Meaning striking down a portion, the individual mandate, of the law would have left a dysfunctional law. So how many times has the supreme Court struck down a portion of a law now leaving the American people being ruled by a dysfunctional law? The supreme Court's only option is to strike down the complete law if any portion is deemed "Unconstitutional". This allows the governmental process to again take up the subject to write another bill that meets the needs of the people by the words of the "Constitution" which then abides by the supreme Court's ruling.

Now I have shown how politics is at the center of the supreme Court. Considering that each supreme Court Justice is appointed by a President (25% of power) and must have the concurrence of the Senate (25% of power) to sit on the bench how do We the People remove politics from our Judicial system?

First as I pointed out the supreme Court can either rule "Constitutional" or "Unconstitutional" on the complete law only, no more supreme Court legislation. This must be an Amendment to the "Constitution" that ties the supreme Court's hands to write legislation and puts written law beyond the supreme Court's power to make changes. This Amendment must also force the supreme Court to quote the written words of the "Constitution" or "Common Law" to base its decision. Their opinions and actions have been proven as political and can no longer be trusted to be based off the "Constitution" or "Common Law". As to whether the Amendment is done through the process of the Federal Government and / or Article V of the "Constitution" makes absolutely no difference. Will this stop it? Maybe not all of it but I believe it will stop a very large percentage of it if not almost all of it. The way the "Constitution" is written it never should of happened in the first place but it did.

I don't see how politics itself can be removed when appointments are politically motivated by a party that may hold the Presidency or the Senate or both. It is the Justice's responsibility to abide by the "Constitution" that is suppose to be guaranteed through their "word" of their Oath of Office. So much for Oaths of Office or a blindfolded Justice system? It's almost like having to shame the supreme Court into doing its job correctly.

Secondly how do "We the People" force a President to abide by the laws of "Constitution" and "Common Laws" when issuing executive orders? The best option would be back in front of a now better functioning supreme Court. Taking illegal immigration as a example. There is no way with the numbers of illegal's that have crossed and with border agents testimony "that their hands were tied by a President's executive order". The supreme Court having to quote written law and no longer able to quote opinion for their decision could side with the current President. The supreme Court's ruling must be on the executive order and not the rule of law. Meaning the court has no power to strike down the law in this type of judicial process. The court must hear this suite brought by either branch of Congress within 30 days of the filed law suite. The court has 10 days to give its decision again based on law and not opinion. The executive order is suspended (optional, decided by the branch of Congress bringing the law suite) when the suite is filed and until the supreme Courts decision is made.

The third is holding a President accountable for his actions with executive orders. To begin with it is not the number of executive orders that are issued that is the problem. It is the one executive order or memoranda that doesn't abide by the law that creates a conflict. As a President it's not hard to know if your executive order or memoranda is in conflict with a written law. If you are trying to get around a law as to not enforce it or a portion of it you are in conflict with the written law. So let's use baseball's three strikes and four balls rule. If at any point in a President's term or terms any three executive orders are overturned by the supreme Court for not following the law. Then from this point forward any executive order from the President must pass Congress with a sixty percent vote before it can be enacted. If the President moves beyond this point with the executive order or any type of orders to a agency and the agency's actions have any reflections of the executive order or changes its normal operation determined by the supreme Court as illegal or not in the normal operation. Then the Agency's Dept. Head shall be removed from any government employment. He shall lose all benefits of and from government, no exceptions. A new dept. head shall be appointed by the branch of Congress that filed the suite and shall report only to a committee of that same branch of Congress for the duration of the President's term or terms. If this condition in government happens three times under one President then the President is automatically deemed incapable of holding the Office of President and the Vice President must assume the Presidency. The Vice President must assume the office with all restrictions on the Presidency still intact until the next election.

To stop the legislative branches from using this as a harassment technique of a President each branch of Congress may only use this process four times during the term or terms of a President. A successful law suite doesn't count as one of the allowed four attempted law suites but a failed law suite does. If the first three law suites fail then the automatic suspension of an executive order is no longer in play due to the branches abuse of the process. If all four attempted law suites of a branch fail then this process is no longer available to the branch and the branch must revert back to the original process in the "Constitution" to suppress an executive order during the remaining term or terms of a President. A President may withdraw a challenged executive order at any time barring that the supreme Court has not began hearing the law suite. The branch of Congress may do the same but if the automatic suspension of the executive order was enforced it does count as one of the three allowed leaving only two automatic suspensions in place.

This action now gives both branches of Congress an avenue to confront a President without having to rely on impeachment and adjudication (too political when relying on political parties to do the right thing) as the only means to rein in the powers of an unconstitutional President.

This process applies to all aspects of government under the Presidents control but this process does NOT apply to the Defense Dept. or any aspect of the U.S. of America's self defense. This process Does apply if these same Military and Civilian powers are used against the Citizens of the U.S. of America including all forms of spying beyond what is allowed under legislated law.

The Founding Fathers twice relinquish government power to the greater number of people in government. Once with Congress's veto overrule of the President and second with Article V of the "Constitution". I believe the Founding Fathers would approve of this method to limit the powers of an Unconstitutional President while also limiting the abuse a Constitutionally legal President must endure.

Government accountability and transparency is essential for good and fair government. Government not being accountable and transparent is essential to politicians enriching themselves and enslaving Citizens through the powers of government at the expense of the Citizens and Taxpayers. Barack Obama stated that his Presidency would be the most transparent in history. That statement should not be a choice but a mandate of government so that the people's government doesn't have the ability to govern in secret. Unless it pertains to National Security and only National Security.

In a attempt to bring all elected officials and employed Federal Government workers into the same Citizenship fold of normal U.S. Citizens not elected or employed by the Federal Government a number or laws most be part of the same Amendment we have started in this discussion.

1st; all elected Federal Government Officials and Employees barring none shall lose their 5th Amendment Rights in regards to their government job or position in government. Upon refusing to testify any Individual of said Positions shall be removed from Government employment and all benefits shall end with any matching retirement money being recovered by Government. This law doesn't effect any civilian situation outside of their government job. The only way public testimony will not occur is in the case of National Security. That testimonial will be held behind closed doors with a prosecuting government committee, the armed forces committee and a Military committee to determine if the information is truly National Security sensitive. If "yes" then the meeting will remain behind closed doors in regards to only the National Security sensitive testimony. If "no" then the testimony must be moved back into the public eye of sight.

If any individual, group or organization that receives any type of government money it must abide by the same "must testify law" to continue any type of government financing and any finances received regarding the subject in question must be returned to the government upon denial of testimony.

This legislation would almost guarantee an open and transparent government. Anyone in government that opposes this obviously likes to hide things from public sight.

2nd; All Bills brought to the floor of either House must be clean Bills. Any added Amendments must have a direct effect on the Bill. All spending Bills must be strictly on topic of the subject of the Bill and any Amendments that are not on the same topic and / or subject may not be added to the Bill.

This would cause more effective spending and less wasted money spent on special interest projects that would not pass Congress on its own merit.

3rd ; Congress shall make no law, the President shall issue no executive order & the supreme Court may make no court decision, that allows a elected official or government employee to have special benefits (no benefit is exempt from this Amendment) provided by government beyond what is available to the American Citizens of the United States. Any Military Benefits are Not Part of this Amendment or any other Amendment unless directly written into the Amendment.

This would stop elected officials from living in a different society with better benefits than what is allowed for American Citizens. If they can pass it on to us this will make them eat what they are feeding us.

4th ; All retirement pay shall be modeled after civilian retirement plans such as but not limited to 401k plans with matching government payments. All matching government payments must not exceed the average percentage paid in civilian plans. All elected officials & employees are limited to one plan with Government matching payments.

The civilian employment system has mostly been a 401k style retirement system for a couple of decades. The change was encouraged by our elected officials for many good reasons and maybe a few bad reasons but if it's good enough for the American Citizen it's good enough for our American elected officials and employees.

5th ; All investments of elected Federal officials and family (wife, sons, daughters and grandchildren) must be revealed to Congress if a bill is brought to the floor of either house that may be in direct conflict (causing or creating a monetary gain for the family) of their vote on the Bill. All profits created from such a vote shall be donated to the U.S. Government and applied to the national debt. Failure to disclose such investments and earnings shall be deemed as fraud and must be prosecuted through the judicial system and none prosecution is not an option.

This will stop elected officials from profiting from their elected position and vote. The officials caught trying to profit using this situation will be prosecuted.

For this portion of the Amendment to the "Constitution" I will quote a portion of the "Constitution" to make my point and reasoning for the change.

"The Senate shall have the sole Power to try all Impeachments. When sitting for that Purpose, they shall be on Oath or Affirmation.

When the President of the United States is tried, the Chief Justice shall preside: And no Person shall be convicted without the Concurrence of two thirds of the Members present".

"Judgment in Cases of impeachment shall not extend further than to removal from Office, and disqualification to hold and enjoy any Office of honor, Trust or Profit under the United States: but the Party convicted shall nevertheless be liable and subject to Indictment, Trial, Judgment and Punishment, according to Law".

"They shall in all Cases, except Treason, Felony and Breach of the Peace, be privileged from Arrest during their Attendance at the Session of their respective Houses, and in going to and returning from the same; and for any Speech or Debate in either House, they shall not be questioned in any other Place".

Reasoning for the changes, 1). Impeachment is too political to determine "right & wrong". 2). The "Constitution" states any individual is liable and subject to the processes of United States' laws. 3). Other than on one of the House floors during a session a Elected Official should be subject to arrest if charged with a crime that requires a average U.S. Citizen to be arrested and booked into jail following the normal process.

As I stated before when the "Constitution" was wrote Elected Officials rode horseback to and from Washington D.C. through what may be a political opponent's territory. A local government could initiate a false charge to hamper the Officials return to Office thus possibly altering a vote total in Congress. This scenario doesn't exist any longer.

6th ; All elected Federal Officials shall abide by and are subject too the same laws which govern the American Citizens and shall be tried & adjudicated in a Judicial Court of law at the individual's expense, taxpayer money will not be used. Upon arrest the individual may return to Office after making bond if needed. If no bond is allowed due to the severity of the offense the respective State of the Official shall by appointment chose a replacement as soon as possible. The replacement shall be picked by either house of State Government but the house that picks must be relative to the position lost. The State House of Representatives shall appoint a Federal House Representative and the State Senate shall appoint a Federal Senator. Also the selected appointment must have the same party affiliation as the individual that was removed from office. If the individual is an independent then the selection may be from any political party. The replacement is only until the next scheduled State election of the position lost is held. Upon a conviction the person shall lose their position in government if the offense requires any jail time other than the original arrest and time to make bail if bail is necessary or allowed for the offense. A replacement Official will be selected as described above. If the offense is related to the individual's office in government in such the individual Abused their Power's of Office or Profited from their Office then this Individual shall never hold a Federally Elected Office, Federally appointed Office or Federally Employed position in Federal Government again. Each House of the legislative branches will retain its ability to punish for disorderly behavior or morality issues which are or are not in conflict with a written law as specified in the "Constitution".

7th; A Balanced Budget Amendment is required to ensure the future of this Nation. A Tax form that is fair, simple and just too all Citizens is a necessity for a thriving economy and Nation. For this Nation too offer jobs by which the civilian population will thrive a tax base must be established that encourages entrepreneurship of the People and business growth for the People creating Jobs for all those willing and wanting to work to improve their lives. Tax deductions must be reduced to weed out the special interest groups that have influenced these same tax deductions through our noble list of government officials of yesteryear and today. I wish the special interest groups could be penalized but too do so will also penalize the American Citizenship with a lack of jobs. Also these special interest groups didn't get these tax deductions without our elected officials allowing it to happen at great rewards to themselves. Just remember this, a 0% tax rate raises no revenue and a 100% tax rate also raises no revenue because nobody works for nothing! That means the rich or the poor! So a balance must be established to ensure a fair return on investment for the job creators yet squeezing every job opportunity and high paying job from the jobs created. With higher employment numbers also comes higher wages to fill those jobs in a Natural advancement of the economy and wages. To accomplish this government must create an economic atmosphere for individual business start ups and existing businesses to expand. What will create this atmosphere is to only allow corporate tax percentage deductions for equipment updates of equipment made in the U.S.A. Allowing a percentage deduction for equipment that lower the emissions of pollutants. Allowing an even larger percentage deduction for equipment that create a larger permanent work force, based on the number of jobs added and wages paid of the added jobs. Allowing percentage deductions for an expanded workforce and workplace. Doing away with any deductions that do not meet these requirements. Now lower the corporate tax rate to somewhere around 20% to 24% with the percentage of deductions coming off these corporate tax rates leaving a minimum tax rate percentage that must be paid of say 15% to 19% depending on the tax rate at the start. This stops companies like General Electric from not paying any taxes, don't forget Barack Obama publicly promoted this company because of it's Green initiative. I would have a totally green initiative if I could make money (Solar & Wind energy) off it and allowed me not to pay any taxes. The object is to get corporate America too invest in their corporation using the American People instead of spending this same money in a absorbent tax rate that benefits only a wasteful government. Government benefits will fall because more people will be working and tax revenues will rise because more people are working and businesses are expanding making more money. Isn't that the objective? Everyone making more money. Now the only way to stop wages from rising is to import a workforce, legal or illegal immigration makes no difference; it undermines the available Jobs & Wages of the American Worker. Hillary Clinton spoke about "Trickle Down Economics" and how it has been tried and doesn't work. It is amazing how these same people that control the velocity of the economy do so while making all the wrong decisions in regards to larger immigration totals and higher tax rates that continually keep the American people unemployed and/or with depressed wages. If they depress wages enough there are a lot of jobs we can't afford to do!

I believe we as a nation must keep the individual progressive tax rate. A person making $100,000 at a flat 15% tax rate has $85,000 to live off of for the year. A person making $10,000 at a flat 15% tax rate has $8,500 to live off of for the year, just a little unfair. So the bottom rate would be maybe 1% as a minimum tax payment so that even they have skin in the game. This also stops people from getting more back then what they paid in. There are safety nets for low income families, food stamps and welfare programs. The collection and funding for government is not a wealth transfer program, the social programs were set up for that purpose not our tax codes. This also should help stop any fraudulent tax refunds of the IRS.

The top rate on an individual should be around 30% with tax incentives in regards to encouraging small business start ups and existing small business of 5% to 7% which would be new to the individual tax rate. It would also still allow child tax deductions and home owner deductions getting the tax rate as low as maybe 23% for someone making $100,000.

Also any state taxes would no longer be written off the National Tax bill causing the states to bring their tax laws more into line with other states.

All these numbers might need a small adjustment but are fairly close to allow money into the economy instead of the lions share being to government which offers little incentive for investment to create expansion of new and existing businesses.

8th; Government elected Officials continually tax the American Citizens to fund an overgrown government. The officials make sure the office of the IRS has the power and resources to track and collect all tax moneys due the Government. Yet, these same Officials have no agency or resources dedicated to track and constrain these same tax dollars when they are being irresponsibly spent by Government agencies and the Military.

Sometime in early 2014 I went to a town hall meeting that had Congressman Jeff Miller a republican from the panhandle of Florida as the speaker. During the question and answer portion of the meeting a retired non-officer Navy individual asked Mr. Miller "What is the government going to do to stop the Armed Forces from spending it's allotted money at the end of the year, intentionally emptying it's coffers, as to ask for additional money for the coming year?" Mr. Miller had no real answer other than saying "We are trying to address the problem". Yet like the Veterans Administration's decades of problems, this problem is not new, it's just the way it's been done in the past and present. But if there is no plan to confront the problem then there will never be a solution for the problem. This question and problem of government stuck in my head for the 20 min. drive home. Upon reaching home I had come up with the answer and an hour later had it written down and emailed to Mr. Miller's local office. But like usual government ignores solutions and the same problems still exist.

The solution is real time tracking of money spent by all government agencies and the Military. This will require accountants with the authority to say no in regards to unjustified spending too empty coffers ensuring added resources for next year for the Agencies or Military. This accountant labor force can be moved from the IRS which is over staffed to the Congressional Budget Office. Then have that office approve and track all spending of the Agencies and Military of our Nation. This portion of the Congressional Budget Office shall report to and be overseen by a Congressional Committee of Congress with a 4.35 to 1 ratio of House of Representatives to Senators that can sit on the committee. The committee will consist of 11 members, 9 Representatives & 2 Senators. This ratio is determined by the same ratio of House of Representatives members (435) to Senate members (100). This ratio also takes into account that the "Constitution" specifically gives the power of the purse of government to the "House of Representatives" in that all Bills regarding spending must originate from the "House of Representatives".

This labor force shall be stationed within all Government Agencies and departments of the Military and Military Bases. They will approve and track everyday expenditures that are funded from a lump sum of money from Congress for the Agency's or Military's yearly operations fund.

The technique that will be used to track these expenditures will be a "Spending Curve" technique enhanced by computer "Spread Sheets" that is common among free market businesses. With daily expenditures needing to be signed off by a Congressional Budget Office employee before the expenditure occurs and not after the fact equals real time tracking of the spending of government.

With all daily expenditures now being tracked the Congressional Budget Office can identify wasteful spending within any government entity. If the curve of the spending curve line moves up it indicates an increase in spending of the government entity during a certain period of time, moving down it represents a decrease in spending. Either curve of the line then can be examined as to what created the curve and if judged to have been wasteful spending then that money can be cut from the government entity's budget as soon as possible or in the following years budget.

At sometime very soon upon the implementation of this program all government entity spending curves will flatten out indicating no abnormal spending. This means no money spent to clear the coffer's of the entity to justify an increase to next year's budget. Now what the taxpayers will have is efficiency in the processes of the daily running of all Federal Government.

9th ; This Amendment doesn't apply to any Military numbers of the Army, Air Force, Coast Guard, Marines, Navy or Veterans Affairs. The number of Federal Government Employees shall be limited to no more than 0.0616% to 0.0636% of all U.S. (based off a pop. of 300 million at 0.060% gives government 1.8 million people to run government not including Border Patrol or the Armed Forces) Citizens. Any percentage above the 0.0616% must go to direct border (disbursed within 2 miles of a land border) control employment. Of the 0.0616% of all Federal Government Employees 0.0016% being 48,000 thousand must be allocated to direct border enforcement with 60% being 28,800 sent for direct southern border enforcement. Of the 4 Border States, Texas will receive 50% being 14,400, New Mexico will receive 3,600, Arizona will receive 7,200 and California will receive 3,600. The other 11,200 will be disbursed for direct border enforcement of the Northern border. The last 8,000 will be allocated for deportation of criminal illegal aliens who survive off criminal activity thus not being able to work would not affect them in their ability to afford to stay. This action will also include all overstayed passports, visas and green cards. 5% of Border Agents of each location may be used for direct support of the Border Agents. Military may also be used to reduce costs but the numbers, placements and job directive must remain the same to be counted as border enforcement numbers.

This addresses the size of government and the open border policy situation with our country, it is imperative that government knows who is entering our nation as to not put the civilian population at a greater risk.

10th; the cost of what is referred to as "anchor babies" is tremendous in regards to our healthcare costs, welfare costs, deficit & debt and immigration laws. This money should be used for and on American Citizens. A child born inside the borders of the United States of America should no longer be deemed a U.S. Citizen without at least one parent being a U.S. Citizen at the time of the birth. I would like this law to be retroactive to all births in the United States after 11/7/1996. This Date is 10 years and one day after the Amnesty Bill of Congress was passed and signed into law by then President Ronald Reagan making about 3 million illegal aliens U.S. Citizens. At no point did the Government of the United States attempt to close the borders to illegal crossing or overstaying of passports, visas and green cards which were suppose to be included in the legislation as promised by government to the American Citizens but it never materialized. This date of 11/7/1996 in fact would be "Unconstitutional" because the laws that govern our Nation say differently in regards to this subject. Any "Constitutional" law passed can't nullify a Citizenship created by an "Anchor Baby" because you can't deny that child's rights under the laws that existed at the time the child was born in this Nation. So only the current date of which a law became enacted is legal under the "Constitution". The fact is our current President has "Unconstitutionally" allowed and encouraged illegal immigration in numbers not before seen by not enforcing current laws (border protection) protected by the "Constitution". His illegal actions will cost the poor Citizens of America needed financial help because the resources will now be divided up among an even larger population of poor people many not being Citizens of this Country.

Many of you may state I'm heartless, a racist or many other things. Well to these people I say "My heart is with the American

Citizens, regardless of race, and this Country First and Foremost". "My Heart and Mind will never deviate from this path". "Nothing I have recommended will curtail or stop legal immigration and once deemed a Citizen through the legal process of legislation and law, regardless of race, they will also be included in that list of American Citizens". "If this alone deems me as racist by the Liberal Left of the Democrat Party which has continually undermined this Nation. I will Happily accept this label as a Badge of Honor and be the biggest racist that I can be with PRIDE.

The realization is we can pass as many laws as we want but without applying them equally to each and every legal citizen we have no rule of law, only law meant to accommodate a smaller portion of our population. So it is truly the character of our elected politicians that ensure our "Constitution" in a civilized society. A corrupt Government can and will create a corrupt "Constitution" to meet their needs.

All the above thoughts or ideas are just that, any and all may need to be adjusted or tweaked. This whole chapter is to start a conversation on options that will improve our government, the way it functions and government's accountability to "We the People".

THE LIBERAL ENDING OF AMERICA

The Liberal Left's intentions for America, being knowingly or un-knowingly, are what drives the American Debt. The Liberal Left has never embraced the Constitution and sees it as a hindrance to what they truly want for our government which is Communism / Socialism. Their embracing of the People with unpaid for benefits thus now buying votes with taxpayer money is beneficial in two ways; it helps them with elections and each time a new unpaid for benefit is given to the public it drives our Debt closer to the point of no recovery. They have done a fabulous job over the decades to get us to this point with misguided voter support.

There is no business, no family household, no countries that can operate with a continuous yearly Deficit and Debt. That doesn't matter to the Liberal Left because bringing an end to America as it is today under that stupid "Constitution" is their ultimate goal. So a financial collapse of America with the collapse of America's Society can also be the means to a end. The unrest and violence that will follow is also just the Means to the End so that the 100 year old Liberal Left Agenda of Communism / Socialism may then take hold with the American "Constitution" out of the way along with OUR FAILED FORM OF GOVERNMENT. With each small step towards Communism / Socialism our percentage of poor goes up and the Middle class is reduced. What societies have the largest percentage of poor? Communist and Socialist societies! What societies have only a Elite Ruling Class, a very small Middle Class and then a always growing faster and larger class of poor? What type of governing has been inserted into the free enterprise system of America since the 1920's? A ever growing Communist and Socialist governing type of society. As one type of governing grows the other shrinks because they can not coexist! Hong Kong was a Free Capitalist society under the British until 2000, today Hong Kong is fighting for its Freedom against a Communist / Socialist government being China. The Liberal Left may change their spots and their tactics but their goals have always remained the same regardless. *ANY TYPE OF* **END** *WILL ALWAYS* **JUSTIFY** *ANY OF* **THE** *NEEDED* **MEANS!!**

CONCLUSION TO FOUR BRANCHES OF GOVERNMENT AND EQUATION

The sentence breakdown of "Articles I, II and III" is the proof the Founding Fathers knew exactly what they were doing when writing the "Constitution". It is also the Proof that anyone using the term "executive branch, legislative branch and judicial branch" as our branches of government have little working knowledge of the document itself. This group includes all of government including elected officials, lawyers, judges, supreme Court Justices, our school systems including colleges with teachers and professors and anyone that may have taught the "Constitution" outside of a class room. This also brings into question their understanding of the Checks and Balances and the processes of the "Constitution". Do my writings discredit the knowledge obtained in regards to the writings of a Founding Father separate of the "Constitution"? No, those are the insights of each Founding Father put in their words. Just keep in mind there might have been some deceit in regards to how many branches were written into the "Constitution" and if there was, who did the deception and who got deceived? That answer will affect the understanding of the writings of every Founding Father who wrote anything before, during or after the writing of the "Constitution" who may have known the answers to these types of questions.

I know the Founding Fathers knew exactly what they were writing by what we were taught with the Founding Fathers statements, a government that would not create another King, elected government with separated powers, powers disbursed evenly along with the functions of government. Now if you were a Founding Father and wanted to divide up power so that no body of government had enough power to take over government would you create three bodies with more total power each or would you create four bodies with even less total power in each body. The Founding Fathers did see and addressed this question, they were to smart not too. Well then, why not five or six branches? Because diluting power too much just makes government too cumbersome and nothing gets done or if it does, it does so at a reduced speed. That is why the Founding Fathers only created six functions with three main functions of government. Not a government trying to make everyone equal as today's government tries to do as an example of an added function. The "Constitution" only guarantees "equal rights" of the people not "equal abilities or desires" which are granted by God and will never be humanly corrected by man. Which explains why there is nothing in the "Constitution" that designates a welfare system.

The Founding Fathers when writing the Constitution weren't real interested in explaining the Constitution as to the exact layout of government. But they explained what they wanted the Constitution to accomplish for "We the People" and what guidelines government can use to accomplish this, including elections. These needs then were addressed by government once "We the People" elected a government because they were included in the "Constitution". The Founding Fathers didn't legislate on these issues because the "people" would have no say if they had done so.

WHAT A NOVEL IDEA TO LET THE PEOPLE GOVERN THEMSELVES THROUGH THEIR ELECTED REPRESENTATIVES AND SENATORS. I HOPE THE one supreme *COURT USES THIS INTENDED CONCEPT IN THEIR INFINATE WISDOM OF THEIR RULINGS.*

The Founding Fathers also created a pathway for future generations to legislate for their needs of their time period in history. Furthermore I don't believe the people who changed the "Constitution" in regards to how it functions had enough knowledge of the "Constitution" to justify any of the changes.

ENDING NOTE FROM ME TO YOU

I hope you have enjoyed and understand my writings on so many different topics. I have offered you the truth to the best of my abilities on these topics. My intentions are to get people thinking on issues that should concern any honest American citizen of this country in an attempt to create a more informed voting base. Even if you don't totally agree with every aspect, it might cause you to research the subject to confirm your thoughts. If you can't back your thoughts or ideas with all the facts on the subject then they are just thoughts absent of truths and possibly absent of realities.

I hope you noticed my repeating of certain phrases throughout my writings on the government and especially the separation of powers. Our government will never function properly when political parties of government are allowed to intermingle the powers of government. One branch taking the powers of another branch to achieve a goal of the Political Party is beyond Treason against all Americans. The

Constitution was written in a manner by our Founding Fathers that kept these powers separated and assigned them to specific branches of government. It was done that way for a purpose, to ensure the rights and freedoms of this country's citizenship meaning no man, woman or people of government are able to take these rights and freedoms away. If you remember at the first of my writings I stated;

"When you are told over and over something you begin to believe it and at some point you accept it as the truth. There is a difference between being told and being taught". "Being told is INDOCTRINATION into a certain way of thinking without any supporting facts, being TAUGHT is backing the curriculum with FACTS that support the Subject then allowing the TRUTH to be Seen!"

Well it works! So if you can indoctrinate someone into a certain way of thinking just by repeating the statement wouldn't it also work for delivering the teachings and facts in the truths of a subject? A teacher in a classroom needing to stress something to their students would repeat it every chance available. If wrong concepts can be taught this way the truth should be easy!

We spent about half the time rediscovering the "Constitution" and how it is suppose to work. That design of governing by our Founding Fathers is a continually giving gift of FREEDOM from them to every past, present and future citizen of this Great Nation. The Document itself is not perfect and can not defend itself against those who see it as an obstacle to Communism or Socialism. It is "The Peoples" responsibility to defend the thoughts of the Founding Fathers which created this Document, to defend our Thoughts, to defend our Nation, to defend our Freedom against those who want to pry these gifts from our hands. This gift of Freedom for it to be True must be True to every citizen. So the bases of our Freedom must be to defend others Thoughts whether correct or not. Defending a Thought is different than enacting a Thought. A thought has no cost, no repercussion until it is acted upon. At that point it will reveal itself as either a good or bad idea. A good idea works anywhere in life, a bad idea doesn't. Our Government is about 40/60 of good and bad ideas in regards to our "written Common Laws". It is the government attitude that nothing changes in government regardless of how bad it is. Just because it is "the just thing to do" or "it is politically correct" has nothing to do with government results, the effectiveness of government or the Constitution itself. "Affirmative Action" was both JUST and CORRECT but at some point becomes the exact thought that now promotes RACISM. Because Government can't endorse one race over another. With the Constitution's inception it did promote one race over another because of the Democrat's thought process on Slavery. The Democrat's thought process has never changed, it still promotes and uses Racism for the party's own gain. With the removal of slavery from the Constitution the document is now and has been Neutral for about the last 150 years in regards to race. With both genders now voting it is no longer sexist.

If an idea of government is bad it doesn't work for all the People. As a Citizen of this Nation it is your RESPONSIBILITY to defend the Constitution. The people seeking political office with the intent of delivering bad ideas or continuing bad ideas of government with your vote against them. But you must know who they are first.

That was the intent of my book, not to only teach you on the processes of government but point out how history and historical events have been rewritten, or over looked entirely, to repaint the Democrat Party in the best possible light.

My other intent with the book is to end the liberal left Democrat movement bringing the Party itself back to the middle of the spectrum allowing all of government to move to the right in the spectrum of government thought. With this book I hope it allows me the opportunity to gain a platform. To point out the politicians being Democrat or Republican who refuse to relinquish the power of government. The power of government being the size and ineffectiveness of government. A smaller more effective government is a better government of the people.

I would like to leave you with one last thought on the spirit of "Faith" and the Liberals constant denial thereof. Liberals make light of a "individual talking to God" as if it could never happen because to many of them "God" doesn't exist. Oil is a byproduct of past life, fossil fuels, past animal and plant life. Science determined this relationship sometime in the last sixty years or so. As I pointed out the Middle East with it vast oil reserves must have been covered with animal and plant life at some time in history being at least million or more years ago. The "Bible's" written history dates back to around four to six thousand years ago and some portions were written by people who made claims they "talked to God".

Answer me this! During a time of limited scientific knowledge being the time period the "Bible" was written. How did a four to six thousand year old book know the Middle East was once covered, a million or more years ago, in animal and plant life as it describes when the "Bible" uses the term "the Garden of Eden"? Today's science has confirmed all aspects of the "Bible" originated from the Middle East including "the Garden of Eden". So a four to six thousand year old book knew this aspect of earth's history four to six thousand years before today's modern science could confirm it!

The Liberal Atheist's feelings of nothingness after death is a reflection of their own denial of "a Greater Power" than themselves. Because Liberals know there is nothing more powerful than themselves!

If you can't answer this question maybe it's time to reexamine yourself Spiritually? As a faith denier you may not be the most important thing in any Universe!

THE END

Printed in the United States
By Bookmasters